Schelling's Organic Form
of Philosophy

SUNY series in Contemporary Continental Philosophy
Dennis J. Schmidt, editor

Schelling's Organic Form
of Philosophy

Life as the Schema of Freedom

Bruce Matthews

Published by State University of New York Press, Albany

For information, contact State University of New York Press, Albany, NY
www.sunypress.edu

Production by Ryan Morris
Marketing by Anne M. Valentine

Library of Congress Cataloging–in–Publication Data

Matthews, Bruce, 1962–
  Schelling's organic form of philosophy : life as the schema of freedom /
  Bruce Matthews.
       p.   cm. — (SUNY series in contemporary Continental philosophy)
  Includes bibliographical references (p.) and index.
  ISBN 978–1–4384–3410–0 (paperback : alk. paper)
  ISBN 978–1–4384–3411–7 (hardcover : alk. paper)   1. Schelling, Friedrich
  Wilhelm Joseph von, 1775–1854. I. Title.

B2898.M395 2011
193—dc22

                                                        2010023365

10 9 8 7 6 5 4 3 2 1

For Manfred Frank

δύο δὲ μόνω καλῶς συνίστασθαι τρίτου χωρὶς οὐ δυνατόν· δεσμὸν γὰρ ἐν μέσῳ δεῖ τινα ἀμφοῖν συναγωγὸν γίγνεσθαι. δεσμῶν δὲ κάλλιστος ὃς ἂν αὐτὸν καὶ τὰ συνδούμενα ὅτι μάλιστα ἓν ποιῇ. (Tim. 32C)

J. Walter Brain

Cambridge, Mass.

Summer 2,012

Contents

x   Contents

Preface

In writing this book, I hope to contribute to the growing effort to decipher one of the most complex and enigmatic thinkers of German Idealism, F. W. J. Schelling. Like the wines of a challenging domain in Bordeaux, the life and ideas of this philosopher have been often overlooked as we reach for the now widely available and thus familiar vintages of a Kant, Fichte, or Hegel. Unlike these three acknowledged giants of German Idealism, Schelling never sought to offer up one unchanging system of philosophy. Over the course of his long career, different years often yielded different results, as he relentlessly worked the *vay vignes* of philosophy, never ceasing to call into question his own ideas in the face of new developments.[1]

Admirers of such an approach to philosophizing are rare. One such connoisseur and self-proclaimed follower of this stratagem was, not surprisingly, another quite enigmatic philosopher, the father of American pragmatism, Charles Sanders Peirce. When asked who had most influenced his own philosophy of nature by William James, Peirce responds that his views were "influenced by Schelling,—by all stages of Schelling, but especially by the *Philosophie der Natur.*" He continues, "I consider Schelling as enormous; and one thing I admire about him is his freedom from the trammels of system, and his holding himself uncommitted to any previous utterance. In that, he is like a scientific man."[2] With these words Peirce lauds precisely that aspect of Schelling's way of doing philosophy that others, most notoriously Schelling's one-time friend and protégé, Hegel, ridicule as a crippling weakness that forced him "to carry out his philosophical education in public"—an embarrassing shortcoming Hegel sought to capture when he awarded Schelling the dubious title of the "Proteus of philosophy." This is the same Hegel who, quite in step with the prevailing winds of modernity, and no doubt reflecting his early career as a Gymnasium schoolmaster, once wrote, "That philosophy, like geometry, is teachable, and must no less than geometry have a regular structure."[3] This position, while perfect for creating a school of thought to be filled out by students drilled in the prescribed method, stands diametrically opposed to Schelling's belief that, since philosophy is the highest act of freedom, the activity of doing philosophy is not only inherently creative, but must always reflect the unique character of the person engaged in this activity. In stark contrast to what would become Hegel's rather megalomaniacal celebration of one method and system of philosophy, Schelling insists that because a philosophy must be "constructed by the individual student himself," any such "system" can only be "perspectival" and thus a limited account of the "universal . . . system of human knowing" (I/1, 447; 457). Highly critical of modernity's embrace of mathematic form as the paradigm through which to understand our knowledge of reality, Schelling embraces an organic and developmental model in which, for example, "all progress in philosophy [is] only progress through *development*; every individual system which earns this name can be viewed as a seed which indeed slowly and gradually, but inexorably and in every direction, advances itself in multifarious development" (I/1, 457). The telos of philosophy lies not in the gradual homogenization of thought into one all embracing logic, but rather in developing a multitude of systems, all of which should offer us ever more diverse and complex ways of understanding our existence.

In undertaking the task of coming to grips with such a singular thinker, it is essential that we allow him to speak for himself, choosing for the moment to avoid the echo chamber of received readings. A strategy to facilitate this is, in a move of intellectual judo, to apply Schelling's interpretive strategies to his own work, thereby helping us to disclose and understand him on his own terms. For while Schelling held that every one of us is called to create our own philosophy, he also maintained that in doing this all of us would be guided in our efforts by one unique yet fundamental idea. As we will see in much more detail, Schelling held that the key to understanding a thinker is to find that one central idea that serves as the axis around which his or her work revolves. And it is precisely this objective I pursue in the pages that follow, namely, to find the fundamental idea that animates and informs his work.

As the title of this book suggests, I argue that Schelling's fundamental idea is the organic form of philosophy. "Life," he writes, is to be understood "as the schema of Freedom" (I/1, 249). With this pronouncement, Schelling serves notice that the first predicate of philosophy must speak to the system of self-organizing nature that is our world. Before self, reflection, clarity, or distinctness, there is "the infinite striving for self-organization" (I/1, 386), wherein nature, as both cause and effect of itself, reveals the form of reciprocal causality indicative of freedom. This "eternal" and thus "indestructible" "form of organization" (I/1, 387) drives the entire continuum of nature, from seemingly inert matter to the most robust self-organizing system of the human spirit, and its most intricate creation, philosophy. This organic form provides Schelling with the conceptual model required to tackle the perennial problem of how to grasp the interconnectedness and unity of our existence and world, as well as all the ensuing dualisms that follow from this underlying oneness. The unifying power of organic form is precisely what Schelling means to express through the term *Identity*, whose relational structure is incapable of being reduced to the linear mechanics of logic, since it exhibits the same property of reciprocity indicative of the dynamic feedback that structures life's capacity for self-organization.

To advance this reading of Schelling I have found it necessary to seek out the proper standpoint from which to examine his earliest work. And while the material I consider is by no means exhaustive of his earliest writings, it does address Schelling's claim to be advancing a new and thus easily misunderstood form of philosophy. As with any original thinker, the labyrinth of Schelling's ideas is very difficult to comprehend while moving through it *sequentially*, at ground level as it were. A more meaningful pattern, however, emerges with the perspective and scope of vision won from a standpoint *above* this pattern. Consequently, I adopt a somewhat synoptic stance in the first chapter, where in the effort to frame the detailed analysis and arguments that follow, I consider Schelling's thought as an integrated whole. In doing this, I allow my presentation to be guided more by the order of argument than the order of Schelling's texts.

As one has already surmised from the first paragraph of this preface, Schelling's almost seventy years of writing and lecturing witnessed quite a few iterations of his philosophy. But as I hope to show in chapters 2 through 6, these iterations were all guided by a fundamental idea or form of philosophy. In what follows, I have limited myself to focusing primarily on the first ten years of his career, from 1794 to 1804. In order to appreciate these determinative years, chapter 2 examines the rich intellectual milieu in which this young prodigy was raised, wherein by the age of eleven he had not only learned six languages, but, more importantly for us, he had already begun to read Plato in Greek. For it is here in his exposure to the ideas of Plato, as interpreted by his varied and numerous childhood mentors and teachers, that we find the raw material of an organic, relational identity that Schelling develops while still a student at the Tübinger *Stift*, using elements of Kant's critical edifice. Chapter 3 is more speculative in its exploration of how and why

Kant himself demands an organic, systematic unity of reason, and the various strategies he proposes to account for this. I pay particular attention to the function of the cosmological concepts of *nature* and *world* in the first *Critique*, and the need to introduce the absolute magnitude of the sublime in the third *Critique*. Chapter 4 examines in detail how Schelling synthesizes Kant and Plato in his commentary to the *Timaeus* and *Philebus*. This text, written in his last years at the *Stift*, is essential to grasping Schelling on his own terms, since it shows us, before he was exposed to Fichte's ideas, his interest in harmonizing Plato's idea of an originary form of all life and knowledge with Kant's call for an organic unity of reason. Chapter 5 investigates how this original synthesis of ideas informs Schelling's first published essay on *The Form of Philosophy in General*. I close in chapter 6 with an overview of how the organic form of philosophy which emerges from the *Form Essay* determines Schelling's work up through his *System of Transcendental Idealism of 1800* and the *Würzburger Lectures* of 1804. In this final chapter I again find myself pushed by the complexity of Schelling's work to "zoom out" to a more synoptic view of his writings, thereby permitting the dynamic of his thought, rather than the configuration of individual texts, to determine my presentation.

Schelling once wrote that if we seek to get at what is truly philosophical in Kant we must "separate the contingencies of form and personality from that which is enduring and essential" in his writings (I/5, 188). This requires that we put ourselves in a position "which Kant himself recognized as possible," namely, one in which we must assume, at least as a working hypothesis, that we can "understand him better than he has understood himself" (A 314/B 370). Perhaps this is the inevitable, yet rather precariously grandiose situation we find ourselves in, when seeking to interrogate and understand a great thinker. It is of course my position in what follows.

Acknowledgments

This book would never have appeared if it were not for the support and guidance of Manfred Frank. He has time and again demonstrated an uncompromising commitment to the principles of friendship and the discipline of philosophy. His learning inspires both respect and a certain wistfulness, in that our current culture no longer values the symphonic grasp of ideas his work exemplifies. At just the right time Louis Dupre provided succinct yet crucial advice that helped bring this work to completion. The text itself has benefited greatly from the insightful suggestions of Joseph Lawrence and Jason Wirth. As always, clarity and elegance of expression are due to the eagle-eye of my first and best teacher of English, Jean Matthews. Finally, a heartfelt thanks to Dennis Schmidt and Jane Bunker at State University of New York Press for helping to make Schelling's works and ideas available to the Anglophone world.

Notes on Sources and Abbreviations

(I/1, 99) References are to Friedrich Wilhelm Joseph Schelling's
Sämmtliche Werke, edited by K. F. A. Schelling, I Abtheilung
vols. 1–10, II Abtheilung vols. 1–4 (Stuttgart: Cotta, 1856–1861).
Abbreviations for other Schelling texts are found in the
endnotes. All Schelling translations are my own, except for
passages taken from Peter Heath's translation of Schelling's
System of Transcendental Idealism (1800) (Charlottesville:
University of Virginia Press, 1993).

AA F. W. J. Schelling, *Historisch-kritische Ausgabe*, edited by H. M.
Baumgartner, W. G. Jacobs, H. Krings, and H. Zeltner (Stuttgart:
Frommann-Holzboog, 1976).

GPP F. W. J. Schelling, *Grundlegung der Positiven Philosophie: Münchener Vorlesung WS 1832/33 und SS 1833*, edited with commentary by Horst Fuhrmans (Torino: Bottega D'Erasmo, 1972).

PO F. W. J. Schelling, *Philosophie der Offenbarung 1841/42*, edited
with an introduction by Manfred Frank (Frankfurt am Main:
Suhrkamp, 1977).

TK F. W. J. Schelling, *Timaeus (1794)*, edited by Hartmut Buchner.
Schellingiana, Bd. 4 (Stuttgart: Frommann Holzboog, 1994).

WA F. W. J. Schelling, *Die Weltalter in den Urfassungen von 1811
und 1813*, edited with an introduction by Manfred Schröter
(Munich: C. H. Beck'sche Verlagsbuchhandlung, 1946).

WMV F. W. J. Schelling, *System der Welalter: Münchener Vorlesung
1827/28 in einer Nachschrift von Ernst von Lasaulux*, edited
with an introduction by Siegbert Peetz (Frankfurt am Main:
Vittorio Klostermann, 1990).

Ak References are to the Akademieausgabe of *Kants gesam-
melte Schriften*, edited by The Königlichen Preußischen (later
Deutschen) Akademie der Wissenschaften (Berlin, 1900–).

KrV Immanuel Kant, *Kritik der reinen Vernunft* (1781). *Critique of
Pure Reason*, translated by N. K. Smith (London: Macmillan

and Co., 1964); A and B refer respectively to the 1781 and 1787 editions, and when cited alone as A 645/B 673 indicate *KrV*, as is customary.

KpV   Immanuel Kant, *Kritik der praktischen Vernunft* (1788). *Critique of Practical Reason*, translated by Lewis White Beck, 3d. ed. (New York: Macmillan, 1993).

KU   Immanuel Kant, *Kritik der Urteilskraft* (1790). *The Critique of Judgement*, translated and with analytic indexes by J. C. Meredith (Oxford: Clarendon Press, 1952).

Logik   Immanuel Kant, *Logik (1800)*. *Logic*, translated by R. S. Hartman and W. Schwarz (New York: Dover, 1988).

MdS   Immanuel Kant, *Metaphysik der Sitten* (1797). *The Metaphysics of Morals*, translated by Mary Gregor (Cambridge: Cambridge University Press, 1993).

Tim.   Plato, *Timaeus*, translated by R. G. Bury. Loeb Classical Library, vol. IX (Cambridge: Harvard University Press, 1989).

Phil.   Plato, *Philebus*, translated by G. P. Goold. Loeb Classical Library, vol. VIII (Cambridge: Harvard University Press, 1990).

1

Life as the Schema of Freedom

Schelling's Organic Form of Philosophy

Subjectivism and the Annihilation of Nature

In recent years, there has been a growing interest in the German philosopher F. W. J. Schelling. One major reason for this renewed attention lies in the symphonic power of this thinker's work, the expanse and complexity of which provides a robust alternative to the anemic theorizing one encounters in contemporary academic philosophy. Too far-reaching to fit into the categories of either German Idealism or Romanticism, Schelling's oeuvre is an example of an organic philosophy which, rooted in nature, strives to support the continuous creation of meaning within a unifying and integrated framework. Realizing that the negative force of critique can never satisfy the curiosity of the human spirit, he insists that philosophy must itself be as capable of continuous development as life itself. Advancing such an ambitious project led Schelling to break away from the conceptual current of modern subjectivism to develop a way of doing philosophy firmly planted in the sensual world of human experience and nature. For it was only from such an organic standpoint that he believed he would be able to overcome and integrate the dualisms that necessarily follow from modernity's standpoint of the subject, posited as the otherworldly source of order and form required to regulate the chaotic flux of life.

As Kant realized, the ideal of unity is the condition of possibility of employing reason systematically. For Schelling, however, Kant failed to pursue the logic of his reasoning to its necessary conclusion, thereby denying continuity between the virtual world of pure reason and the existing reality of nature. Hypostatizing the patterns of his logic, Kant "prescribes" an unbridgeable duality between the object world of *physica rationalis* and the subjective interiority of *psychologia rationalis*.[1] In doing this, Kant limits the unconditional demand both of the Transcendental Ideal and the Kingdom of Ends to the sphere of the thinking subject, thereby demoting the other 'Kingdoms' of nature to the status of mere means to be exploited by humans. While creating a powerful yet limited position from which a disembodied subject can "constrain nature to give answers," the destructive consequences of such an approach vis-à-vis nature were all too clearly visible to Schelling.[2]

In its essence, Kant's Copernican Revolution resulted in what Schelling calls "the pure inversion" of traditional dogmatism,[3] an inversion in which the static and unchanging doctrines of a Wolffian form of scholastic metaphysics are replaced by the "dogmata" of Kant's a priori synthetic propositions which, according to Kant, are as "closed and complete" a "body of doctrine" as the logic of Aristotle.[4] The consequences of this inversion produce an even more destructive dual-plane model of reality than that of dogmatic theology, since it culminates for Schelling in a new form of "dualism" he held to be a "necessary phenomenon of the modern world."[5] Initiated by Descartes, formulated by Kant, and perfected by Fichte, the subjective idealism of modernity denies the objective reality and intrinsic value of nature, since as "a product of the I," the world of nature becomes nothing more than a *"Gedankending"* to be posited by the thinking subject "when needed."[6] According to Schelling, this devaluation of sensuous nature has its roots in modernity's promotion of the thinking human subject to the rank of the absolute, an inflation of the cogito that leads to the vainglorious deification of the human subject at the subsequent cost of what Schelling presciently calls the "annihilation of nature":

> Descartes, who through the *cogito ergo sum* gave philosophy its first orientation to subjectivity, and whose introduction of philosophy (in his *Meditations)* is in fact identical with the later grounding of philosophy in Idealism, could not yet present the orientations entirely separate—subjectivity and objectivity do not yet appear completely divided. But his real intention, his true idea of God, the world, and the soul he articulated more clearly in his physics than through his philosophy. In the comprehensive spirit of Descartes, his philosophy permitted the annihilation of nature, which the idealism of the above mentioned form [Fichte's] extols, just as truly and factually as it actually was in his physics. (I/5, 274)

The annihilation of nature addressed here has at its root the elevation of epistemology above all fields of philosophy, most notably ontology, ethics, and aesthetics. No longer the primary reality of our being, nature becomes something derivative, dependent for *its* being on the thinking subject. This occurs when the subject's cogito becomes the sole arbiter of the being of what is real in our world. The first step in this process occurs when Descartes defines reality as the self-certainty of the cogito, understood as the subject's own reflective knowledge of self. Overcome by the methodological control of knowledge promised by this definitional dance, the price of breadth and depth in terms of what can be parsed by this new epistemological formula seems negligible. Yet if what is real and true can only be that which corresponds to this reflective self-certainty and can only be articulated through the predicates of discursive thought, then the thinking of the unity of nature becomes impossible. The "living band"[7] of a transitive *being*, which as *natura naturans* connects humanity with nature, is thereby dissolved into the discrete moments of logos, of the *relata* of subject and predicate. Thus does the generative relating of the copula *qua* verb become transformed into a static and discrete operator of logical subsumption, while the unbridgeable divide between human subject and the object world becomes the condition of the possibility of true and certain knowledge.

Schelling's point seems to be that when one begins with the dualism of a Fichte, and accepts the disembodied cogito as determinative, then "all knowledge" derived from this principle will remain trapped within an "insoluble circle" of its own fabrication, with the result that the thinking subject, pressed up against the conceptual lens of its own making, can only look out at the world of sensuous nature as if it, the cogito, "didn't also belong to the world" as well (I/6, 144). Drawing attention to what would seem an obvious fact of our existence, namely, that our thinking also belongs to this world, Schelling demands that philosophy not only begin with, but also integrate, that which seems to be so radically *other* than thought, namely the living world of nature. And with this we come to perhaps the most relevant and important reason for the resurgence of interest in Schelling, which is his analysis of how subjectivism sets the theoretical stage for the actual destruction of our natural environment.

As obvious as it is prescient when considered from the beginning of the twenty-first century, Schelling claims in his *Naturphilosophie* that the otherworldly subjectivism of a Descartes or Fichte permits the dismemberment of the organism of nature into its purely accidental qualities, the worth of which equals the profit we reap from their control and manipulation. Nature thus becomes valued merely as an object to be used according to the "economic-teleological" principle whereby, for example, trees in and of themselves have no worth save when turned into furniture (I/7, 18). In this way we reduce the world of nature to nothing more than the material stuff we exploit to satisfy our human desires, ultimately leading to, as we see around our world today, the threat of a real annihilation of nature (I/5, 275). The complicating yet all too obvious fact, however, is that we too are a part of this world, and cannot therefore rip ourselves out of the ground from whence we live and, in good Gnostic fashion, jettison our material existence for the sake of a more perfect theoretical elegance and absolute certitude. If the world of actual life is sacrificed in the name of logical consistency, philosophy is then left to deal "with the world of lived experience just as a surgeon who promises to cure your ailing leg by amputating it."[8] Yet even then, once a philosophy surrenders the chaos of real experience to gain the methodical order of its reflected imitation, it will only find itself trapped within the prison of its own success. For example, while Kant perhaps succeeds in accounting for the possibility of a knowledge grounded in the *reflexio* of the thinking subject, he does so at the price of ever being able to account for actual knowledge, since to achieve this his transcendental edifice would have to integrate what its foundation rejects, namely, the organic world of lived existence and its sensual nature. In direct opposition to Kant's rather dogmatic proclamation that "real metaphysics" can only thrive when it is "devoid of all mixture with the sensual," Schelling challenges philosophy to return, as it were, to its senses, and integrate the metaphysical with the physical, in the hopes of creating a unifying, and thus meaningful, understanding of our world.[9] The supremely difficult yet necessary challenge is thus to somehow to integrate the other of discursive thought, traditionally spoken of as the intuitive comprehension of the sensual. Epistemologically this is highly problematic. As Schelling points out, "If philosophy refuses to amputate existence, then it must begin by ascribing being to those elements of nature that are not known."[10] The seeming impossibility of doing this, however, disappears when one stops equating philosophy with the cogito and its epistemology of certitude, and instead begins to do philosophy with the entirety of our natural faculties, conceptual as well as sensual, cognitive as well as affective. For it is only by pursuing such a strategy that we can begin to account not only for Kant's possible knowledge, but more importantly, that we can begin to wrestle with *actual* knowledge by attempting to lay bare the unity of existence that forms the basis from which all forms of dualism spring. The sensual and the understanding, intuition and concept, the physical and the metaphysical, logos and mythos: these are just some of the more critical dualities that remain inexplicable unless we not only account for the shared ground upon which they interact, but also explain how the opposing members of such dualities work together.

This requires what Schelling calls "an inversion of the principles," which results in the overturning of modernity's ordering of the subject over being, and therewith of epistemology over ontology (I/1 156). In doing this, however, Schelling finds himself forced to begin his philosophical work in the cognitive no-man's-land of pure being, which can only be grasped through intuition, since there is no discursive access to the intransitive being of the copula which unifies subject and object. The grasping awareness of that which precedes the logos of thinking is fundamentally an aesthetic act of *poesis*, whereby the philosopher constructs for himself the intuition of this undetermined oneness. Paralleling the dynamic sequence of *natura naturans* and *natura naturata*, the philosopher's creation is initiated by the chaotic force of the sublime, which in overpowering all limit and measure must be then made complete by the balanced form of beauty. Directed against Kant's woefully inconsistent doctrine of method, Schelling employs synthesis and construction, putting the philosopher beside the geometer, arguing that both must first construct form and space in their intuition, in order to then subject their creations to the analysis of conceptual thought. Like the explosive power of the sublime, this initial moment of aesthetic production provides us with the very real, but very volatile stuff of our intellectual world, since as aesthetic, this subsoil of discursivity remains beyond the oppositional predicates of all thought that otherwise calms and comforts the knowing mind.

Forsaking the artificial certainties of beginning with an act of knowing, shaped as it is by the laws of logic, Schelling begins in the epistemologically problematic realm of being. It is only in that which cannot be determined that he can find the possibility of freedom, and it is freedom that will allow him to meld his strategy with the creative efforts of nature's own generative power, as well as provide him with an opening to establish ethics as the guiding force of philosophy. Freedom thus becomes the "alpha and omega of philosophy" in that it alone can create order within the chaotic field of existence, and thereby provide a unifying basis that can integrate the ensuing orders of ontology and epistemology. Following this strategy philosophy would finally integrate what metaphysics has almost always amputated, thereby freeing it to create a more comprehensive, robust, and ultimately meaningful account of existence.

Necessity and freedom, reason and faith, good and evil, being and becoming: the positive status and reality of the second member in each of these dualities has too frequently suffered a fate similar to that offered to the aforementioned sick leg. The consequence of such philosophical malpractice is too frequently a weakened and crippled philosophy, no longer robust enough to support the transformative meaning Schelling demands of philosophy. Agreeing with those critics of academic philosophy who see in it nothing more than extraneous scholastic debates, he argues that a measure of the truth of a philosophy demonstrates itself in the inability of others to treat it as irrelevant. Addressing the seemingly natural tendency of most philosophies to devolve into such anemic scholasticism, Schelling argues that the question of unity forces us to ask of philosophy this very question of relevancy, thereby compelling us to investigate how an idea or method fits into our overall understanding of existence. The power to do this in an engaging and meaningful manner distinguishes those philosophies that offer us what William James calls "a live option" from those that, incapable of integrating experience into a symphonic whole, do not.

Case in point is Kant's baffling splintering of our experience into two worlds, the phenomenal and noumenal, leaving us with no way of accounting for our knowledge of the fact of freedom, since we only know it to the degree that it reveals itself in the phenomenal world. While Kant's strategy here might successfully rebut Hume's critique of causality, it fails to address our need to understand the reality of freedom, which is something that requires an account of how free will and necessity are integrated. Or again, refusing Kant's attempt to disassociate reason and philosophy from faith and religion, Schelling worked throughout his career to integrate religion and philosophy in such a way that they would no longer have to apologize for each other. Against the prevailing spirit of modernity, he sought to bring logos and mythos back to the negotiating table, working to keep their negative and positive tasks united in an uneasy alliance of belief and doubt. The same holds true for his groundbreaking examination of evil in his *Treatise on Human Freedom*, where, in a manner parallel to his treatment of existence and sensual nature, Schelling refuses to ignore radical evil as a mere privation of the good, and instead acknowledges the all too painful reality of evil's existence and its agonizing relationship with the good. These two vital yet problematic constants in our metaphysical tradition coalesce in a new understanding of the sacred, in which the deity, in order to account for its responsibility as a source of evil, must be conceptualized as a part of the ongoing process of creation that Schelling provocatively describes as a process of "dynamic evolution" (I/3, 61). As source and sustaining force of creation, Schelling's conception of the divine embraces our physical nature in that our world must, from this perspective, be seen as the ongoing self-revelation of that which is most sacred, namely, the source and sustaining power of all life.

The status of nature as the essential medium through which the sacred reveals itself brings us to Schelling's idea of *life as the schema of freedom*: due to the non-linear dynamic of self-organization, life so conceived "manifests the appearance of freedom," no matter how faint and seemingly chaotic (I/5, 527). Life, understood as being "that carries the ground of its *Daseyns* in itself," since "it is cause and effect of itself" (I/2, 40), not only introduces an irreducibly chaotic element into the linear frame of mechanical reasoning, but it also calls into question the limits of such a mechanistic explanatory framework. In Schelling's hands, a mechanistic environment distinguishes itself from an organic system in its reactive obedience to initial conditions and its incapacity for the progressive creation of new and original actions. Like a well-tuned engine that never misfires, a mechanism executes an action "in a circle, so that in every such cycle of actions there is only one action (always repeated)" (I/1, 470). While such a mechanism may break down, it can never break out of its predetermined course. It is also incapable of accounting for the fact of what Schelling calls the "individualization of matter" (I/2, 520), which he holds to be indicative of the "dynamic evolution" of nature. "Even within the same type" he writes, "nature knows of a certain unmistakable freedom, which maintains a certain leeway for differentiation . . . so that no *individuum* is ever absolutely equal to another" (I/10, 378). By positing this low-level freedom in nature as a type of chaotic force that propels the evolutionary differentiation of life, Schelling generates the conceptual resources required to integrate freedom and necessity into a unified account of nature, in which the noumenal and phenomenal intertwine in an organic, and thus chaotic, evolving cycle of self-differentiation.

In this reading, while limited regions of natural phenomena can be explained through mechanistic laws of nature, the entire process of our world's becoming can ultimately be understood in its systematic entirety only when we conceptualize it as a self-organizing, organic whole. Put simply, the progressive development of our world cannot be reduced to a sequence of antecedent causes, since if this were possible, the static structure of the law that governs this causal mechanism would require, like the disembodied cogito, that it not be "of this world" or itself subject to the progressive development which it governs. Thought through consistently, to accept a mechanistic account of the laws of nature would require that we retain some vestige of a dual plane model of reality, as some form of a Platonic realm of eternal laws, which as inalterable axioms would themselves have to be exempt from the very change and evolution we employ them to explain. Schelling refuses to take refuge in such a traditional position not only because it begs the question of how these laws of nature came to be, but because such a bifurcated arrangement rules out the possibility of a future which is not determined by the past, denying the reality of freedom, and thereby removing the possibility of incorporating creativity and purpose into the very fabric of our natural world.

Standing conventional wisdom on its head, Schelling insists that the linear and mechanistic framework of physics can be adequately comprehended only when it is subsumed under the more comprehensive framework of organic life; or in William James's words addressed to C. S. Peirce, Schelling insists that "the inorganic" can only be understood as a "product of the living."[11] Far from being an enigmatic appendix to physics, the dynamics of organic systems must, according to Schelling, become the determinative model that ultimately organizes and accounts for our explanations of the universe. This does not deny the utility and worth of the physicist's investigation into the mechanical regularities of nature that are susceptible to linear, causal explanation. Schelling's point rather, is to draw our attention to the underlying roots of these patterns, which reach deep into nature's dynamic of self-organization. For once we consider the reciprocal form of causation and interconnectedness indicative of organic systems, we can then move from the ontological to the epistemological, and call into question the myth of the objective scientific observer who, from his Archimedean standpoint outside of our system of nature, is alleged to be capable of accounting for the world as it is in itself, devoid of human interests and values.[12]

The ramifications of this shift to an organic paradigm are major. Epistemologically, if we accept the irreducible interconnectedness of nature and acknowledge our starring role in this world—a role, it must be pointed out, demonstrated not in our power for creation, but rather proven by the distressing fact of our seemingly infinite capacity to destroy life—then we become faced with the prospect of what Schelling termed our *conscientia*, or *Mitwissenschaft* with nature. Refusing to accept the absolute skeptic's terms of debate, Schelling reframes modernity's epistemological quandary in accordance with the reciprocal dynamic of self-organizing systems, and our status as the organ of knowing within this system. This is why we are capable of knowing with "direct certainty" that "there are things beyond us," even though this knowledge "refers to something quite different and opposed to us" (I/3, 343). We are capable of knowing that which shows itself to be other than we are because we are "of this world," having been created through the very same dynamic organization that has brought our entire cosmos into being. What unifies knowing subject and known object is this underlying order of organic nature that bonds us with the phenomenal world we live in. Our power to appreciate "the unfathomable intentionality, the unbelievable naiveté of nature in the achievement of its purposes," points to "the view of a true inner history of nature" in "whose formation humanity can look into as into that of a related being" (I/10, 378; I/10, 381). As such we share the ontological DNA of our world, which in accordance with Empedocles' dictum that only like can know like, provides us with the means for our *conscientia*, our knowing of and with nature, since it is nature itself that comes to know itself through our knowing of it.[13] "Poured from the source of things and the same as the source, the human soul has a co-knowledge (*Mitwissenschaft*) of creation" (I/8, 200; I/9, 221). Most clearly demonstrated by the works of the genius, in the autoepistemic structure of nature our function is that of the organ whereby nature comes to know herself. And as so much of twentieth-century science has shown, the infamous epistemological divide between object and observing subject often reveals itself to be more a theoretically required heuristic than a factual ontological divide.[14]

Once we get beyond this epistemological heuristic, Schelling argues that we can begin to appreciate the ethical and aesthetic ramifications of this shift to an organic paradigm. For in overthrowing the supremacy of epistemology over ethics, we open the door to dethroning the Cartesian cogito from its lordly position vis-à-vis nature. In Schelling's reading, the Cartesian cogito or Fichtean ego offer the clearest example of the philosophical pathologies of the modern self. By elevating the individual ego to the center of its solipsistic universe, the self denies its alienation from its source in nature, leading it to pursue its satisfaction by destroying precisely that from which it is estranged, namely, nature. If, however, we examine the ethical ramifications of the organic standpoint, the self begins from a position that acknowledges both our alienation from, and our fundamental dependence on, nature. Coming to terms with our relation to nature forces us to try to understand what in theory is somehow a part of us, yet is experientially and practically a world apart and different from us. At the heart of Schelling's idea of Identity then is this task of realizing the unity of self and nature, and thus grasping how what is radically other is actually related to us.

Beyond the obvious yet unfortunately too often overlooked fact that in destroying nature we harm ourselves, we can see that implicit in Schelling's critique of subjectivism's treatment of nature is the demand to extend Kant's kingdom of ends to all the kingdoms of nature. This follows clearly from his call to cease treating nature merely as a means to serving humanity's "economic-teleological ends," as if it had no inherent value in itself. Schelling makes this point clearly in the *Freedom Essay*, calling for the decentering of the self, and therewith the removal of the self-imposed limitations, created by the cogito, that exclude not only the other of organic nature, but even the more familiar other, as in other human beings. In doing this we begin to overcome our alienation from other beings, and in this important sense Schelling claims that the realization of the unity of self and nature generates a knowledge that is in fact *redemptive*. The only way that we would ever be capable of realizing this, however, would be if we were to understand this not in a theoretical way, in the parlor-game manner, for example, in which a Descartes or a Hume doubts the existence of the world, but rather in an emphatic and experiential way, in which what is known is of such importance that one could never be "indifferent" about it. In the case of our relation to nature, this emphatic knowing is both experiential and redemptive. And with this, we begin to grasp the heretical nature of Schelling's philosophy, since it aims not just at theoretical knowing, but more importantly, it aspires to the creative act of realizing our oneness with nature, which, following Schelling's understanding of nature as the revelation of the divine, means the act of creatively realizing our oneness with the divine. This is something that we will only be capable of doing, however, if we become open to the other of logos, with its obscure language of mythos, which speaks with the voice of nature as it "sensualizes truth."[15] This is a possibility that can only be entertained if unity becomes a telos of philosophy, thereby challenging it to harness the disclosive and transformative powers of logos *and* mythos.

Immanent Reconstruction

The ideal of unifying logos and mythos is only one of the reasons why it is so difficult to understand Schelling on his own terms. Working against the more skeptical and analytical tide of modernity, his acceptance of the mythic, the sacred, and the irrational, as essential and potentially life-enhancing factors at play in our existence, has always caused problems for the reader more in conformity with the dominant

Zeitgeist. Another reason for difficulty is the simple fact that until recently we have not had access to his earliest writings; a fact that partially excuses the standard reading of Schelling as a type of brilliant imitator of other philosophers' ideas, with no real thoughts of his own.[16] Yet Schelling claims in his earliest essays that he is presenting ideas he has been wrestling with for some time before his exposure to a Kant or a Fichte. One of the central points we will explore in the following pages is the extent to which we can justify Schelling's claim to originality, a challenge that requires our examination of not only his earliest writings, but the milieu in which he was raised. But while appreciating the intellectual soil from which Schelling emerges is necessary to grasp the singularity of his thought, it is by no means sufficient. What is required for this is an *immanent reconstruction* guided by the internal coherence and meaning of his writings. Justifiable on its own terms, such a "hermeneutic of retrieval" is explicitly advocated by Schelling when he describes his own strategy of interpreting Kant:

> it has never been my intention to copy what Kant had written nor [my claim] to know what Kant *had* properly intended with his philosophy, but merely [to write] what, in *my view*, he *had* to have intended if his philosophy was to prove internally cohesive. (I/1, 375)[17]

Applying this interpretative technique to his own work, our task is quite clearly to discover what Schelling "had to have intended if his philosophy" is "to prove internally cohesive." While such a task in the case of a thinker like Kant is daunting, it is nonetheless expedited by the astonishingly consistent pattern of thinking employed by this logician's analytic mind. Schelling's oeuvre, on the other hand, presents us with a quite different pattern of thought. Instead of the elegantly brutal purity of Kant's binary architectonic, we face a vertiginous pattern of seemingly contradictory principles and constantly evolving systems. Considered from a distance, it would appear that the attempt to discern *one* "internally cohesive" pattern in Schelling's system is destined to fail.

There are, however, other perspectives from which to view the systemic pattern of his work; the most fruitful no doubt would be from a standpoint *within* his body of work, at the very epicenter of his thinking. Thankfully, Schelling provides us with yet another glimpse into his own strategy of immanent reconstruction when he writes that the only way to truly "honor a philosopher" is to uncover his "fundamental thought":

> If one wants to honor a philosopher, then one must grasp him there, in his fundamental thought (*Grundgedanke*), where he has not yet proceeded to the consequences; for against his own intentions he can go astray in the further development, and nothing is easier than to go astray in philosophy, where every false step has infinite consequences, where one on the whole finds himself on a path surrounded on all sides by chasms. The true thought of a philosopher is precisely his fundamental thought from which he proceeds. (II/3, 60)

The context in which Schelling makes this point is his critique of Hegel's system. Yet like Kant, Hegel is also a logician who desires to develop a set *method* of doing philosophy which, as he put it when still a gymnasium instructor, students can learn as easily as they do geometry.[18] Consequently, if Hegel's philosophy should be as simple to learn as geometry, then the fundamental idea that informs it should also be just as simple to ascertain.[19] To uncover the fundamental thought of Schelling, however, presents us with a much more difficult challenge, since in his mind philosophy is not a techne of mimesis, but is rather the ongoing practice or activity of a person constructing their own philosophical system.[20] The singular nature of his prodigious work thus presents a formidable test and challenge of his own hermeneutic strategy.[21]

Fortunately, Schelling himself once again offers a highly suggestive clue as to how one might approach his apparent "chaos of different opinions." This hint is found in the following extended passage from 1797, in which Schelling provides us with an account of how to read Leibniz in particular and the entire history of philosophy in general—an interpretative strategy that should also deliver the key to unlocking Schelling's own "fundamental thought":

> One must have found Leibniz's 'perspectival center of gravity' from which the chaos of the different opinions, which from every other standpoint appear totally confused, exhibits consistency and agreement. In order to find what Leibniz found—that which even in the most contradictory system is actually *philosophical* [and] also true—one must keep in mind the idea of a universal system that provides context and necessity to all individual systems—as opposed as they may be,—in the system of human knowing. Such a comprehensive system can first fulfill the obligation of uniting all the conflicting interests of all other [systems], to prove that as much as they appear to contradict the common understanding, none of them has actually demanded something meaningless . . . For it is manifest that reason can propose no

question that would not already be answered within it.—Thus just as in the seed nothing emerges that was not already united within it, likewise in philosophy nothing can come to be (through analysis) that was not already present (in the original synthesis) in the human spirit itself. For this very reason, a *common* (*gemeinschaftlicher*) ruling spirit permeates all individual systems earning this name; every individual system is possible only through deviation from the universal archetype (*Urbild*), to which all, taken together, more or less approach. This universal system is, however, not a chain that runs upwards, where it hangs onward into infinity link-by-link, but is rather an *organization*, in which every individual member is in relation to every other [member], reciprocally cause and effect, means and ends. Thus too is all progress in philosophy only progress through *development*; every individual system which earns this name can be viewed as a seed which indeed slowly and gradually, but inexorably and in every direction, advances itself in multifarious development. Who has once found such a center of gravity for the history of philosophy is alone capable to describe it truly and according to the worth of the human spirit. (I/1, 457)[22]

As we will briefly see, Schelling believed that he had found "such a center of gravity" of philosophy, and his choice of words to describe this universal archetype of systematic unity is rich in connotations. As the perspectival center of *gravity*, his universal archetype (*Urbild*) is the *one* integrating locus whose centripetal force permeates the *multiplicity* of systems, no matter how different or contradictory, providing them with the shared (*gemeinschaftlicher*) coherence that unites all of them into what can only be an organic system of human knowing. Like the initial conditions of a self-organizing system, this initial archetype reveals itself, in accordance with the principle of self-similarity, in every subsequent phase of this system's evolution. This account of how to read Leibniz's chaos of contradictions provides us with a clear articulation of Schelling's own perception of what unites all systems of philosophy in every age, including his own; a position that implies that this particular account of the epicenter of philosophy must also hold as the focal point of his own system.

What precisely is this locus? Clearly Schelling is appropriating significant elements of Kant's reified Transcendental Ideal, the *Vernunfteinheit* which is both ground and sum of Kant's system, and which the old master himself described as an organic archetype (*Urbild*) of all reason. In the first *Critique* he provides the following description of this one "form of a whole of knowledge":

> If we consider in its whole range the knowledge obtained for us by the understanding, we find that what is peculiarly distinctive of reason in its attitude to this body of knowledge is that it prescribes and seeks to achieve its systematization, that is, to exhibit the connection of its parts in conformity with a single principle. This unity of reason has always presupposed an idea, namely, that of the form of a whole of knowledge—a whole which is prior to the determinate knowledge of the parts and which contains the conditions that determine a priori for every part its position and relation to the other parts. (A 645/B 673)

What Schelling in the previous discussion of Leibniz calls the "the universal archetype" of all philosophical systems is clearly in harmony with the position Kant here expresses. Moreover, both Schelling and Kant can only speak of this archetype through the use of Kant's dynamic categories of community and reciprocity which explain organic systems. For example, Schelling's "center of gravity" is the self-organizing principle which Kant sees as the "single principle" of a one "form of a whole of knowledge"; a unified whole of knowledge which, according to Kant's account of the apprehension of the reciprocal causality found in a living organism, must be *prior* to our determinate knowledge of its constituent parts.[23] And again: both Kant and Schelling are very clear about the asymptotic quality of this archetype: instantiations of the genus 'philosophy' will strive, yet always fail, to live up to the ideal of systematic unity that reason demands of them.[24]

Perhaps the most reliable demonstration of Schelling's fidelity to Kant's project are his own words that state the decisive role Kant's "ideal of reason" played in focusing his earliest work. In 1847, some fifty years after writing the aforementioned passage, Schelling makes explicit "that point in the structure of the Kantian Criticism on which the later developments" of his system "connect as a necessary consequence"—a point which Schelling designates as "Kant's doctrine of the ideal of reason."[25] But although Schelling may be referring to Kant's ideal of reason, and although Kant would agree with Schelling that this archetype can only be conceptualized and articulated through the dynamic categories of community and reciprocity, Schelling is much more consistent in actually doing this than Kant himself.

Essential to understanding Schelling's starting point is his position that this ideal of "a universal system" is not accessible via Kant's regressive method of logical analysis, which can only engage in a sort of *hindcasting*, always arguing backwards, from the conditioned to the unconditioned.[26] Kant's "chain" of an "ascending series" of successive cause and effect relations, which "subordinated to each other as conditions of the possibility of one another," "runs upwards, where it hangs onward into infinity link-by-link"—such a regressive strategy will never succeed in grasping the unconditioned.[27] It will never succeed because, in accordance with Kant's regressive method, this approach to the unconditioned requires a discursive and subsumptive employment of prosyllogisms that proceed in *antecedentia*, an approach that assumes that the archetype of the unity of all thought can somehow be found in one member in this series of cause and effect relations.

Refusing Kant's exclusive reliance on such an analytic approach, Schelling adopts precisely that method of inquiry that Kant suggests, yet nonetheless explicitly excludes from his critical program: that of the progressive method employed by the dynamic categories. In contrast to the procedure of the mathematical categories, the dynamic strategy articulates the unconditioned unity of system through a *progressive* synthesis, which, beginning with the unconditioned itself, proceeds in *consequentia* to the conditioned. The only class of Kantian category capable of effecting this movement of thought is the dynamic category of community and reciprocal causation (*Gemeinshaft* and *Wechselwirkung*). The challenge in this strategy, therefore, is to grasp in one instant the whole in its entirety (a coordinated aggregate), just as one grasps the relationship of an organism's parts in their unity as a whole. To do this, the whole itself must be presupposed as the standpoint from which the movement of thought must begin.[28] And it is only from this epistemological position that Schelling can employ his *ordo generativus* to account for the "*organization*" of Kant's ideal of reason, "in which every individual member is in relation to every other [member] reciprocally cause and effect, means and ends" (I/1, 457).

Breathing life into Kant's nominalistic Transcendental Ideal, Schelling's use of a genetic method enables him to present this integrating force as a *developing* organization whose trajectory of growth aims at the *future*, a move that not only integrates the transcendental into the very center of the temporal world of living creatures, but conversely, enables Schelling to inject life and its dynamic development into the noumenal world of reason.[29] Consequently, his ideal system of knowing "inexorably and in every direction advances itself in multifarious development," propagating itself in the autopoetic act of self-differentiation that produces an ever greater diversity of knowledge. This universal archetype of reason, construed as the form of this dynamic and self-organizing system, shatters the static and dualistic world of Kant's architectonic. While it makes possible the understanding of a historical development of reason, this strategy also supports the more metaphysical position of a transhistorical category of truth: as the organization of reason grows and individuates, the self-similarity of the archetype of unity, revealed in this system's organization, itself remains constant. And it is this integration and unification of the eternal with the temporal that informs the standpoint from which Schelling can then describe the entire history of philosophy "according to the worth of the human spirit." In doing this, Schelling seeks to demonstrate a unity of existence that overcomes the corrosive dualities of the understanding, and thus to overcome the estrangement that for him characterizes our existence:

> With this acknowledgment of the eternal within all things, however, the philosopher sublates the last estrangement (*Entzweiung*) between the phenomenal world and the things-in-themselves. He recognizes that there are not two worlds, but rather one true world, which is not beyond or above the phenomenal, but is rather right here in this one. (I/6, 274)

This reading of Schelling's hermeneutical strategy suggests the considerable degree to which he is working within the conceptual structure Kant advanced to explicate his ideal of reason. Not only does it confirm the older Schelling's assessment of his initial point of departure, but it also recognizes that Kant's Transcendental Ideal constitutes an essential *element* of Schelling's "fundamental thought." But, as we see, his account of how to explicate the unconditioned element of this ideal differs quite significantly from Kant's. Whereas Kant's ideal is an *analytic* archetype, confined to the unchanging realm of the noumenal, Schelling's ideal is a truly *synthetic* unity, which through its archetype of autopoesis and self-organization informs the evolution and development of all nature, including the noetic system of philosophy. Because Kant's unconditioned, the Transcendental Ideal, cannot *become in time*, it cannot be the center of gravity Schelling deems worthy of explaining philosophy's development past, present, and future. While Kant's Transcendental Ideal and his dynamic categories of relation offer a possibility for articulating Schelling's position, they nonetheless fail to completely satisfy his demand to find the center of gravity for the *history* of all philosophy. One of the more easily discernable reasons for Schelling's insistence that the archetype for the entire history of philosophy be provided no doubt stems from his conviction that he has uncovered the very form (center of gravity) of all philosophical inquiry in the writings of Plato; an eternal form of reasoning he also finds confirmed in Kant's philosophy. Read and understood through the genetic philosophy bequeathed to him by his upbringing, Schelling utilizes a transcendental ideal made immanent to account for how the integration of the physical and metaphysical might occur and thereby engender a wholeness and completeness in philosophy that would make it capable of realizing the ἕν καὶ πᾶν.

Having grasped for the moment the fundamental role this idea of organic unity plays for Schelling, let us turn now to examine in more detail why this same thematic is also central to Kant and the project of German Idealism.

Kant and the Categorical Imperative of Unity in Reason

For Schelling it is in the labyrinth of the subject that we run into the duality as perplexing as it is important for Kant and all of modern philosophy, namely, that of the analytic and synthetic unity of self-consciousness. Although Kant claims "the *analytic* unity of self-consciousness must be preceded by a *synthetic* unity," he fails to explain this proposition adequately, "although," as Schelling rightly points out, "it contains the core of the Kantian philosophy" (I/1, 448).[30]

The "core" demanded here must be a form of unity, capable of generating and sustaining the interplay of dualities at the heart of Kant's work, an originary synthetic unity that must also articulate the form of philosophy in general (*überhaupt*). As Kant himself proclaims in the *First Critique*, there "is a necessary law of reason" that "requires us to seek for this unity," since without such a unity "we should have no reason at all" (A 651/B 679). For "what is peculiarly distinctive of reason" is "that it prescribes and seeks to achieve" the "systematization" of its knowledge, "that is, to exhibit the connection of its parts in conformity with a single principle" (A 645/B 673). This principle, however, must be organic, since in this systematization of knowledge Kant must also be capable of accounting for "the self-development of reason" (A 835/B 863). With this, Kant announces what we might call the categorical imperative of unity in reason.[31]

To fully appreciate this unconditional demand for unity we need to turn to Kant's idea of the *maximum*. This most enigmatic and essentially indeterminate idea is defined in the first *Critique* as a supreme "idea of all ideas," whose function is to insure that all other ideas strive for unconditional completeness.[32] The problem with Kant's nominalistic strategy, however, is that to create systematic unity, this idea of the *maximum* requires a binding force external to—and *other* than—his conceptual structure: to avoid the intellectual vertigo of infinite regress, the unity of ideas cannot itself be guaranteed by yet another idea. At some point, the other of the idea must enter the equation.

In the third *Critique* Kant attempts to provide this maximum with more than merely prescriptive efficacy through the introduction of the aesthetic idea of the sublime.[33] Kant claims here that it is the "absolute whole" supplied by the sublime that will not only reveal the supersensible substrate of nature and our thought, but will also provide the purposive kick required to generate systematic unity. To articulate the magnitude of an absolute whole, however, Kant must elevate the dynamic category of *Community* and *Reciprocal Causation* to synthesize an idea of reason—an honor that he specifically denies it in the first *Critique*.[34] Yet while this move in the third *Critique* corrects the architectural flaw of the first, it also upsets the careful bulwark Kant initially constructed between the mathematical and dynamic categories and their respective methodologies of synthesizing the unconditional. For whereas the mathematical categories merely articulate a *potentially infinite* totality, the dynamic categories can account for an *actual infinite* that belongs to the nature of human existence—a fact that suggests to Schelling that this latter set of categories can be made constitutive of *other domains* of experience beyond the limited instance of the sublime. The following paragraph from the *System of Cosmological Ideas* in Kant's first *Critique* captures the radically different capacities of each class of category with admirable clarity:

> We have two expressions, world and nature, which sometimes coincide. The former signifies the mathematical sum-total of all appearances and the totality of their synthesis, alike in the great and in the small, that is, in the advance alike through *composition* and through *division*. This same world is entitled nature when it is viewed as a dynamical whole. We are not then concerned with the aggregation in space and time, with a view to determining it as a magnitude, but with the unity in the existence of appearances. In this case the condition of that which happens is entitled the cause. Its unconditioned causality in the [field of] appearance is called freedom, and its conditioned causality is called natural cause in the narrower [adjectival] sense. The conditioned in existence in general is termed contingent and the unconditioned necessary. The unconditioned necessity of appearances may be entitled natural necessity. (A 418/ B 446f)

Kant's distinction between these two *cosmological ideas* of world and nature is one of the systematic openings Schelling takes full advantage of in the construction of his method. As we will see, he employs these two ideas in his commentary on the *Timaeus* through his technical use of this very distinction between *Weltbegriff* and *Naturbegriff* to interpret Plato's *maximum* (*TK*, 36), which, in contrast to Kant, Plato provides to his cosmogony through the appeal to the unity of a *living organism*. Construed as the power of self-movement and organization, Plato employs the idea of a living *soul* to supply the absolute magnitude of *Einheit* (oneness) that binds his system into an ordered unity.[35] Synthesizing these two strains of thought, Schelling utilizes Kant's rehabilitation of the dynamic category in the third *Critique* as a justification for *inverting* the dynamic categories over the mathematical, thereby accounting not only for the absolute causality of Kant's freedom, but of Plato's account of the unity of organism as well. Building on Kant's distinction between *Weltbegriffe* and *Naturbegriffe*, he employs the progressive method of the latter to understand *life* itself as a form of Kant's *freedom*, here defined as *"absolute self-action"* (A 418/ B 446). For it is only the dynamic category of reciprocity and community that can articulate how a living organism can simultaneously be both cause and effect of itself, in the type of self-action indicative of self-organizing systems. Exploding the linear causality of the mathematical categories, the multivalent causality of nature as a dynamic whole provides Schelling with an understanding of life, as absolute self-action, as the schema of freedom. And it is this absolute *self-action*—articulated through Plato's triad of forms and Kant's category of *community and reciprocity*—that Schelling then uses to articulate his interpretation of Fichte's formula of identity, 'I = I.'[36] The end result is the application of Kant's inverted categories, beginning now with the dynamic categories of experience and relation, not mathematics and numerical identity, to articulate the Platonic form of self-organization. The *Urform* of the *Form Essay* thus betrays a lineage that begins with Plato's *Philebus* and extends through Kant's critiques.

Schelling finds in Kant's own critical program the textual and logical justification for this inversion: the architectonic of the critical program is baseless if it cannot incorporate what its own internal ordering demands, namely, its unification in, or by, an *absolute magnitude* provided by the *Naturbegriffe* of the dynamic category of *community and reciprocity*. If this method of unification is accepted, it follows that the categories of experience must then ground the abstract mathematical categories, and that the *Naturbegriffe* of these categories—specifically Kant's application of them to the purposiveness of organic life in the third *Critique*—should then provide the *"absolute self-action"* Kant himself advances as the absolute causality of freedom. Following Schelling's reading, this absolute of freedom must then become the principle upon which a transformed critical edifice will be erected, and in which it will culminate; a construction, however, which not according to the regressive method of the mathematical categories, but rather according to the progressive method of the dynamic categories of experience. The resulting system thus develops from the form of a disjunctive (and thus oppositional) logic of community and reciprocity, thereby initiating a genetic dialectic in which form and content, concept and intuition, the intelligible and the sensual simultaneously impact and condition one another in a dynamic and purposive process of *generation*—the only such process commensurate with, and indicative of, its author's mode of existing in the world (intentionality). This and only this, according to Schelling, would be a truly synthetic method, grounded in the absolute of a freedom that is capable of integrating both the dualities of human existence, and of accounting for the unconditional unity philosophy demands of system.

Yet, as we will see, it is Kant's own regressive method that holds him back from satisfying his demand for a single principle that should account for the "form of all knowledge," and therewith provide the systematic unity he himself claims is demanded by reason itself. His insistence that his philosophy only deal with the mathematical world and its sum total of appearances ensures that he will always only deal with the conditioned causal chain of observable natural causes, never grasping the unconditioned causality of nature "viewed as a dynamical whole." His division between the noumenal and phenomenal world appears then to require two different causal realms, one whose causal sequence forever remains inaccessible, while the natural causes of appearances submit to ready observation and analysis. Schelling sees in Kant's division of causality into two different realms, one visible and natural, the other non-observable and thus otherworldly, a problem of philosophy he first encountered in the writings of Plato. Moreover, it is in Plato that Schelling finds a way of integrating these two realms of causation by discovering a form of unity that delivers what Kant could not, namely—in Plato's words now—how "the knowledges collectively are many" (*Phil.* 13e8).

Plato's ὁδός and the Eternal Form of Philosophy

In August of 1792, during his second year at the Tübingen *Stift*, the seventeen-year-old Schelling dedicates a notebook entitled "On the Spirit of Platonic Philosophy" with the following passage from Plato's *Timaeus*:

Wherefore one ought to distinguish two different kinds of causes, the necessary and the divine, and in all things seek after the divine for the sake of gaining a life of blessedness, so far as our nature admits thereof . . .[37]

This particular notebook was one of many Schelling produced during his years in Tübingen that dealt with myth and the *Vorstellungsarten* of the ancient world. Having studied many of Plato's dialogues in their original Greek as a boy, the dedication to this notebook is significant as an index of the determinative role this philosopher plays in the young Schelling's intellectual world.[38]

As we will see later in greater detail, Schelling interprets Plato's distinction between the two classes of divine and necessary causes as paralleling the Kantian distinction between freedom and necessity, while nonetheless reading the former thinker as providing for what the latter philosopher denies, namely, the possibility of integrating the divine *qua* freedom with the necessity of natural causation. Whereas Kant segregated divine freedom and natural causality, assigning them to their own distinct noumenal or phenomenal districts, Schelling seeks to integrate these two seemingly irreconcilable realities of human existence. The challenge is huge, since to do this he will have to account for how the material world of nature could possibly reveal the activity of freedom. But if successful, Schelling believes he will find the key to accounting for how we, as self-conscious and self-determining beings, could possibly come to integrate that which is other than our thinking cogito—be it our emotions, other humans, nature, or the divine.

The importance Schelling places on this idea is demonstrated by the fact that a decade later, in 1802, he explains the title of his *Bruno or on the Divine and Natural Principle of Things: A Dialogue*, by citing this same passage from the *Timaeus*. In a note to this title he writes:

On the Divine and Natural Principle of Things. A passage from Plato's *Timaeus* serves as a provisional explanation [of this title]: "Wherefore one ought to distinguish two different kinds of causes, the necessary and the divine, and in all things seek after the divine for the sake of gaining a life of blessedness, so far as our nature admits thereof. (I/4, 330)

The title of the *Bruno Dialogue* signifies the same determinative interest that guided the seventeen-year-old seminarian a decade earlier, namely, to move beyond the static categories of the understanding by seeking to articulate an organic form of philosophy capable of accounting for how the divine (freedom) and the natural can interact with one another in the generative activity of our world. Only if he is capable of pulling this off can he account for the unity of our knowledge, and this includes our knowledge of the physical as well as the metaphysical, the noumenal as well as the phenomenal.

What is significant for our inquiry is how Schelling locates the means to articulate this organic form in Plato's "way (ὁδός)," which he claims is the eternal form of reason capable of accounting for the unity of difference. In the all-important words he cites from Plato's *Philebus*:

> We notice, he says, that this form, of unity in multiplicity, has every-where governed all speech and investigations from long ago up till our time. This form will never cease to be thought, and has not just now begun, but rather it is an eternal unchanging characteristic of every investigation. The young man who first discovers this form of philoso-phizing, delights as if he had found a treasure of wisdom; his delight fills him with enthusiasm, happily he participates in every investiga-tion, sometimes fastening everything that occurs to him together in one concept, sometimes again dissolving and dividing everything. (*Phil.* 15d8–e5)[39]

Exemplifying the very enthusiasm of the novice Plato here writes of, Schelling sees in these words the solution to Kant's problem of unity, and embraces this eternal form of reasoning as the "center of gravity" of all philosophical inquiry. The centrality of this idea is demonstrated by the fact that he proceeds to refer to it in every one of his earliest writings.

The first reference occurs in his *Magister* of 1792.[40] Two years later, he dedicates a substantial portion of his commentary on the *Philebus* and *Timaeus* to analyzing Plato's use of this form to articulate the genesis of the world.[41] A few months after completing this commen-tary, he puts Plato's triad of forms to work in his first philosophical essay on *The Possibility of a Form of Philosophy in General*, employing them as the implicit framework for his "*Urform*" of all philosophical inquiry.[42] The "principle of unity" that frames his next essay, *Of the I*, betrays the same imprint,[43] while his *Abhandlung* essay explicitly incorporates Plato and this dynamic into his articulation of how the imagination mediates the senses (*Sinn*) and understanding (*Verstand*).[44]

His *Ideas for a Philosophy of Nature* incorporates Plato's use of this form to articulate "that secret band (*jenes geheime Band*)" of the soul, as it unites mind and body into an organic unity,[45] while the title of *The World Soul* speaks for itself. This common pattern that runs throughout all his early works suggests that we should read these texts as the result of the recursive application of this generative form of reasoning to the perennial questions of philosophy.

In his commentary on the *Timaeus*, Schelling reads this organic form of unity in multiplicity as the *"pure, original* form" of Plato's divine understanding which, since it creates both material reality and mind, functions as the common ground to both being and thought. Introducing the Kantian vocabulary into his commentary, Schelling presents this original form of all thinking and being as a universal law or condition of all empirical inquiry. He writes that "this becomes even clearer from the following passage," which he freely translates from *Philebus* 16c5–e5 as follows:

> This form is a gift of the gods to men, which together with the purest fire was first given to them through Prometheus. Therefore the ancients (greater men and closer to the gods than us) have left the story behind, that everything which has ever emerged out of unity and multiplicity (plurality), in that it united within itself the unlimited (apeiron, universal) and the limit (to peras, unity): that thus we too in light of this arrangement of things should presuppose and search for every object one idea. . . . —It was the gods then, who taught us to think, learn and teach like this. (*TK*, 36)[46]

This gift of the gods is the idea that all reality, both mental and material, is permeated by a common structure, which, through its generative form, unifies the entirety of the all into one living organism of divine creation. Schelling understands Plato's portrayal of the dynamic interaction of form and matter through the *cosmological ideas* of τò πέρας, τòἄπειρον, and their generation of τò κοινόν (*das Dritte*), as a paradigm for the generation of the entire chain of being that stretches from the absolute whole of the universe to the producing of every individual entity.

Schelling specifically focuses on how Plato applies this form to account for both the creation of the manifold entities of the world, and the generation of life from the union of the blind soul of matter and the forms of the understanding.[47] It is this later topic of the generation of organic life that prompts Schelling to explicitly draw on Kant's infamous examination of *organism* from §65 of the third *Critique*. His ensuing analysis establishes the parallel structure of Kant's category of *community* and Plato's triadic form:

> We must moreover remind ourselves that Plato looked at the entire world as a ζωόν, i.e., as an organized being, thus as a being whose parts are possible only in relation to the whole, and thus according to their form as well as connection reciprocally produce one another. We must consider, that we, according to the subjective arrangement of our faculty of knowing, can simply not conceive of the emergence of an organized being in any other way than *through* the causality of a concept, of an idea, that *a priori* determines everything that is contained in the being; that, just as the particular parts of the organized being reciprocally produce each other and thus produce the whole, conversely, once again, the idea of the whole must be thought as preceding, and a priori determinative of the form and the parts in their harmony. (*TK*, 33)

The ordering of the whole before the part, required by Kant's category of *community*, provides Schelling with the key that unlocks the order of Plato's triad of causes. From the standpoint of "empirical existence," the element of the triad that presents itself first is that of the third and common element.[48] But from the standpoint of the thinking philosopher, employing Kant's regressive method of analysis, this unity can only be parsed if it can be reduced to a series consisting of its parts. According to Schelling, however, to fully understand the phenomenon under consideration, *both* standpoints must be incorporated, and in their proper order. Thus in the order of empirical existence and investigation, the unity of the whole becomes the necessary starting point and context within which reflection can then take place. From this insight, Schelling concludes that what appears to the regressive method as the successive addition of parts in a series is actually, from the standpoint of empirical existence, a coordinated dynamic whole that interacts with its constituent parts through a multivalent form of causality that allows for their mutual interaction.[49] The integrated, yet trinitarian interaction of Plato's three causes becomes for Schelling the *Urform* of the community of organism, and thus of identity in difference. In short, this original form becomes the paradigm for a dynamic yet monistic dualism capable of overcoming the trenchant dualities of the analytic understanding.

Schelling cites the *Philebus* passage a decade later in his *Bruno*. He uses it here as historical evidence for his contention that there is an eternal form of reason that supplies the *only* standpoint "*worthy* of philosophical consideration."[50] Schelling writes:

> Is it not manifest, that the tendency to posit the infinite in the finite and conversely the later in the former, is dominant in all philosophical speech and investigations? To think this form is [as] eternal as the essence of that which is expressed in it, and it has not just now begun, and nor will it ever cease; it is, as Socrates in Plato says, the immortal, never changing characteristic of every investigation. (I/4, 242)

Schelling proceeds in *Bruno* to argue that this form alone is capable of articulating the "Idea of all ideas," the "only object of all philosophy," the one *qua* "unity (*Einheit*)" (I/4, 243). This, Schelling believes, is the "form of all forms" that both Kant and Plato attempt to articulate within and through their own respective frameworks.[51]

Well read in Plato's work, the young Schelling clearly detects the Platonic spirit at work in Kant's program. As we will see in his work on the *Timaeus* and *Philebus*, Schelling plays Kant against Plato, and Plato against Kant, to generate his own strategy for integrating the natural and the divine, and therewith, the conditioned with the unconditional, a strategy that, in blending Plato with Kant, inverts the latter's singular use of a trichotomy in the category of relation, and synthesizes it with Plato's trinity of the τὸ πέρας, τὸ ἄπειρον, and τὸ κοινόν. The resulting triad is, on the one hand, Schelling's reinterpretation of Plato's eternal mode of thinking, "which belongs to reason itself as such"[52]; on the other hand, the resulting triad is an inversion of Kant's categories, whereby relation displaces quantity as the only possible form of philosophy *überhaupt*. The focal point of Schelling's goal is to account for how, in Plato's terms, the one relates to the many—or in Kant's terms, how the transcendental relates to the empirical—or in Schelling's own terms, how the freedom of the divine interacts with necessity of nature. In this way Plato's dialectical ὁδός of the one and the many becomes the model for Schelling's inversion of Kant's categories and his development of a dynamic philosophy which, in elevating the dynamic categories of relation above the mathematical categories of magnitude, attempts to integrate eternity and freedom with the immanent world of temporality and necessity.[53] As the form of the *ordo generativus*, this triadic dynamic accounts for creation *überhaupt*, a generative process Schelling sometimes refers to as the self-revelation of the divine, and at other times as the *Subject-Objectivirung* of the Absolute. As such, this organic form thereby becomes the conceptual vehicle through which

Schelling pursues his quest of apprehending the divine in nature, and thereby accounting for the ἕν καὶ πᾶν.

The epistemological dilemmas of self-reflexivity are obvious and critical, but they pale in comparison to the ethical consequences of tolerating, and even embracing, the trenchant dualism demanded by modern subjectivism. Schelling holds that there must be a common bond that binds together the seeming difference of subject and object, and that the demonstration of such a unity of difference supplies the basis of knowledge *überhaupt*. These epistemological issues, however, are but preliminary exercises that constitute a propaedeutic to realizing the extent to which this common bond is grounded in our interconnectedness with nature. And as alien as it may sound to contemporary ears, Schelling believes that the realization of this interconnectedness reveals the promise of a redemption that will overcome our estrangement.

The source of the passion with which Schelling assails the subjectivism of modernity for robbing sensuous nature of her sacredness is his (seemingly non-modern) conviction that our world is the self-revelation of the deity. The sacredness of nature so conceived is religious in the etymological sense of this word, meaning "to bind back together." From this standpoint, if nature is the revelation of the divine, then nature herself provides the schema of unity that Schelling places at the core of his system. As a living organism, nature offers an example of a living unity that the discursive categories of the understanding cannot. It is a living unity whose inner dialectic is not the negative sublation of an alienating logic, but rather a dynamic of reconciliation, a positive integration of contraries capable of sustaining a "self-moving, suffering" and "creative unity":

> If only the understanding, deserted by reason, wants to raise itself over and out of the limitedness and the opposition, then the highest point to which it can attain is the negation of the opposition, i.e., the vacuous unproductive unity, whose opposite is posited only as something unholy and not divine, which climbs out from itself, but has in no way taken the contrary up into itself and is capable of truly reconciling it. For reason however, the opposition is just as original and true as the unity, and only in that it grasps both in the same way, and itself as one, does it know the living identity. The opposition must be since life must be; for the opposition itself is life and movement in unity; but the true identity handles itself as integrated, i.e., it posits itself simultaneously as opposition and unity, and thus a self-moving, suffering, creative unity. (I/7, 52)

As opposed to a reason of negation and its ideal of a unity purged of the oppositions that constitute our reality, Schelling insists that a free and binding unity can only be created if we develop a means of integrating the heterogeneous elements that animate and constitute our nature. Consequently, Schelling's system of freedom refuses the Kantian "doctrine according to which freedom consists in the sheer *Herrschaft* of the intelligible principle over the sensual desires and inclinations, wherein the good is derived from pure reason."[54] True freedom is instead the reconciliation of the sensual and the intelligible, aptly articulated through the dynamic category of community and reciprocity, whereby both enter into productive intercourse, thereby restoring the generative unity that is the condition of possibility of creation *qua* life.

Organic Unity and Nature's Redemption

According to Kant, the euthanasia of pure reason is the consequence of reason's unrestrained application of the objective synthesis of appearances. Although this strategy initially shows great promise in generating unconditional unity, its rather simplistic projection of the subjective forms of reason onto the objective phenomenal world eventually self-implodes under the weight of the internal contradictions that emerge from its sustained employment. At this point, Kant predicts that reason will be so "constrained" by its own self-contradictions that it will lose the resolve even to seek to establish a principle of unconditioned unity. Despondent with its seeming impotence to attain what it desires, reason will "abandon itself to a skeptical despair."[55]

Contrary to his best intentions, Kant's Copernican Revolution helped initiate the very chain of events his prophecy warned against. His global employment of a reflective modality of thinking set the stage for its enthronement as the actual structure of not only human consciousness, but also all of reality. His alchemical inversion of the possible experience of conceptual "reality" as the condition of actual experience provided the structures of support for the subsequent animism of the concept as the actual life-giving force of nature. And his transformation of the divine *omnitudo realitis* into a linguistic *Inbegriff* of all possible predicates is an ideal that has led to the deification of language as the absolute source and mediator of "meaning."

The speculative thesis of this work is that there exists in the work of Schelling a possible schema for a new configuration of unity and freedom capable of overcoming the destructive void of contemporary philosophy. The schema for such a possible unity lies in his conception of a *decentered Self* whose consciousness is conceived on the model of productive self-organization vis-à-vis the wider self-organization that is nature. Construing reality as essentially organic allows Schelling to articulate successfully both the normative and descriptive unity of humanity and nature as members of a larger totality. In response to his contemporaries' circular attempts to articulate self-consciousness, Schelling develops a genetic history of the self whose unity is rooted *jenseits* the grasp of self-reflection; the roots of our consciousness lie embedded in a strata of our nature that provide the common ground which unites human *qua* species with the world. The impossibility of knowing these roots, reflexively, and the error of making this liminal level of our existence dependent on our ability to know it thus reflected is a theme that runs consistently throughout Schelling's career:

> For all the failed attempts to answer this share the mistake of attempting to explain conceptually what effectively precedes all concepts; they all betray the same incapacity of the spirit to transcend discursive thinking and to ascend to the immediacy that exists within us. (I/1, 376)

The immediacy that exists within us is the possibility of grasping a unity that "effectively precedes all concepts." This defense of immediacy and the attempt to restrain discursivity from encroaching upon the domain of what he will term *das Unvordenkliche* (that before which nothing can be thought), requires a way of grasping the other that reframes the reflexive tropes of modernity. Consequently, as an alternative to Kant's Transcendental Ideal and its formal logic of reflection, Schelling posits an "ideal of the world" that is an ideal of immanent transcendence realized through a logic of production, which takes the generative power of organic nature as its template and the promise of a balanced and integrated unity as its telos.[56]

His medium of choice for the expression of his vision is textual, and through it he strives to create not just a new philosophy, but also a new form of philosophy that would, by incorporating the numinous dimension of myth, usher in an era of the realization of the divine in nature. While such sentiments are evident throughout his writings, perhaps nowhere are they as clearly stated as in the concluding paragraph of the *Oldest System Program of German Idealism* (1797). Here Schelling and company advance a prophetic vision in which the dualities of myth and reason, of the ideal and the sensuous, have been overcome by an "eternal unity" brought on by a "new religion":

Before we make the Ideas aesthetic, i.e., mythological, they are of no interest to the *people*, and on the other hand, before mythology is reasonable, the philosopher must be ashamed of it. Thus enlightened and unenlightened must finally shake hands, mythology must become philosophical and the people reasonable, while philosophy must become mythological in order to make the philosophers sensuous. Then eternal unity will reign among us. Never the despising gaze, never the blind trembling of the people before its wise men and priests. Only then do we expect *equal* development of *all* powers, of the individual as well as the individuals. No power will be suppressed any more, and general freedom and equality of spirits will reign! A higher spirit sent from heaven must found this new religion among us, it will be the last, greatest work of humanity.[57]

This new religion spiritualizes nature in a *Versinnlichung* of its truth. Its gospel preaches no otherworldly dualism, but rather a radical immanence of transcendence. Betraying the decisive influence of Plato, it is explicitly demanded that his ideas—and those of his contemporary interpreter, Kant—be made sensuous. Only this will realize the infinite within the finite in a manifestation of beauty, thereby providing sensuous access to the infinite divine.

As we will see in the next chapter, the telos of this youthful crescendo of idealism has its roots in the philosophical theology of the Württemberg Pietists, Oetinger and Hahn. And as we will see in the chapters that follow, this vision of a new religion and mythology of a sensualized truth does not fade as Schelling's career advances. He later explicitly connects the program of his *Naturphilosophie* with this new mythology, and argues in his *Philosophy of Art* that a "future symbolism and mythology" will emerge from the foundations established by his speculative physics, writing:

> Neither do I hide my conviction that in the philosophy of nature, as it has been developed from the idealistic principle, the first, distant foundation has been laid for that future symbolism and mythology that will be created not by an individual but rather by an entire age. (I/5, 449)

Here, just as in his *Oldest System Program*, Schelling denies the possibility that an individual alone can be responsible for a new mythology. Elsewhere, however, while reemphasizing this point, he provides an opening for his own individual activities, writing that the best a "truly creative individual" can hope for is "to create his own mythology, and this can occur using virtually any material or content, thus also that of a higher physics" (I/5, 446). The content or material of such poesy and mythology also remains consistent with the Platonic and Kantian overtones of the *Oldest System Program*: it is "the world of ideas" that can also "be viewed as a world of gods" (I/5, 451). But the future mythology will never allow itself to be "designed simply according to the instructions of certain ideas of philosophy" (I/5, 446). Rather this new culture "await[s] its gods," leaving it to the *"Fügung der Zeit"* to determine the ultimate "synthesis of history and nature" (I/5, 449), of necessity and freedom, that will usher in the post-Christian era of the spirit, in which, true to Hahn's prophecy, the "rebirth of nature" will be recognized as "the symbol of eternal unity":

> Whether this moment of time, which for all developments in science and works of humanity has become such a strange turning point, whether it will not also be so for religion, in which the true Gospel of reconciliation of the world in its relationship to God will draw near, in which the temporal and merely external forms of Christianity collapse and disappear,—this is a question which must be left for every individual, *who understands the signs of the future*, answer for themselves.
>
> The new religion, which already announces itself in singular revelations, which is the return to the first mystery of Christianity and its completion, will be recognized in the rebirth of nature as the symbol of eternal unity; the first reconciliation and dissolution of the primordial strife will have to be celebrated in philosophy, whose sense and meaning only *that* person will grasp, who recognizes in nature the life of the newly arisen deity. (I/5, 120; emphasis mine)

The telos of his vision is the overcoming of the estrangement and alienation Schelling first addresses in his *Magister*; the realization of this vision is once again the realization of nature in its sacred status as the deity externalized, the spirit of the divine made flesh.

And this is what makes Schelling a heretic in the eyes of the orthodoxy of the Enlightenment: his understanding of the intimate relation between religion and philosophy.[58] Just as the only possible form of generative *geistige* activity must engage the binary structures of our thought process, kicking them into a complementary and thus productive opposition, so too with the relation between religion and philosophy. As stated in his *Oldest System Program*, the "new religion" will require that mythology [religion] "become philosophical and the people reasonable, and philosophy . . . become mythological [religious] in order to make the philosophers sensuous." Neither will be reduced to the other, rather both will limit and challenge the other to work towards their united, progressive development. Religion, without the critical discipline of philosophy, has a well-documented destructive effect on life, manifesting itself in the fevered frenzy of blind faith and the zealous acts of religiously motivated hatred that litter our past and populate our present. Conversely, philosophy devoid of the animating force of the divine and living spirit becomes an act of intellectual onanism, failing to fulfill the challenge of creation, settling instead for the immediate gratification of an illusory power and control that ultimately leads to its own demise, as it grows increasingly irrelevant to the life it fails to integrate, much less engender. Instead of generating a vision for the present and future, it collapses into just another scholarly pursuit of the fossilized truths of the past.

At the close to his *Freedom Essay* (1809), Schelling makes a rather pointed remark regarding the possibility of philosophy in his day, which might be even more relevant now:

> If the dialectical principle (that is the differentiating understanding which, precisely because of this, organically orders and forms) as well as the archetype towards which it is directed, are both simultaneously withdrawn from philosophy, so that it no longer has either measure or rule in itself, then there remains nothing else for philosophy to do save attempt to orient itself historically, and to take as its source and guiding principle *tradition*. (I/7, 307)

If we remove the telos of philosophy, the "archetype" of divine unity "towards which it is directed," we then deprive it of its power to attract, to generate hope, and thereby to transform the present, as well as provide an opening for a changed future.[59] Such a negative philosophy becomes a historical subject, since its truth lies not in the present or possible future, but rather only in the past. The philosopher then becomes a scholar of the history of ideas, his role devolving from creator of new visions and meaning, to that of a parasite living off the host body of the historical truths of tradition. Having lost all connection to the immediacy of truth, such a philosophy must then resign itself to a lifeless and uninspired form of ancestor worship.

Schelling, however, finds this possible future of philosophy—although a very real threat in his own day—to be overshadowed by a very different possible future, in which philosophy rediscovers the immediacy and living force of truth as revealed in nature. The decisive contrast lies between the immediate knowledge of truth as revealed in nature, or a faith in the truths of the past as mediated in texts. His rather heretical strategy to move ahead is to cast this estrangement in the subject-object terms of our relation to nature: the *Entzweiung* is between the illusive asymmetrical relationship we have posited to exist between the human subject and the object of nature. This is the context in which his critique of modern philosophy since Descartes occurs: that making the subject absolute will lead to the *annihilation* of nature. The *estrangement* requiring resolution, however, is not *within* the human self *per se*, but rather between the human subject and the object of nature. In the closing paragraph of his *Freedom Essay* Schelling expresses this eloquently, connecting the "possibility of immediate knowledge" with access to a "revelation" of truth more originary than that of the religions of historical faith. The revelation of which he speaks is to be sought in the forces of nature:

> We entertain the greatest respect for the profound significance of historical investigations; . . . we believe that truth lies nearer to us and that we should first seek the solution for the problems that have become vital in our time among ourselves and on our own soil, before we wander to such distant sources. The time of merely historical faith is past as soon as the possibility of immediate knowledge is given. We have an earlier revelation than any written one—nature. It contains archetypes that no one has yet interpreted, whereas the written ones have long since received their fulfillment and exegesis. If the understanding of that unwritten revelation were inaugurated, the only true system of religion and science would appear, not in the miserable garb pieced together out of a few philosophical and critical conceptions, but at once in the full significance of truth and of nature. (I/7, 307)[60]

And what does nature as the manifestation of divine life produce in human consciousness but, at a lower level of complexity, myth, and at a higher level, revelation. As Schelling writes regarding the relation between mythology and revelation in his *Philosophy of Revelation* (1841–1842), in myth the "presentations (*Vorstellungen*) are products of a necessary process," whereas revelation "presupposes an *actus* outside consciousness and a relationship which the most free of all causes, God, has himself freely given to mankind."[61]

Echoing Plato's call to seek the two classes of causes, the natural and the divine, Schelling here, some fifty years after composing his notebooks in Tübingen, once again assigns the divine as the source of a free and thus immediate knowledge, capable of overcoming the limits of an estranged consciousness, chained as it is to a reality determined by the necessary causes of tradition and convention. Obviously, such knowledge, unmediated and free, breathes life into the imagination and creativity required by every act of discovery or revelation, be it scientific or artistic. The *actus* for this creative development Schelling locates in the most potent freedom, the divine freedom of God, with the result that knowledge, unmediated, free, and creative, becomes redemptive in its power to bring unity to humanity's limited and fractured consciousness. And since the arena of this transformative knowing is this world, this knowledge is ultimately a *Mitwissenschaft*, a *conscientia*, through which humanity realizes its essential unity and dependence on nature.

By definition, the voice of prophecy is rarely clear and the views of a heretic are seldom comforting. At first glance, our presentation of Schelling's "new philosophical religion" may appear total nonsense: he uses terms we are familiar with, but arranges them differently, establishing connections and relations among concepts we normally don't perceive as having anything to do with each other. How can nature be a revelation? How can immediate knowledge provide us with a truth that will somehow solve the problems of our time? How can one understand the unwritten revelation of truth in nature? Finally, how can one coherently think a God who is the free cause or *actus* of humanity's potential consciousness of the most liberating knowledge of all, divine knowledge? Particularly if we think of god as nature, so that the source of revelation is from an *actus* beyond our consciousness, namely nature?

The key to addressing these questions lies in Schelling's embrace of the immanent ideal of organic unity, whose completeness, understood in the sense of balance and integration, supplies the conceptual resources to ground ethics in the aesthetic productivity of life, understood as the schema of freedom. As we will see later in chapter 4, Schelling latches onto Plato's creator deity who, in contrast to the ethically ambiguous character of the Abrahamic God, is a singular deity who desires that creation be as "like unto himself" as possible (*Tim.*, 29e). This divine desire Schelling reads as positing an ideal of completion for creation, in which it should be as full and complete, in the sense of τὸ ὄν, as the creator deity is. It is here in his reading of Plato's creation that we see Schelling begin to elevate beauty over the good, as he calls upon Plato's description of τὸ ὄν as τό καλόν, rather than τὸ ἀγαθόν. Schelling suggests with this that the ethical term τὸ ἀγαθόν is too limited and one-sided, whereas τὸ καλόν speaks to beauty judged according to balance and proportion, and thus better suited to capture the *arrangement* of τὸ ὄν,[62] a *completeness* in creation that requires the uniting and integration of the seemingly dualistic domains of the *intellectual and the sensual*. This is the conclusion of Schelling's attempt to unearth the integrating principle of Plato's cosmogony: beauty, understood as completeness, requires that both the sensible and intellectual be united to form one whole, integrated entirety. And it is the aesthetic which, better than the ethical good, speaks to the common ground, the *supersensible substrate*, that unites nature and our thought, since not only can the aesthetic balance dualities, but following both Plato and Kant, the sublime realization of this oneness results in an enthusiasm, a *Begeisterung*, which, as this term's etymology indicates, has the divine as its cause, and is easily linked to Schelling's understanding of intellectual intuition. And it is precisely this experience, this sublime realization of the oneness of our natures, which overcomes our alienation and redeems us, making us whole again with our nature.

In his *Oldest System Program* Schelling takes on the mantle of prophecy, proclaiming the advent of a new religion, one whose text is nature, which as living, provides us with the schema of our freedom. Life strives for a self-differentiation that engenders freedom, which always looks forward towards the future. As we will see in the final chapter of what follows, Schelling holds that the tense of the absolute is futurity, an open-ended orientation to *what should be* that requires a rethinking of traditional teleology. Grounded in Schelling's weaving of freedom into the very fabric of nature, this new teleology departs from the hindcasting of the Aristotelian model, in which the telos is already prefigured in the formal cause. To say that futurity is the tense of the absolute is to acknowledge that the absolute is, as every self-organizing system, incessantly engaged in the process of development and further self-differentiation. As Schelling's account of creation in the *Timaeus* makes clear, it is precisely this incessant creating that is complete, and thus beautiful. But *complete* in this process of development does not mean the telos of this process is *completely determined*, a situation that for Schelling could only generate "complete boredom."[63] Completeness in this process speaks instead to the possibility of the future as the arena in which *what should be* is realized as *what is*. And it is in this sense that this new teleology is perhaps best called *utopian thinking*.

Informed by his analysis of Plato's triadic *way* of doing philosophy, Schelling injects a triadic ordering into his own system that follows seamlessly from his organic form of philosophy. Driven by Kant's dynamic category of relation, he sets the unlimited power of nature and the limiting force of history into a relation of reciprocal causality, out of which emerges the third that binds these two, namely, art. As he wrote in 1797, "There should thus be a *philosophy of nature and a philosophy of history*. As the third which emerges from both one must add the *philosophy of art*" (I/1, 465).[64] This ordering complements the dynamic at work in his *Oldest System Program*, in which the anticipated *eschaton* can only occur if aesthetics integrates the truths of philosophy and religion, creating a balanced and complete work that makes the truths of both concrete. Yet it is this creative process that, as most free, is least stable, and thus least predictable in its outcome. The aesthetic vision is in this sense utopian in that this thinking gestures at a place, a future that does not yet exist. And in the same sense that Kant's Kingdom of Ends can only be read as a secularized Kingdom of God, this utopian thinking is to be understood as a secularized form of prophecy in which a thinker creates the telos, the purpose, and the vision of what his philosophy, what his life, should become. Schelling's organic form of philosophy challenges philosophy to become productive, to self-differentiate in the most potent way possible, through the creative power of the aesthetic, so that the noetic ideas of reason are made sensuous and concrete, thereby offering the hope of transforming reality itself.

Ideas *in situ*: Embedded Thought

In the *Form Essay*, the essay that put the nineteen-year-old seminary student on the philosophical map, Schelling makes the rather provocative claim that it is grounded in ideas that he has been thinking about "for some time" (I/1, 87). Contrary to the traditional reading of Schelling as a sort of brilliant imitator and synthesizer of ideas advanced by Kant, Fichte, and perhaps Jacobi and Spinoza, Schelling himself claims that his first philosophical essay deals with thoughts and ideas that predate his exposure to these thinkers. Ideas which, as he acknowledges, have been recently stimulated by the writings of Maimon, Fichte, and Schultz, but whose original quality and depth can only be fully understood and appreciated in the context of the culture that helped shape his singular vision of philosophy. Consistent with the principles of immanent reconstruction, the second stage of our work begins in situating his ideas in the intellectual soil that gave birth to them.

The young Schelling was brought up in an intellectually and religiously charged atmosphere, where he was exposed to both the learning of traditions past and the critical edge of contemporary scholarly

methods. Central to our effort at making sense of his claim to originality is his early study of Plato, which began at the age of eleven, and
whose depth and importance we can now more fully appreciate given
the recently published notebooks he composed while a student at the
Tübingen *Stift*. And while a careful examination of his commentaries
on the *Philebus* and *Timaeus* is the subject of chapter 4, we must first
turn to the intellectual milieu of his upbringing so that we might
approach his commentaries on Plato from the most productive angle.
His acculturation steeped him in teachings heavily influenced by two
leading figures of his community, Philipp Matthäus Hahn (1739–1790)
and Friedrich Christoph Oetinger (1702–1782); teachings which, when
examined in the context of Schelling's reading of Plato and Kant, help
us not only to come to a better understanding of the genesis of his
philosophical world, but also help to explain some of the more controversial aspects of his work. As we will see in the next chapter, it was in
his most formative years that he was exposed to Oetinger and Hahn's
idea that life is the first predicate of not only the divine, but of creation
itself, a position that in elevating the will and its freedom over reason
and its laws creates an intellectual environment in which life naturally
emerges as the schema of freedom. Both Oetinger and Hahn make use
of an "*Ordo Generativus*" which, more fundamental than the mechanistic *ordo mathematicus* of a Cartesian or Newtonian physics, uses a
genetic logic to understand the living world around us as the ongoing
revelation of the divine. Grounded in the sacred status of nature, these
two thinkers interpret the evolutionary dynamic of this revelation
through a triadic framework based on the very same Platonic texts
Schelling will use to articulate the organic form of his philosophy.

The conviction with which Schelling wields a remarkably similar
genetic framework no doubt results from his exposure to Oetinger and
Hahn's ideas, but perhaps even more importantly, it springs from the
deep respect and fascination he had for Hahn in particular, whom he
not only met as a young boy, but who was a regular correspondent
with Schelling's relatives. The source of this respect and fascination
was due not only to this man's presence, something which Schelling
vividly recalls several decades later, but also to this man's alleged experiences of a direct intuitive grasp of divine, fundamental truth. It was
believed that Hahn had experienced twice in his life what was called
the *Zentralschau*, an intuitive insight that, like Aristotle's encounter
with the *nous poetikos* and Spinoza's *scientia intuitiva*, provides access
to a truth which, unmediated and undisturbed by discursivity and
predication, permits one to actually experience the divine ἕν καὶ πᾶν.
The reality of Hahn's experience provides the background to Schelling's

embrace and defense of *intellectual intuition* as a necessary source for a comprehensive epistemology capable not only of integrating logos and mythos, but also of understanding the voice of nature as it speaks through the genius, both as artist and prophet. Also significant for the young Schelling was Hahn's role as a self-proclaimed heterodox prophet whose freethinking led to the censorship of his writings by the Württemburg church. But perhaps most important for deciphering a central puzzle of Schelling's philosophy was Hahn's status as a renowned *Naturphilosoph*, a natural scientist of true acclaim, whose empirical investigation of nature was guided by the belief that humanity's role in creation is to complete its evolution by coming to know the divine *through* nature. So taken by the remarkable figure of Hahn, the fifteen-year-old Schelling, after Hahn's death, published a poem eulogizing him in the local newspaper, a significant poem in that Schelling dedicates his life here to following Hahn's path of investigating both the "forces of nature" and the "harmony of the soul."[65] As perhaps no other historical document, this brief *Jugendgedicht* provides us with the key to understanding Schelling's lifelong commitment to *Naturphilosophie*, and the attendant challenge of integrating the irreconcilable dualities of nature and soul, or, in Plato's words from the *Timaeus*, of integrating the *same* and the *other* into one.

In this first chapter, I have purposely compacted the telos of Schelling's thought into a synoptic account in order to focus our investigation on the perplexing yet important question of the fundamental characteristics of his thought. In this way, the telos of his thinking will hopefully facilitate our efforts to construct an accurate portrayal of his initial defining interest, a proposition which Schelling himself considers essential to understanding the work of any great thinker.[66] The assumption central to this quest is Schelling's conviction that *life is the schema of freedom*, an understanding of life as that which manifests the active presence of freedom, and which parallels the influx of the divine in the immanent world of nature. As such, an organic form of philosophy is the only form capable of accounting for the self-organizing reality of our world, both in its divine and in its natural manifestation, in a systematically unified manner. As we will see in the next chapter, Schelling's understanding of nature as the self-revelation of the divine is in many ways the result of the tradition he was raised in as a youth. And while many of the religious and seemingly mythic ideas we encounter may, in the words of the *Oldest System Program*, momentarily "embarrass the philosopher," the understanding we gain of the rich *geistige* soil which gave birth to Schelling will go a long way in helping us to understand this challenging thinker on his own terms.

2

Beginnings

Theosophy and Nature Divine

The Acculturation of a Prophet of Nature

We begin at ground zero. To engage in an immanent reconstruction of the inner dynamic of Schelling's philosophy we must first attempt to bring to light the background from whence his ideas emerged. This exercise will prove all the more worthwhile since in this chapter we survey a cast of figures whose passions and beliefs do much to solve many of the puzzles apparent in our subject's work.

In what follows we explore the upbringing and acculturation of Schelling, paying particular attention to three determinative forces: 1) the scholarly study of ancient languages and text criticism, 2) Pietism and the freedom of the unmediated experience of the divine, and 3) Theosophy and the divinity of nature. The study of ancient language inducted the young Schelling into the ordered and disciplined world of thinking and its ability to travel through time; the second factor stands opposed to the first: the unmediated experience of the divine provided Schelling with a normative paradigm of the priority of experience over reflection. The last influence unites the previous two: through his exposure to the person of Philipp Matthäus Hahn (1739–1790), Schelling was presented with an ideal of one who dedicates his life to pursuing the divine in both sensuous and intellectual nature. It is perhaps this figure more than any other who provides the young Schelling with the model of a thinker who is a philosopher of nature both seen and unseen, who pursues the absolute through the study of the natural sciences, while simultaneously pursuing the same end through the study of sacred texts. Hahn's attempt to synthesize these seemingly opposed activities into one life parallels his interpretation of Plato's doctrine of the binding of mind and ensouled matter through the "eternal band" of life *qua* soul in the *Timaeus*. The impact of this man on the young Schelling was so great that at the age of fifteen, he wrote and published a eulogy in his honor. The contents of this eulogy are brief but illuminating. What they tell us is that Schelling started very young with the conviction that life, understood as the power for self-organization, always precedes the subsequent reflections of reason. An inquiry into these roots will go far in correcting the monochromatic portrait of this multifaceted thinker, helping us to understand much of the complexity of his thought that gets lost when we fail to read Schelling on his own terms.

The Discipline of Language and Actuality of the Past

> Freedom is the highest good of humanity; but only independence of the will from the understanding is freedom.
>
> Affixed in remembrance,
From your true friend,
20 August 1788
F. Schelling[1]

Schelling entered these words of condolence into the family record of a recently deceased colleague of his father. The idea that freedom is the highest possible good of mankind seems entirely predictable coming from a thinker who argues that "freedom is the alpha and omega of all philosophy."[2] Indeed, the position that the logic of the understanding enslaves the will and hinders it from determining itself would appear to be quite the expected position of a thinker who grounds his philosophy in the unfathomable footing of freedom. Yet all semblance of normalcy vanishes when we examine the date of this condolence and realize that Schelling was but thirteen years of age he wrote these words.

Before Kant's second and third *Critiques*, a year before Jacobi's *büchlein* on Spinoza, and many years before Fichte's works, this youth posits freedom as the *summum bonum* of humanity, and sets as its condition the will's power to overcome its dependence on the understanding. Where does a youth of this age come up with such thoughts? The received portrait of Schelling's beginnings as a philosopher portrays him as an acolyte kneeling before Fichte. More sophisticated renderings of his intellectual pedigree have Fichte flanked by Kant and Jacobi's Spinoza, with perhaps Leibniz, Hölderlin, and Schiller lurking nearby in the background. In the orthodox scripting of the beginnings of German Idealism, Schelling's role lacks any significant distinguishing characteristics or unique identity: he is merely the bridge between Fichte and Hegel in the development of Idealism. While too much importance should not be placed on this one sentence written by a young adolescent, the complexity of thought here expressed demonstrates the need for a new reading of one of the most complex thinkers in modern thought.

Born in 1775 in Leonberg, a small town outside Stuttgart, Friedrich Schelling was a bit of an anomaly. Raised as the firstborn son of a family whose forefathers had served for generations as pastors of the church, the young boy was the obvious benefactor of his father's devoted attention, as well as his "substantial library" filled with an extensive collection in both classics and current works in theology and philosophy.[3] Later a professor of Oriental language and philology at the cloister school in Bebenhausen, the elder Schelling proved an exceptional role model. After his father began teaching him Latin and Greek, at the age of eight Schelling is sent off to the Latin School in Nürtingen, where he is befriended by Hölderlin, five years his senior.[4] After a little more than two years, his instructors send him home, as they have nothing left to teach him. Not knowing what to do with the boy, his father allows him to sit in on classes at Bebenhausen. Thus at the age of eleven he finds himself attending class with eighteen-year-olds and writing proofs of the divine origin of the Bible in Latin. He learns both Hebrew and Arabic, and becomes so proficient in composing Latin and Greek dactylic hexameter that he was able to "translate German dictation immediately into Latin Hexameter."[5] Thereafter it is Plato, Aristotle, Thucydides and Pindar in the original Greek, and Leibniz's *Monadology* in Latin. At fourteen, he is given permission to attend the seminary at Tübingen. In his wisdom, the elder Schelling waits until his gifted progeny is fifteen to send him off.[6]

The fact of Schelling's exceptional intellectual talent is essential to understanding his future development. His insatiable curiosity and lust for knowing was matched only by an almost sponge-like capacity to absorb new ideas. These traits were further cultivated by Schelling's tendency to spend time in the company of adults, always eager to engage in conversation and debate on philosophical topics.[7] What was most decisive, however, in shaping this young mind was his extensive fluency in ancient languages. An established scholar who could read Latin, Ancient Greek, Hebrew, and Arabic, the elder Schelling imparted to his son the essential scholarly habits and disciplines required to master the major texts of the ancient world. In addition to developing the critical skills required to interpret the morphologic and lexigraphic meanings of six languages, he was exposed to the panoramic vista of the different worlds of other ages and cultures. While the surface meaning of a term can be determined by formal analysis, the true challenge and art to "reading" such texts lies in the imagination's capacity to momentarily leave the logic of the present culture, and attempt to open itself to other ways of interpreting the reality of our existence and world. It was in this art that Schelling first proved his genius.[8]

To be capable of reading and writing the original language of an ancient text is of course to encounter a historical record of etymological strata and sedimentation that discloses facets of our intellectual past that are inaccessible via translation. To have such encounters constitute your upbringing and acculturation inevitably shapes a consciousness acutely sensitive to history; that is, a consciousness acutely aware of both the changing *and the unchanging* variables manifested in historical accounts. The exposure as a child to such an extensive record of written history no doubt informed Schelling's understanding of how the force of time shapes our consciousness and significantly contributed to his conception of the liberating role the past plays in generating visions of possible futures yet to come.

Considered as complementary facets of one exceptional mind, Schelling's intellectual gifts created a rich and fecund soil in which any worthy germ of an idea would quickly take root and grow according to the singular quality of that fertile environment. This was not the intellectual climate of reflection and imitation. It was instead an intellectual ecosystem conducive to grafting and cross-pollination, producing entirely new syntheses and ideas.

The Tradition of Pietism: Freedom as the Unmediated Experience of the Divine

> We know nothing other than what is in experience, says Kant. Very correct; but what is being in experience is precisely what is alive, eternal or God. (I/7, 245)

> The vacuous person, that denies it [power of God], expresses it, without knowing it; he is not able to connect two concepts rationally other than through this idea [of the copula]. (I/7, 83)

Ground zero for the beginnings of the Pietist movement is the text *Pia desideria*, written by Philipp Jakob Spener in 1675. Reacting to the Lutheran church of his day, Spener advocated a plan of reform whose goal was to counter the then dominant obsession with purity of doctrine. He held that this fixation on dogma and tenet distanced the individual from the source of true religion; a source which Spener believed was the direct and unmediated communion of an individual's soul with God. In this understanding of the relation between the human and the divine there can be no mediating structures of dogma, ritual, or clergy. According to Spener, where there is such mediation the faith which it nurtures is anemic, and thus easily controlled by those who lead the community of believers. Such feeble faith and its control was the antithesis of Spener's understanding of religion in which the determinative characteristics of faith are precisely the vitality and freedom afforded by the unmediated experience of the numinous.[9]

The Pietist orientation has obvious epistemological ramifications. How one determines truth derives from the certainty generated not by calculation (*ratio*) according to a rule, but rather from the pre-reflective certainty of unmediated experience. The yardstick for measuring truth thus begins beyond the reach of reason in the *bedrock* certainty of lived experience, and only thereafter feeds into the regions of our experience dictated by the discursive movements of predication, calculation, and prediction. The certainty of the combination of terms which characterizes acts of discursive reason is thus derivative of a more primary certitude that, to borrow a phrase from Wittgenstein, "is the prototype of a way of thinking and not the result of thought."[10] In this scheme of things the reflective or combinatory certitude of reason relates to the certitude of experience as parasite does to host body: rational doubt is parasitic on a pre-reflective certainty of unmediated experience.[11] To invert this order and propose that certainty is parasitic on doubt—or worse, to argue that the certitude of life and death is subservient to the certitude of the law of the excluded middle—is to engage in a pathology of thinking that emasculates life and generates, at best, an anemic theory of concepts, a theoretical "castle in the air" that mistakes "words for concepts, and concepts for realities."[12]

This epistemological ordering of the priority of unmediated experience over the derivative modality of discursive reflection is determinative for Schelling's philosophical orientation. The dynamic of this order, however, by no means denigrates the role of the reflective understanding; indeed, for there to be a dynamic there must be tension, and for this to emerge, there must exist relative parity between its constituent forces, a relative parity that in this case integrates the living force of immediate experience with the limiting precision of conceptual thinking. The focus of such *geistige Kraft* was in the life of the young

Schelling exemplified by a constellation of heterodox Pietists informed by the latest manifestation of the heterodox spirit, Jakob Böhme's Theosophy.

Halfway between Tradition and the Enlightenment: Theosophy and the Divinity of Nature

The family Schelling was raised in could not determine on either its maternal or on its paternal side when its lineages first became clergy: for as long as records had been kept their respective ancestors had been engaged as officers of the church. It was from both sides of the family tree that the Schelling family harvested their extensive circle of intellectual and spiritual contacts, all united by a common passion for the life of the spirit, both theoretically and practically. The culture Schelling was raised in strove to integrate the most disciplined of intellectual activities with the invigorating experience of the numinous. The life of Schelling's father provides a telling example of this posture.

As pastor, J. F. Schelling was true to his family's Pietist roots; but as a scholar of ancient languages, he was also true to the rational methods of the new text criticism. The resulting orientation was paradoxical in that he employed the non-traditional tools of reason to mine the mythic truths of his Bible's traditions. As a Pietist, J. F. Schelling sought freedom as the unmediated experience of the divine. As a scholar however, he pursued exegetical strategies that employed reason as the key to unlocking and liberating the truth from tradition's interpretation of scripture. In the former approach, he sought an unmediated freedom informed by his tradition; in the latter, he sought to free the truth from tradition through the use of reason. In brief, the elder Schelling stood halfway between tradition and the Enlightenment, in search perhaps of a position that would combine the best of both orientations.

A successor of Oetinger as the Prälat in Murrhardt, J. F. Schelling was a *geistige* figure in his own right, both spiritually and intellectually.[13] His theological position was informed by both his Pietist tradition and his general interest in the work of Johann Albrecht Bengel (1687–1752), one of the "fathers" of the Württemberg church. His intellectual views were informed by the critical biblical hermeneutic developed by Johann David Michaelis (1717–1791), a professor in Oriental languages at Göttingen.[14] Within an environment steeped in the traditions of both scholarship and Pietist spirituality it was virtually impossible to encounter intellectual figures that were unfamiliar with the writings of Jakob Böhme (1575–1624). This of course includes Schelling's father.

Just as Spener himself had studied the writings of Böhme, so too had most every significant figure of the circle of acquaintances and friends surrounding the Schelling family.

A case in point would appear to be the Pietist theologian Bengel, whom the senior Schelling followed in refraining from most of Böhme's more extreme speculations.[15] As a leading figure of Württemberg Pietism, Bengel judged the truth of any speculative position by whether or not it could be made consistent with the writings of Holy Scripture. In addition, although he was skeptical of the truth of Böhme's teachings, he was nonetheless intimate with them. His disputation, written in 1707 while a student at Tübingen, dealt with both mystical theology and Böhme's position towards it.[16] Years later Bengel carefully couched his evaluation of Böhme's work in an ambiguous form, successfully balancing the need to express caution regarding his teachings while still affirming their limited value: "I cannot rightly manage with Jakob Böhme's writings. He has positions which obviously do not agree with Scripture, but on the other hand, he also has some positions that are thoroughly beautiful."[17] The ambiguity of Bengel's judgment of Böhme is characteristic of Pietism's official position on Böhme and his Theosophy. On the one hand Böhme's reading of Holy Scripture was deemed to be unjustified and thus contrary to the accepted doctrines that derived from the Pietists' accepted reading of the Bible. From this perspective, Böhme was judged a Theosophist and condemned as encouraging a type of spiritual bacchanalia in which doctrine no longer played a formative role. On the other hand however, there was an appeal in Böhme's understanding of God as absolutely free and immanent within creation which was undeniably attractive to many of the Pietists' leading theologians. From this perspective Böhme's work represented the most recent contribution to the spiritual underground of heterodoxy whose lineage unites the Pietists with the Gnostics and Alchemists. It made little sense for those who placed such an absolute value on the freedom of religious experience and expression, and who themselves were subject to religious persecution, to follow the traditional practice of condemning these teachings wholesale as heretical. Instead there appears to have been an uneasy truce established which allowed Böhme's Theosophy to be addressed only to the extent that it conformed to Pietism's doctrine.

Although Bengel certainly did not follow Böhme's teachings, many other figures in Schelling's upbringing did. Plitt reports that the Schelling family entertained the likes of Kreises, Oetinger, and Hahn. Oetinger, who was both a close correspondent with Bengel and a recognized authority on Böhme's teachings, was acquainted with the family through professional ties; as previously noted, the elder Schelling had succeeded Oetinger as the Prälat in Murrhardt. Although it is clear from the record that the elder Schelling was not personally close to Oetinger, it is just as evident that J. F. Schelling was familiar with his work. Given the intimate economies of scale within the Württemberg Pietist church, and the passionate commitment of all involved in their faith, it would follow that a published professor of a cloister school would have had an excellent understanding of the work of a personal acquaintance as controversial as Oetinger. This is particularly clear in light of their shared interest, as followers of Bengel, in the techniques of biblical criticism. Indeed, it seems more than likely that he himself had some of Oetinger's books in his "substantial library"; a suggestion made more plausible by his son's written request of 1802 that his father procure for him "some of the most select philo-theosophical writings of Oetinger."[18]

J. F. Schelling would have had a particular interest in Oetinger's understanding of *Heilgeschichte*. Whereas Bengel saw history developing dialectically, in a struggle between good and evil, and which becomes more intense and extensive with each successive stage of development, Oetinger held a more linear understanding of historical progress. In his work, the history of the world unfolds in different epochs, culminating in the *"Johannesoffenbarung"* and the aeon of the *Heilige Geist*, when the rule of law and justice will reign supreme throughout all creation. For Oetinger, history thereby proves itself as a theodicy of God's justice:

> Finally everything that in manifest ways has appeared to stand opposed to universal law (*allgemeine Recht*) will fade away; the different forms of government will be done away with ... so then will each one in their place become similar to the whole, so that God is everything in all (*alles in allem*).[19]

Oetinger raises here a theme that Hahn will develop extensively, namely, the idea that the *alles in allem* of Corinthians 15:28 does not mean that sensual nature will be spiritualized into some ethereal heaven, but rather that spirit itself will be made sensual: the Second Coming is not that of a deity becoming human, but of the divine itself realizing itself in nature. Oetinger alludes to this when he writes of each individual becoming "similar to the whole": the completion of God's revelation in creation is the condition in which a perfect symmetry is established between the part and the whole.[20] This idea becomes determinative for the younger Schelling's later philosophical writings on the sacral dimension of his *Naturphilosphie*.

Oetinger's theosophical vision however, was not merely just an intellectual factor in the Schelling household. As for all variants of Pietism, the ultimate goal of *book learning* was to become more pious in one's life. The tangible and concrete presence of Oetinger's teachings was made personally known to the Schelling family through the maternal line. There was first the brother of Schelling's mother who visited often and was renowned throughout the region as a fervent admirer of Oetinger.[21] As an enthusiastic proponent of Oetinger's teachings it seems more than likely that this uncle of the young Schelling would have focused his attentions on a youth so obviously gifted; a task facilitated by the young Friedrich's practice of associating almost exclusively with adults. Combine these two factors of a zealous evangelist and a young and malleable mind craving intellectual stimulation, and the possibility of a thorough cross-pollenization becomes extremely likely.

But the most direct and extensive exposure of the young Schelling to Oetinger's teachings had to have occurred during the two years he spent away from his family while attending the Latin School in Nürtingen. There he lived with another of his maternal uncles, the Deacon Köstlin, who was also known to be a member of those Pietists who closely followed the works of "the leading Pietists of the time, Oetinger and Hahn."[22] Given Plitt's reports that the Latin School proved no challenge to the young Schelling, and that the boy consequently spent most of his time in the company of books and adults, we find it once again hard to imagine that the this young scholar would have come away after a two-year visit without having acquired more than a passing familiarity with the framework of Theosophy.[23]

Accepting this likely scenario of Schelling's upbringing, we must now consider specific themes Oetinger propagated that may have taken root in Schelling's young and receptive mind.

Oetinger's Genetic Epistemology and the Unmediated Knowing of the *Zentralerkenntnis*

The term "life" is for Oetinger the determining predicate of every dimension of creation, from the external world as organism, to our mind as an organ of our body. He describes this process of universal becoming in terms of an *"ordo generativus,"* not a mechanistic *"ordo geometricus or mathematicus."*[24] As he was apt to repeat, formal logic alone will never account for the dialectically developing struggle of forces that generate nature, since logic only serves to measure and define dead things and relations.[25] To account for a living God and its creation he instead insisted on employing a *genetic* modality of knowing that, since it paralleled the genetic development of nature, could also provide a direct and unmediated knowledge of the actuality of our world. Oetinger placed his interpretation of Böhme's *Zentralerkenntnis* at the apex of his epistemological hierarchy. As the modality of knowing reality "without images" and "without imagination" it provided the unrefined and unmediated stuff of discursive thinking.[26] It was thus the way of knowing "through which one knows not one after the other, like dull reason through inferences" but rather as one knows directly, lacking the mediation of any discursive ratio or use of images.[27] Such an immediate knowing is associated by Oetinger with the inspiration one *receives* through the *logon sophias* of the Holy Ghost (1 Cor. 12:8): one does not will this modality of knowing to happen, rather God wills to make it happen to you.[28] Following in the tradition of Plato's account of the divine manias and enthusiasm, and of Aristotle's *nous poetikos* as mediated by Meister Eckhart, Oetinger construed this non-discursive modality of knowing as affecting the individual in his *entirety*. The resulting impact of such a seeing supplies Oetinger with his paradigm of absolute truth and certainty: "The *Zentralerkenntnis* is the highest degree of the universal feeling of truth."[29] While Oetinger's epistemology does not dismiss discursive thinking and empirical knowing, he does nonetheless relegate them to a *preliminary level* of knowing. They are a preparatory level of knowing that retains a claim to validity only as long as they acknowledges their status as such, agreeing thereby to limit their scope of applicability and claim to relevancy.

It was this *Zentralerkenntnis* that provided the epistemological power and expanse of Oetinger's system of thought, the goal of which was to structure all the various different branches of knowledge to see "'All in each thing and each thing in All."[30] Gesturing at the same vision pointed to by the programmatic ἕν καὶ πᾶν, this phrase captures the ambitious scope of a system of thought that attempts to account for all of creation; a system of thought Oetinger calls an *Intensum*, a term he choose to emphasize that the object of his system is "an all-comprehending spiritual living organism."[31] This conception of an *organic* system is required by a system of thought that attempts to account for a living God and its creation. To be consistent with its subject, this *Intensum* must be animated by the opposing forces that generate and sustain all life, thereby allowing for the productive use of logical opposition and contradiction *within the system*, as the generative process of sustaining the system's growth; a point that leads to the rather paradoxical position of the systematic necessity of contradiction, in that a system that lives on the productive use of contradiction could only rid itself of all contradiction by seeking its own destruction. Opposition of force and position is the necessary condition of life; remove it and the system loses its capacity to produce new insight, decaying into a fossilized dogma.

Divinity as Freedom in Nature: The Priority of Freedom over Wisdom

Following Böhme, Oetinger transposed Newton's centripetal and centrifugal forces into the polarity of God's generative power of creation and movement: "God, in that he reveals himself, has moved himself freely to such an eternal movement."[32] Accordingly, life and self-movement are "the first and highest idea of God."[33] Because this power for self-movement resides within God he is not a "necessary essence, who has no freedom."[34] On the contrary, God's essence *lives from freedom*: God is the freedom of life. In contrast to the rationalist conception of the deity—most notably that of Leibniz—Oetinger maintains that "Wisdom is not first in God, but rather freedom."[35]

Freedom is thus not only a way of accounting for God's justice in the positive reality of evil, but it is also the sufficient condition for love.[36] Eros is thus given a role in creation as one of the primordial principles that, struggling with the contractive force of evil and darkness, eventually succeeds in realizing its expansive power as the unifying light of knowing.[37] Life is characterized by opposition and polarity, but this opposition is impossible if there is nothing that binds these opposing forces together and tempts them toward their ultimate reunion. Creation and its evolution thus conform to what C. S. Peirce called an "agapastic theory," in which only the power of Eros is strong enough to convince opposites to commingle.[38]

Oetinger's account of creation is extremely important to our topic: his cosmogony suggests strong similarities with both Plato's *Timaeus* and Schelling's early writings. The first and most important parallel occurs in his description of the freedom of God—as distinguished from his creation—as the tensive interplay of the forces of the divine life held together by a binding he repeatedly refers to as an "indissoluble bond."[39] Creation occurs when God dissolves the "bond of the forces"[40] that originally unites them in a state of "indifference,"[41] thereby allowing them to spill forth and separate into the productive forces of nature.

Oetinger places great importance on this indissoluble bond as the principle for distinguishing the created from the creator.[42] The presence or absence of this unifying bond distinguishes the divine life from human life: "Truth is that in the inaccessible light of God all the forces are in an indissoluble bond, as the origin of darkness, cold, heat, and color."[43] But in creation the forces separated: "Forces are led out of the forces of his majesty into the creature, and in this way those forces are . . . in the creature no longer as in God."[44] In God this "bond of eternal forces (*das Band der ewigen Kräfte*)"[45] is formed by the logos, the word, which unites the duality of forces into one integrated unity. In creation however, this bond has been dissolved and the unity disrupted, thereby setting the duality of forces free to reveal God through the creation of our world.[46] Oetinger concludes that "Nature is a third out of two."[47]

This brief account of Oetinger's understanding of the dynamic of creation parallels the aforementioned essential elements of the form of reasoning found in Plato's *Timaeus*. The most obvious is Oetinger's use of "das Band" and Plato's use of ὁ δεμός. Both use this relation to describe—in Plato's words—a *mean that in uniting two extremes* becomes a third. This form or process, while characterizing all forms and processes of creation, finds its ideal instantiation in the generation of life as the third μέσος that binds the two extremes in what Plato refers to as the soul (principle of movement).[48]

Both Plato's and Oetinger's accounts suggest strong affinities with Schelling's construction of the principle of identity in his philosophical system. When we finally turn to Schelling's commentary on the *Timaeus* the parallels will become even more striking. As much as we would like to pursue these parallels here, such a segue would divert us from the task at hand. In the case of Oetinger, there are clear parallels with Schelling: the conception of God as the generative source of life;[49] the unmistakable family resemblance between their conception of *an organic Intensum or system*; the similarity between their epistemological frameworks in general; and especially Oetinger's use of a genetic modality of unmediated knowing and Schelling's use of intellectual intuition.[50]

It is clear that the young Schelling was raised in a culture that was not only receptive of Theosophical teachings, but was also actively engaged in the further development and propagation of such ideas. As we have seen, the capacity for learning the young Schelling displayed can only be described, so to speak, as that of an *intellectual sponge*: place him in an environment of ideas and he will quickly absorb the essential elements that constitute that intellectual ecosystem.[51] We have argued that through his consistent exposure to the culture of Theosophy the young Schelling must have acquired at least a broad understanding of many of the central tenets of this philosophical system. But our current aim is not only to make the argument that Schelling was significantly influenced by the culture of Theosophy, but to provide historical evidence of direct influence. Although there are strong textual similarities, there is no demonstrable historical evidence to establish conclusively a direct dependence of Schelling on the work of Oetinger at this early stage of his career. The available evidence remains circumstantial at worst, and tantalizingly convincing at best.

No matter how difficult it is to imagine that this voracious student would fail to absorb any understanding of these ideas that permeated his upbringing, we need a demonstrable historical connection to this intellectual tradition to substantiate our claim of a direct influence.[52] There remains however, one possible historical figure whose impact on the young Schelling is capable of being demonstrated: not Oetinger, but his onetime student and the *other* "leading Pietist," Philipp Matthäus Hahn (1739–1790).

The possibility of Hahn's having played a formative role in defining the initial orientation of Schelling's thinking is strongly suggested by both documented historical evidence and substantive thematic affinities between Hahn's teachings and Schelling's philosophical work. Schelling's family was most likely directly acquainted with Hahn through Schelling's godfather and great uncle, Friedrich Philipp von Rieger. An established figure within the Württemberg community, Rieger was a "contemporary and intimate friend of Bengel," who often visited with Oetinger, and who belonged to a congregation that followed Hahn's teachings.[53] From Hahn's own journal we learn that he had entertained the Schelling family at least on one occasion.[54] But the most significant and convincing historical evidence of the role Hahn played in Schelling's early development is to be found in the most curious and astonishing eulogy the fifteen-year-old Schelling felt moved to write upon Hahn's death in 1790. This eulogy, the youth's first published writing, provides us with the historical link we have been looking for.[55]

Schelling's Eulogy and the System of Philipp Matthäus Hahn (1739–1790)

Philipp Matthäus Hahn embodied the spiritual and intellectual passions of Schwäbian Pietism. Standing between the religion of his tradition and the scientific researches of the future, Hahn was an iconoclastic figure whose reputation was known throughout the region. He was part mystic and part scientist, part theologian and spiritual leader, and part businessman and engineer.

His spiritual path began with Böhme's "Way to Christ" which, in Hahn's own words, caused his "religious awakening" as a young student at Tübingen.[56] Thereafter he served as Oetinger's assistant and devoted himself to exploring the chthonic depths of Böhme and the Kabbalah. His natural disposition towards such matters came to fruition when, unlike Oetinger, Hahn himself actually experienced the *Zentralschau* or mystical vision which served as the epistemological apex of Böhme and Oetinger's teaching. Hahn went on to preach and write, developing a theology which, based on his own personal visions, eventually brought him into conflict with the censors of the Württemberg church.[57]

Yet parallel to these spiritual adventures, Hahn proved himself to be a rigorous and practical scientist whose research and activity in the fields of astronomy and engineering led to a successful business constructing machinery. It also led to a commission from the Duke of Württemberg in 1769 to construct "astronomy machines" to predict the movements of the heavenly bodies, and the demonstration of a "calculating machine" for Kaiser Joseph II in 1777.[58] His work in mechanics and engineering was held in such esteem that he was twice offered a professorship in these fields.[59] He refused both positions, however, because his true interests could only find their satisfaction in the pursuit of the *divine in* nature, free of the ideological constraints of working in a university setting. The trajectory of his research precluded explaining nature as a mechanism, demanding instead that nature be understood as the ongoing revelation of the divine life.

What is significant here for our argument is how Hahn's approach to the study of the divine anticipates the way in which Schelling goes about pursuing his philosophical career. Hahn refused to devote himself exclusively either to the life of the biblical scholar and spiritual teacher or to the life of the natural scientist investigating the inner workings of nature. Grounded in his conviction that creation is itself the self-revelation of his God, he pursued a complementary strategy whereby he addresses both the spiritual and the material dimensions of the "object" of his study. While the study of the holy text was important, there was also the text of nature. For whereas the former offers up but a sacred history of God's revelation in the past, the text of nature is the self-revelation of the deity in the concrete here and now. In brief, and to borrow Schelling's dedication of his notebooks on Plato, Hahn pursued the very strategy Plato recommended in the *Timaeus* when he wrote:

> Wherefore one ought to distinguish two different kinds of causes, the necessary and the divine, and in all things seek after the divine for the sake of gaining a life of blessedness, so far as our nature admits thereof. . . . (*Tim.* 68e5–69a1)

A Theology of Life

The role of *life* in Hahn's theology determines his entire system. Following the teachings of Oetinger, he holds that there is no understanding of a world within space and time, nor of a God beyond the world, that would not have life as its determinative characteristic. His primary assumption is by now a familiar one: as a Heracletian struggle between opposing forces, "life is an incessant battle of the active and passive [forces]."[60] The duality of forces, whose active presence in our life characterizes its actuality, are manifestations of the original dualism of forces in God. No doubt derived from Böhme's interpretation of Newton's attractive and repulsive forces, Hahn uses this divine struggle to account for creation itself.[61] The beginnings of this creative struggle emerge from a free decision of the deity. Building towards a triadic portrayal of God, Hahn traces the original act of creation back to the deity's "calm desire of eternal freedom," in which God makes the choice to "reveal himself and become conscious of his highest perfection."[62] In a radical departure from orthodoxy Hahn holds that the creation of our world is the result not of an overabundance of goodness, but of a *lack* in the creator, a missing element of self-consciousness which this deity can only overcome through the act of revealing himself *to himself* through his work of creation.[63] From this concept of creation, the possibility of a process of development *within the deity* itself follows.

Central to his explication of this cosmogony is his account of the condition under which we must posit God as making a free choice for creation: a free decision requires the distinction between God as revealed *in* space and time and God *beyond* space and time. Beyond space and time Hahn presents God as a nothing (*ein Nichts*), a conception of the deity that follows Böhme's "*Ungrund*," and its spiritual ancestor, the Kabbalistic *Ein Sof*. The face of God beyond space and time is *empty* as far as our metaphysical speculations are concerned: "We can know nothing of God a priori, rather only a posteriori, since God beyond his economy of revelation is hidden from all creatures: 1 Tim 6."[64] Following a logical move as old as the *Timaeus* cosmogony, Hahn reasons that the divine cause of creation must itself be of a different order than that which it brings into being. To posit the freedom of real development and change, there must be a defining variance that transcends a logic of pure immanence.

To account for this original division in God, Hahn employs the conceptual tools of the trinity as a foil for describing the variance that drives the divine life and creation. The strategy he employs shows his debt not only to Böhme's work, but more specifically, to that of Oetinger. As always occurs in such attempts at describing a beginning beyond language and thought, Hahn employs various sets of metaphors to describe the different aspects of the generative vortex from which God produces creation. He presents the divine life as three different wills, forces, or as a threefold spiritual "personality (*Ichheit*)."[65] The first *Ichheit* signifies the "ground of the deity, the invisible God" that, beyond being, "is invisible because all the forces are concentrated within it, and out of which—as from a beginning point, in which everything lies, but is not yet differentiated—every revelation of God, namely a twofold divine force of life, incessantly comes forth."[66] In this unusually clear yet complete formulation, Hahn articulates his interpretation of Kabbalism's cosmogonic doctrine of *Tsimtsum*.[67] To account for the creation of a world that is somehow separate from the deity that creates and sustains it, Hahn must posit a *limit* or *fissure* within the deity. The condition of possibility of revelation is in fact the imposition of a limit, the clearing of a region within the deity in which creation might occur. *Tsimtsum* etymologically means "concentration" or "contraction," the term Hahn uses to describe the primordial state of the infinite construed as an infinitely contracted point. As such, this first *Ichheit* of the deity is utterly beyond being and knowing. Visually construed, this first personality is total darkness devoid of all light.[68] It is God "outside his revelation," that is outside (before) his creation, beyond (before) the conditions of space and time, and thus inexplicable within a language determined and informed by the logic of these conditions.

This contracting of the first *Ichheit* is an imposition of limit that divides the original unity or oneness of the deity into a duality or polarity of opposing and generative forces. The darkness of the first starting point is thereby illuminated, whereby this second *Ichheit* becomes the source of light, the logos, or word. The relation of the first *Ichheit* to the second *Ichheit* is like that of the dark storm cloud from which bolts of lightning are generated in Ezekiel 1:4.[69] This dualism of opposing forces Hahn further characterizes as the *Ebenbild*—the double—of the first personality.[70] This doubling is the producing, the generation of a likeness in the same way as the father generates a son who then becomes his mirror image. The second *Ichheit* in turn generates the third and last personality of the Deity, that of the Spirit, who is finally the "externality of God" that reveals itself in and through creation.[71]

Procreative Logic: Hahn's "ordo generativus"

The processive epigenesis of the deity continues into and throughout creation as the living revelation of God. The world of nature thus becomes the arena of the life of God in which he comes to know himself by means of his creation. The world of nature thereby assumes a thoroughly processive character whose development Hahn can only describe as a history of the divine life. As witnessed by Hahn's scientific activities, the most direct way to comprehend the history of the divine life is to comprehend the life of nature.

His vocabulary of organic metaphors of life and ontogenesis is intended to clash directly with the abstract *Neologie* of Wolffianism and the dualism required by a mechanistic conception of life and nature. Systematically considered, Hahn holds that only the concept of life, and not logic, can account for the divine act of creation. Logic cannot comprehend the genetic transition from one to two, whereas the actual procreative forces of life, *by definition*, can and do effect this transition. Logic functions in the ether of reflection, in which an initial duality must always be presupposed of an *archetype* and its reflected *echotype*. Hahn's system however, functions in a monistic continuum capable of accounting for duality through its organic conception of *production*. What is presupposed in his organic methodology is not an original dualism, but rather an original living being that by definition is a unity sustained by a plurality of forces. Since rationalism and its methodology of reflection must start with a duality, it lacks the explanatory power to account for an initial act of creation that would provide the point of unity that frames duality. In so many words, logic is too impotent to generate the growth from the one to the many. Through his use of a living God as the paradigm of organic life, Hahn provides a paradigm in which organism is the determinative model for understanding how unity can be conceived as mediating difference; a theoretical problem that arises whenever we try to figure out why the strict logical dichotomy of mutual exclusion refuses application to the complementarities of lived experience.

Systema Influxus: The Immanent Harmony of the Trichotomy Body, Soul, and Mind

The contrast between Hahn's system and those of a Wolff or Leibniz is perhaps best illustrated by his understanding of the organic unity of soul and body: viewed from the standpoint of the particular neither can be conceived as having existence independent of the other, but viewed from the standpoint of their unity they form "a third" *qua* organic whole. Once again illustrating how the genetic framework demonstrates more explanatory power than the mechanistic, Hahn argues that whereas a Leibniz must assume a mysterious *systema harmoniae* to account for how the two different realities of body and mind correspond, his monistic dualism enables him to create a *systema influxus* in which body and soul are as intimately related as the dualism of forces that generate life. In his own words, they are but "two sides of one coin"[72], whose intimate "*gegenseitige Reflexion*" he explains through the relationship of the betrothed in marriage.[73]

As we remarked earlier, Plato ultimately provides the archetype for this triadic relationship. Hahn himself explicitly acknowledges his debt to Origen's version of Plato's anthropological trichotomy, and comments that this more ancient conception places "humanity closer to God" than the church's doctrine of an "anthropological dichotomy."[74] If God is conceived of as a trinity of forces or personalities, it follows that humanity, as the *Ebenbild* of the deity should also display a parallel structure. His account of how "man consists of three men" demonstrates the extent to which Hahn is working within the Platonic tradition, and provides us with an example of how he understood Plato's use of the ὁ δεμόσ to describe the "band" of life that unites body and spirit:

> *The spirit of man*, that though invisible is the original stuff and archetype and *spiritus* rector of everything, *one could compare to the Father. The soul of man*, which is a *medium conjungendi* for 2 *Extrema*, and is participated in by both extremities and is a subtle corporeal image of the spirit: this *would be the Son. But the body of man* is a likeness of the soul, and consequently also of the spirit, and as a house of the soul and of the spirit it *would then be the Holy Ghost*, the transfigured creation, the body and dwelling of God, *Eph:* 2.[75]

Paralleling the three personalities in God, Hahn describes here how the soul is a medium that binds together two extremes. This construal of the soul follows Plato's conception as found in the *Timaeus* even closer than Oetinger's. Granted, Oetinger's use of the term "band" to describe the conjoining power of soul is justified in the quantitative sense in which Plato uses the term ὁ δεμόσ in the *Timaeus*.[76] Plato first uses this term in the sense that Oetinger does: to describe the trinitarian dynamic he posits as the only way to conceive not only creation, but also how there can be unity in the multiplicity of that creation:

> However, it is not possible that two things alone should be conjoined without a third; for there must needs be some intermediary bond (δεσμόν) to connect the two. And the fairest of bonds (δεσμῶν) is that which most perfectly unites into one both itself and the things which it binds together. (*Tim.* 31c)

While Hahn's usage of course agrees with Oetinger's, his choice perhaps reflects a more scientific approach to the subject, glossing Plato's specific account of how soul unites mind (the "Same") and body (the "Other") through a continuum of means (averages):

> He cut off yet further portions from the original mixture, and set them in between the portions above rehearsed, so as to place two Means in each interval,—one a Mean which exceeded its Extremes and was by them exceeded by the same proportional part or fraction of each of the extremes respectively; the other a mean which exceeded one Extreme by the same number or integer as it was exceeded by its other Extreme. (*Tim.* 36f)[77]

While the literal reading of the mathematical formula specified by Plato is to this day read as a specification of the "harmonic mean," the figurative reading Hahn gives targets the general function of the band as mediator between the spirit and body. And it is the cohesive force of *"das Band"* that unifies the material and immaterial elements of life in what Plato calls "the bond of life" (*Tim.* 73b3).

The use of this "third" member of Plato's trichotomy by both Hahn and Oetinger is consistent with Plato's use of it in the *Timaeus*. For example, Oetinger's employment of the "indissoluble bond" of God's powers as the principle for distinguishing the creator from the created parallels Plato's account in the *Timaeus*, when in the following passage God makes this address:

> [T]hose works whereof I am framer and father are indissoluble save by my will. For though all that is bound may be dissolved, yet to will to dissolve that which is fairly joined together and in good case were the deed of a wicked one. Wherefore ye also, seeing that ye were generated, are not wholly immortal or indissoluble, yet in no wise shall ye be dissolved nor incur the doom of death, seeing that in my will ye possess a bond (δεσμόυ) greater and more sovereign than the bonds wherewith, at your birth, ye were bound together. (*Tim.*, 41c9–b8)[78]

The soul of man is thus a *typus divines*, the *Ebenbild* of God.[79] As a doubling of God, it has the potential to duplicate the divine life; just as the act of creation is freely made by God, so too does man freely choose and create his world.[80] The movement of creation from darkness to light, from God's unfathomable ignorance to his revelation of himself to himself through creation, plays itself out on the human level in the life of each individual person.

Life in the Anticipation of the Eschaton:
The Prophet of Freedom and Nature Divine

All of the followers of Bengel had to come to terms with his prediction that the Final Judgment prophesied in the book of Revelation
would occur in 1836. Most, like Schelling's father, for obvious reasons
did everything they could to distance themselves from such biblical
literalism. Although Hahn himself refused to fully endorse Bengel's
prediction, the influence of the apocalyptic theme on his cultural land-
scape was palpable and had to have influenced his theological work
to some degree. As noted earlier, Hahn claimed to have enjoyed the
mystical insight afforded by the *Zentralschau* into the inner workings
of divine reality. Bracketing for the moment the truth of that claim, it
was readily apparent that Hahn was possessed of at least a mechanical
genius that earned him entry into the highest circles of his society. Add
to this that Hahn operated under the conviction and passion generated by his insight into the divine nature, and that his writings and
teachings were the subject of several official complaints and eventual
censorship, and there emerges a picture of a man who could quite easily
perceive himself as a persecuted prophet, attempting to speak the truth
to the ignorant before the final day of reckoning.

After his censure in 1781, which forced him to publish all future .
works anonymously, entries in his journal testify to a growing
perception of himself as one caught in the uncomfortable role of the
prophet. As the criticism of his teachings increased in 1784, he confided
as much in the following entry in his journal: "I see therefore, that
they are full of suspicion . . . since they are priests and my concern is
that of *prophecy*, which has always found resistance."[81] The critique
Hahn articulates in his prophetic voice is essential to comprehending
Schelling's seeming obsession with *Naturphilosophie:* Hahn's is a
critique of the naturalism of the Enlightenment that, with its global
subsumption of experience to conceptual analysis, threatens to
strip nature of its status as the medium through which God reveals
himself. In 1784 he confides in his journal that "I see increasingly
how naturalism encroaches all around."[82] The target of his scorn are
those figures who, like Leibniz and Wolff, embrace the tenets of the
Enlightenment, advocating a thoroughly rational theology in which the
divine is removed from the world of nature, while religion proves itself
to be superfluous since, rationally understood, it is nothing other than
a form of morality. When advanced consistently naturalism denies the
existence of the soul, while rationalism denies the need for revelation.

Reality is thereby reduced to the limited sphere of experience delimited by the intersecting subsets of what reason can comprehend and what the senses can provide us from experience. Any aspect of our reality that somehow falls outside the intersection of these two regions of truth is stripped of its possible claim to significant importance. But it is precisely in these repressed regions of our life that Hahn sees and experiences the power of the sacred that fuels his argument that our human life is far richer than what reason has insight into and what our senses can deliver to us from experience.

Hahn's criticism of the Enlightenment's removal of nature's divine status focuses on the unintended consequences of this movement's attempt at liberation: for Hahn the only real freedom is a freedom that participates in the absolute freedom of the divine. Remove the divine and the chance of real freedom disappears with it.

For Hahn however, humanity is only conceivable in its connection with the divine, via its *Ebenbild,* through which it shares in God's divine freedom. The liberation of man that Hahn calls for occurs through a process of divinization; a process initiated by the divine logos and actualized in life as a process of knowing. Through the knowing of the will of God one realizes the *"gottliche Ebenbild"* in man.[83] This divine image is not only the epistemological condition for man's knowing of the divine, but is also the condition of man's freedom: in sharing the image of God man shares in his absolute freedom. With each successive expansion of our knowledge of God, the knower becomes that much freer.

The knowledge of God is approached via an inner and outer route. The outer route is mediated by *nature* which, as the "externality of God" is the revelation of the deity's third personality. The inner route is mediated by Holy Scripture which, as the logos of the deity's Sophia, is the revelation of God's second *Ichheit.* Both the inner and the outer routes aim at the *Zentralschau* into the original unity of the first *Ichheit.* For it is in this spiritual intuition that the opposition of creative forces is balanced in the "calm desire of eternal freedom." If nature and the world of creation is denuded of its divinity, and thereby its sacred status as the revelation of God, then man as nature, as creature, is also stripped of his freedom. He becomes nothing more than an object subject to the mechanical laws of science and the marketplace. As we have seen, for Hahn there could be no living body without a living spirit, just as there could be no living spirit if there were no living body; to deny the reality of either was to deny the possibility of providing a systematic and comprehensive account of reality.[84] The ultimate goal of his system however, was to provide a way of understanding and encouraging the spiritualization of nature in the face of naturalism's attempts to reduce the spirit to the material.

Only if humanity pursues the sacred will its ultimate destiny be attainable as presented in the biblical vision of the Kingdom of God; a vision which Hahn construes as the realization of Paul's prophecy that in the end time *creation itself* will be set free and made complete.[85] Hahn envisions this telos of creation as the "fulfillment of all creation with God's glory, in which the entirety of his creation becomes a temple of God, so that God in his depths of completeness, sweetness, beauty, wisdom and power, reveals himself and communicates with his creatures."[86] In so many words, Hahn here anticipates God's full revelation of himself in and through nature, whereby nature is made complete and thus fully divine.

If this common relation that orients humanity with the divine is abolished, humanity and nature lose that force that not only limits and holds in check our species' claim to absolute power, but also fills humanity with a power that animates our intellectual life, the world of the *Geist*. In the absence of a decentering force that refuses to be subsumed under our conceptual structures—a decentering force that for Hahn was the divine as manifest in nature—the human subject will inevitably rise to idolatrous proportions and seek to satisfy its insatiable desires through the technological exploitation of creation. The overriding concern of Hahn's work in the last decade of his life was to somehow incorporate what is true in the *"Berliner Aufklärung"* in order to overcome its destructive shortcomings, and to thereby usher in what he considered to be the *true enlightenment*, which would lead to the realization of his vision of a complete and divine nature.

The means to this were to be found in new ways of thinking he believed would have to be advanced by the philosophers and theologians of the next generation. And curiously enough, in 1774 he predicted that a Christian rereading of Spinoza's pantheism would most likely provide this "new way of thinking."[87] A few years later, this suspicion blossomed into an unshakable conviction when he encountered Herder's use of Spinoza. In a letter from 1780, Hahn asks, "Why do they fear Spinoza? Not all of it is consistent with Scripture, but truth is to be met in every *Selbstdenken*."[88] As his life winds towards its end and Hahn becomes more despondent about the current state of his religious tradition, he remains optimistic because of figures such as Herder.[89] In 1788, two years before his death, Hahn is convinced

that the childish ceremonial Christianity of the Catholics and Protestants will fail, that a knowledge of God in spirit and in truth will

emerge. That a Spinoza, a Herder could find thinking and nourishment for their spirit in it, as it is described in Herder's booklet about
God,—is already proof that this religion will emerge and the human
understanding will raise itself out of its childhood and will come into
its manhood.[90]

All that is required are the prophets of this new religion to emerge,
who will provide knowledge of God in spirit and truth, thereby raising
humanity in its spiritual maturity from childhood to adulthood.

Schelling's Eulogy of Hahn (1790) and the Passing of the Flame of Prophecy

We finally return to Schelling and pose the following question: what
could possibly move a fifteen-year-old to compose a eulogy for a religious and scientific figure of Hahn's stature? Perhaps he was inspired
by Hahn's writings, or maybe he was moved to write by Hahn's "charismatic presence." Then again, it may have been the entire *Gestalt* of
both Hahn's teachings—known perhaps from the theological discus-
sions the young Schelling was witness to—and of this man's spiritual
presence. The historical record suggests the latter possibility as the
most likely.

Hahn's spiritual presence: Schelling was not the only person
to have held Hahn in such high esteem. In the circle of family and
friends of the family, Hahn exuded a "chthonic sensuousness" which
differed drastically from Oetinger's dry academic tone.[91] The reason
for this is that in contrast to Oetinger, Hahn had actually experienced
the *Zentralschau* that had informed Böhme's teachings. Oetinger, in
his analysis of Böhme's alleged experiences, defined this experience of
mystical cognition using Plotinus's term *Henosis* and the Christian *unio
mystica*, writing that it is "an intuiting, a momentary all-seeing cognition of the ground of all things."[92] Hahn reportedly enjoyed several
such mystical experiences, the first of which he describes as follows: "I
saw into the most inner birth and into the heart of all things, as if all
at once the earth had become heaven and as if I saw the omnipresent
eternity in which God revealed himself."[93] Whether out of spiritual
pride, personal rivalry between teacher and student, or maybe even
based on reasoned argument, Oetinger himself doubted that Hahn ever
had truly enjoyed the vision of the *Zentralschau*. Nevertheless, it was
clear that many others did believe this based both on Hahn's otherwise
levelheaded strategies in engineering and his overpowering sense of
spiritual authenticity. For in contrast to Oetinger's secondhand analysis

of the epistemological source of his own system, Hahn's teachings were grounded in his own alleged experience.

It was in October of 1784 that Schelling and his family visited Hahn; the young boy was but nine years old. What type of experience would it have been for this nine-year-old, who even at this young age had a remarkable grasp of Latin and Greek? Clearly, Schelling would have been aware of this man's stature, and would have known of his purported status as one who had actually been inspired and blessed by God with the *Zentralschau*. The impact this person would have had on a young boy of Schelling's intelligence and spiritual nature must have been immense, particularly if, after having visited that person with his parents, and perhaps spoken with him, he came away believing that this man had actually enjoyed such experiences. The experience could mark a child of a certain disposition for life, giving him personal and irrefutable proof of the reality of the divine and the way it can inspire and move humans to piety and greater wisdom.

By all indications, it appears that such was the impact and experience the young Schelling enjoyed. The magnitude of the impact generated by the encounter and acquaintance with a man like Hahn was such that it not only led Schelling to compose the eulogy when he was fifteen, but it remained with him his entire life. Twenty-seven years after his visit, in 1811, Schelling attests to the impact this man had on him in a letter to G. H. Schubert: "I do not know Burgern; but that he was a friend of Hahn tells me enough. I saw this great man as a small boy with hidden incomprehensible reverence (*geheimer, unverstandener Ehrfurcht*); and strangely enough, the first poem I ever wrote in my life was at his death. I will never forget his look (*Anblick*)."[94] That Hahn made a lasting impression on Schelling is clear. What we must now explore is the extent to which his teachings influenced his development as a thinker.

Although Schelling attests in 1811 that he "saw this great man as a small boy with hidden, incomprehensible reverence" the content of his eulogy suggests that by the age of fifteen he had become more knowledgeable of his teachings.[95] Though the very form and extent of a brief forty-line eulogy rules out the possibility of demonstrating a thorough and studied understanding of Hahn's system, its content both reinforces the spiritual impact he had on the youth—he alludes to Hahn's visions—and confirms our suggestion that Schelling was indeed familiar with his system.

The eulogy betrays the form of a poem divided into ten stanzas, each consisting of four verses. Two positions in the poem are of particular relevance: stanzas three through five and the concluding two lines. In the third stanza, on lines 10 and 11, Schelling makes a clear reference to Hahn's experiences of the *Zentralschau* and the vision of the creator they provided:

> Ha, in light alters the transfiguration,
> Stands in angel's robe before God's throne
> 10 Gaze now freer through the world—indeed allowed
> Him some views of the creator while here![96]

These visions provide the source for his understanding of nature, which Schelling then proceeds to elaborate in the fourth stanza. In these four short lines Schelling addresses Hahn's teachings on the nature of God and his presence in creation, which is revealed through the "*Kräfte der Natur*" that animate everything from the outer cosmos to the valleys of the earth, revealing the "purest traces of the deity" in nature:

> Did he not dare to speak, with astute demeanor
> Still mortal, the forces of nature?
> Did his eyes not plunge through the cosmos and earth's dale
> 15 Searched and found the purest trace of the deity?[97]

From the manifestation of divine forces in the outer world of nature, Schelling moves to consider the interior force of Hahn's spiritual being. Once again alluding to the inspired knowledge imparted to Hahn through his visions, Schelling writes of how this knowledge exuded or made itself palpably noticeable in his physical presence, writing of the nourishing fire of divine spirit evident in his eyes and his "*Tief Blik in dem Angesicht*":

> Heard he not the harmony of the soul? Heard
> And understood he not the language of the spirit?
> Did you never see the fire, that nourished his eye,
> 19 Never see the profound look in his countenance?[98]

Schelling closes his eulogy to Hahn by committing himself to emulate the example presented by Hahn's life, thereby dedicating himself to the pursuit of wisdom, following in the footsteps of Hahn:

> 36 But his name lives here! Often celebrate
> His majestic memory,

> So often then to renew the resolve,
> To thus dedicate ourselves to wisdom here!

What then is the significance of this eulogy for understanding the development of Schelling's thought? Beck, who rediscovered this unknown poem and published it in 1955, argued that "the poem discloses in its content a previously sought X in the development of Schelling: Pietism and Theosophy as a locus in his spiritual development."[99] But as of yet this poem has received little commentary, or, as Jantzen points out, no mention at all in the Schelling bibliographies of Schneeberger and Sandkühler.[100] Jantzen's own appraisal of the poem echoes the orthodoxy of received wisdom when he states that the content of the poem demonstrates Schelling's weakness for modalities of understanding nature that do not conform to the tenets of the Enlightenment or rationalism:

> The adoration for Hahn not only makes clear his rootedness in Pietist thinking; it is simultaneously the first evidence of a continuous fascination that obviously proceeds from a reconstruction and knowledge of nature that according to its intention is by no means of the enlightenment or rational.[101]

Jantzen's evaluation of Schelling's approach to nature could not be more accurate, but not in the way Jantzen intends. Whereas Jantzen intends his comments as a criticism of Schelling's understanding of nature, Schelling himself would have taken it as a compliment, at least to the degree that he shared Hahn's conviction that the rationalist's understanding of nature could, at best, only provide a partial mechanistic understanding of nature, while at worst, it could lead to an exploitive and potentially disastrous abuse of nature.

Prophet of the New Religion of Nature: Matter Spiritualized

The significance of this eulogy lies in illuminating the standpoint from which Schelling will approach the world of orthodox philosophy and theology in Tübingen and beyond. What immediately suggests itself is that both Oetinger and Hahn were deeply indebted to not only the traditions of Gnosticism, Alchemy, Böhme, and Kabbalism, but were also significantly influenced by Platonism proper, and the *Timaeus* in particular. Schelling himself it appears was decisively impacted and influenced by the work of Hahn. It is of course highly doubtful that this influence is to be traced to their one meeting when he was but nine years old (but then, how many people do we remember meeting over twenty years ago, hence, when we were just nine years of age?). It could have been his uncle, the Deacon Köstlin, in whose home he lived for two years while attending the Latin School in Nürtingen, who introduced him to the works of Hahn. Regardless of who it was, we know that it was also about this time in Schelling's life that he started to seriously read Plato in Greek.

The themes of the divine and nature that defined the environment in which Schelling was raised will begin to manifest themselves in the themes and topics of his research and essays during his "pre-philosophical" years at Tübingen. There he begins his serious investigation of the *Vorstellungsarten* of the ancient world. He develops a method of text criticism and interpretation that he calls "Historical Interpretation" and employs it in his analysis of myth. Here his primary concern is to disclose the truth of myth as the necessary product of divine nature's *Versinnlichung* of truth. Central to his methodology is his insistence that we are so constructed as beings of nature that we are capable of divining the truth nature has made sensual through these earliest manifestations of mythic language.

Parallel to Hahn's interpretation of the myth of the Fall, Schelling writes his *Magister* on the same topic and supplements Hahn's reading with that of the Ophite and Valentinian schools of Gnosticism.[102] Following the later two schools of thought, Schelling reads the myth of the Fall not as the result of a sinful inability to follow divine commandments, but rather as one of the earliest attempts at Theodicy. In doing this, he argues that the original author of the first oral traditions of this myth had a quite different understanding of how reason relates to evil and sensual nature.

Finally, he delves into a serious study of Plato's philosophy, devoting considerable attention to the various ways in which Plato accounted for divine inspiration and prophecy. Thus two years after eulogizing Hahn, Schelling embarks on the independent study of how to account for the two most significant (or seductive) gifts Hahn enjoyed, thereby suggesting at the very least a strong personal identification with Hahn's position in this life. As his later use of intellectual intuition demonstrates, the possibility of *experiencing* the divine, as demonstrated in Hahn's life, becomes in Schelling's hands the primary weapon against Kant's idea of philosophy as a conceptual science of pure reason. The essence of this position is clearly stated in his *Letters on Dogmatism and Criticism*:

We all have a secret and wondrous capacity of withdrawing from temporal change into our innermost self, which we divest of every exterior accretion. There, in the form of immutability, we intuit the eternal in us. This intuition is the innermost and in the strictest sense our own experience, upon which depends everything we know and believe of a supersensuous world. (I/1, 318)

This is perhaps the clearest articulation of the foundational premise of Schelling's epistemology, which predates by many years his later exposure to a Jacobi or a Fichte. Although over his career he will change the ways in which he understands the "knowledge" provided by this higher form of cognition, he never removes this vital source from the body of his system. Without the possibility of a nondiscursive knowing, Schelling would be forced to accept the reflective dualisms required by post-Cartesian epistemologies and thereby deny the possibility of an unmediated access to experience. Hahn, having himself experienced the *Zentralschau* central to Pietist spirituality, provided Schelling with a living example of a modality of knowing that defies subsumption under any "orthodox" scheme of either the Church's dogma or the Enlightenment's categories of reason.

The Pietists' insistence on a direct and unmediated relationship to divinity, their conviction that this direct relationship was an immediate *immanent* presence of the divine revealed through nature in their life, and their further insistence that this experience was also the highest form of knowing: all of these points required a grounding of "*Erkenntnis*" in precisely that which cannot be integrated into the orthodox framework of rational knowledge. His eulogy of Hahn provides us with an important insight into how he understands the relationship between these two types of knowing. Schelling writes of how Hahn scoured the sensuous world of nature in search of the "purest trace of deity," which he located in "the forces of nature." In the individual things of the world of nature Hahn disclosed that which permeated and united all of nature: the deity *qua* force of nature. In one sense, we can read Hahn's knowing of the deity through the forces of nature as alluding to the *Zentralschau* which permitted him to experience the divine ἕν καὶ πᾶν. In this, the apogee of the spirit—or the creative act of *Conscientia*—Hahn experienced the overpowering surplus of life, as if he were participating directly in the self-revelation of the divine. It is this experience of the sacred that Schelling holds out as the ideal of his work. This highest, most potent knowledge is not just the theoretical grasp of an idea ultimately irrelevant to one's existence, but is rather an actual experience of the holy which, as overpowering and ecstatic as the experience of the sublime, is something *sui generis*, and as such, is radically alien to the symmetrical reflections of discursive consciousness.

As far as we know Schelling understood Hahn's *Zentralschau* as Oetinger did: like a critic at a theater production, attuned to every possible nuance in performance, but ultimately just a spectator, not a participant. Nonetheless, there are as many different modalities of "knowing" the unity of creation as there are those in search of it. The essential point for the interpreter of Schelling is to try to make clear what he could possibly mean when later in 1802 he speaks of knowing this unity:

> What remains is only that which sublates all alienation, since only this is truly one and immutably the same. Only from this one can a true universe of knowledge, an all-encompassing form develop. Only what proceeds out of the absolute unity of the infinite and the finite is immediately through itself capable of symbolic presentation, capable therefore of that towards which every true philosophy strives, [and which is] objective in religion, an eternal source of new intuitions and a universal *typus* of all that is to become, in which human action expresses the harmony of the universe and strives to cultivate it. (I/5, 115)

From this passage, it is clear that the ideal he sets for his philosophy is to provide an exemplar of how it may be possible to overcome the alienation of human existence. The key to this is the apprehension of *das Ganze*, the irreducible and animating unity that binds the cosmos into one. Such a knowing of the generative whole is inaccessible to the logic of sequential thought. The fruits of such experience can only be communicated through symbolic and aesthetic works whose form and power extend beyond the reach of analytic and synthetic propositions. The telos of these symbolic presentations is to provide an anticipation of what humanity is to become in the future; a telos that requires humans to act and order their lives so as to best express the harmony of the universe. In addition, it is ultimately only the apprehension of the thoroughgoing interconnectedness and unity of creation that generates the insight needed to accomplish this.

This leads us to our last and perhaps most controversial point that the eulogy suggests concerning Schelling's understanding of who he was and the meaning, the telos, of his life. Raised in a subculture of paradox in which scholarly discipline and spiritual enthusiasm generated a productive clash of values, the scholarly work of his father brought acceptance and recognition, while the spiritual and theosophical work of Hahn and others brought censure and notoriety. Yet the impact of Hahn's person on the young boy seems to have been more than just significant. The figure of this man offered the young Schelling an exemplar of one blessed with genius and spiritual visions, a persecuted prophet who proclaimed the truth to the ignorant.

From what we have seen, the young Schelling led a terribly anomalous life as a child, separated from other children his age, associating primarily with adults and the ideas he discovered in the vast number of books he consumed. It strains the imagination to suggest that this young genius was not aware of his gifts and talents. From all reports, Schelling was throughout his life possessed of a magnitude of self-confidence that fluctuated from engagingly charismatic to abrasively arrogant. By any measure he was clearly possessed by a vision that compelled him to realize its content in much the same way as those engaged in artistic endeavors describe their pursuits, and in much the same way as he himself will describe in his *Oldest System Program*.

Following Schelling's goal of integrating the mythos of religion with philosophy's logos, we now turn to Kant in order to clarify the conceptual underpinnings that support Schelling's construction of an organic form of philosophy. As we have seen, central to this task is coming to terms with the epistemological challenge of apprehending the organic unity of reason and knowledge. And if Schelling is to succeed in his attempt to make mythology "become philosophical," then he must develop a philosophical account of how it is that we may come to grasp the unity expressed in sacred myths.[103] In other words, the young Schelling must create a way of employing the Kantian framework so that "the philosopher" in him may no longer "be ashamed" of the starkly mythological elements in his own upbringing. While indeed important, the more theosophical ideas of life as the first predicate of a nature which, valued as the self-revelation of the divine, provides us with both the schema of freedom and the organic form for conceptualizing and realizing the redemptive harmony of the ἕν καὶ πᾶν—all these more mythic and sensuous ideas require a justification which can only occur if Schelling can supply them with systematic support. Moreover, if we are to fully grasp the reasons given in his *Form Essay* for his inversion of Kant's system, then we too must become clear about the problematic nature of Kant's quest to coherently account for how his philosophy achieves a systematic unity capable of harmonizing the dualisms which threaten to undermine the foundation of his architectonic.

3

The Question of Systematic Unity

§83. Principle of These [Reflective] Conclusions
The principle underlying the conclusions of [reflective] judgment is
this: It is impossible for many to conform in one without a common
ground; rather, what appertains to many in this manner will be necessary out of a common ground. (*Logik*, §83; Ak IX, 132)

By way of introduction or anticipation, we need only say that there
are two stems of human knowledge, namely *Sinn* and *Verstand*, which
perhaps spring from a *common, but to us unknown, root.* (A 15/B 29;
emphasis mine)

Systematic Unity and the *Urform* of Reason

The problematic quest for a common ground to Kant's system runs
parallel to all three critiques. Within the framework of the first and
second *Critiques*, it appeared as if the absolute causality of freedom
would provide the necessary capstone required to transform his
"aggregate" of faculties and elements into a true "system." In the third
Critique however, Kant removes freedom from center stage and recasts
reflective judgment in its place. Finally making explicit his proclivity to
derive freedom from reason, Kant in this last critique argues that it is
finality (Zweckmäßigkeit), and not *freedom*, that is the unifying force
of critical reason.

In the transcendental deduction of the faculty of judgment's a priori
principle Kant posits a "need of understanding" that determines its
"necessary aim." He defines this goal as "the possibility of the unity
of experience, as a system according to empirical laws" (*KU*, 183). To

satisfy this need Kant derives the a priori principle of the "finality of Objects (here of nature)."[1]

It is this principle that will justify Kant's efforts to discover "a ground of the unity of the supersensible that lies at the basis of nature"; a foundation that will provide the basis upon which empirical science can "divide its products into genera and species" (KU, 176; 185). Indeed, it is this a priori principle of finality *Zweckmäßigkeit* that establishes the possibility of what Kant properly calls the organized whole of 'nature' (in its subjective sense). Through this principle of finality, reflective judgment leads the particularity of nature's sensible manifold back to the standpoint of a systematic unity in which that particularity can be understood. Whereas the determinative judgment of the understanding *descends* from the universal to the particular, subsuming and thereby erasing the heterogeneity of the sensible manifold, the reflective judgment of reason is forced to *ascend* from the individual to the universal ideal of systematic unity, but without the defining determination of sensible intuition. The guide for reason's ascent is instead the rule provided by the ideal of beauty.[2]

Kant however, is not only interested in justifying the efforts of the empirical scientist and his reliance on the theoretical knowledge of the understanding. More importantly, he must demonstrate how pure reason's *arche* prescribes an a priori *law* for freedom "as the supersensible in the Subject, so that we may have a purely practical knowledge."[3] For this to be possible there must exist a ground in the supersensible that "determines the causality of things of nature to an effect in conformity with their appropriate natural laws, but at the same time also in unison with the formal principle of the laws of reason"—namely, the law or causality of freedom (KU, 176; 195).[4]

Whereas the sensible is denied an influence on the intelligible, the supersensible ground of freedom is assigned the role of somehow *determining* the laws of sensible nature, while at the same time not *violating* them. Kant finesses this point by positing the effect of the causality of freedom as the final telos to "manifest" itself in the sensible world, a manifestation of the supersensible that *is not*, however, a revelation or miracle that defies the order of nature. Rather freedom as the final telos of the sensible world "presupposes the condition of the possibility of that end in nature," narrowly construed as the *nature of man*, not of nature in the objective sense (KU, 196). With this appeal to the finality of both freedom and nature, Kant unites in the faculty of reflective judgment the practical interest of reason and that of the theoretical interests of the understanding:

This faculty, with its concept of a finality of nature, provides us with the mediating concept between concepts of nature and the concept of freedom—a concept that makes possible the transition from the pure theoretical [legislation of understanding] to the pure practical [legislation of reason] and from conformity to law in accordance with the former to final ends according to the latter. For through that concept we cognize the possibility of the final end that can only be actualized in nature and in harmony with its laws. (Ibid.)

In this dense but central passage, Kant lays out his attempt to navigate the transition from the many of the sensible manifold to the unity of the final telos of humanity. He argues that through its a priori principle of finality, reflective judgment supplies the "supersensible substrate" with the possibility of determination *through the intellectual faculty* (ibid.). Reflective judgment thus provides the mechanism whereby the supersensible—left undetermined by the understanding—is made *available* for determination by our intellect. However, it is not the formative action of theoretical reason that determines this supersensible substrate; rather it is determined "a priori by its practical law" (ibid.). By preparing the intelligible ground for possible determination by the final telos of reason *qua* freedom, the faculty of judgment "makes possible the transition from the realm of concept of nature to that of the concept of freedom" (ibid.). But unfortunately Kant fails to make clear precisely what this mechanism of reflective judgment is and how its principle of finality prepares the supersensible for possible determination. The success of his entire critical "system," however, rests on these two crucial points.

Life Is the Schema of Freedom: The Will of Desire and the Causality of Freedom

Kant specifies two modalities of reflective judgment, the aesthetic and the teleological, with the latter being dependent on the former for generating the concept of finality. Both however, are ultimately dependent on the will's faculty of *desire* that drives them to seek the final end of reason in freedom. It is only through the power of will's desire that man has the capacity to be the cause of a representation whereby it can determine itself. As an inhabitant of the sensible world, this power of the will's desire can only be articulated in connection with the *faculty of life*, insofar as "[l]ife is the faculty of a being by which it acts according to the laws of the faculty of desire. The faculty of desire is the faculty such a being has of causing, through its representations, the reality of the objects of these ideas."[5] The causality of life's desire is the sensuous *schema* for the causality of freedom. Reduced to "a faculty of" a noumenal "being," life exhibits a "causality" of a desire, "a striving (*nisus*) to be a cause by means of one's representations."[6] By definition, desire seeks its satisfaction, and the attainment of desire's want or need generates pleasure.[7] It is this dynamic of desire's need and the pleasure of its satisfaction that unifies aesthetic and teleological judgment; the feeling of pleasure attained by the subject in such acts of judgment serves as the sensible *schema* for the understanding's a priori subjective principle of finality: "The attainment of every aim is coupled with a feeling of pleasure" (*KU*, 187). Due to the ideality of freedom however, Kant must elevate life and pleasure to the higher level of desire, in order to remove them from the sensual and provide them with a purely intellectual reading.

He does this in his *Metaphysics of Morals*, where he defines an "intellectual pleasure" in contrast to the more familiar "practical plea-sure . . . necessarily connected with [the] desire" of an object of sense: "On the other hand, that pleasure which is not necessarily connected with the desire of an object, and so is not at bottom a pleasure in the existence of an object of a representation but is attached only to the representation by itself, can be called merely contemplative pleasure or inactive delight."[8] In blatantly Aristotelian terms, Kant here describes a contemplative pleasure that, devoid of a sensible object, finds the attainment of its end in the contemplation of the pure form of the representation itself.[9] While the actual *feeling* caused by the "inactive delight" still remains sensible, the "intellectual pleasure" is itself the effect of an "antecedent determination of the capacity for desire."[10] This causal determination of intellectual pleasure by the higher capacity for desire is judged by the understanding to be "a general rule (though only for the subject)" that articulates what Kant calls "an interest" (*MM*, 40). The representation that constellates this "general rule" is an *object*, which "must be called an interest of reason" since it is "based on pure rational principles alone."[11] In the third *Critique* Kant also determines this "inactive delight" of contemplative, intellectual pleasure as "*taste*."[12] With this, he makes perfectly clear the systematic connection of the moral and aesthetic: at their core both aesthetic and moral judgment are determined by the same "ground" or interest of pure reason.[13]

In the third *Critique* Kant first presents the ground of aesthetic plea-sure as the unintended harmony between an object generated by the internal intuition of imagination and the conceptual form understanding

applies to it through reflection *qua Vorstellen*. This harmonious equi-
poise of conflicting faculties is their response to the apprehension of
beauty. In this context he argues that since pleasure is the *unintended*
result of the free play of the imagination and understanding, the form
of the object found in this *Vorstellung* is considered to have universal
validity: "The object is then called beautiful; and the faculty of judging
by means of such a pleasure (and so also with universal validity) is
called taste" (*KU*, 190).[14] The determinative subsumption of particular
to universal has no need of the pleasure of finality, since the work of
the categories occurs according to the involuntary machinations of
our cognitive faculty. However, since there is no empirical object to
determine a concept of finality, the reflective judgment has need of
the individual's subjective guidance to create the rule for the ascent to
finality *qua* systematic unity. This subjective guidance begins in the
pleasure of discovering a beautiful object.

This pleasure emerges from what is "purely subjective in the representation of an object" since it has been created by an intuition of the
imagination. It is the pure "form of an object of intuition" that provides
the "aesthetic quality" that constellates pleasure (*KU*, 188). This
apprehensio of the pure form of an object of intuition occurs "in the
imagination"; but pleasure arises only if imagination, "as the faculty
of intuitions *a priori*," is unintentionally brought into accord with the
understanding" as "the faculty of concepts" (*KU*, 190). The feeling
of pleasure occasioned by the beautiful object becomes the source of
the concept of finality that accounts not only for aesthetics, but also
for the teleological judgments that belong "to the theoretical part of
philosophy" (*KU*, 194). Most importantly, the satisfaction that reason's
desire finds in the ground of the feeling of pleasure generated by the
beautiful serves for Kant as a symbol of morality:

> The spontaneity in the play of the cognitive faculties whose harmo-
> nious accord contains the ground of this pleasure, makes the concept in
> question, in its consequences, a suitable mediating link connecting the
> realm of the concept of nature with that of the concept of freedom, as
> this accord at the same time promotes the sensibility of the mind for
> moral feeling. (*KU*, 197; cf. §59)

Kant captures the irreducible position of the individual through his
analysis of the role *subjective taste* plays in this ascent to finality. Yet
Kant at the same time insists that the ground of this pleasure is an a
priori representation of finality that is valid for all humanity. And with

this, we encounter the antinomy of aesthetic judgment: the same representation of finality that pleasurably satisfies understanding's want of unity is the *same* ground for the manifold of *individual* subjective taste. The question we have to examine now is how Kant accounts for and resolves this obvious contradiction.

The Antinomy of Aesthetic Judgment

§29. Peculiar Character of Disjunctive Judgments
The members of the disjunction are altogether problematic judgments of which nothing else is thought but that they, taken together, are e*qual* to the sphere of the whole as parts of the sphere of a cognition, each being the complement of the other (*complementum ad totem*) . . .

The division in disjunctive judgments thus indicates the coordination not of the parts of the whole concept, but all the parts of its sphere. There I think many things through one concept; here one thing through many concepts, e.g., the definitum through all characteristics of coordination. (*Logik*, §29; Ak IX, 107)

The principle of taste demands that every individual be entitled to one's own subjective position and, at the same time, claims that every such subjective judgment necessarily makes a universal claim to validity. The resulting antinomy is clear: the maxim of the thesis demands that since everyone has his own taste, such judgments cannot be "based on concepts," for if they were they would be open to definitive resolution by "means of proof."[15] The maxim of the antithesis however, insists that since aesthetic judgments make "a claim to necessary validity for everyone," they must be somehow based on concepts that can be contested (but not disputed).[16] Simply put: the thesis of sensible intuition demands the singularity of subjective taste whereas the antithesis of understanding's logic requires a universal claim to validity.

Each of these maxims is the result of the different ways in which Kant's reason treats sensible intuition and the concepts of the understanding. Whereas the concepts of the understanding can be fully and elegantly determined by the predicates of sensible intuition, *sensible intuition cannot determine itself as singular*; a problem that raises once again the question of how Kant can integrate the heterogeneous factors of *Sinn* and *Verstand* into his critical infrastructure.

He is constrained in this by the mathematical ideal of his first *Critique* that, as system principle, requires the subsumption of qualitative difference under the principle of a homogenizing magnitude, so that one transcendental subject can "yield connection of heterogeneous knowledge in one consciousness."[17] Only if this act of a homogenizing subsumption is possible can the ideality of objects of sense be extracted from the indeterminate "*Stoff*" of the senses; a possibility that in turn provides the evidence for Kant's claim that there can be a priori determinations of the forms (mathematical) of phenomena.[18] This possibility of a homogenizing subsumption however, must presuppose a "transcendental rational concept of the supersensible" that is the noumenal form—the *Ding-an-sich*—as the active fundament of all sensible intuition.[19] This *intelligible* fundament however, is, strictly speaking *unintelligible* to discursive thinking: like the πρότασις ἄμεσος of a demonstration, as the basis of the predicates of sensible intuition, the noumenal substrate cannot be determined by the same sensible predicates for which it is the condition.[20] Consequently, the noumenal substrate must remain "intrinsically undetermined and indeterminable" by those predicates.[21] It is this field of sensible intuition, however, that is the source of the individual, subjective pleasure that characterizes the taste of Kant's aesthetic judgment. Whereas his theoretical reason simply ignored the problematic status of this circular dilemma, an account of reason employed in aesthetic judgment cannot: the individuality of pleasure must somehow be integrated into the systematic unity specified by his architectonic.

Kant's solution, like the late defenders of the Ptolemaic system, is to add yet another type of *concept* to his theoretical edifice: the antinomy of taste arises from the mistaken demand that reason somehow be limited to the *one type* of fully defined concept required by the judgments of the understanding in the first *Critique*. To reconcile the contrary demands of aesthetic judgment he proposes a new form of concept that submits to predication, but not to the theoretically complete determination of the concepts of reason. On the contrary, this new class of concept is by definition incapable of ever being completely determined. Moreover, because it betrays the "form" capable of generating a "double sense," reason must approach it from more than one "point of view."[22] Employing the *progressive* use of the disjunctive form of judgment, Kant can now dissolve the antithesis of taste by attaching "opposite predicates" to this one new type of concept:

> The thesis should therefore read: The judgment of taste is not based on *determinate* concepts; but the antithesis: The judgment of taste does rest upon a concept, although an *indeterminate* one (that, namely, of

the supersensible substrate of phenomena); and then there would be no conflict between them.[23]

While "inherently indeterminate," the substantive content of this new concept is "a general ground of the subjective finality of nature for the power of judgment," which is none other than "the supersensible substrate of phenomena."[24] Such an undeterminable concept—which is nonetheless capable of somehow expressing the intelligible basis of experience—is what Kant calls an "aesthetic idea." And what this new type of idea articulates is nothing less than the concept of the *supersensible ground that unifies the concepts of nature and freedom.*

This new class of idea is a "counterpart (pendant) of a *rational idea*"; it is a *Vorstellung* of the imagination in its active mode as "a productive faculty of cognition."[25] Kant further clarifies the status of imagination by stating that the aesthetic idea is the result of a new kind of "internal intuition" for which "no concept can be wholly adequate."[26] Thus does this new class of concept *qua* aesthetic idea receive a new modality of "internal intuition." The irreducible distance between the "*Stoff*" of this new class of internal intuition and reason's concepts "emulates," according to Kant, "the display of reason in its attainment of a maximum."[27] The inadequacy of predicates to determine completely the internal intuition of the aesthetic idea emulates the inability of theoretical reason to attain its maximum, and therewith fully determine its ideas.

The idea of the maximum is crucial to understanding the regulative force that characterizes the (albeit) limited developmental telos of Kant's architectonic; a point of concern that directly impacts Kant's reinterpretation of Plato's "architectonic ordering" of the world according to *ideas*, and Schelling's further development of "the eternal form of knowing" that incorporates elements lifted from both predecessors according to his own "organic ordering." To grasp the import of the maximum and its relation to the ideas of reason we must now return to the first *Critique* and examine in detail Kant's reinterpretation of Plato's theory of ideas.

The Unity of the Ideas of Reason and the Transcendental Ideal as the Form of Forms

But only the totality of things, in their interconnection as constituting the universe, is completely adequate to the idea. If we set aside the exaggerations in Plato's methods of expression, the philosopher's spiritual flight from the ectypal mode of reflecting upon the physical world-order to the architectonic ordering of it according to ends, that is, according to ideas, is an enterprise which calls for respect and imitation. (A 318/B 375)[28]

To explicate Kant's understanding of the ideas we will first describe the *elements* he uses to articulate what is arguably one of the oldest themes of philosophy: defining the abstract relation of the One to the Many, which simultaneously determines the logical relation of identity and difference (genera and species). True to tradition, Kant opts to work within the trinitarian framework that allows for the one system principle to be articulated by its three constitutive principles: the system principle of the Transcendental Ideal realizes its unity through the regulative employment of its three Ideas of reason that account for its logical and transcendental articulation.[29]

In outline, Kant's Transcendental Ideal names what he calls the transcendental concept of reason, which is "the *totality* of the *conditions* for any given conditioned."[30] This transcendental concept of the *unconditioned* is mediated by the transcendental ideas of reason, which Kant circuitously defines as the necessary concepts of reason "to which no corresponding object can be given in sense-experience" (A 326/B 383).[31] Working together, the transcendental ideas of reason occupy themselves with effecting the "absolute completeness" of the system of reason (A 328/B 385). This normative goal of completeness finds its most adequate expression in the achievement of the *"unity of reason"* (ibid.).

Just as the understanding is the source of experience through its categories (according to its form) and transcendental principles, pure reason is the transcendental source of the regulative ideas of reason which, since they are not determined by a sensuous object, have no objective constitutive efficacy. These ideas are instead heuristic models, whose normative status guides inquiry towards the unconditional, thereby insuring that no attained limit of analysis or synthesis will ever be conceived as final or insuperable:

They are thought only problematically, in order that upon them (as heuristic fictions), we may base regulative principles of the systematic employment of the understanding in the field of experience. Save in this connection they are merely *Gedankenden*, the possibility of which is not demonstrable, and which therefore do not allow of being employed, in the character of hypotheses, in explanation of the actual appearances. (A 771/B 799)

Just as the source of the categories were the four logical forms of all judgments of the understanding, the form of the first trinity of transcendental ideas are taken from those of the three syllogisms of reason. The resulting pairing reads:

Categorical	Hypothetical	Disjunctive
Immortality	Freedom	God
unity of the soul	the manifold of the phenomenal series of conditions	the continuity of forms in a system

Kant derives these transcendental ideas of immortality, freedom, and God from the three forms of *Vernunftschlüsse* in order to establish not only the logical infrastructure for the Transcendental Ideal, but to also lay the groundwork for these principles—first and foremost that of freedom—to bridge the theoretical concepts of nature with the moral ideas of practical reason.[32] To do this Kant distinguishes between three *functions* of each transcendental idea:

1) *The transcendental*: as transcendental ideas proper, these synthetic a priori propositions enjoy objective but indeterminate validity when employed as rules for actual experience (A 680/B 708);
2) *The logical*: as logical principles of reason that prescribe the methodological rules of reason's systematic unity; and
3) *The moral function*: as maxims of reason, these synthetic a priori propositions enjoy a purely subjective, heuristic status when applied to possible experience.[33]

Substantively, Kant claims that each idea of pure reason displays the double aspect of a moral and logical visage: the moral aspect of these ideas is captured by the concepts of immortality, freedom, and God, to which correspond the logical principles that ground unity (genera), manifoldness (species), and continuity (continuum).

Transcendental Modality: Unity as *Grundsatz* of Reason

As the understanding imposes conceptual unity onto the manifold of sensation, so too must reason establish systematic unity among the manifold of the understanding's concepts. As alluded to earlier, there is an essential difference between how the understanding and reason each go about achieving their respective goals; a distinction Kant refers to in the first *Critique* as the difference between the apodeictic and hypothetical uses of reason.[34]

The categories of the understanding determine their respective objects through a form of judging modeled on the derivation of the particular from the universal. This process assumes that the universal is both provided and certain, and all that remains for judgment is to subsume the particular under this universal, thereby providing it with a necessary determination. This is the regressive synthesis of the analytic method, which Kant employs in what he calls the "apodeictic use of reason" (A 646/B 674).[35] Within the scope of the universal concept that determines each category, Kant is thus able to supply cognition with the apodeictic certainty he promises to deliver in his introduction.[36] The problem of course is how to provide for a certainty of knowing regarding the systematic unity *among* these twelve categories of the understanding. Having established the certainty of the twelve "parts" of the understanding, Kant must show how these parts come together to form a system grounded in an even higher order of unconditional *Einheit*.

To do this Kant must depart from the regressive synthesis of his analytic method and instead avail himself of a progressive synthesis that begins with a universal of an undetermined concept—that "is admitted as problematic only"—namely, a universal concept that is the "mere idea" of systematic, unconditional unity (ibid.). As an idea incapable of being determined by the forms of the categories, reason has no certain knowledge of this universal concept, and thus no way of ascertaining its rule that should determine the plethora of particulars that constitute its scope; all it can consider are the particular instantiations of the actions of the categories and then compare these considerations with a rule it *guesses* to be the rule of the concept of unity.[37] The problematic universal concept that this employment of reason aims at however, is none other than the unconditional systematic unity of Kant's entire system, as constellated by the Transcendental Ideal. The irresolvable problem Kant faces goes to the very core of his attempt at the *self-grounding of reason*, namely, the problem of stating the type of synthesis whereby he will 'know' the unity of knowing through reason and reason alone.[38] Clearly, *if* the unity of reason is unconditional, the type of knowing Kant suggests must be markedly different from the pedestrian subsumption of the understanding.[39]

The only kind of knowing he can make use of to do this is to be found in his discussion of the system of reason's ideas as *Naturbegriffe*—a point that will later be essential to our discussion of Schelling's interpretation of Plato's Ideas.

Weltbegriffe and Naturbegriffe: The Limits of a Mathematical
World in the Face of the *"Absolute Selbsttätigkeit"* of Nature

Kant uses the term *Naturbegriffe* to describe the Ideas of Reason in the
first section of *The Antinomy of Pure Reason*. Preparing the ground
for his resolution of the antinomies, Kant continues his division of
reason into its mathematic and dynamic operations. Following the
division in the tables of judgments and categories, he assigns "in the
narrower sense" the *Weltbegriffe* of the "great and the small" to the
mathematical categories of quantity and quality, whereas the *Naturbegriffe* he assigns to the dynamic categories of relation and modality (A
420/B 448). To the former he assigns exclusive use of what he calls a
regressive synthesis, to the later, a progressive synthesis.

The transcendental ideas of the *Weltbegriffe* address "the totality
of the regressive synthesis" that allows reason to infer the existence of
the unconditioned from the occasion of every conditioned synthesis.[40]
This mathematical series operates within the sphere of appearances *qua*
conditioned, and ascends from these conditioned to the unconditioned,
positing an "absolute totality of the synthesis on the side of the conditions" as appearances (A 335/B 392). This synthesis presupposes that the
"unconditioned" that emerges from its successive series *is ultimately of
the same kind as the members of its series*: the unity it presupposes is
successive. Consequently, this series is *"a parte priori"* without limits or
beginning; it is an infinite series of relative magnitudes which, although
it can be "given in its entirety," is nonetheless "never completed" (A
417/B 445). As such, Kant calls this infinite regress only "potentially
infinite," thereby removing the possibility that the mathematical form of
synthesis could ever "produce" an actual infinite, that is, the totality of its
synthesis will never be actually unconditioned. The unity this regressive
synthesis presupposes is successive, thereby precluding the possibility
that, at least via the operations of mathematical reason, the Transcendental Ideal will be heterogeneous to its conditions. "In the context of
the antinomies of pure reason Kant ignores the progressive synthesis of
the dynamic series, suggesting that its "significance will appear later" (A
420/B 448).[41]"

What makes the "dynamic series" of the *Naturbegriffe* suited to
articulate the reflective judgment guided by the ideas of reason is that
the condition of this series is also the problematic idea of unconditional
unity. And what attracts Schelling's attention to this method of analysis
is how in contrast to the mathematical series, the idea of unconditional
unity is *heterogeneous* to this method's "series," since it is a *purely*

intelligible idea which is not itself part of the series of conditioned particulars (A 531/B 559). In a reference no doubt to the *supersensible strata of the noumenal,* Kant calls this unconditioned "a condition of appearance outside the series of appearances" (ibid.). In contrast to the potential infinite of the mathematical series, this dynamic series has a "first member" that provides it with an absolute magnitude, thereby distinguishing it from the *Weltbegriffe* of the comparative magnitudes of "the great and the small." This first member provides for the dynamic categories "in respect of causes, *absolute Selbsttätigkeit* (freedom), in respect of the existence of alterable things, absolute natural necessity" (A 418/B 446).

The heterogeneity of the first member of these series is primarily determined by its status as a whole (*ein Ganzes*), and the relationship this status determines vis-à-vis its particulars: it relates to its particulars in a "descending" yet simultaneous relation of community, not as the beginning member of a mathematical series that ascends in a sequence of time. Kant states that the progressive synthesis requires one to consider the world "as a dynamical whole" (ibid.), by which he considers "the sum of appearances insofar as they stand, in virtue of an inner principle of causality, in thoroughgoing interconnection" (A 419/ B 446, fn. B). Kant's challenge in the first *Critique* has been of course to—contra Hume—provide this "inner principle of causality" with its transcendental grounding. He does this in the *Regulative Employment of the Ideas,* in his presentation of the transcendental *Grundsatz* of reason as *the one form of knowledge as a whole.*

The *Urform* of Reason: αἱ συνάπασαι ἐπιστῆμαι

What is at stake for Kant is not one of the aforementioned three ideas of reason, but rather the transcendental *Grundsatz* of the systematic unity of reason, which will itself *regulate the regulative deployment of the ideas*: what he needs is a principle of principles, or, in the vernacular of the tradition, a form of forms. The question is, however, can there be a "proposition" that articulates *Einheit*?

His first step in addressing this aporia requires the alchemical transformation of the strictly logical into the transcendental. After having distinguished the apodeictic from the hypothetical use of reason, Kant proposes that the regulative demand for systematic unity is "a mere idea" that generates "a *projected* unity, to be regarded not as given in itself, but as a problem only" (A 647/B 675). Yet Kant quickly qualifies the status of this projected unity, however, calling it nothing more than a "*logical* principle" that is only a prescription of unity made by human reason that simply *suggests*, in an instrumental sense, that the objects of nature comply (A 648/B 676). The grounding principle of reason however, cannot rest its claim to validity on mere heuristics. The grounding principle of reason must provide *objective* validity:

> But to say that the constitution of the objects or the nature of the understanding which knows them as such, is in itself determined to systematic unity, and that we can in a certain measure postulate this unity a priori, without reference to any such special interest of reason, and that we are therefore in a position to maintain that knowledge of the understanding in all its possible modes (including empirical knowledge) has the unity required by reason, and stands under common principles from which all its various modes can, in spite of their diversity, be deduced—that would be to assert a transcendental principle of reason, and would make the systematic unity necessary, not only subjectively and logically, as method, but *objectively also*. (Ibid.; emphasis mine)[42]

Kant transforms this logical principle of reason into the transcendental in three moves: 1) establish the principle of systematic unity as logically and subjectively valid, 2) *postulate* this principle as having objective validity, and 3) test against experience. Kant's "evidence" to justify the extension of this subjective principle of reason to include the objective structures of empirical objects is indirect: since reason presupposes this principle without our consent, and since nature seems to oblige us by conforming to this principle, it must then be "one of nature's own laws" (A 650/B 678). The essence of his argumentative strategy is summed up succinctly in the following presentation of his reasoning on this matter:

> The law of reason that requires us to seek for this unity, is a necessary law, since without it we should have no reason at all, and without reason no coherent employment of the understanding, and in the absence of this no sufficient criterion of empirical truth. In order, therefore, to secure an empirical criterion we have no option save to presuppose the systematic unity of nature as objectively valid and necessary. (A 651/B 679)

In what amounts to an apagogic proof, Kant seeks to justify his position by disproving its opposite: to deny the possibility of systematic unity is to deny the possibility of reason, understanding, and empirical truth.[43]

The transcendental principle of reason is thus for Kant nothing less than the possibility of all episteme; a position which implies that this *Grundsatz* specifies, in the Platonic sense, the *one form of knowledge as a whole*.[44]

The reflective form of judgment required to determine the rule of this *Grundsatz* testifies to the scope and nature of this problematic universal concept that is the transcendental principle of reason: this concept must be that of an unconditioned *Einheit* that *indeterminately specifies the form of all determinate knowledge*. This is clear from Kant's description of the *Vernunfteinheit*:

> If we consider in its whole range the knowledge obtained for us by the understanding, we find that what is peculiarly distinctive of reason in its attitude to this body of knowledge, is that it prescribes and seeks to achieve its systematization, that is, to exhibit the connection of its parts in conformity with a single principle. This unity of reason has always presupposed an idea, namely, that of the form of a whole of knowledge—a whole which is prior to the determinate knowledge of the parts and which contains the conditions that determine a priori for every part its position and relation to the other parts. (A 645/B 673)

The homogenizing effects of the English language's philosophical vocabulary successfully obscures the variegated richness of Kant's words in this key passage; a richness that focuses the points of contact between Kant, Plato, and Schelling, and their shared interest in discovering a form of the unity of knowledge.[45] The unity of reason *has always* presupposed one idea of one form of episteme considered in its entirety. This *eternal form of knowledge* is the necessary epistemological condition for the determinate knowing of the individual elements of *epistêmê* because, as the framework for their interpretation, this whole determines both the position of each determinate element and their systematic interconnection. And indeed, precisely this is the central point of Kant's argument: the disparate categories of the understanding require reason—as it "has always (*seit jederzeit*)"—to unify them according to *the one form of knowledge as a whole*.

In adopting this presupposition Kant asserts a "transcendental principle whereby such a systematic unity is a priori assumed to be necessarily inherent in the objects" of sense (A 650/B 678). Since this principle however, carries its "recommendation directly within" itself, intuition cannot provide a "schema" that would prescribe the rules required to establish "the complete systematic unity of all concepts of the understanding" (ibid.; A 665/B 693). If this transcendental principle is presupposed as necessary to secure an empirical criterion for truth, then Kant must develop a mechanism whereby the *transcendental ideas* can articulate the rules, and thereby fulfill their regulative duty. Somehow, the transcendental ideas must provide a rule for their application to the concepts of the understanding.

To do this, Kant must provide an account of how one negotiates the transition from the *Einheit* of reason to the multiplicity of the categories. In anticipation of one of the central questions Schelling raises in the *Timaeus Commentary*, Kant must answer the question how "the forms of knowledge collectively are many" (*Phil.* 13e8).[46] To do this Plato employed his triad of forms τὸ πέρας, τὸ ἄπειρον and τὸ κοινόν. Now Kant must also show how the manifold of knowledge and sciences are somehow united as one. At the heart of the Kantian program lurks an aporia as old as philosophy itself—a point that is not missed by Schelling.

The Logical Visage: The *Prinzipien* of Unity, Manifoldness, and Continuity

After having demonstrated that the logical principle of systematic unity "presupposes a transcendental principle," Kant must descend again to his native land of the logical and account for how "the logical law of genera and species"[47] is capable of providing the "methodological device"[48] required to prescribe the "systematic unity to the manifold knowledge" of the understanding (A 647/B 676). To achieve this, not only must the respective extremes of the unity and multiplicity of our knowledge be considered separate from one another, but there must also be a regulative principle capable of *mediating the two*, preserving their difference while upholding their similarities.[49] Ignoring the ancient formulation of this problem in the unscientific terms of the One and the Many, Kant opts for the scholastic treatment of this time-honored aporia, and translates unity into the "logical principle of genera, which postulates identity," and manifoldness into the countervailing principle of "species," which posits "diversity in things" (A 654/B 682).[50] Both principles command the understanding to address diversity no less than the identity of its concepts, thereby demonstrating reason's "twofold, self-conflicting interest . . . in *extent* (universality) in respect of genera, and . . . in *content* (determinateness) in respect of the multiplicity of species" (ibid.).[51]

Kant resolves this self-conflicting interest of reason by introducing a third term, the mediating logical principle of *"affinity,"* or the *"continuity* of forms" (A 658/B 686). It relates to homogeneity and specification just as the third category of each class relates to the previous two: it is the product of the addition of the first to the second.[52] Thus the third logical principle, the continuity of forms,

> arises from union of the other two, inasmuch as only through the processes of ascending to the higher genera and of descending to the lower species do we obtain the idea of systematic connection in its completeness. For all the manifold differences are then related to one another, inasmuch as they one and all spring from one highest genus, through all degrees of a more and more widely extended determination. (Ibid.)[53]

In articulating the logical principles of systematic unity, Kant attempts to provide the three rules that will asymptotically circumscribe the systematic unity of the unconditioned totality of the Transcendental Ideal.[54] As Kant makes clear, it is the continuity of forms, ordered by the disjunctive syllogism, that successfully comprehends the Transcendental Ideal.[55] What he does not make clear, however, is the status of these logical principles. As he notes, "what is strange (*merkwürdig*) about these principles is that they seem to be transcendental, . . . and yet possess, as synthetic a priori propositions, objective but indeterminate validity, and thereby serve as rules for possible experience" (A 663/B 691). But if they can in fact be "employed with great advantage to the elaboration of experience" as mere "heuristic principles," then the truth of these principles of logic must be *objectively validated* to justify their binding legislation.[56] Once they have received their validation, Kant can then elevate them from the status of principles of logic to principles of reason.

As the resolutions of the antinomies of pure reason demonstrate, the principles of pure reason are "never constitutive in respect of empirical concepts" (A 664/B 692).[57] Consequently Kant is forced to find a different way to "secure" their "regulative employment, and therewith some sort of objective validity" (ibid.). Because these pure *Vernunftbegriffe* are "derived . . . from the interest of reason in respect of a certain possible perfection of . . . knowledge," he is compelled to exchange the truth of correspondence (with an object of possible experience) for a coherence theory of truth. Regulating this coherency is the logical idea of continuity construed as the *idea of the maximum* that will guarantee the formal, systematic unity of reason.[58]

The Idea of the Maximum as the *Analogon* of the Schema for the *"Prinzipien der Vernunft"*

As we have seen, at this point in the first *Critique*, the principles of pure reason employed in their transcendental function are incapable of executing their regulative duty, since intuition cannot provide a "schema" that would prescribe the rule "for the complete systematic unity of all concepts of the understanding" (A 665/B 693).[59] Arguing once again from the principle of systematic elegance and symmetry, Kant demands that "there can and must nonetheless be an analogon of such a schema" that will account for the regulative employment of the idea (ibid.).[60] What he is obviously looking for in this analogon is something similar to a schema that could somehow fulfill its function of a rule for employing the ideas.

In the *Analogies of Experience*, he confronts a similar problem. According to his architectonic, since empirical intuition cannot generate the evidence of apodeictic necessity that mathematical intuition can, the categories that explicate experience have only a regulative function in establishing the relations and connections between empirical objects. This is achieved through a procedure of applying analogies consisting of two *qualitative* relations in which only three of the terms are known. Consequently,

> we can obtain a priori knowledge only of the relation to a fourth, not of the fourth member itself. The relation yields, however, a rule for seeking the fourth member in experience, and a mark whereby it can be detected. An analogy of experience is, therefore, only a rule according to which a unity of experience may arise from perception. (A 179/B 222)

Regarding pragmatic belief, Kant also turns to analogical reasoning, and writes that the analogon is employed when "there is no existing means of arriving at certainty in the matter," since we are dealing with an idea "about which nothing can be done by us" (A 830/B 858). This indeed would appear to be the case in terms of the principles of pure reason.[61]

The analogon Kant proposes for the *Grundsatz* is that of "the idea of the maximum in the *division* and *unification* of the knowledge of the understanding under *one* principle" (A 663/B 693; my emphasis).[62] His justification for this idea of the maximum follows analogically from his treatment of the understanding: just as sensibility is the object of the understanding, the understanding is the object of reason. The idea of the maximum determines the *Vernunfteinheit* to simultaneously divide and unite the knowledge provided by the understanding under the principle of systematic unity (ibid.). The idea of the maximum will insure that what is divided and united will be done so with absolute completeness.[63] As an analogue of a schema, the idea of the maximum provides Kant with a rule for fully determining what is "greatest and absolutely complete" in the understanding; to insure that this *Vernunfteinheit* will be thought completely and that the continuity of forms will be linear, all "restrictive conditions which provide indeterminate manifoldness" and discontinuity *will be* "ignored (*weggelassen*)" (ibid.). Indeterminate sensual nature is of course not integrated into the pure a priori of transcendental reason. Yet this idea of the maximum does include *determinate manifoldness*, since it integrates division and unification under the one principle of continuity of form, in accordance with the three logical principles of unity, variety, and continuity.[64]

These three principles of reason thereby provide Kant with "an analogon of a schema of sensibility" (ibid.). When the categories of the understanding are applied to "the schema of reason," however, instead of generating knowledge of an object as the understanding would with its sensible object, it yields in this instance only "a rule or principle for the systematic unity of all employment of the understanding" (ibid.). It is at this juncture that Kant departs from the traditional conception of the transcendental object *qua* maximum, and insists that it *does not* refer to any empirical object.[65] While the principles of reason regulated by this maximum "prescribe a priori to the understanding thoroughgoing unity in its employment," they only have an *indirect* effect on the objects of experience (ibid.). These principles of reason thus offer up a schema "for which there is no object, not even an hypothetical one," thereby enabling the subject merely "to represent to ourselves other objects in an indirect manner, namely in their systematic unity, by means of their relation to this idea" (ibid.). Limiting their once-removed claim to objective reality, these ideas of reason only "indicate the procedure whereby" the application of the understanding to empirical objects will be brought into "complete harmony with itself" (A 664/B 694). To indicate however, is not to determine. Consequently, Kant must demote these principles of reason—formally considered—to the status of *subjective principles* of reason, which he titles "maxims of reason" (ibid.).

What then is the idea of the maximum of reason to which the aesthetic idea should attain and the artist emulate? It is the idea of absolute and complete division and unification of all knowledge generated by the understanding under one principle.[66] The idea of the maximum is thus the schema of the systematic unity of reason.[67]

The Transcendental Ideas: The Figurative Guarantors
of Reason's Extension

In the idea of the maximum Kant not only provides the one and the many with a rule for systematic integration, but he also sets the stage for a new class of deduction for the ideas of reason; a new class of deduction that demonstrates their "indeterminate objective validity" (A 669/B 697). In this deduction, and in contrast to the logical principles considered earlier, these ideas of reason now—Spinoza-like—are provided with their *"object in the idea"* (A 670/B 698). What this means is that the three ideas of reason now suddenly *have schemas*, but still lack objects.[68] The object, which we use indirectly to represent the transcendental idea to ourselves, is determined by whether it "leads us to systematic unity" and provides an "extension of empirical knowledge":

> This, indeed, is the transcendental deduction of all ideas of speculative reason, not as constitutive principles for the extension of our knowledge to more objects than experience can give, but as regulative principles of the systematic unity of the manifold of empirical knowledge in general, whereby this empirical knowledge is more adequately secured within its own limits and more effectively improved than would be possible, in the absence of such ideas, through the employment merely of the principles of the understanding. (A 671/B 699)

The schema of the systematic unity of reason—the idea of the maximum—thus becomes the criterion for determining the objects of the ideas of reason. The objects of these ideas of course do not exist, they are rather only "analoga of real things, not as in themselves real things" (A 674/B 702). The transcendental objects of the transcendental ideas of soul and God are, as "analoga of real things," only to be considered *as if* they had true existence. Nonetheless, these objects of the transcendental ideas are essential to the completion of the "one single interest" of reason, namely, to achieve maximal systematic unity (A 666/B 694).

Consider a possible transcendental object of the transcendental idea of God, that of a "supreme intelligence (*intellectus archetypus*)" (A 695/B 723). Transforming Anselm's logic of the maximum, Kant argues that as the object of the transcendental idea of God, the thought of the divine understanding becomes the schema "of the regulative principle of the greatest possible empirical employment of my reason" (A 679/B 707). Following the aforementioned logical principle, Kant *must* posit the idea of God for not only its pragmatic value in the domain of practical reason, but also, more importantly, he must posit this idea for the pragmatic value it provides *theoretical* reason. Lacking a way of generating a schema for merely logical principles, Kant requires the figurative schema of the ideas to employ his principle of systematic unity:

> For if the greatest possible empirical employment of my reason rests upon an idea . . . that of systematically complete unity, . . . I may posit it only as a something which I do not at all know in itself, and to which, as a ground of that systematic unity, I ascribe, in relation to this unity, such properties as are analogous to the concepts employed by the understanding in the empirical sphere . . . and since this idea depends merely on my reason, I can think this being as *self-subsistent reason*, which through ideas of the greatest harmony and unity is the cause of the universe. (A 677/B 705f)

The irony is thick: the only way for Kant to provide a rule for his *Grundsatz* of systematic unity is by an appeal to the object of this idea, figuratively construed *via* the predicates of the traditional deity. Granted, Kant denies that the predicate of existence can be meaningfully applied to this concept, but he nonetheless agrees with tradition that there is no way to know and predict the object of this concept in a theoretical and positive fashion. The only way to articulate his principle of systematic unity is through the same *via analogica* of a traditional theology whose pedigree stretches back to at least Aristotle. For systematic reasons shared with that tradition, this idea of God is again the capstone of his edifice; remove it and his structure loses all unity and coherence. The idea of God thus becomes the condition of possibility of his entire theoretical attempts to rebut Hume and ground the empirical employment of reason. Of course, as an idea it lacks reality (*Wirklichkeit*), being instead a totality devoid of any substantive content. The objects that provide schemas for the employment of this idea are pure forms, lifeless outlines of terms once used in the attempt to capture the ecstasy of life and sublime rapture of the sacred (think Plotinus, Rumi, Eckhart, Luther). The transcendental object of the Transcendental Ideal (*Prototypon Transcendentale*) is none other than the God of Monotheism transformed into a nominalistic idea:

> I think to myself merely the relation of a being, in itself completely unknown to me, to the greatest possible systematic unity of the universe, solely for the purpose of using it as a schema of the regulative principle of the greatest possible empirical employment of my reason. (A 679/B 707)

Kant not only adopts the summit of tradition's conceptual hierarchy, he also makes use of the triadic structure of this hierarchy's uppermost tier. Just as Plato first construed the One or the Good as the "form of forms" responsible for providing the systematic unity of his metaphysical system, Kant likewise incorporates the idea of the maximum *qua* Transcendental Ideal as his system's "idea of ideas." The idea of the maximum is required to "indicate" the rule or "conditions of the greatest possible unity of reason" (A 670/B 698). Its function parallels that of traditional metaphysics' "form of forms": it orders all other ideas of reason according to this charge, insuring that all ideas of reason enjoy a distinct type of "completeness" in their determination, "to which no possible empirical knowledge ever attains. In them reason aims only at systematic unity, to which it seeks to approximate the unity that is empirically possible, without ever completely reaching it" (A 568/B 596). His justification for this however, is strictly epistemological, since without the integrating and binding force of this idea his entire edifice will collapse into a disconnected pile of faculties and elements. This in turn generates the following problem: as a subjective maxim, the principle of systematic unity provides the complete and perfect determination of *possible objects* of experience, but, like an aesthetic idea, its *objective validity* can only be determined in an indeterminate and vague manner:

> The unity of reason is the unity of system; and this systematic unity does not serve objectively as a principle that extends the application of reason to objects, but subjectively as a maxim that extends its application to all possible empirical knowledge of objects. Nevertheless, since the systematic connection which reason can give to the empirical employment of the understanding not only furthers its extension, but also guarantees its correctness, the principle of such systematic unity is so far also objective, but in an indeterminate manner (*principium vagum*). (A 680/B 708)

With this, we encounter Plato's dynamic of the divine cause: *the condition of knowing itself can never be known determinately*. Though Kant's position would agree with Plato's on this point, the new meaning Kant gives to this old maxim is provided here by the phrase "indeterminate manner": as a regulative principle and maxim this principle's function lies in providing that unattainable goal which furthers and strengthens "in infinitum (indeterminately) the empirical employment of reason" (ibid.). Constellating the third *Critique*'s dynamic of *Zweckmäßigkeit*, the indeterminate aspect of the rule lies in its maximal demand for infinite and unconditional completeness. As such, it can never be fully limited or conditioned by predication. The object of this idea, the "transcendental thing," the object of the maxim, is posited as being the "point of view from which alone" systematic unity "can be further extended" (A 681/B 709). Kant writes: "In short, this transcendental thing [supreme intelligence] is only the schema of the regulative principle by which reason, so far as lies in its power, extends systematic unity over the whole field of experience" (ibid.). Finally, echoing the problematic status of the idea of systematic unity (A 646/B 674), the object that Kant employs to articulate the rule of the transcendental principle of reason is clearly identified as itself depending on a postulate whose "status" is at best "problematic":

> This object [the transcendental object], as thus entertained by reason (*ens rationis ratiocinatae*), is a mere idea; it is not assumed as a something that is real absolutely and *in itself*, but is postulated only problematically (since we cannot reach it through any of the concepts of the understanding) in order that we may view all connection of the things of the world of sense *as if* they had their ground in such a being. (A 681/B 709)

Systematic unity ultimately derives from, and is dependent on, a postulate of *problematic* status. This follows from Kant's understanding of the "the hypothetical employment of reason" insofar as it "is regulative only" (A 646/B 674). The critical issue is: how convincing is the regulative status of a postulate that Kant himself admits enjoys only problematic status? Does this problematic postulate satisfy Kant's stated goal of the first *Critique*, namely, to provide an account of reason's self-grounding? Having successfully employed the method of analysis to dissect the organism of reason, does his appeal to a regulative idea of systematic unity supply the power needed to integrate and reunite its manifold of elements and faculties? In light of the stated goals of the third *Critique*, we can only conclude that Kant would have himself had to answer these questions in the negative.

We have made this journey through the underbrush of the first *Critique* in search of a context in which to frame our discussion of the aesthetic ideas. We assume that Kant introduces a new class of concept in the third *Critique* only because he saw a systematic need that none of his elements from the first two *Critiques* could provide. As I pointed out before we dove into the first *Critique*, the same explanatory framework Kant advances to account for his aesthetic work—just as it was for Plato—forms the epistemological basis for *his entire critical edifice*: all hope of systematic unity vanishes unless Kant can provide a binding account of a supersensible substrate that will integrate his bifurcated "doctrine of nature" that divides our reality. Just as Plato had concluded, Kant finds that only τό καλόν is capable of delivering the centripetal force necessary to reconcile the divisions and oppositions that define our reality. As he notes in the introduction to the third *Critique*, what he seeks to articulate therein is the common point of reference that lies at the intelligible basis of our nature (*KU*, 176). What remains to be seen is whether this intelligible basis of our nature—and our freedom—is only an idea or ideal that can be thought and postulated to exist, but whose true existence and workings lie buried in a hidden art of our nature forever inaccessible to our human knowledge. To do this we must address the status of the aesthetic ideas. Most importantly, we must finally address Kant's one and only demonstration of the *progressive synthesis* of the dynamic categories in their application to the *idea of the sublime*.

Aesthetic Ideas, the Sublime, and the Internal Intuition of the Supersensible Ground

Whereas Kant never accounts for the generation of the ideas of reason, he tells us that the aesthetic ideas are generated by what he calls the principle of *Geist* that animates the psychic substance of soul: spirit "sets the mental powers . . . into a play which is self-maintaining and which strengthens those powers for such activity."[69] As the "faculty of presenting aesthetic ideas," spirit incites the productive powers of the imagination and the understanding to generate ideas that, like the ideas of reason, will help bring about "an extension of thought."[70] Like the maxims of reason, these aesthetic ideas always exceed in their representation what can be determined conceptually; but unlike the maxims of reason, aesthetic ideas can never be completely predicated. As the product of "internal intuition . . . no concept can be wholly adequate to them," just as no intuition can ever be adequate to the concepts or ideas of reason.[71] Imitating "the display of reason in its attainment of a maximum," the aesthetic idea serves as the schema that prescribes the "rule" for art and its beauty.[72]

As we have seen, the idea of the maximum seems to be the linchpin of Kant's critical edifice: it regulates not only the ideas of reason, but unites them with the new aesthetic ideas. But how do they differ, these two sets of ideas? Kant gives us the clue when he writes that "no concept can be wholly adequate" to the aesthetic ideas, just as no intuition can ever be adequate to the concepts or ideas of reason. The symmetry here parallels Kant's division in the first *Critique* between the regressive and progressive methods employed by the mathematical and dynamic categories to articulate the unconditioned. And it is to the dynamic categories that we must turn if we are to fully appreciate Kant's new attempt at supplying his idea of systematic unity with the power to generate the idea of an absolute whole of unconditional unity (the whole *qua* τὸ ὅλου), a power he finds in the *experience* of the sublime, which, in its palpable infinity, renders the purely relative magnitude of the mathematical categories inapplicable. In the face of the sublime, the relative categories of the mathematically great and small will not suffice to establish an unconditioned magnitude.

Once again, we must return to the first section of the *Antinomy of Pure Reason*, "The System of Cosmological Concepts." Preparing the field of understanding for his antinomies Kant here focuses only the *Weltbegriffe* of the mathematical categories of magnitude. As we have already seen, his analysis of the ideas of reason and the idea of the maximum were also presented through the mathematical categories of magnitude. In a passage Schelling depends on mightily, Kant notes that there are complementary ideas associated with the dynamic categories whose synthesis of the unconditioned is not quantifiable, but is rather that of *freedom*:

> We have two expressions, world, and nature, which sometimes coincide. The former signifies the mathematical sum total of all appearances and the totality of their synthesis, alike in the great and in the small, that is, in the advance alike through *composition* and through *division*. This same world is entitled nature when it is viewed as a dynamical whole. We are not then concerned with the aggregation in space and time, with a view to determining it as a magnitude, but with the unity in the existence of appearances. In this case, the condition of that which happens is entitled the cause. Its unconditioned causality in the [field of] appearance is called freedom, and its conditioned causality is called natural cause in the narrower [adjectival] sense. The conditioned in existence in general is termed contingent and the unconditioned necessary. The unconditioned necessity of appearances may be entitled natural necessity. (A 418/B 446f)

The distinction relevant to the sublime regards how each modality conceives the unconditioned *qua* infinite. The mathematical synthesis construes the unconditioned on the model of linear time: it is homogenous to the unlimited members of its series in that it is a "part of the series—a part to which the other members are subordinated"(A 417/B 445). Kant labels this an "infinite regress" that provides only a "possible infinite." In contrast, the dynamic synthesis construes the unconditioned on the model of *space*: it is heterogeneous to the members of its aggregate of coordinated parts, which are "not subordinated to one another" like the members of the causal series of magnitudes, since they are not "the conditions of the possibility of one another" (A 414/B 441). The heterogeneity of the unconditioned in this configuration allows Kant to conclude that, in this synthesis, there is "a first member of the series" that can be delimited as either the limit of the world, the simple, or "the *absolute self-action (Selbsttätigkeit)*" of freedom (A 418/B 446). This irreducible difference of the "first member" and the series it conditions delivers in all these ideas an infinite that is not merely *possible*, but is instead, in respect of existence, "absolute *natural necessity*" (ibid.).

Both kinds of categories are of course regulated by the idea of the maximum. However, it is just as obvious that whereas the mathematical categories only provide the unending regress of a possible infinite, the dynamic categories deliver the limit of a maximum as an *actual infinite*. This difference Kant uses in the third *Critique* to account for how his new aesthetic ideas will do what the ideas of reason could not: be productive causal agents of unity through the capacity to generate aesthetic pleasure "τῶν ὅλων τὶ καὶ τελείων."[73] However, whereas the idea of beauty delivers a *concept* to the understanding, it is the idea of the sublime that supplies reason with an *intuition* of the aesthetic surplus of the whole. This is most evident in §26, *The estimation of the magnitude of natural things requisite for the idea of the sublime*.

Echoing his account of the *Weltbegriffe* in the first *Critique*, Kant begins this section by making explicit the implicit identification of the logical and the mathematical methods of determining measure: both are incapable of ever arriving "at a first or fundamental measure, and so cannot get any definite concept of a given magnitude" (*KU*, 251). The movement of discursive thought is its definition: since it never stops, it never attains to an absolute measure. All it can ever process are the relative movements of a continuum whose extremes are provided by another modality of knowing, namely, that of intuition:

> The estimation of the magnitude of the fundamental measure must, therefore, consist merely in the immediate grasp that we can get of it in intuition, and the use to which our imagination can put this in presenting the numerical concepts. (Ibid.)

Kant designates the apprehension of this first measure as subjectively determined through intuition, a modality of "estimation" he calls aesthetic. Disregarding the division of the mathematical and dynamic categories of the first *Critique*, Kant proceeds to repeat the points we just covered:

> Now for the mathematical estimation of magnitude there is, of course, no greatest possible (for the power of numbers extends to infinity), but for the aesthetic estimation there certainly is and of it I say that where it is considered an absolute measure beyond which no greater is possible subjectively (i.e., for the judging subject), it then conveys the idea of the sublime and calls forth that emotion which no mathematical estimation of magnitudes by numbers can evoke (unless insofar as the fundamental aesthetic measure is kept vividly present to the imagination): because the latter presents only the relative magnitude due to comparison with others of a like kind, whereas the former presents magnitude absolutely, so far as the mind can grasp it in an intuition. (*KU*, 251)

The mind can grasp the absolute magnitude only in intuition. With this, Kant identifies the structure of the aesthetic with that of the modalities of the dynamic categories he uses in the first *Critique* to account for freedom, and in the third *Critique*, the *reciprocal causality* of organic life. All of these accounts are patterned after the form of the disjunctive syllogism—the only syllogism that allows him to think the oppositional dynamic of members of a whole that, "taken together," constitute "the sphere of the whole as parts of the sphere of a cognition, each [part] being the complement of the other (*complementum ad totum*)."[74]

The aesthetic apprehension of magnitude does not occur *successively* in a linear time sequence, but as a whole. If it were to follow the infinite dynamic of the logical estimation of magnitude, and produce an unending series of formal schema, it would never touch what is materially final and thus pleasing. Instead, in a key turn of phrase, Kant insists that the aesthetic apprehension beholds "the many in one" (*KU*, 254), an intuition that the voice of reason itself demands:

> The mind, however, hearkens now to the voice of reason, which for all given magnitudes—even for those which can never be completely apprehended, though (in sensuous representation) estimated as completely given—requires totality, and consequently comprehension

in one intuition, and which calls for a presentation answering to all the above members of a progressively increasing numerical series, and does not exempt even the infinite (space and time past) from this require-ment, but rather renders it inevitable for us to regard this infinite (in the judgment of common reason) as completely given (i.e., given in its totality). (*KU*, 254)[75]

What reason demands is a *Vorstellung* of the intuition of "the many in one": a single beholding that would present the infinite as actual and completely given. We can see how this "demand of reason" now satisfies the principle of transcendental reason's demand for maximal systematic unity. In contrast to the problematic status of the ideas of reason and their assorted objects, the *actual perceptive experience of the many in one* provides the binding force the voice of reason demands; a perceptual experience—a seeing in the Platonic sense—of a one that is of course an *Einheit* integrating the many into an actual system. To ground this ability to apprehend the many in one, however, Kant must first supply a new "supersensible faculty" of the mind responsible for this perceptive knowing of *das Ganze*:

> the mere ability even to think the given infinite without contradiction, is something that requires the presence in the human mind of a faculty that is itself supersensible. For it is only through this faculty and its idea of a noumenon, which latter, while not itself admitting of any intuition, is yet introduced as substrate underlying the intuition of the world as mere phenomenon, that the infinite of the world of sense, in the pure intellectual estimation of magnitude, is completely comprehended under a concept, although in the mathematical estimation by means of numerical concepts it can never be completely thought. (*KU*, 254f)

Acknowledging the limitations of his logical-mathematical *Verstand*, Kant must concede the existence of a faculty of higher synthesis that is capable of doing what his regulative ideas of reason could not: provide a structural mechanism for the *production* of systematic unity. Within the logical-mathematical parameters of the first *Critique*, it would be sheer nonsense to posit a subsumptive determination of unconditional unity; hence his ideas of reason and their problematic employment in regu-lating the systematic unity of reason. By the third *Critique* however, after having further developed the central role of freedom—what he could only hint at in 1781 as its *"absolute Selbsttätigkeit"*—Kant real-izes that he will have to make use of the explanatory resources of the dynamic categories if he is to succeed in delivering a (somewhat) constitutive unity to his system through the productive power of aesthetic creation.[76] What Kant calls the "necessity" of the sublime is what feeds and supplies the maximum, the idea of the absolute whole that should unify reason, and which is available only through the violent surplus of the sensual, a surplus that can only be articulated through the dynamic categories (*KU*, 266).[77] The only way Kant can provide this is to allow a new modality of perception, whereby we are capable of perceiving an "absolute whole" via the idea of the sublime:

> the proper unchangeable fundamental measure of nature is its absolute whole, which, with it, regarded as a phenomenon, means infinity comprehended. But, since this fundamental measure is a self-contradictory concept (owing to the impossibility of the absolute totality of an endless progression [i.e., the limits of the mathematical synthesis]), it follows that where the size of a natural object is such that the imagination spends its whole faculty of comprehension upon it in vain, it must carry our concept of nature, to a supersensible substrate (underlying both nature and our faculty of thought) which is, great beyond every standard of sense. Thus, instead of the object, it is rather the cast of the mind in appreciating it that we have to estimate as sublime. (*KU*, 255)

Through his appeal to the idea of the sublime, Kant finally succeeds in incorporating a mechanism whereby the productive imagination—the *Ein-bildung*—is finally allowed to form the contraries into one unity. What the imagination produces is a *symbol* of the supersensible substrate that integrates the same and the other of thinking and nature, which, following the dynamic of disjunction, are each "the complement of the other (*complementum ad totum*)."[78]

Thinking the infinite is to extend the imagination and mind beyond the bounds of the empiricist's domain. The surplus of imaginative force required to achieve this parallels that of the sensory overload received in the aesthetic experience of the sublime. For these reasons, Kant argues that even enthusiasm (*Begeisterung*) is sublime when viewed from an aesthetic standpoint, since

> it is an effort of one's powers called forth by ideas which give to the mind an impetus of far stronger and more enduring efficacy than the stimulus afforded by sensible representations. Aesthetic judgment thereby employs the imagination to generate the idea of the sublime; an idea that in turn refers to the faculty of theoretical reason a self-contradictory idea of a unifying ground of thinking and nature; an

idea that works in accord with the ideas of reason (indeterminately indicated), i.e., to induce a temper of mind conformable—to that which the influence of definite (practical) ideas would produce upon feeling, and in common accord with it. (KU, 256)[79]

Kant however, refuses to take this idea of an identity between subject and object as necessitating the extension of "true sublimity" to adhere as an objective predicate of nature herself (ibid.). All nature provides is the intuition of the sublime, it is reason itself that refines and processes it into the idea of the sublime. Sensual intuition is thus once again used as a "natural resource" that is merely a means to the end of sustaining the virtual world of conceptual experience. Having conceded the essential role sensible intuition provides in supplying the unthinkable (unvordenkliche) "first or fundamental measure" that establishes the absolute parameters of the relative measures of logical thought, Kant nonetheless sees no role for it once it has, like Aristotle's prime mover, initiated the infinite series of conditioned measurements.[80] Although the aesthetic estimate of an unconditioned, infinite whole produces the raw material of the idea that he hopes will supply solidity to his critical edifice, Kant insists that ultimately it is the mathematically sublime that wins out over the aesthetic, concluding that this

> systematic division of the cosmos conduces to this result. For it repre-
> sents all that is great in nature as in turn becoming little; or, to be more
> exact, it represents our imagination in all its boundlessness, and with
> it nature, as sinking into insignificance before the ideas of reason, once
> their adequate presentation is attempted. (KU, 256)

Dependent on the certainty of categorical predication, the mathematical analysis ultimately subordinates the dynamic and contingent synthesis of an aesthetic judgment, thereby solidifying the top-down hierarchy of subsumption that determines Kant's architectonic. The possibility of a reciprocal, common interaction between nature and mind announced by the idea of the sublime is refused in order to maintain the symmetry of his system and his allegiance to the Baconian ideals of modernity. Sensual nature and the imagination thus sink into oblivion as sources of the possible expansion of humanity's rational facilities.

As a transition to Schelling's *Timaeus Commentary*, there remains one last thicket to traverse in Kant's dense growth of ideas: that of the seeming reciprocal causation (*Wechselwirkung*) of the genius, nature, and art. If the symmetry of his system is as absolute and consistent as this last quote would suggest, then we must read Kant's account of the genius as a figurative interpretation of an allegorical figure similar in truth content to his account of Satan in the *Religionsschriftt*.[81] However, this reading would seem hard to square with the tone of his presentation of the genius in the third *Critique*, where he appears to argue that the genius is actually informed by nature—the very nature he elsewhere claims does not have, *an sich*, the actual *Kraft* of the sublime.

Genius: Autoepistemic Organ of Nature?

Kant defines the *genius* as the only type of person capable of both experiencing the internal intuition of the "general ground of the subjective finality of nature" and of also expressing it in a work of art.[82] Similar to the role of the poet in Schelling's construal of Plato's theory of divine inspiration, Kant presents the genius as enjoying a "natural endowment" or "innate mental aptitude . . . through which nature gives the rule to art" (*KU*, 307). In clear harmony with Plato on this point, Kant maintains that the genius, having received this gift *of* nature, can only *by* nature (involuntarily) receive insight into the *intelligible* ground of nature through an internal form of intuition. While still under the sway of nature's control, the genius's creative activity is informed and guided by the rule expressed in the aesthetic idea; in this way, "nature gives the rule to art," inducing the "production of the beautiful" (ibid.)

The gift of producing such beauty is the result of "the nature of the individual" genius. The genius is thus the *conduit* through which the "element of sheer nature . . . forms the point of reference" in art that achieves the *integration* of the singularity of *Sinn* and the universality of *Verstand*. It does this by constellating "the harmonious accord of all our faculties of cognition."[83] Whereas the determinative judgment serves theoretical reason's interest in the logical "perfection of the object" by means of promising the complete predication of the object's concept,[84] aesthetic judgment seeks "the harmonizing of its representation in the imagination with the essential principles of judgment generally in the Subject."[85] The ideal is here no longer the promise of a complete predication in the future, but is instead the experience of an immediate and real harmony. Consequently, in this regard the telos of the aesthetic ideas are "essentially different from rational ideas of determinate ends."[86] The telos of the rational ideas lies in the securing of the "ideality of objects of sense as phenomena," in order to demonstrate the "possibility of [the] a priori determination" of their respective forms. The telos of the aesthetic ideas however, lies in securing the possibility of both the "*a priori* validity for everyone" of judgments of taste, *and* the free play of imagination that generates the subjective feeling of finality characteristic of the experience of beauty.[87]

Only the imagination is capable of pulling off this balancing act of blending the demands of the subjective particular with the objective universal. This is achieved in part by its ability to reconcile the determinacy of a concept with the indeterminacy of intuition, just as it does in producing the schema that mediates, through the auspices of time, the spatial stimulus of the senses with the "pure" concepts of the understanding. However, whereas the production of the schema is an objective and involuntary act of the transcendental ego, the internal intuition of the supersensible, of the intelligible substrate of reality that unites human with nature, is somehow subjective and objective, voluntary and involuntary at once. While the production of the aesthetic ideas is the decisive factor that enables imagination to generate the *subjective* finality associated with the beautiful, this producing itself is determined by "nature" in the guise of the genius. But this nature is ultimately the intelligible substrate, the noumenal domain of the *an sich* of reality that is the source of the *individual's transcendental freedom and character*, the nature of which can never be known directly, but rather only through our actions and—more clearly or enjoyably perhaps—through the experience of beauty.

It is this systematic support that once again suggests Plato as Kant construes the idea of beauty not as the schema of the Good, but as the *symbol* of morality.[88] For if the experience of beauty and the sublime is our only (limited) access to the intelligible substrate of our reality—the fundament of our reality that is both our "holy" transcendental freedom and our noumenal character—then the experience of beauty must also somehow be the opening for the revelation of the Good. Moving away from the awkward use of the *analogon* in the first *Critique*, Kant here distinguishes between schemata and *symbol*: both are intuitions, the former "of which contain direct . . . presentations" of the a priori concepts so perceived, whereas symbols "contain . . . indirect presentations" of the intelligible substrate.[89] The free play of the imagination lost in the enjoyment of a beautiful work of art is thus a symbol for Kant of the autonomy that characterizes the morally good. No longer "subjected to a heteronomy of laws of experience" that characterize the phenomenal world, the faculty of imagination elevates the mind to an autonomous pleasure wherein imagination "gives the law to itself," providing a more noble pleasure than that determined by the authority of the senses.[90]

Even if one does not receive the gift of nature enjoyed by the genius, the nature within the observer of created beauty grants access to the noumenal world of freedom in which one may catch a glimpse of his or her transcendental character. The observer's own free nature, grounded as it is in the unknowable strata of the supersensible, is aroused by the anticipation of experiencing its transcendental character, which is generated by the autonomous freedom indicative of the beauty of art. It is this harmonious accord, generated by what Kant calls the "unconditional finality of fine art," which justifies the beautiful work of art's "claim to being bound to please everyone," since according to Kant this "harmonious accord is the ultimate end set by the intelligible basis of our nature." This claim is at once both aesthetically and ethically binding, thus uniting the ethical and aesthetic, and the judgment of both to the normative claim of universal validity.

There still remains the problem of how strictly to interpret Kant's analysis of genius. We have suggested a rather speculative reading that conforms more to the presentation of genius Schelling adopts; a portrayal that calls on Kant's position that the genius enjoys the natural ability to access and then express the supersensible and intelligible basis of our nature. This is a cycle of production that, if taken literally, assumes a circular form of creative feedback between human and nature. If it is nature that speaks through the genius in order to express the identity of nature and human through the supersensible ground—and if the telos of art is to serve the ultimate goal of man's moral destiny, that is, to perfect his nature as an animal species by subsuming it under his moral nature—then through the genius nature effects *its own* transformation. Kant provides for such a *gemeinschaftliche* interaction (for the genius must have some degree of freedom and autonomy in his production, otherwise the beauty so generated would be a symbol of pure heteronomy) through the more robust faculty of intuition he describes in this context. Indeed, with this new extension of this faculty's powers, Kant offers up an internal intuition capable of granting indeterminate insight into the nondiscursive *intellectus archetypus*, which he identifies with the "supersensible substrate of all the subject's faculties . . . underlying both nature and our faculty of thought."[91]

Thus whereas in the first *Critique* the *intellectus archetypus* is the conceptual schema for the transcendental idea of God, in the third *Critique* it appears that the nature of the genius provides the Empedoclean condition of knowing whereby nature becomes accessible through internal intuition. This indeterminate insight is mediated by the symbolic aesthetic ideas: concepts that because they are modeled after the *dynamic categories* are capable of reconciling and establishing a "harmonic mean" between the eternal (and thus nondiscursive) realm of the noumenal and the linear world of phenomenal reality. Unlike the ideas of reason—whose form submits to a mathematical synthesis—the dynamic synthesis that informs the aesthetic ideas makes them the only vehicle whereby Kant can articulate the *intuition of the absolute whole* of a maximal smallest magnitude, or conversely, the maximal largest magnitude of the unconditioned. Through this capacity for perceiving the absolute whole the soul enjoys the pleasure of finality (τελείων *qua* ὅλον) that is the symbol, not only of morality, but of the systematic unity of Kant's critical system. Ultimately, the idea of the beautiful articulates the absolute whole of an *Einheit* that encompasses the absolute *self-action* of freedom.

As we will see in the remaining chapters, Schelling employs these elements of Kant's critical program to justify his inversion of Kant's edifice, thereby freeing the dynamic categories of experience, organic life, and freedom to provide the cohesion and integration required by any truly systematic philosophy. As we have seen, Kant's architectonic is baseless if it cannot integrate what its own ordering demands, namely, its unification in an *absolute magnitude* provided by the dynamic categories of *community* and *reciprocal causality*. For it is only the dynamic categories of experience that have the power and flexibility to parse the purposiveness of organic life, and provide the "*absolute self-action*" Kant himself advances as the absolute causality of freedom we encounter when nature is seen as a dynamical whole. In Schelling's reading, it is this absolute causality of freedom that is the principle upon which a transformed critical edifice can be erected, which, however, will be informed by an organic form of philosophy. The system which emerges will develop from the form of a disjunctive (and thus oppositional) logic of community and reciprocity, thereby engendering a genetic dialectic in which form and content, concept and intuition, the intelligible and the sensual, simultaneously impact and condition one another in a dynamic and purposive process of *generation*. This and only this, according to Schelling, will be a truly organic philosophy, grounded in the absolute of a freedom that is capable of both harmonizing the dualities of human existence and of accounting for the unconditional unity philosophy demands of system. To fully flesh out the resources Schelling draws on to construct his organic form of philosophy, we must now turn to his reading of Plato.

Schelling sees in Kant's division of causality into two different realms, one visible and natural, the other nonobservable and thus otherworldly, a problem of philosophy he first encountered in the writings of Plato. Most importantly perhaps, it is in Plato that Schelling finds a way of integrating these two realms of causation by discovering a form of unity that delivers what Kant could not, namely—in Plato's words now—"how all the knowledges are one."

4

The *Timaeus Commentary*

Wherefore one ought to distinguish two different kinds of causes, the necessary and the divine, and in all things seek after the divine for the sake of gaining a life of blessedness, so far as our nature admits thereof. (*Tim.*, 68e5–69a1)

To Seek the Divine in Nature

The subject matter we now turn to is contained within two notebooks Schelling compiled during his first two years as a student at the Tübingen *Stift*. The first carries the title of *Vorstellungsarten of the Ancient World* while the second is called *The Spirit of Platonic Philosophy*. These note-books document the attempt to apply his historical method to a select cross-section of ancient texts—mostly Platonic and early Christian—that depict how *knowing,* in the widest possible sense of the word, was presented in the ancient world. Just how wide Schelling construes the field of his investigation is shown by the subtitle of notebook §28, which reads: *Of Poets, Prophets, Poetic Inspiration, Enthusiasm, Theopneusty, and Divine Influence on Men in General.* Though these terms would suggest to us a theological or religious inquiry into the varieties of religious experience, in the historical context of the Platonic dialogues they acquire a more relevant meaning: since for Plato the true is divine, within the context of his dialogues there is no possibility for there to be a true knowledge that is not divine in origin.[1]

The perspective from which to understand Schelling's reading of Plato is provided by a quote from the *Timaeus* that he used in August 1792 to dedicate his notebook on *The Spirit of Platonic Philosophy*:

Wherefore one ought to distinguish two different kinds of causes, the necessary and the divine, and in all things seek after the divine for the sake of gaining a life of blessedness, so far as our nature admits thereof.[2]

As mentioned earlier, the importance of this passage is not simply that of a student's momentary fixation on a pregnant turn of phrase. His use of it as a point of reference to his own work a decade later in the subtitle of the *Bruno* dialogues testifies to the significance he attached to it. Evocative of his eulogy to Hahn, this passage is perhaps the earliest sign of Schelling's intent to develop a system of philosophy capable of articulating how the binding unity of the divine reveals itself in this world of nature. It also points to Schelling's attempt to supply Kant's program with systematic unity. As we have seen, Kant attempted to do this through an appeal to the unconditioned realm of the supersensible that was couched in the explicit terms of Plato's ideas. Through the ideas Kant attempted to demonstrate how the categories of the understanding are to be united and "employed in dealing with experience in its totality" (A 321/B 378). Somehow, the ideas were to form the cohesive infrastructure that binds and integrates the conditioned activity of the categories into the unconditional demand of reason for systematic unity.

Well versed in Plato's writings, Schelling clearly senses the Platonic spirit at work in Kant's program. Throughout these writings on Plato, he plays Kant against Plato and Plato against Kant to generate his own strategy for integrating the natural and the divine, or, to use Kantian terms, to integrate the conditioned world of phenomena with the unconditioned kingdom of the noumenal. Schelling's analysis of Plato's distinction between divine causes and those of nature bears the imprint of Kant's distinction between the concepts of the understanding and the ideas of pure reason. The class of natural causes, like the categories, is applicable directly to experience and can therefore be known directly. In contrast, Plato's divine causes, like the ideas of reason, are not applied directly to experience, and are thus incapable of being empirically known. Whereas the causes and ideas of the empirical realm have no concern with the unity of their respective systems, both Kant and Plato must account for how the class of primary causes or ideas are organized and united as one unified system.

Before plunging into Schelling's commentary, we need to clarify the textual context of his citation. The context in which this passage appears is a concluding paragraph of the second of the *Timaeus*'s two logos. After a first cosmogony from the perspective of the divine and creative intelligence (νοῦς), Plato indulges himself in a discussion about necessity (ἀνάγκης) by considering "probable accounts of Becoming"

(59d).[3] Upon finishing this probabilistic account, he concludes with typical modesty:

> But should any inquirer make an experimental test of these facts, he would evince his ignorance of the difference between man's nature and God's—how that, whereas God is sufficiently wise and powerful to blend the many into one and to dissolve again the one into many, there exists not now, nor ever will exist hereafter, a child of man sufficient for either of these tasks. (*Tim.*, 68d2)

The human impossibility that Plato refers to is that of articulating the transition from the divine one to the many of the world of becoming. The characteristic that separates these two classes is the capacity to be the cause of one's own action. The divine is what Plato calls the singular form of the most good and beautiful, which he further defines as the first cause and "principle of life."[4] This highest class of cause (αἴτιον τῶν πάντων) enjoys the capacity to move and determine itself. Subsumed under this one form of forms are the subsidiary causes of reason, soul, beauty, greatness etc., which Plato refers to in themselves (καθ αὐτὸ) to signify their absolute or unconditioned nature.[5] As the unconditioned cause of action and form of the empirical world however, this class of realities is not capable of being detected through empirical intuition. This is in contrast to the "secondary" class of *necessary* causes that constitute the conditioned, empirical realm of observable phenomena. These are the "auxiliary causes" (ζυναιτίων) that form the "class of things which are moved by others, and themselves, in turn, move others because they cannot help it" (46d). The four elements of fire, water, air and earth are the primary representatives of this class. The question of the one and the many is thus a question of how to account for the relationship of the divine and the necessary classes of causes in Schelling's citation, which in its full context reads:

> the demiurges of the most fair and good took them over at that time amongst things generated when He was engendering the self-sufficing and most perfect God; and their inherent properties he used as subservient causes, but Himself designed the Good in all that was being generated. Wherefore one ought to distinguish two different kinds of causes, the necessary and the divine, and in all things seek after the divine for the sake of gaining a life of blessedness, so far as our nature admits thereof, and to seek the necessary for the sake of the divine, *reckoning that without the former it is impossible to discern by themselves*

*alone the divine objects after which we strive, or to apprehend them or
in any way partake thereof.* (68e–69a4; my emphasis)

Taken in its context Schelling's citation presents several important
themes. First, the question of the one and the many is primarily an ethical
matter, namely to account for how creation could share in the goodness
that Plato considered to be both the first and final cause of the cosmos.
Second, as self-determining, this divine class of cause offers Schelling
an historical anticipation of Kant's causality of freedom: the Good is not
only the condition of ethical action, but is also the cause of the "absolute self-action (*absolute Selbsttätigkeit*)," which is the capacity for the
unconditioned act of self-movement.[6] Third, the passage demonstrates
the extent to which he has accepted Hahn's mantle and his approach to
nature as the self-revelation of the divine: since the only avenue open to
reach the divine leads through the changing world of the secondary causes
of necessity, the study of the workings of observable nature becomes the
only avenue of knowing the divine.[7] Lastly, as the unconditioned cause
of the phenomenal world, these intellectual "objects" are impossible to
know directly; rather, just as Kant's ideas, they can only be approached
indirectly through their effects. While all these themes will be addressed
in what follows, it is to this last point we now turn.

The distinction Schelling draws between causes divine and necessary
must be set into orbit round the defining axis of his thought, the question of freedom. Plato's distinction between divine and necessary causes
relies primarily on the criterion of self-movement: that cause which is
unconditioned is divine whereas the conditioned causes of mechanical
interaction are necessary. The contrast here is between action that
is free of conditioning cause and action that is not. In other words,
Schelling's dedication should be read as not only referring to the world
of sensual nature as the productive manifestation of the divine, but it
must also be construed as referring to the divine causes that permeate
this world, yet are unconditioned and thus *free* of the restricting neces-
sities of empirical causes. On this reading the free and divine cause is
the productive agent par excellence insofar as it powers the creation
of the world in general, and the world of humanity's creativity in
particular, in accordance with the ideas of beauty (τό καλόν) and the
good (τὸ αγαθὸν).[8]

The focus of Schelling's inquiry into the epistemology of the divine is
Plato's analysis of techne and a divine power (θεια δυναμις) as possible
agents of creative activity. By techne Schelling means "producing
something through a . . . series of causes and effects,"[9] whereas divine
agency covers all phenomena excluded from this definition of techne:

In general Plato considers everything in the human soul as divine activity, or rather presents it as such, that emerges in our ideas lacking any empirical cause and lacking any empirical development (like virtue), or at least lacking easy to notice empirical causes, and lacking easy to notice empirical development (as for example, Enthusiasm)—in short everything in which the empirical data is either completely missing or is difficult to find.[10]

The point of reference Schelling adopts to articulate Plato's account of creativity is the more contemporary idea of the genius. In this respect he is once again reading Kant against Plato. Accepting this, we can read Schelling as investigating what we now call the *logic of discovery*. Consequently, included within this thematic of creation is not simply beauty, but *new knowledge* as well: the field of human activity Plato construes as being subject to a "divine explanation" includes not only the creative arts, but also the "art" of knowing. And it is in this context that Schelling presents Plato's analysis of how the philosopher comes to know the object of his desire, namely the ultimate cause of the systematic unity of our reality, the ἑν καὶ πᾶν.

Schelling's treatment of Plato on this subject is significant for what it tells us about the former's understanding of how a philosopher could be said to be a prophet, and divine truth could be said to be revealed. Indeed, prophecy and revelation are the two defining terms used by Schelling to articulate Plato's conception of divine knowing.[11] They articulate the same distinctions made in the case of the poet regarding the difference between activities dictated by a techne and those that are not. In the pages of his *Studienheft* immediately following his commentary on the sublime Platonic *Begeisterung*, Schelling introduces the prophet:

> The universal concept of prophets in general is for Plato this one: one who speaks for the gods, *interpres decorum*. This illuminates for example, the passage in the *Philebus* where Protarchus says: 'and I ask you, Socrates, to be our prophet yourself' (28d); as one sees from the context "interpreter of the Gods," since previously Socrates had spoken from 'his God' (from the Daemon dwelling within him). ('You exalt your own God'). (28b)[12]

What Schelling alludes to in this jumble of notes is the manner in which Plato portrays Socrates in his quest to speak not about the truth of opinion, but about the truth of episteme. And since this truth is of divine origin, it is incapable of being known *via* the techne of inferential knowing of conditioned causes at home in the world of empirical intuition. Thus, when Plato portrays Socrates in search of knowing the Ideas, we find him invoking the gods for assistance:

> Soc. Well, what shall we say is the nature of the third made by combining the two?
> Pro. You will tell me, I fancy, by answering your own question.
> Soc. Nay, a god will do so, if any god will give ear to my prayer.
> Pro. Pray, then, and watch.
> Soc. I am watching; and I think, Protarchus, one of the gods has this moment been gracious unto me. (25b)

The god Socrates refers to is of course his own Daemon that Schelling construes as the agent of his prophecy (28b). What is of the utmost importance, however, is the way Schelling interprets the particular term Plato uses here to describe the "graciousness" of Socrates' Daemon. The term Plato employs to describe this state of grace is φίλος, meaning beloved, dear or pleasing, declined in its nominative form. In this context, Plato is clearly describing how the material of prophecy is provided only as a gift to those who are pleasing to the divine. Significant is that this term is used in precisely the same form and context in a passage in the *Timaeus* which Schelling refers to *three times* in this notebook as providing the key to understanding the source of prophecy as both a revelation and as a gift.

Following his intent to flesh out the relationship between the classes of divine and necessary causes, Schelling's commentary focuses on the one question that Plato never answers: how the elements and the ideas interact with each other. As we noted earlier, Plato distinguishes between primary and secondary causes. The primary divine cause is "self-identical form, ungenerated and indestructible, neither receiving into itself any other from any quarter nor itself passing any whither into another, invisible and in all ways imperceptible by sense, it being the object which it is the province of *noesis* to contemplate" (51e8f). The secondary causes are the four elements that imitate the primary cause, but are "objects perceptible by sense, generated, ever carried about, becoming in a place and out of it again perishing, apprehensible opinion with the aid of sensation" (52f). Each class of cause forms an object of the mind that has its own way of being known, with the secondary causes of necessity being accessible to all humans, whereas the primary cause is participated in by "only the gods and but a small class of men" (51e4). This small class of men to whom the gods grant the gift of participating in the self-identical *eidos* are those whom the gods find dear or pleasing. This much we have seen already. But on the same page of his notebook cited above, a page that deals with the general concept of prophecy in Plato, we find the following citation preceded by a loose translation that says more about Schelling's intentions than Plato's. The subject of the passage is how we know the primary causes, and it is normally translated as follows:

> the principles which are still higher than these [the secondary causes] are known only to God and the man who is dear (φίλος) to God. (53d7)

Schelling accurately transcribes this passage in Greek, and then makes the very liberal translation:

> The relationship of the visible elements with the ideas, says Plato, only God knows, and those to whom God wants to reveal it.[13]

The introduction of revelation to describe the original dispensation of divine episteme may or may not reflect a systematic intent on Schelling's part. Nonetheless, it suggests at the very least that in this context Schelling makes use of an understanding of revelation that differs markedly from the received understanding of Lessing, Kant or any of his enlightened followers. While it would appear that Schelling might agree with Lessing's characterization of revelation as a form of "education . . . coming to the individual man," he would disagree that its content and goal is the development of "mere truths of reason."[14] Kant on the other hand, presents revelation in a light completely at odds with Schelling's. According to the former, revealed religion is a form of epistemological short-cut: it merely presents humanity with a truth "that men *could and ought to have discovered* . . . of themselves merely through the use of their reason."[15] This would follow, however, given Kant's adherence to the mathematical synthesis of the *Weltbegriff*: pure reason is confined within the infinite series of conditioned and thus relative thinking (discursive), incapable of access to a first member qualitatively different from the series—except, as we have seen, through the aesthetic idea of the sublime.

Contrary to Kant's naturalistic reading, Schelling presents the truth of the divine *noesis* as being inaccessible to the techne of empirical research, confined as it is to the infinite series of appearances. Like the inspiration of the poet and genius, the source of the divine cause is beyond the sensible sphere of conditioned causation. Suggestive of the "capstone" of Aristotle's epistemology, the *"nous poetikos,"* Schelling here describes an epistemological trajectory in which the knowing comes to—not from—the knowing subject.[16] From this perspective, Kant's claim that revelation presents immanent truths of reason which humans can discover on their own would have to be qualified. Schelling's reading would support the knowledge of the empirical world governed by secondary causes and elements, but it would deny that human reason has the capacity to know the primary causes of the intelligible world *in the same manner.* The ideas of this intelligible class of *arche* can instead only be known in a manner analogous to the way in which the poet creates his poem: through a modality of cognition that does not use predicates or images taken from the empirical world, but instead utilizes the divine element within the knower to "apprehend by thought itself the nature" of the divine cause "in itself."[17] This a modality of knowing clearly different from Kant's description of the aesthetic idea of the sublime, but perhaps similar to the unspecified modality of cognition of the dynamic synthesis capable of accessing an absolute first member of the causal chain, which, in a functional sense, does precisely what Plato's divine causes do.

In the pages of his notebook that fill out his commentary on the *Timaeus* Schelling refers to the above passage twice. In both references he drops any mention of revelation and instead places emphasis on the class of men to whom the Gods grants this knowledge, calling them the "favorites of the Gods."[18] Removed from the context of a discussion of prophecy and divine inspiration, Schelling addresses in these notes a well trodden thematic whose parameters have been largely set by established scholarship.[19] Here Schelling is quite thorough about analyzing these two different causes and the modalities of knowing each entails given their respective objects. And it is in this discussion that we encounter what is the clearest presentation of a Platonic construal of pure intellectual cognition. He begins by asking "whether or not there are intelligible forms of the elements":

> Plato answers the question in the following manner. He answers it purely through the *fact (Datum)*, that there is in the human faculty of knowing, [. . .] two types of knowing (*Erkenntnis*)—experience and pure, independent of experience, knowing—[which] are so different, that one can explain it in no other way than through the assumption of thoroughly different objects of these [types of] knowing. *Experience* is for him δοχα, and because there is again a difference between

different perceptions, of which some (as mere appearance of intuition) provide no contribution to experience, in its more precise meaning, [this experience is] δοχα αληθης; pure knowing, what he otherwise also calls episteme, he here calls νους. The former brings nothing other than persuasion (πειθω), the later conviction (theory, διδαχη); the former devoid of firm reasons, the latter through such firm reasons. The former changes, the latter is unchanging; the former is participated in by every human, the latter only by the Gods and the few humans who, as Plato otherwise says, are *favorites of the Gods*. There must then be *objects* that always remain the same, that do not come to be (empirically) and can be just as little ever destroyed, objects, that accept nothing else than themselves, and go over into nothing else . . . . objects that are completely invisible and certainly cannot be objects of sensual intuition—[these] are pure objects of the intellectual faculty of knowing.*[20]

In this loose translation of 51d–52, Schelling presents us with his construal of an "intellectual faculty of knowing" whose object—the *eidos*—can only be grasped through an act of *noetic* seeing. The asterisk above refers to a note in which Schelling sarcastically critiques—once again—those "very learned" scholars who still nonetheless maintain that Plato held these intellectual objects, these ideas, to be substantial and to actually exist. This occurs, he reasons, because these scholars "cannot distinguish the *representation* of the idea from the idea itself (the form of our faculty of representation from the object of that representation)" (*TK*, 72). The ideas, the objects of noetic seeing, are thus similar to Kant's forms and Reinhold's *Vorstellungsvermögen*. To leave no room for doubt, immediately following this loose translation of the passage Schelling transcribes it in its entirety in Greek, closing with the last sentence in which Plato's term for Schelling's "intellectual faculty of knowing" is ἡ νόησις. He concludes, "Plato could certainly not explain himself more clearly than he has in this passage" (*TK*, 72).

This modality of noetic cognition, of νόησις, no doubt holds the key to understanding how there can be a knowledge of the ἐν and unity of the ordered systems of philosophy. This is a modality of knowing that Plato and Kant must somehow avail themselves of if they are to supply unity to their respective systems. As the first systematic proponent of such cognition, Plato not only acknowledges, but sets his entire system into orbit around this *noetic seeing of the unity*. Kant, as we know, is another story. The one point we must raise here before moving on to Schelling's commentary on the *Timaeus*, is how strikingly similar

Kant's account of the "pure a priori use" of his transcendental ideas and their unchanging, eternal status sounds to Plato's account of the divine ideas.[21] The conveyers of truth for Plato, the εἶδος, are like the Kantian Ideas of reason, in that both are the condition of possibility of true episteme. Like the axiom of a demonstration these conditions of knowing—the ideas, whether Platonic or Kantian—cannot be known directly. While Plato ultimately appeals to the poet and divine inspiration to account for such direct knowledge, Kant, in his last critical effort, must finally resort to genius and the revelatory dimension of the sublime to awaken our awareness of "a ground of the unity of the supersensible that lies at the basis of nature" (KU,176).

Schelling's Commentary on the *Timaeus*

The importance of Schelling's *Timaeus Commentary* is hard to understate. Written in the early winter of 1794, just four to six months before his essay, "On the Possibility of a Form of All Philosophy," this text demonstrates the formative impact Plato had on Schelling's understanding of the necessary role the "ideas of reason" play in generating systematic unity.[22] His interest is indicated by the passages of Plato's texts he addresses; a point that contrasts with what the title given to this commentary indicates. Although he is driven by an interest in understanding Plato's cosmogony, over one third of the references he makes are taken from the *Philebus*, a dialogue whose subject is the ideal relationship of pleasure and wisdom. The connecting thread, however, is clear, namely an investigation parallel to Kant's analysis of the logical principles required to think systematic unity: In the *Philebus* Plato discusses how to articulate the unity of the plurality of episteme through a triad of logical principles which, in the *Timaeus*, he employs to generate his cosmogony in both its ontological and epistemological aspects.

Schelling embraces Plato's characterization of the generative triad of τὸ πέρας (the finite), τὸ ἄπειρον (the infinite), and τὸ κοινὸν (what is common), as the eternal form of all reason (τῶν λόγων αὐτῶν ἀθάνατόν τι); he derives from its formal aspect Kant's mathematical categories and applies its relational form as the generative 'Kräfte der Natur' that permeate and animate all creation.[23] Following the organic cosmology of his youth, he construes Plato's *World Soul* as the archetype of Kant's infamous section on organism from the third *Critique* (§65), seeing in both an organic relation of part to whole whose principle of self-organizing causality (*gemeinschaftliche Wechselwirkung*) articulates life's systematic integration of oppositional forces, as demonstrated by an organism's capacity to be both cause and effect of itself.[24] Plato's World Soul, considered as the system of the world, becomes the paradigm of an organic system of thinking Schelling uses to account for the *immanent preestablished harmony* of Plato's cosmos—a reading he justifies through an appeal to Plato's triad of primary causes and their pervasive determination of the form of every "organ" of the being that is creation. As our signature DNA is written in a code believed to permeate our current cosmos, so too do the elements of Plato's cosmos bear the imprint of the triad of divine causes. Since every entity is the result of the interaction of the limited and the unlimited, every entity presents a relative mean (identity) of the complementary aspects of form (thinking) and matter (being).

The ideational progeny of Schelling's affair with Plato populate the work of his entire career. The form he discovers in Plato becomes the lens through which he reinterprets Kant's Transcendental Ideal as not merely a regulative ideal, but as an "ideal of this world," as a genetic and organizing principle of life, and thus of creation (*TK*, 35). With this, he raises Kant's dynamic categories of relation above those of mathematical magnitude, and thereby establishes a new processional ontology that, just as one must with the idea of organism, begins with the absolute magnitude of the whole *qua* unconditioned Absolute. All of his work on the dynamic potencies of creation, which permeate our being and thinking, from most simple to the most complex organization, is presented via this form of episteme. Whether it be the generative *Urform* of all philosophy in 1794, the articulation of *Geist* as "das Band" that unites body and mind in his first *Naturphilosophie* of 1798,[25] the principle of Identity in 1801, the "Threefold Band" of the *natura naturans* of 1806,[26] or the unfolding of God's potencies in 1842[27]: all accounts follow this one organic form of systematic unity that Plato uses to express the "reciprocal relationship between the one and the many."[28]

We begin this chapter where we left off in the last. In an interesting parallel to Kant's aesthetic ideas, Schelling focuses his initial analysis of Plato on the role *beauty* (τὸ καλόν) plays as the "Ideal" that determines the *completeness* of his systematic account of creation.

The Divine Ideas of Reason

The principle according to which one must evaluate the kind of presentation in the *Timaeus* Plato provides at [28c3]: "Now to discover the Maker and the Father of this Universe were a task indeed; and having discovered Him, to declare Him unto all men were a thing impossible."[29]

With this introduction, Schelling begins his commentary on the *Timaeus*. Faithfully adhering to the words of his dedication that focus his inquiry into Plato's philosophy, Schelling addresses his distinction between the primary and secondary classes of causes in order to immediately designate two classes of correlative "ideas." He cites Plato's words in Greek, which in a standard translation read:

> Now first of all we must, in my judgment, make the following distinction. What is that which is Existent always and has no Becoming? And what is that which is Becoming always and never is Existent? Now the one of these is apprehensible by thought with the aid of reasoning, since it is ever uniformly existent; whereas the other is an object of opinion with the aid of unreasoning sensation, since it becomes and perishes and is never really existent. (27d3)[30]

Schelling's chosen point of entry places him in precisely the same epistemological dualism common to both Plato and Kant: the division of reality into the static realm of the "pure concepts of the understanding" and the constantly changing sphere of sensation. In the first few sentences of this commentary, Schelling provides an explicit indication of the extent to which the Kantian framework informs his reading of Plato:

> Here Plato explains the ov itself for something that is the object of the pure understanding, which is pure and completely knowable and not even the object of an uncertain and incomplete opinion. These are all characteristics that fit the ideas of the *pure* understanding and of *pure* reason. (*TK*, 23)[31]

Schelling's intent is obvious: to find a "fit" between Plato and Kant. Thus before he even begins to discuss *Plato's ideas*, Schelling examines how easily Kant's version fits into and conforms with the framework of Plato's system; a hermeneutic which suggests a definite *Vorverständnis* that posits significant similarity between these two masters. As if moving through a list of common system elements suggested in Plato's words, Schelling proceeds to compare each to a possible Kantian equivalent, until he finally moves to describe Plato's ideas as "pure concepts" that do not belong among the objects of intuition, considered "purely as such" (ibid.). Since they are engaged in the process of becoming, and thus not yet complete, the objects of sensible intuition can at best justify only a δοχα or πιστισ, whereas the ideas can support an episteme.[32]

Contrary to Aristotle's misunderstanding of Plato's idealism,

Schelling's reading of the *Timaeus* demonstrates that for Plato every-thing, including preexisting matter, is infused with form.[33] The challenge for Plato in this dialogue is not to oppose form to matter, but rather to account for the relationship between something that is outside our discursive parameters of space and time to things that are within the space-time continuum of becoming and knowing. Or, as the words of Schelling's dedication to his *Timaeus Commentary* indicate, the chal-lenge is to account for the relation between the divine cause that stands outside the observable domain of space and time and the observable causal series of conditioned nature.

The perplexing and decisive question is therefore how to explain the *relation* of what is outside space and time with the world of becoming. This question is perplexing because the seeming fluidity of this rela-tion refuses to be subsumed under the static mathematical categories of magnitude and determinate predication. As we have seen, the synthesis these categories effect requires homogeneity both among the members of its unending series, *and the series considered as a totality*—a formal requirement that renders this synthesis incapable of integrating the "first magnitude" of a totality qualitatively different from the very series Kant argues is required to establish the limits of a continuum. But this is precisely Plato's characterization of the relation between the primary and secondary classes of causes: Whereas the latter do in fact constitute an unending chain of conditioned causation, the former divine causes are qualitatively different—unconditioned—and thus cannot be addressed via the regressive method of the mathematical categories.

Schelling's analysis of Plato's ideas as guarantors of systematic unity—of there being an efficacious ἓν καὶ πᾶν—presupposes this logical analysis. But before Schelling can examine Plato's presentation of the divine ideas, he must first account for Plato's principle of *unity* which demands that the created cosmos be a complete synthesis of pure being and becoming. He locates this principle of unity in the determi-native role *beauty* plays in Plato's argument for why there is this world of a sensuous *and* intelligible nature, rather than nothing at all.

τὸ καλόν as the Ideal of Unity and Completeness

With the divide of reality into the space-time world of the senses and the non–space-time zone of absolute completeness, Plato creates for himself the explanatory lacuna needed to account for the process of creation and becoming.[34] What is striking in his reading of Plato's account of the initial stages of the Demiurge's creative activities are the words Schelling uses to describe them. As we saw above in his extraction of the German term *Offenbarung* from a Greek text in which no such equivalent term appears, Schelling occasionally allows himself great latitude in his translations. When he mistranslates consistently, he tells us of course more about his own intentions than Plato's. The two terms he interjects at this point are *ideal* and *completeness*, using the former to explicate Plato's 'paradigm', and the latter to clarify Plato's frequent use of beauty (το καλόν) and its cognates.

The first object of his inquiry is Plato's unequivocal presentation of eternal being (τί τὸ ὂν ἀεί) that is not subject to the necessary causes of the observable world. As always identical with itself (κατὰ ταὐτὰ ἔχον; 29a7), this being must be the converse of *what becomes*, from which follows for Schelling that this being is best described as something fully complete. The distinction he develops here posits a continuum of completeness in which the objects of reason are those that can be "completely" known, whereas the objects of sensation, being "incomplete," are incapable of being known in this sense at all.[35] Schelling places great importance on this point: he uses the root term *complete* (*vollkommen*) seven times in the first thirty lines of the commentary.[36] One negative factor that could drive his choice of terms is his conviction that another possible predicate—existence—is a term entirely unsuited for application to being (τὸ ὄν).[37] From a positive standpoint however, it is clear that Schelling equates *completion* with Plato's use of the substantive τὸ καλόν: "Plato attributes *completion* (τό καλόν) only to that which . . . [is] . . . independent of all experience, of all sensuality" (*TK*, 24). This association of completeness with beauty is lent a suggestive Kantian appearance when the Demiurge's παράδειγμα—which Plato describes as of necessity beautiful—is called an *ideal* by Schelling. From this it follows that if eternal being, *jenseits* of all empirical nature, is the ideal of the Demiurge, then "the work that he makes after this [ideal] must become *complete*, since all completeness is agreement with the ideal" (ibid.). Semantically, while there are similarities between a paradigm and an ideal, there are also significant differences.[38] A paradigm can indeed serve as an exemplar, but we seldom posit an exemplar that is unattainably complete, whereas it appears that this is precisely the Kantian meaning Schelling affixes to 'ideal.' More importantly, however, is the substantive principle Schelling has established in this identification of the fully complete status of the ideal of the created cosmos, namely, that whatever may become of the copy, *completeness* will become the ideal that determines both its creation and its development. As we will soon see, this reading of completeness as a constitutive principle will have a surprising and yet decisive effect on his account of creation.

Having now introduced the terms of completeness and ideal to describe being (τὸ ὄν), Schelling makes the next logical step and extends their meaning to beauty (τὸ καλόν) and the good (τὸ ἀγαθόν). In the passage Schelling deals with here (roughly *Tim.*, 27d5–31), Plato uses the adjective *beautiful* (καλόν) three times, its superlative form *most beautiful* (καλλιστόν) five times, while the adjective *good* (ἀγαθὸν) is only used three times, to account for God's motivation to create:

> He was good, and in him that is good no envy ariseth ever concerning anything; and being devoid of envy He desired that all should be, so far as possible, like unto himself. (*Tim.*, 29e)[39]

In contrast to the ambiguous ethical character of the Abrahmic God, Plato posits a singular deity who desires that creation be as "like unto himself" as possible. Schelling reads this divine desire as positing an ideal for creation that demands that it be as complete as the god is (in the sense of τὸ ὄν). This reading is supported by the fact that Plato's preferred term in these passages to describe being (τὸ ὄν) is τὸ καλόν, rather than τὸ ἀγαθόν. Indeed, etymologically τὸ ἀγαθόν was used by Homer to indicate whether a person was *well born* or whether a thing was *servicable*.[40] Τὸ καλόν, on the other hand, has always been primarily a term affirming the beauty of a person's *outward form*, judged according to its fairness and balance.[41] The meaning of τὸ καλόν is not only more extensive than that of τὸ ἀγαθόν, but it is also a more accurate term to describe the *outward form* and *complete balance* of τὸ ὄν. Substituting Schelling's term complete for the plethora of cognates of τὸ καλόν which Plato uses to describe this initial act of creation transforms the reading of this passage significantly: instead of encountering "most beautiful" and "most fair" as predicates of being, we read of the *most complete*. More significant, however, is how this reading of these passages drastically changes the way Schelling presents the actual act of creation. Schelling reads Plato's use of τὸ καλόν as an ideal that demands *completeness* in creation, thereby requiring the uniting and integration of the seemingly dualistic domains of the *intellectual and the sensual*. He writes:

> Καλον expresses not only beauty, but in general completeness, complete orderliness. One sees this clearly in the following, since he posits the καλον as one and alone participating in the form of the understanding. He says of the demiurge, 'As he considered, therefore, He perceived that of such creatures as are by nature visible, none that is irrational will

be more beautiful, comparing wholes with wholes, than the rational [30b]'

The sense is namely this: the demiurge thinks that there could be no visible world (εχ των κατα φυσιν οπατως ολος), incapable of participating in the forms of the understanding, that would be a more beautiful work than a [visible world] united with this one (νουν εχος ολος). (TK, 28)[42]

This is the conclusion of Schelling's attempt to unearth the integrating principle of Plato's cosmogony: beauty, understood as completeness, requires that both the sensible and intellectual be united to form one whole, integrated entirety. Faced with the divide between the incompleteness of the preexisting matter and the ideal of completeness presented by being, Plato's demiurge must follow the ideal of that eternal being and create a world that will be as complete as its paradigm; to be complete creation must become a integrated whole that fully unifies both the intellectual and the sensual. If—operating for example, under the traditional understanding of an ideal of perfection—one were to exclude the sensible from the intellectual or vice versa, the world would not be as beautiful—considered as a whole, as a unity—as when these two domains are united in one complete cosmos. The only idea capable of integrating such disparity under its scope of meaning is the complete wholeness of the ideal of beauty (τὸ καλόν).

This emphasis on Plato's ideal of integrating both the physical and the metaphysical into one world occurs repeatedly. Schelling refutes Plessing's reading of the interaction between the unlimited matter and limited form, because it assumes that the common element that emerges from their interaction has somehow *been purified of its chaotic lack of limit*. Schelling objects, citing reasons already discussed, and then makes the additional point that "all reality is something unlimited (ἄπειρό τι)" just as much as it is "something limited (πέρασ τι) (TK, 62).[43] To be complete, creation must consist of both rational form as well as irrational matter. To form a complete unity, the Same and the Other must be bound into a perfect harmony, not silence. That which is common (τὸ κοινόν) emerges from the interaction of these two forms, yet does not negate or nullify them; rather it integrates them into a unity that must continue to be both limited form and unlimited matter.

In taking this position, Schelling accepts that the order of our world is not exclusively determined by the form of the finite limit. It is instead a world informed by the productive interaction of the two opposing forces of the finite and the infinite; chance and the irrational are just as an essential component of creation as is the necessity of the rational. Schelling makes this clear in defense of Plato's cosmology. If we accept Schelling's reading of Plato as positing the ideal of a complete world as his "ideal of the world," significant interpretative consequences follow, such as the overturning of the majority of the simplistic dualisms associated with Plato's thinking (*TK*, 35). Instead of the founder of the two-world theory so easily absorbed by Augustine and the early Christian Church, we find an anomalous rendering of creation determined by the ideal of completeness and unity.

Plato however, has only introduced the two elements of the unintelligent (ἀνόητον) and the intelligence (νοῦς). To create a unity he needs a third element to bind these two into one. He finds this third in the relational form of soul.

The World Soul as "The Ideal of the World": Organic Life as Principle of Systematic Unity

> But it is not possible that two things alone should be conjoined without a third; for there must needs be some intermediary bond (δεσμὸς) to connect the two. And the fairest of bonds (δεσμῶν) is that which most perfectly unites into one both itself and the things which it binds together; and to effect this in the fairest way. (*Tim.*, 31c)[44]

Schelling argues that Plato held beauty *qua* completeness to be the principle whereby the disparate domains of sense and reason should be integrated. Beauty however, appears to be better suited to the role of a regulative ideal than that of an active force that could persuade the Same and the Other to work together. As if on cue, after stating that the most complete cosmos will unite these two opposing forces, Plato immediately introduces soul as the agent of this unification:

> As he considered, He perceived . . . that reason cannot possibly belong to any apart from Soul. So because of this consideration He constructed reason within the soul and soul within body as He fashioned the All, so that the work He was executing might be of its nature most beautiful and excellent. (*Tim.*, 30b1–6)

Schelling finds compacted within these few lines indications that he believes leads to a radically new conception of Plato's cosmogony in which matter itself is *ensouled before* its commingling with the order of νοῦς. His line of reasoning begins with Plato's position that whereas there can be soul without the divine νοῦς, there can be no νοῦς without soul.[45] From the fact that soul is a necessary condition of νοῦς Schelling infers that soul must somehow predate νοῦς. Since Plato considered matter to be "something totally heterogeneous" to the ordered form of the divine νοῦς, there had to be an unordered form of movement that animated matter before their commingling.[46] This original form of matter is soul, which as the cause of motion (ἀρχὴ κινήσεως) is the original principle of a blind, unconscious, and irregular move-ment that inheres within matter *before* the imposition of the divine understanding. If movement is equal to change, this original form of soul can then be considered as the "*principle of change in the world in general.*"[47] What the divine form brings to the original form of soul in matter is the limit (πέρας) of law-like order. Schelling points out that Plato assumes that the forms of the divine understanding "have for themselves alone no causality," and are therefore dependent on the form of chaotic movement and change of matter.[48] Consequently, neither the divine νοῦς, or the chaotic matter, could alone bring forth the next form, that of *life*. The act of creating is then the melding together of blindly changing matter and the static order of the νοῦς. The *banding together* (συνιστάς) of both these classes of ideas gener-ates the living cosmos with both soul and νοῦς (κόσμον ζῷον ἔμψυχον ἔννου, 30b9).

The introduction of the idea of an intelligent creature (ἃ νοητὰ ζῷα) introduces the problem of how this limited idea of a living crea-ture relates to the unlimited variations of living creatures that populate the cosmos. In a word, we are faced with the genus-species question of how this one idea relates to its many sensible instantiations. Plato himself rhetorically asks after which individual living creature did God model this universal idea of living creature (30c2), and answers: no idea produced from a part is worthy of this cosmic idea of the whole (τῶν μὲν οὖν ἐν μέρους εἴδει πεφυκότων). His reasons for stating this are clear: an individual species of animal is incomplete (ἀτελει) when compared to the completed whole (ἕν). Plato's choice of words here not only confirms Schelling's construal of καλόν as completeness, but they indicate Plato's understanding of the essential link between *finality* and *beauty*: "For nothing that is like the incomplete could ever become beautiful" (30c4). In these few words Plato unequivocally establishes *finality qua* completeness as the necessary condition of τὸ καλὸν, and it is precisely the quality of incompleteness that the individual species of animal betrays when compared to the highest genus of living creature, that of the living cosmos.

Schelling finds it extremely significant that Plato addresses this question of how the one universal living creature relates to the multitude of species in creation through the organic framework of life: before even raising the question of how the one and the many, or the limited and unlimited, relate *in the abstract terms of pure reason*, Plato articulates this question in its most elementary, biological terms. Perhaps following Pythagoras' use of the biological term for begetting and procreation, ὁ γόνος, to name and describe unity, Plato frames the question of how genus relates to species through the model of how the organs of a living creature relate to and interact within an organism as a whole.[49] As he makes clear in the following passage, it is only this modality of unity, of being a complete whole, that warrants the superlative most beautiful (τὸ κάλλιστὸν):

> But we shall affirm that the Cosmos, more than aught else, resembles most closely that Living Creature of which all other living creatures, as one and generically, are portions (καθ᾽ ἓν καὶ κατὰ γένη μόρια). For that living creature embraces and contains within itself all the intelligible Living Creatures (νοητὰ ζῷα πάντα), just as this Universe contains us and all other visible living creatures that have been fashioned. For since God desired to make it resemble most closely that intelligible Creature which is most beautiful and in all ways complete (καλλίστῳ καὶ κατὰ πάντα τελέῳ), He constructed it as a Living Creature, one and visible, containing within itself all the living creatures which are by nature akin to itself. (30c6–d5)

Clearly, Plato held that one visible creation that melds together matter and νοῦς is more beautiful (because more complete) than a world limited to one or the other component. The only way Plato can present this idea is to speak of the created cosmos as a living creature—which as a copy of "the idea of ζῴου ἁ ζῷον νοητοῦ"—has within itself all the thinkable living beings—νοητὰ ζῷα πάντα—that are the forms of the genii of all visible living beings.[50] This is also the only way Plato can make sense of how the universal ideas of the νοῦς interact with those that deal only with matter. On the one hand, for Plato the "understanding for itself alone has no causality," but if it is to ever become visible in something, this can only happen if it is united with "a principle of activity" (*TK*, 29).[51] Matter provides this through its unconscious principle of change viz. soul (ψυχή). From the other perspective however, the blind, unconscious psyche of matter, in and of itself, could never have brought forth life: the form of the νοῦς was required to limit, focus and raise the soul of matter to the intensity of life. According to Schelling, it is this, *life itself*, which is *simultaneously* the unifying force that *individuates* the things of the world:

> Every singular entity of the world was thus not the work of matter, but was rather really a *banding together of particular pure laws* into one entirety, i.e., it was the work of an *idea*, of a *representation* of the banding together of particular pure laws into one entirety. Beyond this the banding together of laws into one entirety occurred according to *rules*, the banding together of these laws itself were thus again the work (not of matter) but rather of a pure *form* of *unity (Einheit)*, [the] work of an *intelligence*. (*TK*, 33)

Schelling's use of the term *Zusammenstimmung* is an obvious translation of Plato's συνιστάς (*Tim.* 30b), which the later uses to describe the "banding together" of the living cosmos. What Schelling describes here is the banding together of particulars into a more comprehensive and complete whole. Reiterating the process of unifying matter and νοῦς in more detail, this more elaborate coordination of elements is organized by the form of pure unity (*Einheit*). The austere elegance of Plato's method of presentation (*Darstellungsart*) however, leaves Schelling wanting for a richer and more complex vocabulary to articulate both this pure form of unity and how the World Soul interacts with its members. Schelling finds such an interpretive framework in Kant, and turns in the next line to his concept of a *"self-organized being,"* taken from the last *Critique*, §65, *Things considered as physical ends are organisms.*

Section §65 has long been considered one of the most concise statements of the program of Kant's third *Critique*. In it we find the elements of Kant's dynamic category of reciprocal causality and community applied to that modality of phenomenon they are best suited to explain: that of a living organism. As we have seen, this relational category employs a synthesis of a whole that is qualitatively different from its parts—and yet somehow the same. Whereas the mathematical categories allow for a successive, unilateral determination of the totality of members in a series—such that the sum of its parts determines the totality—the dynamic categories in contrast deny this possibility, thereby necessitating a bilateral or reciprocal relationship between the parts considered as parts, and the whole considered as whole. Consequently, the order of knowing such an entity requires that one first begin with the whole, and then work to the individual parts. One must begin with unity and then work back to the members who derive their sustenance from their interaction with that unified whole. Thereafter one can abstract from their unity and analyze its constituent members.[52] Schelling's brief transcription of this seminal statement of the only *dynamic* modality of Kant's otherwise static system is determinative for the future development of his *dynamic philosophy of nature*. Indeed, this passage should be read as the embryonic beginning of that philosophical framework. Schelling writes:

> We must moreover remind ourselves that Plato looked at the entire world as a ζωον, i.e., as an organized being, thus as a being whose parts are possible only in relation to the whole, and thus according to their form as well as connection reciprocally produce one another. We must consider, that we, according to the subjective arrangement of our faculty of knowing, can simply not conceive of the emergence of an organized being in any other way than *through* the causality of a concept, of an idea, that *a priori* determines everything that is contained in the being; that, just as the particular parts of the organized being reciprocally produce each other and thus produce the whole, conversely, once again, the idea of the whole must be thought as preceding, and a priori determinative of the form and the parts in their harmony. (*TK*, 33)[53]

Schelling sees in the progressive ordering of Kant's dynamic categories the order of unity in general: one must presuppose the absolute whole and then proceed accordingly. The opposite strategy of a regressive synthesis will, in principle, never attain to the standpoint of that absolute whole, which is the only standpoint from which the organization of the living being can be understood. Schelling cites this principle of an *ordo generativus* and acknowledges that Plato was "forced to assume the idea" of unity (ἕν, *Einheit*), that orders the World Soul. It is only through the a priori assumption of such an organized being that Plato can integrate and unite the "living ideas" of reason "into one whole, for one purpose" (ibid.). This point of order illuminates why Plato's hierarchy of ideas must be conceptualized as the ordered relationship between the parts and whole of an organism, for it is only in this way that their systematic unity can be thought; consequently, the 'idea of ideas' or 'form of forms' will always be of unity *qua* the whole. The other ideas will then relate to this whole as the subordinated concepts of a disjunctive judgment relate to the sphere of the judgment, or, as Kant describes this relation in the *Critique of Pure Reason*, the ideas will be "coordinated with, not subordinated to" this system principle.[54]

This idea of unity, however, must be "thought as preceding, and a priori determinative of the form and the parts in their harmony" (*TK*, 33); if we seek to think an organic whole, the *idea* of the whole becomes the condition of thinking the parts. But in contrast to the unilateral movement of simple causality, the reciprocal causation (*Wechselwirkung*) of the category of community (*Gemeinschaft*) demands that these parts must in turn influence the concept of the whole. Plato's idea of a living cosmos fulfills this condition: it provides him with the condition for thinking the ideas of all living creatures, and for how they in turn can be thought to relate to the idea of the entire living cosmos. But this living, thinking World Soul, since it is "one and visible," cannot itself be the highest cause of life and intelligence. Rather this visible living cosmos must have as its source a nonvisible, yet *still living model*.

It is this first and highest idea of a living cosmos, which Plato identifies as the divine understanding, that Kant subsequently refers to as the *intellectus archetypus*, and which Schelling—in a perhaps intentional inversion of Kant's Transcendental Ideal—calls the "the ideal of the world" (*TK*, 35).[55] What is apparent, however, is that a quantitative logic of analysis is incapable of making the qualitative leap from the part to the whole required by a complete principle of systematic unity. Systematic unity can only be articulated and made binding through the use of an organic form of logic that begins with unity, and then proceeds to the divisions (*Urtheil*) of its parts. This point of "order" is essential to understanding not only the context from which Schelling's *Form Essay* emerges, but it is also the key to understanding his reading of Plato's cosmogony as presenting the *immanent preestablished harmony* of a monistic dualism: a framework that requires us to invert Kant's architectonic in order to grasp what systematic unity is.

Immanent Preestablished Harmony:
The Condition of Possibility of Einheit

It was a magnificent idea of Plato's, that could easily send him into an inspired state (*Begeisterung*), that he should look for the harmony of the beings of nature (*Naturwesen*), not merely amongst themselves but also of each individual with itself, not with the method of empirical research, but rather in the investigation of the pure forms of the *Vorstellungsvermögen* itself. No wonder that he expressed

this sublime idea in a language which, uncommon to the usual philosophical language, actually soars,—that his language itself is the work
of a philosophical inspiration (*Begeisterung*),—that *through* such
a discovery of a supersensible principle of form and harmony of the
world in ourselves [such a language] necessarily must have arisen. (*TK*,
34, 1–10)

Echoing Kant's analysis of the sublime's power to disclose the supersensible and inspire *Begeisterung*, Schelling turns to Plato's discovery
of the sublime, supersensible principle of form and harmony.[56] He sees
this articulated in Plato's insight that the entire cosmos must be seen
a unity, as an organized being (ζωον), whose individual members are
possible only in relation to the whole. The supersensible, non-empirical
principle itself is the pure form of *Einheit*, construed as an organized,
noetic being, that lies at the basis of the visible beings of nature, and
serves as the condition of our being able to conceive the disparate
elements of the empirical world as building an integrated whole unified
for one purpose. This *intellectus archetypus* is a noetic organism whose
form, according to Plato's cosmogony, determines the organic form of
humanity's mind.

Schelling is quite aware of the anthropomorphic risks of Plato's
strategy. Indeed, in words only a Kantian could write, he advances the
following hermeneutic key to interpreting Plato's work: "The key to
understanding the entire Platonic philosophy is the observation that
he everywhere projects the subjective sphere onto the objective. In
this way, for Plato the proposition (of course long present before him)
emerged that *the visible world is nothing other than a copy of the
invisible world*" (*TK*, 31). But whereas Kant stops at this descriptive
surface and accepts the divide between subjective and objective worlds
ordained by his pure reason, Schelling cannot. The nagging question he
is driven to answer is not only what is the condition of the possibility
of this so successful correspondence between the subjective and objective, but also what led us to the projection in the first place. Schelling
continues this passage, writing:

But no philosophy would have come across this statement [that *the
visible world is nothing other than a copy of the invisible world*] if it
didn't have its philosophical basis in us. In so far namely, the entirety
of nature, just as it appears to us, is not only the product of our
empirical receptivity, but rather more properly speaking a work of our
Vorstellungsvermögen, in so far as it contains pure forms (of nature)

grounded originally in itself, in so far does the world belong in the representation of a higher capacity than mere sensuality, and nature becomes presented as the typus of a higher world, which the pure laws of this world articulate. (*TK*, 31)

The thematic vein Schelling is mining here is an old one: that the cognitive software nature programmed us with betrays the signature forms of that author. Because of this genetic similarity in code, the pure laws we abstract from our world inevitably lead to the idea that 'nature is the typus of a higher world'. The supersensible principle that supports this, however, is the idea of ἕν, of unity, that Schelling maintains is a universal concept that must come in the *order of creation* before the individual instantiation of a species, and in the *order of human knowing*, before sensual intuition. This follows from the logic of organic unity: we must 'think' the whole before thinking the parts of a living entity. Indeed, this is why Schelling finds Plato's construal of the unity of the cosmos as a living organism so convincing: as if confirming an eternal form of reason, it corroborates Kant's dynamic logic, just as Plato's position in turn supports Kant's.

Schelling makes this reciprocal corroboration explicit when he refers to his passage from the *Philebus*, and argues that Plato here makes the possibility of the universal concept of unity the "condition of the universal law according to which humanity carries out its empirical investigations" (*TK*, 35). In short, if there is no universal concept of unity, then there can be no empirical research or knowledge. The universal law Schelling is referring to is the same "pure law" he has mentioned twelve times in the previous two pages of his commentary; a pure law that is to be understood as the idea or form of unity:

> Every singular entity of the world was thus not the work of matter, but was rather really a *banding together of particular pure laws* into one entirety, i.e., it was the work of an *idea*, of a *representation* of the banding together of particular pure laws into one entirety. Beyond this the banding together of laws into one entirety occurred according to *rules*, the banding together of these laws itself were thus again the work (not of matter) but rather of a pure *form* of *unity*. (*TK*, 33)

It is this pure form of unity that is the "universal law" Schelling cites as Plato's condition of all our empirical researches and knowing. There must be a form common to all sciences that unites them as sciences; that is, there must be *a form of the whole of knowing*. The conceptual terrain Schelling is traversing is precisely the area Kant covers in his analysis of the "Regulative Employment of the Ideas" in his first *Critique*: "This unity of reason always (*seit jederzeit*) presupposes an idea, namely, that of the form of a whole of knowledge—a whole which is prior to the determinate knowledge of the parts and which contains the conditions that determine a priori for every part its position and relation to the other parts" (A 645/B 673). Kant's idea of "the form of a whole of knowledge" is precisely what Schelling believes he has found in his investigation of Plato. Specifically, he locates it in the answer Plato provides in the *Philebus* to his rhetorical question of how "the knowledges collectively are many" (*Phil.* 13e8, translation modified).[57]

These ideas and forms are not simply subjective Kantian categories. In a tone of explicit agreement, Schelling argues that in contrast to Kant, these forms were applicable for Plato to both the subjective and *objective* world. Plato's construal of the fourth form of generative cause as the form of the divine understanding demonstrates that these forms are "not only forms of our understanding, but are rather universal *Weltbegriffe*, from which the existence of the entire world is capable of being explained" (*TK*, 63). This follows directly from Plato's justification in the *Philebus* of his position that mind is the cause and principle of creation. He makes this defense through a rebuttal of those that maintain the cosmos is without order and thus not one, or a unity (*TK*, 29). The strength of his position depends entirely on his contention that creation is ensouled, and thus an organized being; a position that is not the result of a naïve projection of the subjective forms of understanding onto the objective structures of the cosmos, but is rather an explicitly self-conscious attempt to account for the symmetry between the order of our inner and outer worlds of experience; a symmetry that is not of our own making, but is rather the result of the order of the world around us.

The premise of his argument is the continuity of elements that constitute nature and man: as living beings we are of the same substance and nature as the elements of the rest of creation (29b). As natural beings of this world, we are shaped and governed by the same forces and natural laws that shape and govern nature, and it is on the basis of this isomorphic structure that our knowledge rests. Concede this premise, and Plato's second proposition follows: that we are not the source of these elements and living nature, but rather the world beyond us is the source of ours and all other creatures (29c8). Having established these two points, Plato addresses the question of the unity of creation, using the organic unity of the living body as the paradigm of this ἕν. "When we see all the aforementioned elements gathered into a unity, do we not call them a body (σῶμα)?" (29d8). If yes, then we should apply the same reasoning to the universe considered as a whole, that "would likewise be a body, being composed of the same elements" as ourselves (29e). Based on his second proposition, Plato asks whether our body derives nourishment from the larger body of nature or vice versa. He concludes that since we derive body—and therewith unity—from the larger organism of nature, the same relationship of dependence must exist regarding soul and mind: humanity is not the source of ensouled mind, rather the larger organism of nature is the source of this ordering power within us (30d3f). Consequently, the form and order of this ensouled mind derives from the objective forms of nature.

This position follows from the premise of Schelling's interpretation: that the ideal of creation itself is complete wholeness. Given that the ideal of the world is to fully integrate the sensible with the intellectual, we are permitted to make inferences between these two realms. Once again pointing out how Plato's use of these forms is so entirely different from Kant's, Schelling articulates how these forms serve as the common structure of both Plato's epistemology *and* his ontology: "according to *his* [Plato's] philosophy, which subordinates the sensible and the supersensible world under the one form of the most complete unity," such "inferences from empirical objects to pure concepts that are independent of experience" are entirely justified (*TK*, 63); this in contrast to a philosophy that must *refuse* the validity of inferring from empirical objects to concepts independent of experience, since it insists on divorcing matter from mind for the sake of logical expediency, thereby refusing to integrate the sensible and the supersensible in a higher unity.

The Ideas: Existence Is Not a Predicate

Schelling interprets the Platonic *ideas* as the Kantian condition of possibility of scientific knowledge *qua* universal concepts, which must somehow precede our discovery of them. "Plato," Schelling writes,

> must indeed view these universal concepts as originary concepts that are present before experience, which do not first come into being through the objects of sensible intuition, but rather themselves have first made the objects possible, since only through the causality of previously existing concepts could the individual objects of the world come into

being, so that an empirical understanding could once again discover them in objects through comparison and abstraction. (*TK*, 35)[58]

We have already suggested that Schelling finds two classes of ideas in the *Timaeus*: 1) those that are the basis of the world considered in its material aspect, and 2) those ideas that are the basis of the world considered in its formal aspect. The former class includes the intelligible living creatures (ζῷα νοητά), and can thus refer or relate to particular objects, whereas the latter can never refer to individual objects "AS SUCH. (As for example, the idea of the Good, of quantity, of quality, of causality and so on)" (*TK*, 31). The former ideas populate the "one visible intelligence of the World Soul, while the latter populate that of the divine understanding" (*TK*, 35). In general, we can conclude that Schelling held the former class of ideas to refer to the visible world of necessary causes, and the latter to the divine causes of the understanding of the *intellectus archetypus*.

Schelling twice interjects the specter of *Schwärmerei* into his discussion of the ideas, each time with the intent of dispelling the widespread but simplistic caricature of Plato's ideas that conceives them as existing, yet invisible exemplars of *individual* beings. This is, according to Schelling, a category mistake of the first order. Consider the predicate of existence. Following Kant's argument in the first *Critique*, Schelling writes that the moment the predicate of existence is applied to something supersensible, it "loses all physical meaning and retains merely a logical one" (*TK*, 44). A logical meaning of the term *existence* adds absolutely nothing to the subject it is attached to. "The concept of existence applied to the idea of god is an abyss for human reason—it surrenders itself either to the most excessive *Schwärmerei*, or it goes not one step further beyond the limits of the idea" (*TK*, 44). Before the predicate *existence* is applied to an idea, it enjoys an ideal or logical existence. The addition of the empirical predicate of reality *qua* existence adds nothing to the modality of the idea's existence: it is still not real, but rather simply ideal.

This in turn leads to Schelling's second debunking of a caricatured construal of the ideas. This one occurs when one attempts to apply a descriptive predicate of an existing *individual* entity to a *universal* idea:

If Plato had assumed that an objective, invisible, but physically existing foundational entity (*Grundwesen*), that contained the character of its entire genus, lay at the basis for every entity of the world, then this would have been a *Schwärmerei*, i.e., it would have been the projection of the purely sensual, of what belongs solely to empirical intuition, onto the supersensible. (*TK*, 32)[59]

According to Schelling, Plato consistently denies the validity of projecting individual empirical predicates onto universal intellectual ideas. In his reading, there is an idea only for each individual genus of objects which, precisely because it is the idea of the genus, is also the idea that lies at the bottom of every individual object.[60] But even if Schelling denies the possibility of successfully projecting the individual onto the universal, he does see a very important place in Plato's work for the projection of the universal idea onto the objects of the sensible world, but only with the proper justification.

The Threefold Form of All Knowing

Before we plunge into our analysis of Schelling's reading of Plato's beloved way of doing philosophy (his ὁδός; *Phil.*, 16B), we must examine Schelling's rather anomalous use of the term *form* to describe Plato's universal law of unity. His use of *form* in the translations we are about to consider follows the pattern he demonstrated earlier: he often interjects a term where there is none to be found in the original Greek text, thereby betraying his own interpretive agenda. His employment of the word *form* in these passages is perhaps the clearest example of this practice: he employs it ten times in thirty lines of text, frequently when there is no correlate term in Plato's original text.[61] We suggest that his usage here indicates this commentary as a link between Kant's inquiry into "the form of a whole of knowledge" and Schelling's *Form Essay*, in which Schelling not only advances a form of the whole of knowledge, but an essay in which he also asserts that Kant "stopped at the statement that the original *Urform* of all philosophy is available; he did not connect it with any supreme principle" (I/1, 104). The charge that Schelling levels against Kant is that he stopped too soon in his inquiry into what this *Urform* could be, that he cleared the way for its possibility—and even established its necessity as a condition of all knowing—and then did not specify what it is.

The "supreme principle" Schelling mentions in the *Form Essay* is the *universal law* he cites in his *Magister* in 1792, and which he analyzes in the following passages from the *Timaeus Commentary*. The universal law to which Schelling refers in his *Magister* is what Plato literally calls in the *Philebus* "a gift of the gods" he considers to be an eternal form of reasoning that guides all thought and inquiry (16c4). Most importantly perhaps, Schelling believes that this *Urform* will provide him with a first principle through which he can provide a solid foundation or premise to the results of Kant's critical program. This will only be possible if he can provide an organic account of this *Urform* that will demonstrate that it is not simply a form of our subjective understanding that we project onto the world, but that it is more accurately the productive structure of objective nature itself. Only if he succeeds in this will he successfully produce a monistic dualism that avails itself of an immanent preestablished harmony. By all relevant indications, he appears to believe he has found the paradigm of such a genetic account in Plato's cosmogony.

Schelling declares that this universal form of reasoning is for Plato a "thoroughly commanding idea (*herrschende Idee*)" that determines his triadic formula for thinking the productive relationship that holds between a unity and its parts (*TK*, 36).[62] Schelling translates from the *Philebus*:

> We notice, he says, that this form, of unity in multiplicity, has everywhere governed all speech and investigations from long ago up till our time. This form will never cease to be thought, and has not just now begun, but rather it is an eternal unchanging characteristic of every investigation. The young man who first discovers this form of philosophizing, delights as if he had found a treasure of wisdom; his delight fills him with enthusiasm, happily he participates in every investigation, sometimes fastening everything that occurs to him together in one concept, sometimes again dissolving and dividing everything. (*Phil.*, 15d8–e5)

Schelling proceeds to argue that Plato held this form of inquiry to be a "*pure, original* form" of the divine understanding, which in creation the Demiurge applied both to matter, and to the human understanding (*TK*, 36).[63] As a pure original form applied both to matter *and* to our understanding, this universal law functions as the condition of all logical and all empirical inquiry. As such, it is the common point of identity between empirical being and rational thinking; to indulge the old adage, this structural unity is the coin of which thinking and being are its two faces. Schelling writes that "this becomes even clearer from the following passage," which he translates from *Philebus* 16c5–e5:

> This form is a gift of the gods to men that together with the purest fire was first given to them through Prometheus. Therefore the ancients

(greater men and closer to the gods than us) have left the story behind, that everything which has ever been emerged out of unity and multiplicity (plurality), in that it united within itself the unlimited (ἄπειρος, universal) and the limited (το πέρας, unity): that thus we too in light of this arrangement of things should presuppose and search for every object one idea. . . . —It was the gods then, who taught us to think, learn and teach like this. (TK, 36)

Contrary to Schelling's promise, this passage from the *Philebus* fails to provide us with a precise articulation of what Plato's original form is. What is clear, however, is Plato's position that this form of all inquiry (σκοπεῖν) is divinely given, and thus itself is the form of the *intellectus archetypus*, a member of the first class of Plato's divine causes. Following Plato's distinction between necessary and divine causes, to search for the latter cause by means of the necessary causes of the empirical world would here become a search for the ἕν and unity in the manifold of things. This emerges from the key phrase in this passage that correlates the relation of the one and the many with that of the limited and the unlimited, asserting that this polarity is the generative source of all creation that eternally inheres in all things.[64] It follows that this polarity is the one integrating form that, since it originally generates the all of creation and continues to sustain and inhere therein, is itself the binding principle of unity common to everything in the world. Schelling elaborates:

The idea of the combining of *unity and manifoldness* or plurality is a thoroughly commanding idea in Plato that he not only applies logically, but also . . . as a concept of nature (*Naturbegriff*), and everywhere considers as the first form that circumscribes all Nature, through whose application to the formless matter brings forth not only particular objects, but also makes possible the relationship of objects to one another and their subsumption under genii and species. (TK, 36, 18f)

Schelling's choice of the term *concept of nature* (*Naturbegriff*) is extremely significant. As we have seen, the distinction between *Naturbegriff* and *Weltbegriff* is not obvious, since Kant only uses it once in the entire first *Critique* (A 420/B 448). Its importance, however, is immense to Kant's future attempts at a *transition* to empirical reality. Schelling's selection cannot be random, since he uses it in its technical employment to describe "nature when it is viewed as a dynamical whole" (A 419/B 446f). His use of the term *Weltbegriff* earlier, and the distinction he makes here between that previous *logical* use of the idea, in contrast to its employment here in this case to its current application to a dynamic whole, strongly suggests that we have here our first evidence of Schelling's adoption of an essential standpoint and set of categories that will be determinative for the rest of his career. This reading confirms our position that Schelling is interpreting Plato through the framework of the logic of Kant's dynamic category of reciprocal causality, a standpoint from which the idea of the whole, of *"the first form that circumscribes all nature,"* is indeed what must be presupposed and then used as the framework for empirical research. This will become even clearer in the next chapter when we move to consider his first philosophical essay, the *Form Essay*, and discover just how careful a reader he is of Kant's critical system.

As Schelling reminds us, however, Plato employs this *Urform* for both logical and empirical investigations, emphasizing the inescapable necessity of presupposing *unity qua* whole before embarking on a discussion of even the logical relationship between genus and species. And to do this we must first provide a more complete account of Plato's *Urform*.

Plato's *Urform*

The reason why Schelling draws the *Philebus* into his analysis of Plato's cosmogony is that this dialogue contains the most extensive discussion of Plato's understanding of this original form that he declares a "gift of the gods." The subject he addresses in the second logos of the *Philebus* is sensation: how to articulate the unity of the seemingly inchoate continuum of our senses. He begins by establishing his explanatory forms. The first two he takes as the "gift of the gods" that "revealed" two principles inherent in all being, the infinite and the finite.[65] To this he adds *a third* made "by combining these two" (23df). Here we see the point of contact that justifies Schelling's reading of Plato's forms as following the ordering of whole to part as specified in Kant's analysis of organic nature: in an inversion of the order of discovery that matches the order of creation in Plato's cosmogony, the third form is the whole that must be posited as the first cause, of condition of the ensuing multiplicity of the triad.[66]

By subsuming the appropriate objects under the first two forms of the limited and the unlimited, Plato unites the infinite under the relative series of differences that constitute the *quality* of unlimited degree that characterizes all sensation: there is no limit for any comparative sensation of, for example, "hotter and colder."[67] The finite Plato unites under the heading of *quantity*, that is, anything that provides a "definite number or measure in relation to such a number or measure" (25a10). The third form is then what *relates* and unites the previous two, putting "an end to the differences between opposites and making them commensurable and harmonious" (25e).

Schelling notes that in Plato's words "one sees very plainly traces of the Kantian principle of quality," namely, their common use of the infinite form of judgment and the category of reality (*TK*, 60).[68] The form of the finite Schelling identifies with the Kantian principle of quantity, thereby associating these first two forms with Kant's mathematical categories. The third form of "το κοινον" is associated with the dynamic categories of existence and experience, specifically that of reciprocity and causality. Consistent with Kant's ordering, Schelling points out that Plato considered these forms "as forms of all existing things and as forms under which one must think the origin of the world" (*TK*, 63). The third form in particular, the τὸ κοινὸν, is the "first concept under which the present world, according to its form and matter, must be subsumed" (*TK*, 63). When viewed from the standpoint of the present world, the dynamic categories are prior to those of the mathematical, suggesting again that the order of investigating this actual world must begin with the unity of experience, and then proceed to the separation of that unity into its constituent elements through the use of the two most abstract classes of categories available, finite quantity and infinite quality.[69]

Schelling makes this point repeatedly in his criticisms of Plessing's interpretation of Plato's ideas as substances that exist in a divine understanding. These four forms are "concepts" that according to Schelling, Plato would understand as "ideas" in the Kantian sense (*TK*, 68). "Under πέρας and ἄπειρον he understands nothing other than pure *formale Weltbegriffe*, and under αἰτία nothing other than *Verstandsbegriffe*, under which one must, in *his* philosophy, objectively conceive the connection of these two in a κοινόν" (*TK*, 69f). Schelling concludes that one can think the first two formal ideas of the πέρας and the ἄπειρον as separate "only in the *Vorstellungsvermögen*" (*TK*, 70), but "if the talk is about *empirical* existence, then they both are present only in connection with each other" in the κοινόν (ibid.).

The categories however, act as agents of differentiation of the manifold; Plato's four forms on the other hand, primarily serve as explanatory concepts with which he can account for the unity of that manifold. Taken separately these four forms can act as the principles of each class of category in Kant's table. Considered together they can also fulfill the same function as Kant's *Weltbegriffe*, and provide a mechanism for articulating the absolute systematic unity of νοῦς *qua* reason; a systematic unity which is of the whole, unconditioned universe:

> From the above it becomes clear that Plato wants to maintain that these four forms are to be considered as concepts under which one can subsume everything which exists in the world; in brief, they are to be referred not to individual objects but rather only to the whole universe. (*TK*, 68)

Schelling here makes perfectly clear the degree to which he accepts Kant's enthusiastic admission of imitating Plato in the first *Critique*. The ideas of Plato's eternal form of reasoning are the very ideas Schelling sees unified by Kant's problematic categories of relation, which, as we will see in the next chapter, Schelling pays particular attention to in his first philosophical essay, *On the Possibility of a Form of Philosophy in General*. It is in this essay that he provides the justification for his inversion of Kant's program, citing the internal systematic reasons that lead to this, as well as the textual clues left by Kant himself in the updated B version of the first *Critique*. To the young Schelling, as eager as he is to create and announce the advent of a new epoch of philosophy and freedom, Kant's new words in this edition to the effect that his categories provide "all the *momenta* of a projected speculative science" (B 110), occurring as they do in a new section dedicated to discussing the problematic nature of the categories of relation, indicate that Kant's imitation of Plato extends to the oldest archetype of philosophical reasoning itself. And with this, he has the *Urform* of all reasoning that will answer the question of the possibility of a form of all philosophy; an original answer to a question which, as I will show in the following chapter, suggests the degree to which a new and more accurate grasp of Schelling's position will enrich our understanding of the roots of German Idealism.

5

On the Possibility of a Form of All Philosophy

The *Form Essay*

§11

This table of categories suggests some nice points, which may perhaps have important consequences in regard to the scientific form of all modes of knowledge obtainable by reason. For that this table is extremely useful in the theoretical part of philosophy, and indeed is indispensable as supplying the complete plan of a whole science, so far as that science rests on a priori concepts, and as dividing it systematically according to determinate principles, is already evident from the fact that the table contains . . . *the form of a system . . . in the human understanding*, and accordingly indicates all the momenta *of a projected speculative science*, and even their order, as I have elsewhere shown. (B 109)[1]

Schelling's Original Insight

Schelling's first philosophical publication, *On the Possibility of a Form of Philosophy in General*, is traditionally read as the youthful work of a follower of Fichte.[2] At first glance, such a reading appears to be justified. He does make ample use of some of Fichte's central ideas, most notably the absolute positing of the I and its formulaic expression 'I = I.' But as we have seen in his earliest texts, Schelling has been busy at work developing his own ideas for some time before his actual exposure to Fichte. A point that, if clearly demonstrated, would lend credence to Schelling's claim that the *Form Essay* is actually grounded in ideas that he had already been thinking about "for some time"

(I/1, 87). In fact, when examined in the light of writings such as the *Timaeus Commentary*, which predate the *Form Essay* by as much as three years, it appears that the customary reading of Schelling as simply a brilliant follower of Fichte can no longer be maintained.

As we have seen, the *Timaeus Commentary*, finished sometime in May or June of 1794, is a work free of any Fichtean vocabulary.[3] Fichte's *Recension des Aenesidiemus* appeared in early February of the same year, while his "Ueber den Begriff der Wissenschaftslehre oder der sogenannnten Philosphie, als Einladungsschrift zu seinem Vorlesungen über diese Wissenschaft," appeared in May.[4] As the *Form Essay* is dated September 9, 1794, this provides a three-month period during which Schelling could have read one, or both, of Fichte's works.[5] From both a substantive and historical standpoint, however, it appears that Fichte's *Recension* had more of an impact on Schelling's *Form Essay* than the *Grundlage*. First, there is evidence that Schelling did not even have a copy of Fichte's "Ueber den Begriff der Wissenschaftslehre" until the end of 1794. In a letter to Hegel dated January 6, 1775, he speaks of having finally received the first part of the "Wissenschaftslehre" from Fichte himself. He writes, "I read and found that I had not failed my prophecy."[6] If this timeline of events is accurate, this would mean that Schelling refers to Fichte's *Recension des Aenesidiemus* when in the *Form Essay* he writes: "My opinion regarding that part of the problem, which the *Theorie der Vorstellungsvermögen* has left for some future elaboration of *die Elementarphilosophie*, has been strongly confirmed by the newest work of Professor Fichte" (I/1, 88). This points clearly to the *Recension*, in which Fichte indeed critiques *Aenesidiemus* on some points, yet also agrees with other issues Schultz raises against Reinhold's theory. The focus of dispute in this nexus of essays is the possibility of formulating Kant's mysterious "common ground" that should unite the duality of the intuitive facticity of our senses and the conceptual forms of our understanding. All parties involved agree that there must be an ultimate principle, derived from this common ground, to unite both the form and content of philosophy. Schelling states that Reinhold's *Elementarphilosophie* merely repeats Kant's case for the possibility of the form of philosophy, failing, just as Kant before him, to extend the "investigation to an ultimate principle of all form" (I/1, 88). Such a form Schelling believes will help him overcome philosophy's inability to show "how the content of a philosophy is possible," thereby correcting a critical failure that has "hitherto hurt philosophy extraordinarily" (I/1, 88). The inability of philosophy to integrate content references a theme central to Schelling's program, which he addresses as early as his *Magister* of 1792, when he complains of philosophy's inability to reconcile our "sensual nature" and its desires with the "domineering voice of reason," thereby denying the essential role the sensual plays in "our development to completeness."[7] Anticipating his use of Plato's ideal of completeness in the *Timaeus Commentary*, Schelling here insists that philosophy must get beyond the simply elegant yet repressive strategy of subsumption in order to develop "a solution of the entire problem of the *possibility of philosophy in general*," which would satisfactorily integrate "both sides of the problem" of form and content, the analytic and the synthetic, into a unified system (I/1, 88). And it is in precisely this regard that Fichte's *Recension* helped him, as he claims, to develop his own thoughts on this matter more fully. Referring to Fichte's work, Schelling writes:

> This work surprised me all the more pleasantly in that it became easier for me to penetrate into the depth of this investigation by means of my own preconceived ideas. Though I may not fully have succeeded in this endeavor, perhaps I did advance farther than would have been the case without these preconceptions. I was thus able to pursue the purpose of this investigation, namely to arrive eventually at a solution of the entire problem of the *possibility of philosophy in general*, a topic with which I had already been somewhat familiar. It was this work that led to a more complete development of my thoughts on this problem, and I found that this effort was rewarded, that this work became more understandable in the same measure as I had developed my own ideas earlier. I derived this advantage from the excellent review of *Aenesidemus* that appeared in the *General Literary Magazine*. (I/1, 88–89)

This passage clearly demonstrates Schelling's position that he considers Fichte's work as *not* having provided a solution to the problem that Schelling addresses in the *Form Essay*. What the *Recension* does provide him with, however, is a new way of formulating his own "preconceived ideas," which in turn led "to a more complete development of my thoughts on this problem," as found in the *Form Essay*. Schelling evidently considers that what he is doing in this essay is not only *different* from what Fichte suggests in the *Recension*, but that he accomplishes what Fichte has not, namely, proposing a form of philosophy that will integrate both form and content.

There are two lost *Specimina*, the written exam required to receive the *Magister* that Schelling took in the fall of 1792, whose titles provide even more evidence that confirms this initial focus of Schelling's earliest work.[8] The first betrays a title very similar to that of the *Form Essay*, and reads "Über die Möglichkeit einer Philosophie ohne Beinamen, nebst einigen Bemerkungen über die Reinholdische Elementarphilosophie." The similarity between the first clause of this essay's title and "Über die Möglichkeit einer Form der Philosophie überhaupt" is obvious. The interest in establishing the possibility of a philosophy conditioned by nothing save itself seems to be the common thread linking these two projects. How Schelling may have conceived of establishing such an unconditioned philosophy is indicated by the title of the second *Speciminen*, "Über die Übereinstimmung der Critik der theoretischen und praktischen Vernunft, besonders in bezug auf den Gebrauch der Categorein, und die Realisirung der Idee einer intelligibeln Welt durch ein Factum in der lezteren."[9] This title suggests that the question of the mediation between Kant's realm of the intelligible and that of the sensual has been of long-standing interest. We have already seen this in his pursuit, also in 1792, of how Plato accounted for this same mediation between his unconditioned (free) divine ideas and those of nature. Significant also is Schelling's use of the term "Realisirung der Idee einer intelligibeln Welt," a phrase that appears not only in the *Oldest System Program*, but one that also leads into his idea of "die realisirende Vernunft," which, as we will see in the next chapter, plays such a central role in his *System of Transcendental Idealism* (1800). Most important, however, is the acceptance of the Kantian *fact* of freedom. Just as Kant used the disjunctive form of syllogism to dissolve the third antinomy of freedom—as well as to articulate the Transcendental Ideal—Schelling will advance this form of disjunction as the original form (*Urform*) of all reasoning, capable of parsing not only freedom's dynamic, but also the systematic unity of philosophy in general. The traditional reading of the relationship between Fichte and Schelling assumes by necessity that Schelling had no demonstrable agenda of his own, thereby discounting his own introductory remarks that this essay expresses thoughts "I had already pondered for some time" (I/1, 87). This reading is due in large part to the simple fact that until recently we have not had access to Schelling's earlier writings and have consequently been unable to assess critically his claims to originality. A primary objective of the current investigation is to offer a new reading of Schelling's early development in light of the works examined in the previous chapters, a new reading that no longer interprets Schelling through the narrow lens of Idealism, Fichtean or otherwise. As difficult as it is potentially illuminating, we have to begin reading Schelling on his own terms, from the immanent perspective we have been pursuing. What this requires is the broadening of our own interpretative categories to include the possibility of a thinker whose thought still challenges our understanding of both him and his era. The complexity of Schelling's way of thinking is best grasped through his use of an organic form of reasoning, structured by a *disjunctive logic of identity* that articulates the self-organizing dynamic of freedom and necessity as it extends throughout the entire spectrum of reality. The essence of his strategy is the use of a trichotomy of principles to generate ideas that far outstrip, in both complexity and richness, a system assembled via a method of dichotomy. From this standpoint, we no longer face the dilemma of having to ignore the seeming contradiction between his Philosophy of Nature and Transcendental Idealism advanced by the standard reading.[10] We must instead allow our reading to be informed by the heterodox Pietist culture of his upbringing, and in particular, the decisive role Hahn played in providing him with the example of the philosopher who pursued a two-track inquiry into the nature of the divine. For it is only when we have taken Schelling's stated dedication to pursuing this path that we can begin to grasp, and then employ, Schelling's logic of disjunction to transform the most confusing dissonances of his work into complementary aspects of the whole of his philosophy, a reading that should, at the very least, be faithful to the manner in which he awkwardly presented his philosophy as a *real-idealism*.

The *Urform* of All Forms

> The thoughts expressed in this essay have been renewed in my mind by the newest publications in the philosophical world. I had already pondered such thoughts for some time. I was led to them through the study of the *Critique of Pure Reason*, in which nothing seemed more obscure and harder to understand—from the very start—than the attempt to lay the foundation for a form for all philosophy without having anywhere established a principle (*Princip*) that would not only furnish an *Urform* as the root of all particular forms, but would also give the reason for its necessary connection with the particular forms that depended on it. (I/1, 87)

Schelling begins his presentation by addressing the very themes that have driven our investigation thus far. He targets Kant's first *Critique* and its attempt to establish the transcendental principle of reason that should provide "the one form of knowledge as a whole" (A 645/B 673). This in turn suggests his treatment of Plato's attempt to answer the same question of how "the knowledges collectively are many."[11] Once again, in Schelling's words, the aporia is how to derive "the forms of unity and multiplicity" from a supreme principle (I/1, 111).

Unfortunately, like Plato's youth who has just discovered the ὁδός of the One and the Many, the enthusiasm with which Schelling attacks this perennial problem of philosophy presents the reader with a formidable, but not insurmountable, challenge. Blessed with a genius of mind and spirit, the intellectual athleticism with which this now nineteen-year-old scholar executes the leaps and turns of this compact essay often obscures the sequence of his argument. Using the insights we have gleaned from our reading of his earliest works we must retrace more clearly the territory he covers in those spirited leaps in thought to reconstruct the pattern of his reasoning. To do this we must again draw into play those points of Kant's critical program that Schelling's maneuvers tacitly assume as their support and justification. We must also rely on our analysis of his reading of Plato to complete our surgical reconstruction of the connective tissue that holds his argument together. Accordingly, we approach Schelling's presentation thematically, beginning with his supreme principle from which he will derive the *Urform* of all knowing *qua* philosophy. Excluded from consideration is Reinhold's suggestion that this supreme principle be derived "from an already present *concept*" (ibid.). It must instead be derived, not from Fichte's *deed* (*Tathandlung*), but from a "fact (*Tatsache*)."[12] This fact, however, is not the Kantian fact of freedom. It is rather the fact that we are necessarily a "living being (*Wesen*)."[13] Using this necessary fact of life as a schema *of* freedom, Schelling derives from it the *principle* of freedom (I/1, 110).[14] This principle, with its "absolute causality" of freedom, expresses the I's power of self-positing (I/1, 97). This capacity of the I corresponds nicely with Kant's account of the *world* as *nature*, namely, a dynamic whole in which freedom becomes the "absolute self-action (*Selbsttatigkeit*)" of freedom, and "existence" becomes an "absolute *natural necessity*" (*KrV* A 418/B 446). Schelling's strategy transforms Kant's when he demands that by "absolute necessity" the *Urform* must be deduced "from a principle which expresses a fact" (I/1, 111). The absolute causality of freedom fulfills this demand as a *possibility* in the *necessary* fact of the I's organic capacity to be both cause and effect of itself: "It is posited not because it is posited [from without] but because it is itself the positing agent" (I/1, 97).[15] And it is this principle from which Schelling will "furnish an *Urform* as the root of all" philosophy; it is the supreme principle of freedom that expresses the possibility of the unconditioned self-positing of the I, from which Schelling must now derive the form of all knowledge.[16] We have seen all these elements, in this arrangement, in the previous chapters. In the frame of the dedication to his *Studienheft* on Plato's philosophy, the self-determining action of the I is an expression of its unconditioned (and thus divine) causation, which is independent of the observable techne of the conditioned causal chains of empirical nature.[17] In the *Timaeus Commentary*, what is both cause and effect of itself is the ζῷον of Plato and the organic life of Kant's third *Critique* (§65). This Platonic understanding of life construes it as the connective tissue (τὸ κοινόν) uniting the intelligible form of the limited (τὸ πέρας) and the ensouled content of the unlimited (τὸ ἄπειρον), a principle of organic unity that was the basis for Plato's argument for the unity of both the cosmos and our body of knowing. Most importantly perhaps, there is Kant's method and category singularly capable of accounting for an unconditioned magnitude—the very same method and form Schelling consistently uses to articulate the dynamic whole of organic life: the form of the relational category of *community* (*Gemeinschaft*) and its *reciprocal causality* (*Wechselwirkung*), employed through the disjunctive logic of the progressive method. The common denominator of all these elements is the form of organic unity, a form that requires a grasping comprehension as unconditioned as it is inexponible. This is an epistemological directive, which, as we have seen, insists that the understanding of the parts of any system is dependent on first comprehending the whole. This is a requirement that, as we will see, has serious systematic ramifications for both Kant and Schelling. Accordingly, Schelling points out that in deriving this form he cannot, as Kant and Reinhold did, proceed exclusively "in a formal respect" employing the regressive method of the mathematical categories. Rather, in order to solve the problem that has "hitherto hurt philosophy extraordinarily"—namely, its exclusive reliance on formal analysis—Schelling must begin in accordance with the progressive method of the dynamic categories. This requires a starting point which is nothing less than the unconditioned itself, which can be grasped only as one grasps the absolute measure of the sublime, in an experience that supplies an intuitive *arche* beyond the immanent sequence of discursivity; an *arche* whose chaotic content provides the force needed to integrate the *same* and *other* of form and content. In short, he must employ an embryonic variant of a genetic method he will later place at the center of his system as the *method of construction*. Beginning in the intuitive certainty of unmediated contact with the unconditioned, this method of construction proceeds progressively in a manner parallel to that of the geometer, a process Schelling obliquely refers to in the following passage:

> Should we go back from axiom to axiom, from condition to condition to the highest, absolute categorical axiom? Only we would then have to begin necessarily from *disjunctive* propositions, i.e., that axiom would

never,—insofar as it is determined neither by itself (for then it would be ultimate) nor by one that is higher (for then we would already have the higher one we are looking for)—be qualified to become *the first point of a regressive investigation*. Nonetheless, the first characteristic that lies in the concept of an absolutely unconditioned proposition shows of itself the quite different way in which it must be sought. For such a criterion must be given only by its own criterion. But it has no other criterion than the criterion of absolute unconditionality. (I/1, 96; my emphasis)[18]

Following the circular logic of an inexponible measure, Schelling rules out the possibility of a regressive synthesis. As we have seen in Kant's discussion of the cosmological concepts of the mathematical categories, such a synthesis can never attain to an actual unconditioned. Indeed, the absolutely unconditioned can never be reduced to the exponible qualities of a discursive principle *qua* proposition. The only example we have seen of a synthesis that somehow assimilates the *actual infinite* of the unconditioned is in Kant's treatment of the sublime. The defining characteristic of the unconditioned that Schelling seeks is specified by Kant as follows:

> If, however, we call anything not just great, but, without qualification, absolutely, and in every respect (beyond all comparison) great, that is to say, sublime, we soon perceive that for this it is not permissible to seek an appropriate standard outside itself, but merely in itself. *It is a magnitude comparable to itself alone.* (KU, 97; emphasis mine)

Kant demands an unconditioned the criterion of which is given "only by its own criteria." How does Kant investigate this unconditioned magnitude, which, as he points out, "awakens *a feeling of a supersensible faculty within us*" (ibid.)? Through a *progressive synthesis* employing a method we have discussed earlier, but must now investigate in more detail if we are to grasp the movement and flow of Schelling's argument in the *Form Essay*.

Kant's Progressive Method: The Removal of the Time Condition as the Condition of Comprehending an Absolute Magnitude

In his *Logic* Kant defines the progressive method as equivalent to the synthetic (*Logik*, §117; Ak IX, 149). Whereas the analytic or regressive method begins with the conditioned, and moves backwards in sequence to "principles" (*a principiatis ad principii*), the progressive method moves forward "from principles to consequents" (ibid.). However, Kant's programmatic definition of the synthetic method begs the question: if synthesis is defined as contrary to analysis, it follows that whereas the regressive method begins with the conditioned, the synthetic *must begin with the unconditioned*. Although this is precisely the starting point Kant himself calls for in his *other* discussion of the progressive method—namely, his brief analysis of the *Naturbegriffe* in the *System of Cosmological Concepts*—he excludes such a progressive method from the purview of his transcendental philosophy.[19] To maintain the ascetic purity of a transcendental reason that functions exclusively through "concepts devoid of intuitions," Kant denies his transcendental philosophy the power of engaging in the type of a priori synthesis that the mathematician and geometer employ in the act of constructing their concepts.[20] In what would *appear* to be a direct contradiction of his alleged claims to employ a synthetic method in the first *Critique*, Kant states in *The Discipline of Pure Reason* that[21]

> We shall confine ourselves simply to remarking that while philosophical definitions are never more than expositions of given concepts, mathematical definitions are constructions of concepts, originally framed by the mind itself; and that while the former can be obtained only by analysis (the completeness of which is never apodeictically certain), the latter are produced synthetically. Whereas, therefore, mathematical definitions make their concepts, in philosophical definitions concepts are only explained.[22]

Kant's transcendental philosophy, as a science based on "discursive principles," may not rely on the "intuitive principles" or axioms constructed as they are by the mathematician.[23] Consequently, transcendental philosophy's "synthetic method" must begin with *discursive principles*. But since these principles (ideas) are in theory completely exponible, they are incapable of delivering the very unconditioned magnitude of the supersensible that Kant must somehow incorporate into his system, if it is to transform itself from a mere aggregate of disparate principles into a systematic whole united by a common ground and telos. In violation of his stated doctrine of method, he must avail himself of a content with unconditioned magnitude if his structure of forms is to be "organically united in a system of human knowledge" (A 835/B 863).[24]

As we saw in chapter 3, Kant finally succumbs to this systematic necessity in the third *Critique*, introducing the sublime as "the estimation of the magnitude of the fundamental measure"—an unconditioned magnitude we access "in the immediate grasp that we can get of it in intuition" (*KU*, 98).[25] In a clear violation of his doctrine of method, this intuition of an absolute measure is an *inexponible* representation of the imagination that provides the forbidden "third mediating knowledge (*drittes vermittelndes Erkenntnis*)" of intuition (A 732/B 760). The resulting inexponible representation cannot be reduced to concepts (a reduction that "is equivalent to giving its exponents"), since this could occur only if it could be reduced to a regressive series susceptible to analysis. This breach in the symmetry of Kant's architectonic provides Schelling with precisely the opening he requires to integrate positive content into his form of philosophy. The only other element of his architectonic that Kant describes as inexponible is that of substances in *Community*, which, unified through the simultaneous interaction of reciprocal causality, contain nothing on which to base a series ("und keines Exponenten einer Reihe haben"; A 414/B 441). Because of their inexponible nature, Kant rejects this category (along with substance, but not causality) as "not adapted to a transcendental idea" (ibid.). Why? Because it cannot be reduced to a series: "That is to say, in it reason finds no ground for proceeding regressively to conditions" (ibid.). Kant could only employ these dynamic categories of experience in a progressive manner, *in consequentia*, in a method that he actually ridicules, since it would only lead to "the whole series of all future alterations" (A 337/B 394). Compared to determining past events through the regressive method, such an inherently open-ended strategy would only lead to uncertainty, a fact that renders the progressive method "gratuitous and unnecessary" to the conservative interests of Kant's 'pure' reason (A 411/B 438).[26] Ignoring for the moment Kant's contradictory treatment of these categories and the sublime—he rejects the former as incapable of generating an idea of reason because it is inexponible, but requires the latter precisely because it is inexponible—it appears that Schelling grasped their common form and characteristics. As we have seen in the last chapter, he rightly interpreted the relationship of substances in a reciprocal causal system as a simpler model of the same relationship that holds in Kant's organism. As we also saw in his analysis of Plato's description of what he called our *sublime supersensible* faculty, he is fully aware of Kant's connection between the power of the sublime to provoke an awakening of the supersensible within us and an experience that often releases a pleasantly violent surplus of spirit *qua Begeisterung*.[27] The common epistemological requirement of these elements—apprehending a reciprocal causal system, organism, and the sublime—is their common need to effect what Kant calls "a comprehension of the manifold in unity" (*KU*, 107). Only if we can comprehend the reciprocal establishment (*wechselseitige*

Begründung) of whole and part—*simultaneously* with the interaction among the parts themselves—only then can we understand the dynamic whole that is organic nature. Likewise, only if we can absorb the actual infinite of the sublime in a grasping 'of the whole' can this experience fulfill its cognitive and systematic duties. What this requires however, is that Kant must shatter the static form of our pure a priori intuition of time. To fulfill his need of an *actual maximum*, he must qualify intuition's sequential processing of time and permit an experience in which the time-condition is removed. To satisfy reason's need for the actuality of the supersensible, he must allow for a "single intuition that holds the many in one" in a simultaneous "comprehension" (*KU*, 101); an intuition whose resulting *Vorstellung* resists reduction to a mathematical series, since it cannot be reduced to a *sequence of the time series*:

> Measurement of a space (as apprehension) is at the same time a description of it, and so an objective movement in the imagination and a progression. On the other hand, the comprehension of the manifold in the unity, not of thought, but of intuition, and consequently the comprehension of the successively apprehended parts at one glance, is *a retrogression that removes the time-condition* in the progression of the imagination, and renders coexistence intuitable (*KU*, 107; emphasis mine).[28]

This is the "retrogression" that Kant *implicitly denies* in his analysis of space in the first *Critique*, yet demands in the third *Critique* to supply the sublime with the "violence" needed to not only disclose the supersensible substrate, but to also generate the unifying telos that should integrate his system into an organic whole.[29] With the removal of the linear time sequence, nature as an infinitely interrelated whole becomes intuitable, and thus capable of providing reason with the cognitive dissonance required to awaken the faculty of the supersensible. This result produces precisely the view of nature that Kant describes in the first *Critique* when it is considered through the *Naturbegriffe* of the dynamic categories of experience. It is nature "viewed as a dynamical whole," in which *there is* an unconditioned magnitude that serves as the "first member of a series," which "in respect of causes" is "*absolute self-action (freedom)*," and in respect of "existence" is "absolute natural necessity" (A 418/B 446). As the first member of a series, this unconditioned magnitude discloses what the regressive synthesis of the mathematical categories cannot, namely, the absolute magnitude of the *actual infinite*. Thus whereas the *discursive principles* of the mathematical *Weltbegriffe* can only produce what Kant calls the "potentially infinite" of a series whose regress is never complete, the estimation of the sublime through the dynamic categories supplies reason with the concepts required to *think the infinite as an absolute whole*, and thereby awaken the human faculty of the supersensible. As we have seen in chapter 3, Kant holds that the mere capacity to think the infinite without contradiction

> *is something that requires the presence in the human mind of a faculty that is itself supersensible.* For it is only through this faculty and its idea of a noumenon, which **later,** *while not itself admitting of any intuition*, is yet introduced as substrate underlying the intuition of the world as sheer phenomenon, that the infinite of the world of sense, in the pure intellectual estimation of magnitude, is completely comprehended under a concept, although in the mathematical estimation by means of numerical concepts it can never be completely thought. (*KU*,103f; my emphasis in bold and italics)

Notice the time sequence specified in the intuition of the noumenal: *only later* does it not admit of intuition. But to awaken the supersensible and stimulate our awareness of the idea of the noumenon, there must be, on some level, an original intuition of that substrate. Only the dynamic estimation of a progressive method—a method that begins with the "immediate grasp" in *intuition* of the unconditioned noumenal substrate—can deliver, in Schelling's words, "the ultimate unity of knowledge," in both its form *and content*, which he seeks.[30]

Kant of course denies the possibility of this. Like a true defender of his faith in the doctrine and *dogmata* of pure reason, Kant cannot accept what his system nonetheless needs in order to make sense of his own description of an organic "*self-development of reason*" (A 835/B 863). To achieve this truly organic quality, it would have to incorporate a feedback mechanism whereby the discontinuity of the sensual acts is a needed counterbalance to reason's excesses. Schelling addresses such an excess in his *Magister* of 1792, pointing out that "the domineering voice of reason concedes but an all too small share" to our "sensual nature" in "our development to completeness."[31] But to do this, sensible intuition would have to be actually incorporated into the entire edifice of the system, and not merely as a coarse and unrefined servant, whose labors bring food to the back door of the big house, yet is forbidden from entering and participating in the further preparation and enjoyment of its toil. The faculty of intuition would have to be recognized as the faculty of *the whole* whose activity—whether we acknowledge it or not—always runs parallel to that of our discursive understanding, functioning as the connective tissue that unites the discrete momenta of the time sequence. Accepting this duality for the moment, neither supersensible nor sensual nature manifests the characteristics of the continuity that would allow for its graphic representation on Lambert's two-dimensional graphical grid.[32] The violent surplus of power released by the unconditioned being of the actual infinite characterizes the awe-inspiring force of nature that even Kant concedes he needs to provide the finality, and therewith the completeness, which will serve as the capstone of his edifice. But whereas Kant's regressive method ultimately fails to achieve this, Schelling believes that the progressive method, grounded in the immediate intuitive grasping of the unconditioned, will succeed in integrating the intellectual with the sensual; a unification that occurs in a progressive method of construction, whose origin he locates in the internal intuition of the supersensible substrata *qua* freedom. Although this genetic moment of *internal intuition* is absent from the *Form Essay*, its presence and agency is presupposed by Schelling's entire presentation.[33] As we demonstrated through our analysis of his account of Plato's apprehension of the divine causes in the *Timaeus*[34]—an analysis written just months before the *Form Essay*—Schelling accepts an epistemological framework that demands the possibility of an "intellectual faculty of knowing" whose object, the Platonic forms, can only be grasped through an act of *noetic* seeing. And while this initial phase in his method of intuiting the unity *qua* supersensible will not come into explicit focus until his next essay *Of the I* (written only six months later), it is this activity that supplies him here, in the *Form Essay*, with the *unconditioned intuitive principle* from which he begins his progressive demonstration of the unifying form of all philosophy. As we have seen, this immediate grasping through intuition of an absolute magnitude satisfies Schelling's demand for an absolute whose "criterion must be given only by its own criteria." Moreover, as an unconditioned first member of a series, it satisfies Schelling's requirement of "absolute causality" (I/1, 88), whose existence as a *fact* of living nature is "absolutely necessary" (I/1, 110; cf. *KrV*, B 446). Most importantly, because Schelling's progressive method begins from the standpoint of absolute unity, he can, in Kant's words, integrate "the many as one," and thereby establish the form of the unity of all knowledge (ἓν καὶ πᾶν). As such, his method takes off from "a retrogression that removes the time-condition," thereby rendering the unconditioned unity of the I's act of absolute causality *qua* self-positing open to intuition, but *not to reflective thought*.[35] As Schelling points out, the nature of his investigation requires us to adopt *two different orders of time*:

> To be sure, the act that appears to the philosopher first (as far as time is concerned) is the act of consciousness, but the condition of the possibility of this act must be a higher act of the human *Geist* itself. (I/1, 100, n. 1)

As *kairos* violates *chronos*, the instantaneous time of the higher act of *absolute self-action* not only violates the linear time-series of discursive thinking, but it functions as its *condition of possibility*.[36] As we will see in the next chapter, Schelling only makes these points explicit in his *System of Transcendental Idealism*, when he derives his categories from the production of time consciousness itself. In addition, the circumvention of the time-series demands the type of epistemic positionality Schelling later expresses through his *two complementary positions* of the standpoint of production and the standpoint of reflection. Building on Spinoza's distinction between *natura naturata* and *natura naturans*, these two different standpoints of viewing the same phenomenon are also implicit in his analysis of the interaction of Plato's triadic *Urform*.

As we saw in the last chapter, in his interpretation of Plato's forms as Kantian 'ideas,' Schelling explicitly makes the very technical distinction between the mathematical *Weltbegriffe* and the dynamic *Naturbegriffe* (*TK*, 68):

> Under περας and απειρον he understands nothing other than pure *formal Weltbegriffe*, and under αιτια nothing other than *Naturbegriffe*, under which one must, in *his* philosophy, objectively conceive the connection of these two [το περας and το απειρον] in a κοινον. (*TK*, 69)

From the subjective standpoint of reflection the first two formal ideas of τò πέρας and the τò ἄπειρον are separate "only in the *Vorstellungsvermögen*" (*TK*, 70), whereas from the objective standpoint of production, "if the talk is about *empirical* existence, then they both are present only in connection with each other" in the τò κοινòν (*TK*, 70, Schelling's emphasis). In the *Form Essay* he makes precisely the same distinction regarding these two standpoints of the subjective and objective.[37] From the standpoint of the absolute necessity of empirical existence neither the infinite nor the finite, the unconditioned nor the conditioned, are separate. Consciousness of empirical existence is rather the product of the interaction of the unconditioned and the conditioned, so that every particular thing (τόδε τι) is the result of, and thus manifests characteristics of, both the finite and the infinite. From the standpoint of the *Naturbegriffe* of empirical existence, the finite alone would self-implode into a black hole of absolute involution, while the infinite alone would disperse into sheer nothingness. Schelling repeats this relationship in the *Form Essay* between the interaction of the *Ich* and *Nichtich*. These two forms separate only in the abstractions of the *Vorstellungsvermögen* as *Weltbegriffe*. In reality, they always form one organic unity.

Schelling applies this same epistemic positionality to the fact (*Tatsache*) of self-positing. From the standpoint of reflective consciousness, this original act of self-positing is inaccessible, whereas the "elements" that originate and are generated in the act of abstracting—elements that result from the activities of reflective consciousness itself—are plainly observable to the philosopher in the linear sequence of the time series. As a result, the philosopher of reflection will see precisely those separate forms that define his consciousness: from the standpoint of discursive reflection, the elements of consciousness are indeed as separate as the discrete moments of the time series, and thus offer no evidence of their common ground (eternity).[38] From the standpoint of production however, the philosopher 'sees' the original unity of the unconditioned positing of the I, and comprehends the simultaneous emergence of both principles *qua* whole as they reciprocally produce and limit one another. Accordingly, the philosopher of reflection employs a regressive method of analysis that, grounded in discursive principles, can never account for the necessary unity of our knowing, but must instead only presuppose it. Schelling on the other hand, argues that he can account for the *necessity* of this unity from his standpoint of production, employing a progressive method of construction. A method which he only hints at in his *Form Essay*.[39] If we do not make this embryonic method of construction explicit, the sequence and clarity of Schelling's argument in this his first philosophical essay will appear opaque at best and nonsensical at worst. Our reading is consequently an aggressive surgical reconstruction that hopefully animates, rather than anesthetizes, the spirit and intent of Schelling's argument.

Reciprocal Establishment of the *Urform*

Before we plunged into the murky waters of transcendental method, we had taken the first step in reconstructing Schelling's account of the supreme principle of freedom, expressed in the fact of the self-positing of the I, from which he must now derive the *Urform* of all philosophy. To capture the essence of this fact of the I's self-positing, he states that "the form of all philosophy" must be "the form of being unconditionally posited as such" (I/1, 109). What is required is a "form of being posited (*Gesetztseyns*)" that articulates the internal accusative of the I's self-positing in an unconditioned form; a form, however, which is still capable of incorporating the *content* that will express how the I can be simultaneously both cause and effect of itself (I/1, 93). This *Urform* he articulates through the highest axiom in its most general expression as A = A.[40]

The circularity of this form testifies to its suitability to articulate an unconditioned unity whose 'criterion must be given only by its own criterion.' From the standpoint of reflection, the *rotary* nature of formally defining any actual absolute must be *problematic*. This is especially true when one is attempting to establish the highest form of all knowing, a form of knowing that by definition must not be conditioned by anything else. Like the reciprocal causality of life, in which organic life is both cause and effect of its being—and which consequently offers the only dynamic to articulate the most potent expression of life, namely, the absolute self-action of human freedom—the form of all knowing must also display a similar dynamic in the circularity of its self-definition as absolute. The genius of Schelling's approach is that this is a circular form that can bridge the absolute freedom of the self-positing I and the absolute characteristic of the form of all knowing, since both require an unconditioned form of unity. Most importantly, like the postulate upon which his future system will rest, this absolute *Urform* hopelessly begs the question when considered formally from the analytic standpoint of reflection:

> Some will ask: How do you prove that? By the original form of human knowledge! True, I reach it only by presupposing such an absolute unity of knowledge (that means the original form itself). This is indeed a circle. However, this circle could be avoided only if there were nothing absolute at all in human knowledge. The absolute can be determined only by the absolute. There is an absolute only because there is an absolute (A = A). This will become clear in the sequel. (I/1, 92, n.1)

By definition, the absolute can never be discursively proved.[41] Like the space of the geometer, the absolute is the necessary condition of every proof and logos, and as such cannot itself be directly demonstrated.

The extent of the proof of the absolute Schelling offers is an apagogic strategy as old as Plato's defense of the One in the *Parmenides*: deny its existence and the autistic echo chamber of vacuous dissemination follows.[42] The goal of the argument Schelling advances, however, is not to prove the unprovable absolute. On the contrary, before he can "clarify" his reading of this formula of A = A, he must first demonstrate the inability of the *regressive method* to do justice to the actual content of the absolute. If he succeeds in relativizing the global claims of reflective analysis, he succeeds in providing the opening required to advance his own heterodox strategy.[43] To do this he must first establish what the form of the absolute *qua* unconditioned unity would have to be when considered from the standpoint of reflective analysis. He does this in the previous passage through the adaptation of Kant's own definition of an absolute magnitude: if only the unconditioned unity can determine the unconditioned unity, then the only formula appropriate for expressing this is A = A. This is an analytic judgment that in stating the identity of concepts is, to use Kant's words, a tautological judgment that appears to be "void of consequences."[44]

The Progressive Method of Disjunctive Identity

Having established the form of his highest axiom, we can now finally answer the question we previously posed regarding the methodology Schelling employs. To review, our initial query was prompted by his own rhetorical allusion to method:

> Should we go back from axiom to axiom, from condition to condition to the highest, absolute categorical axiom? Only we would then have to begin necessarily from *disjunctive* propositions, i.e., that axiom would never,—insofar as it is determined neither by itself (for then it would be ultimate) nor by one that is higher (for then we would already have the higher one we are looking for)—be qualified to become *the first point of a regressive investigation*. Nonetheless, the first characteristic that lies in the concept of an absolutely unconditioned proposition shows of itself the quite different way in which it must be sought. For such a criterion must be given only by its own criteria. But it has no other criterion than the criterion of absolute unconditionality. (I/1, 96; my emphasis)

Schelling explicitly states he cannot begin with a *conditioned disjunctive* proposition and search *regressively* for the unconditioned.

"Nonetheless" he writes, the very nature of the "absolutely unconditioned proposition A = A shows" the method that must be used. Our
reading of this typically opaque pronouncement of manifest clarity is
the following: in light of his technical use of the terms *disjunctive* and
regressive, and taking into consideration his position that the nature of
the unconditioned proposition indicates the direction in which one must
proceed, his method must begin as Plato's did. That is, Schelling must
begin from a triadic relational form whose disjunctive logic articulates
the unconditioned unity of an organic whole, from which Schelling can
then *progressively* unfold the consequences that follow.

This reading is possible, however, only if we reinterpret the form of
identity as stated in the absolute proposition A = A. Clearly, from the
perspective of a reflective analysis, the idea that the form of this proposition actually expresses the characteristics of a disjunctive proposition
is far from obvious. However, Schelling is not approaching this aporia
from the exclusive standpoint of reflection. The content and depth
he seeks to integrate into philosophy pushes him beyond the myopic
standpoint of the cogito to include the standpoint of production. In
brief, Schelling reconfigures the parallel structures of Spinoza's *natura
naturata* and *natura naturans* and Kant's regressive and progressive
syntheses into the complementary logic of disjunction, whereby the
resulting standpoints of reflection and production generate, so to speak,
biopic vision. Alone, each standpoint fails to do justice to the dynamic
of existence, but working together as two organs of a larger organism,
they accurately perceive the reality of our world. Reflection is regressive, production progressive. At work is an ambidextrous strategy
that, while incorporating both the regressive and progressive methods,
must begin with the progressive in order to secure the condition of
the whole, which will then permit him to comprehend its constituent
parts. From the standpoint of the progressive method we will be able to
better understand Schelling's arguments for why and how the proposition A = A actually expresses a disjunctive form. Only after we have
comprehended his argument can we then evaluate its cogency from the
standpoint of reflection. The first step in this process is to reconstruct
his argument. To do this it is advisable that we avail ourselves of the
regressive method, and begin once again with his conclusion, and then
work backwards.

The *Urform* of Relation

Our point of orientation is Schelling's Kantian reading of organic
nature in Plato. Life, understood as self-action, is the common rela-

tion (τὸ κοινὸν) that unites the form of the limited (τὸ πέρας) and the content of unlimited (τὸ ἄπειρον), which in turn is the basis for Plato's argument for the immanent preestablished harmony of both the cosmos and our system of knowledge.[45] Both of these arguments address the respective points Schelling must integrate, namely, the connection between the freedom of the self-positing I and a unifying *Urform* of all knowing, which will integrate both the form and content of philosophy. To reiterate the conclusions reached earlier, only organic life presents us with a unity of difference that can be both cause and effect of itself, a fact which to comprehend requires us to sacrifice the discursive movements of reflective analysis and grasp the whole as the condition of the existence of its parts. It is the comprehension of a living being (*Wesen*) that supplies us with the paradigm of a systematic whole whose unity is unconditioned by the divisive determinations of discursive thinking. Consequently, the elucidation of the unity of organic life and freedom requires that the form of the disjunctive judgment, and its correlative category of *community and reciprocal causality*, must assume priority over the other forms and categories of Kant's system. If the self-positing of the I is the expression of the supreme principle of freedom, it follows that the form that articulates life and freedom must be the model for the *Urform* of all philosophy. This is precisely the conclusion Schelling reaches:

> If one looks at Kant's table of these forms, then indeed one finds that, instead of placing the *Urform* as the principle of the other forms, Kant placed it among the others, as one on a par with them. Upon more careful investigation, one finds not only that the forms of relation are the foundation of all others but also that they are identical with the *Urform* (the analytic, the synthetic, and the two combined). (I/1, 107)

The *Urform* is a relational unity comprised of the very same forms (ideas) specified by Plato, but filled in and articulated with Kantian elements: the analytic *qua* infinite, the synthetic *qua* finite, and a third arising from the union of the first two (the mean *qua* (δεσμῶν). As a relational unity, one can only comprehend it through an extreme type of intuition (Kant's "higher act of the human spirit") that delivers the shock of the sublime and its accompanying "retrogression that removes the time-condition" (*KU*, 259). This is the justification for Schelling's contention that the *Urform* is "given . . . simultaneously with and inseparable from the content of all knowledge" (I/1, 105). Consequently, each one of the *Urform*'s three forms is derived from a symbol in the ultimate axiom 'I = I.'[46]

Those axioms are:

1. A form that is absolutely unconditioned, the form of the positing of an axiom which is conditioned by nothing but that axiom, and which therefore does not presuppose any other content of a superior axiom, in short, the form of unconditionality (axiom of contradiction, analytic form).
2. A form that is conditioned, which can become possible only through the content of a superior axiom—form of conditionality (axiom of sufficient reason, synthetic form).
3. A form that combines the two forms—the form of conditionality determined by unconditionality (axiom of disjunction, connection of the analytic and synthetic forms). (I/1, 104)

Schelling is not only struggling here with creating a new form of reasoning, which he can only refer to through the relational terms of combining and connecting (*zusammengesetzt, Verbindung, Gemischte*), but he is also dealing with one of the oldest challenges of philosophy, namely, negotiating the transition between idea and *form*. Of these three ideas *qua* forms, only that of the new composite form, *based on the axiom of disjunction and the unity of community*, is a *Naturbegriff*, and is, as such, applicable to the absolute necessity of empirical existence. The other two forms are *Weltbegriffe* from which—just as he does in the *Timaeus Commentary*—Schelling derives the mathematical categories of quantity and quality (I/1, 107f). These are the two ideas that in apt circular fashion are precisely the reflective forms analyzed in discursive thinking and Kant's critiques.

To explicate both the reasons for and consequences of this inversion of the Kantian categories, we need now to examine the philological and logical reasons Schelling provides to justify his strategy.

Philological Justification

Fortified by Kant's claim that his critical program was a mere propaedeutic intended to clear the way for the construction of a future system of philosophy, Schelling appears to read Kant as Philo of Alexandria read Moses. In a form of allegorical interpretation, Schelling searches for the rough spots, the contradictions and *hints* in Kant's text, which perhaps, as Philo would have it, were intentionally left behind by the master to indicate to the alert and worthy where the "higher meaning" was to be found. Schelling finds such a clue in §11of the *Table of Categories*, in the *second edition* of the *Critique of Pure Reason*, which was added along with §12, after Kant had finished his *Metaphysical Foundations of the Natural Sciences*. Familiar with that work and *the problems* Kant encountered when he attempted to apply his mathematical categories of pure reason to the dynamic world of actual experience, Schelling considered the addition of these new sections in the B edition to be of systematic significance. Kant himself clearly states in the preface to the *Metaphysical Foundations* the central problem of his attempted *transition* from theory to experience:

> no employment of pure reason can ever concern anything but objects of experience; and insomuch as nothing empirical can be the condition in a priori principles, these cannot be anything more than principles of the possibility of experience generally. This alone is the true and adequate foundation of the determination of the boundary of pure reason, *but it is not the solution of the problem as to how experience is possible by means of these categories, and only by means of them. . . . Therefore I shall take the earliest opportunity to make up this defect* . . . [so we will not be] placed in the . . . disagreeable necessity of taking refuge in a preestablished harmony because of the surprising agreement of appearances with the laws of the understanding, even though the latter have sources quite different than the former.[47]

The "problem" Kant concedes here has at its core the question: how does *empirical experience* depend entirely on the a priori forms of the understanding to transform the raw content of the senses into cognitive knowledge capable of satisfying his normative definition of 'experience'? The sequence of this process in Kant's theory is as clear as it is problematic: first form, then content, then synthesis into a knowledge acceptable to his normative status of possible experience. The problem, however, is as obvious as it is familiar: what is the common ground between the forms of understanding and the content of experience that enables (justifies) the synthesis (agreement) of the former with the latter? Kant addresses this problem "at the earliest opportunity" by adding to the A version of the *Table of Judgments* the two new *concluding* sections, §11 and §12—an insertion strategically placed right before his *Transcendental Deduction of the Pure Concepts of Understanding*. And what does Schelling find when he turns to the newly inserted §11 but an opening paragraph in which Kant provides his *clue* that the table of categories contains all the elementary concepts of the understanding in their completeness, nay, even the form of a system of them in the human understanding, and accordingly indicates all the *momenta* of a projected speculative science, and even their order, as I have elsewhere shown [in the] ... *Metaphysical First Principles of Natural Science.* (B 110)

It is this passage that Schelling refers to in the *Form Essay* immediately after he has inverted and supplemented Kant's ordering of the forms of propositions. He expresses his amazement that Kant establishes "this *Urform* of all knowledge" and then "does not specifically ** indicate the connection of the particular forms of knowledge (which he presents in a table) with that Urform" (I/1, 105). The asterisks in Schelling's text refer to a footnote in which he references the previous passage from the new §11, and asserts that it

actually contains a reference to this *Verbindung* [now composite disjunctive form] and to its importance in regard to the form of all science. Such passages in which such references occur—like single rays of light which the admirable genius sheds on the whole (corpus) of the sciences—vouch for the correctness of those traits by which Fichte (in the preface of his above mentioned essay) tries to characterize Kant. (I/1, 105, n. 2)

But why is Schelling convinced that it is the form of disjunction that Kant alludes to in the previous passage from §11? It is most likely because Kant provides in this new section his solution to the problem of *a common ground* that unites the *form* of the mathematical categories with the *content* provided by the dynamic categories. A common point of unity from which Kant claims these different categories emerge: "This difference" between the mathematical and dynamic categories "must have some ground in the nature of the understanding" (B 110). In his attempt to supply this common ground of form and content Kant addresses the obvious asymmetrical dissonance between the fact that, on the one hand, "all a priori division of concepts must be by dichotomy"—as testified to by his division of the *Table of Judgments* into the *two* subsets of the mathematical and the dynamic—yet on the other hand, each class of category always has *three* categories. In contrast to the method of analytic division employed (allegedly) everywhere else in his a priori science, when it comes to allocating the classes of categories, Kant must employ a method of *production* in order to allow the third category to emerge (*entspringen*) "from the combination of the second category with the first of its class" (ibid).

How does Kant account for this asymmetry? By an appeal to a "special *actus* of the understanding (*besonderen Aktus des Verstandes*)," which is quite different from the *actus* "exercised in the case of the first and the second" (B 111). He writes:

> It must not be supposed, however, that the third category is therefore merely a derivative, and not a *Stammbegriff* of the pure understanding. For the combination of the first and second concepts, in order that the third may be produced, requires a special act of the understanding, which is not identical with that which is exercised in the case of the first and the second. (B 111)

Kant's attempt at shedding clarity on the asymmetry of a priori division and the trichotomies of the categories raises more questions for Schelling than it solves. With this attempted explanation, Kant must now maintain that the third category is *simultaneously* both a *Stammbegriff* and the product that emerges from the combination (*Verbindung*) of the first two categories of a class. This dilemma becomes even clearer in the examples—all pertaining to phenomena addressed by the category of *disjunctive community*—he provides to clarify this new clarification:

> nor can I, by simply combining the concept of a cause and that of a substance, at once have an understanding of *influence* (*Einfluß*), that is, how a substance can be the cause of something in another substance. Obviously in these cases, a *separate act of the understanding* is demanded; and similarly in the others. (B 111; emphasis mine)

What this separate and special act of the understanding *is*, however, Kant never tells us. All we can infer is that on the one hand, the third category is original and irreducible to the first and the second, but on the other hand, it is the result of the interaction of those two categories. And it may perhaps be at this point that Schelling began to see the "rays of light" generated by Kant's genius shining through this otherwise opaque clarification. The source of this light is the subject that Kant inexplicably turns to in the next sentence: the third category of relation, that of community and reciprocal causality, and the problematic logical form that determines this category, that of the disjunctive syllogism. In the rest of the section Kant wrestles with trying to explain how this logical form and category work—*the only such extended discussion in the entire first* Critique.[48]

Schelling must have asked himself: why is Kant adding this section, with this particular content, as a solution to the problem he admits in his *Metaphysical Foundations*? Why is the question of how a third can arise from two—and yet also be considered original—connected with an explication of disjunction and *community*, in a section that begins by hinting at the form of a future speculative science? Informed by his intimate familiarity with the Platonic use of the triadic form of reasoning, Schelling must have read Kant's explanation here as proof of this form's power to account for *a unity of difference* in its articulation of a dynamic and relational *Einheit*. Only the disjunctive form of *community* can articulate the unity of a common ground that coordinates its constitutive and complementary parts, thereby accounting for how *Sinn* and *Verstand* could simultaneously emerge from their reciprocal production of each other. Kant's only mistake as far as Schelling is concerned, is he fails to see that the third element in this triad (the common unity) is the condition of the first and the second element. Kant fails to see this since he only considers this aporia from the standpoint of reflection and its division of all propositions into the simple dichotomy of analytic and synthetic. Schelling, however, contends that there is a third form, which corresponds to Plato's *Urform*, and is a disjunctive composite of the analytic and synthetic forms that, as we will shortly see, can only be grasped through a "retrogression of the time-condition." Faced with the inability of his system to provide a foundation for the natural sciences, Kant was forced to admit that the understanding must be capable of a different standpoint that could account for the generation and apprehension of relational concepts such as 'influence.' This predicable in particular is of the species whose function it is to 'fill in the gaps' of our object-oriented sequence of reflections. Like unity, relation, and field, 'influence' is a word tasked with the impossible job of signifying something that is no 'thing'. While such predicables fail to disrupt the quantifiable world of possible experience and pure reason, the dynamic nature of experience presents quite a different world with exponentially more complex challenges.[49] His first attempt at this transition (*Übergang*) from the theoretical to the actual proved unsuccessful due to his system's inability to grant full citizenship—with the right to constitute experience—to the productive standpoint of the dynamic categories. To integrate the categories of relation would have required an entirely new architectonic for his critical edifice—a task perhaps too monumental of a redesign for a man of Kant's nature and age. Just as he avoids the systematic ramifications of employing the progressive method in his analysis of the aesthetic idea of the sublime, Kant here too refuses to address the obvious flaws in his design. To do so would have required the dissolution of the dualism on which his critical enterprise rests, and the integration of the very *content* he deems unworthy of pure reason—which is precisely the content that Schelling insists is *essential* to establishing a form of the systematic unity of knowledge. Whereas this philological analysis helps complete our genealogical account of Schelling's *Urform*, it does little in the way of explaining how Schelling goes about advancing it in the *Form Essay*. To this most complicated and convoluted thicket of ideas we must now turn.

Epistemic Positionality and the Removal of the Time-Condition

Perhaps the most serious flaw in Schelling's *Form Essay* is his failure to explain to his reader the *epistemic positionality* his entire essay presupposes and consistently uses. Making use of the progressive method he engages in Kantian-like "special acts of the understanding" that are unintelligible to the reflective analysis of the regressive method. To reiterate our conclusions based on the epistemology of the sublime, the immediate grasping in intuition of an unconditioned, *dynamic whole* initiates a retrogression that ruptures the time sequence. This allows for the comprehension of the simultaneous coordination of phenomena governed by the category of *community and reciprocal causality*. Like a witness to a crime, although Schelling's description must move sequentially, the facts he relates are the result of an insight afforded by an act that occurs in the flash of an instant.

Schelling grounds his argument in the supreme principle of freedom that, parallel to Plato's divine ideas, expresses the fact of the unconditioned causality of the self-positing of the I. His axiom 'I am I' is an attempt to articulate the form of this absolute self-positing, whereby the I fully becomes both cause and effect of itself. The method he employs is progressive, beginning with an unconditioned proposition whose content is identical, but whose form is of a new type of proposition modeled after the disjunctive form of judgment. Using the *Naturbegriff* of the category of *community and reciprocal causality*, this axiom is treated as the organic form of a dynamic whole; that is, it is treated as if it were the unconditioned unity of a living being with self-consciousness. The method Schelling applies is the same he used to derive the categories from Plato's forms and his analysis of Plato's ζῶον: from the standpoint of the *Naturbegriffe* that order the unmediated experience of empirical existence, the relational whole (τὸ κοινὸν) of the living organism is the only necessary unity. From the standpoint of the *Weltbegriffe* that determine reflective thought, however, what was one necessary unity in existence now becomes divided by abstraction in the *Vorstellungs-vermögen* according to the categories of quantity (analytic/form) and quality (synthetic/content). As we have seen through Kant's analysis of the "retrogression" and the removal of the time sequence, the "special act of the understanding" that is operative in this changes our perception of the time series. From the empirical standpoint of the *Naturbegriffe*, the organic being is comprehended all at once, in a grasping of the many in the one dynamical whole, in which one comprehends simultaneously the whole and its parts as they reciprocally generate and condition each other. When analyzed from the standpoint of reflection however, the time sequence of this discursive frame requires that the instantaneous and inexponible dynamic of the whole be reduced to exponents of an aggregate "sum total" of parts. Thus if one relies exclusively on this regressive method of reflection, failing to supplement it with the progressive method, then the sequential dualities of consciousness ordered by reflection become hypostasized, leading to the inverted world of modernity's cogito.[50]Schelling addresses this difference in time sequence only once, and then in a footnote: "To be sure, the act that appears to the philosopher first (as far as time is concerned) is the act of consciousness, but the condition of the possibility of this act must be a higher act of the human *Geist* itself" (I/1, 100, n. 1).[51] The higher act of the human spirit Schelling appeals to here functions with the same epistemological fluidity as the special "act of the understanding" (B 111) Kant adds to the second edition of his first *Critique*. Like the interaction of τὸ πέρας and τὸ ἄπειρον in Plato, neither form nor content precedes the other from the standpoint of production and empirical existence. Rather, just like Plato's triad of divine causes, they mutually induce one another, arising in the same act as a *whole*, thereby rupturing the continuity of the successive series of time and conditioned causes. Schelling's three forms of the *Urform* are thus a transformation of the three divine causes of Plato: both sets of ideas account for the empirically unaccountable effects of what must therefore be an unconditioned causality. For normal empirical consciousness all this occurs beyond its view, occurring in the unconscious, which, as we will see in the next chapter, Schelling systematically employs to make sense of this standpoint of production in his groundbreaking *System of transcendental Idealism* (1800). As with his analysis of Plato, only from the standpoint of the reflection, of looking to an event in the past as mediated through the time sequence, do we encounter the mutually exclusive relation between the *Ich*/content and the *Nichtich*/form. Worse, when viewed like this, *after* the fact, this separation of form and content is accepted as an original duality of form and content.[52] This rupture of the time series caused by the influx of a timeless simultaneity supplies Schelling's explanatory model with the resources to account for the "absolute causality" of the self-positing of the I. Following his analysis of Plato's divine causes, the active presence of timelessness is noticed only by its effect, insofar as certain actions of living beings are observed for which there are no empirically observable causes. It is only from this standpoint outside the time sequence that he can account for how content and form may arise from a common ground qua Urform—an equiprimordial polarity of terms (Wechselbegriffe) that can be viewed alternately as τὸ πέρας and τὸ ἄπειρον, conditioned and unconditioned, synthetic and analytic, Sinn und Verstand, and so forth. What Schelling must demonstrate is how the axiom 'I = I' can generate both terms of these opposed series, beginning with form and content, before moving to the unconditioned and the conditioned. His criticism of previous attempts to do this assumes this higher standpoint of production and the efficacy of the category of community to articulate the reciprocal epigenesis of elements:

> The mistake therefore, of all previous attempts at a solution of the problem of a principle (Grundsatz) of all principles obviously consisted in always trying to solve only one part of the problem (sometimes the part concerned with content of the principle, other times concerned with the form of the principle). No wonder, then, that the individually advanced formal principle lacked **reality** or the material principle lacked **determinateness**, as long as the reciprocal grounding of the one through the other was not recognized. (I/1, 95; italicized emphasis original, bolded mine)

Schelling's choice of terms is illustrative of his ambition to provide a form of philosophy that will integrate form and content: he seeks a form for articulating the determinate reality of our empirical existence. While there are a host of other aims his disjunctive form of philosophy will have to account for, the primary task in the Form Essay is to account for the necessity of experience anterior to the necessity of the logical. The simultaneity of reciprocal grounding (wechselseitige Begründung), based on the frequency with which he uses it, is perhaps the central conceptual feature of the category of community employed to attain this goal. What Schelling seeks to circumvent is the regressive and futile strategy of moving sequentially from one principle to the next in the effort to establish unity. Moving in an infinite series of conditioned conditions the philosopher of reflection creates for herself an impossible task of generating a unity out of the two terms of a duality. By the very rules of the game—axiom of contradiction—the analysis of reflective consciousness can always only capture one term of a polarity *at a time*. The progressive method, however, can comprehend *both* in their reciprocal unity that *qua* unity is actually a trinity of forms; a relational unity that harmonizes quite well with the Platonic teachings of Schelling's youth, namely, that to generate a synthesis always requires three terms.[53] Following the sublime dynamic of the whole and the logic of community and reciprocal causality, Schelling suspends the time series of reflective thought in order to provide a more comprehensive account of how these terms relate necessarily in empirical experience.

The condition of simultaneity enables the shift in explanation away from the *subordinating* logic of determining terms towards a more dynamic and open-ended order of their reciprocal *coordination*. Such a strategy in turn broadens the focus from the product of the two terms produced by the reciprocal grounding to the actual process of *producing itself* (*natura naturans*). This broadening of focus requires that the nature of the relating itself be considered as *a third* element in the axiom 'I = I'. Construed transitively, the *relatum* provides for the flexibility required of a unity of the whole scope of the axiom, while the *relata* are understood as the complementary characteristics of the coordinated relationship. Shifting emphasis away from a static unity of subsumption to a more fluid unity of coordination, this strategy incorporates the binding action of the *relatum*, while retaining the *difference* between the *relata*. The *Urform* of self-positing must then elevate the transitive relating of the copula to a status worthy of its role as the whole that simultaneously mediates and conditions the parts of predicate and subject; a point that Schelling addresses when he writes:

> Aenesidiemus could rightly say that the axiom, being a proposition, must have a subject and a predicate. But how can their connection be possible unless I presuppose a form which expresses the relationship of subject and predicate? (I/1, 93)

What Schelling demands is a *form of being posited* that will not be simply subsumptive or, what amounts to the same thing, blind to difference. His use of the disjunctive form is an attempt to specify a form of relating subject to predicate that will establish a connection (*Verbindung*), but one that maintains and coordinates the difference between the two terms:

If . . . I want to express a definite content or meaning, then that meaning should be different from any other meaning. How is this possible? How can I posit a meaning as different from any other without presupposing a form of positing, through which every definite meaning is determined from everything else that can be posited? (Ibid.)

This question goes to the very essence of Schelling's project, namely, what is the condition of positing difference? Only if the form of unconditioned positing can address this, will it succeed in integrating its content. That is, only if there is a content to this unconditioned positing, will there be a *positive something* to suffer the differentiation *qua* negation in the reciprocal act of the conditioned limiting the (relative) unconditioned.

Linguistically construed we could say that only if there is a positive meaning in the subject can the predicate's determination have *something* to negate. Schelling's contention is that we can only posit a differential meaning if there is a reality, a content, that is posited simultaneously with a form of determination. As he pointed out earlier, all regressive attempts at establishing a form of philosophy have failed because they posited sequentially, thereby beginning with form and then generating nothing more than a determinate concept void of all content and reality. Others began by positing content and generated a reality devoid of a determinate articulation. In either case, the condition of positing difference was left unfulfilled. This condition can only be met if both form and content are posited as *gleich ursprünglich*, as coming into being in a simultaneous act of spontaneous reciprocal engendering. Kant's treatment of difference is emblematic of the regressive approach. Kant targets the conditions of determining the homogeneity of quanta, convinced that this alone will provide for the conditions of knowledge. And he is correct as long as he seeks only "a science" in which we "*know* only the *cognitions* but not the *thing presented* by them" (*Logik*; Ak IX, 72). If, however, it is the thing or the *content* that we in fact seek, then we must move from a dichotomy to a trichotomy to incorporate *das Dritte*—the τὸ κοινὸν—of empirical existence. Kant no doubt was aware of the risk that in foregoing content to guarantee determinate cognition, he would also forego the chance of developing a philosophy with the ability to integrate difference or generate systematic unity. Schelling takes on a different risk in pursuing the more comprehensive and global problem of the form of a unity that can integrate both the Same and the Other of form and content, and in doing so generate the determinate reality of the "thing presented." His approach to this problem is clear: only if a beginning of simultaneity is assumed can there be a system that produces knowledge with a specific content, since both form and content must

> mutually establish the other. In that way the ultimate axiom not only expresses the entire content and form of philosophy but also gives itself in this very fashion its own content and its own *specific* form simultaneously. (I/1, 94; emphasis mine)[54]

This reciprocal form of this unqualified unity captures the dynamic of the absolute causality that is the mark of the unconditioned self-positing of the I. This *Urform* must be capable of integrating form and content because the relation it articulates is not static, but dynamic. The *relatum* in disjunctive mutual causality is capable of a *transversal fluidity* that allows it to mediate two directional forces at once, thereby supporting a unity of difference. Due to the three-way interaction of terms and copula, the flow of determination is not unilateral as in subsumption, but is rather reciprocal as in coordination. Like Hahn's androgynous Deity, this *relatum* unites and mediates both polarities—a "*medium conjungendi* for 2 *Extrema*"—thereby constituting a threefold unity.[55] Only a transitive copula can achieve this, and only the form of mutual engendering can articulate the dynamic of such a natural whole. Kant himself speaks to the necessity of this transitive copula in his account of the relationship of parts and whole as articulated by the category of *community*: "since no one of them can be contained under any other, they are thought as coordinated with, not subordinated to, each other, and so as determining each other, not in one direction only, as in a series, but reciprocally" (B 112).

The process of reciprocal grounding generates two essential points. The first regards the form of the unconditioned unity: if these parts mutually engender one another, the *form*—but not content—of their relationship matches perfectly that of the unconditioned unity of A = A. This provides for the form of unconditioned unity that determines and unites every form of knowledge. Second, if the *relatum* in this form of the absolute is transitive, then it is capable of coordination and not merely subordination. Only then could there be a philosophy capable of generating knowledge with a specific content via a copula that mediates *transversal* difference. This transitive copula expresses the form of absolute positing, since it is this *relatum* that provides for the (circular) absolute causality of how the I can be *both cause and effect* of itself. Self-positing is not an act of regressive subsumption; it is instead "a higher act of the human *Geistes* itself" that somehow emerges out of a productive combining (*Verbindung* as band or δεσμὸν) of unity, whose reciprocal causality, while manifest in the self-organizing actions of all organic beings, is most clearly appreciated in our freedom as self-determining moral beings. Considered against this backdrop of the dynamics of organic form, we can perhaps more clearly grasp Schelling's attempt to expand and flesh out the consequences of this way of reasoning. To do this, however, we must follow him as he leaves the standpoint of production and descends to the reflective explication of this instantaneous act of self-positing. The goal of this "deduction" is to establish the three forms of axioms that together constitute his *Urform*. To present the simultaneity of what he is attempting to describe, however, we should consider this deduction as one might synchronized snapshots of one person taken from three different perspectives right as that person, say, jumps off the edge of a cliff. The first snapshot is of the perspective of the unconditioned self-positing of the absolute *Ich*. From this angle, Schelling derives the axiom of contradiction and the form of unconditionality, which can only be expressed in analytic form. The second snapshot captures the view of the *Nichtich*. From this perspective, he derives the axiom of sufficient reason and the form of conditionality expressed in synthetic form. The final picture focuses on the consciousness of the existing person. Here he combines the two previous axioms into an axiom of disjunction and derives a conditionality determined by unconditionality, a consciousness that can only be expressed in an unspecified "composite form" consisting of both the analytic and synthetic forms.[56] As Schelling reminds us only too infrequently, the generation of these forms is, from the standpoint of consciousness, *spontaneous* and indeed *ongoing*; or as he states at the end of his "deduction":

> As the original form of all thinking, Kant set up the analytic and the synthetic. Where do they come from and where is the principle on which they rest? .... This form is given by the [three] supreme axioms of all knowledge, simultaneous with and inseparable from the *content* of all knowledge. (I/1, 105)

Form of Being Unconditionally Posited: 'I = I'

According to its modality, the form of unconditional positing falls under the form of possibility (I/1, 108). This is due in part to the fact that it is the exemplar (*Vorbild*) of the categorical form of judgment. Although the ultimate condition of all reality, even the axiom "I=I," to the extent "that it is posited unconditionally, has only possibility" (I/1, 108).

It is the active realization of the categorical imperative that supplies the fact of the absolute causality of the self's freedom, and it is this freedom that provides his axiom with its unconditioned *content*. This absolute causality is the distinguishing criterion of the unconditioned, and expresses the *highest power* of the organism's capacity to be simultaneously the cause and effect of its actions. This unconditioned content supplied by the I's self-positing is simply the I. Since, however, the unconditioned content mutually engenders its form, the positing of the unconditioned I generates its unconditioned form of 'I = I.' This is the basis for the derivation of the axiom of contradiction and the form of the analytic proposition.

Form of the Conditioned: *NichtIch = Nicht Ich (Nichtich ≠ Ich)*

The form of the conditioned becomes the exemplar for the hypothetical syllogism. Consequently, Schelling transitions to the *Nichtich* via a hypothetical argument. The point of his tortuous argument here is to introduce *heterogeneity* into the derivation of consciousness. Schelling asserts that the conclusion of the argument produces the conditioned content of the "*Nichtich* as such" that serves as the "possible content of some axiom as such" (I/1, 98). To the extent that the *Nichtich* is opposed to the unconditioned form of the I, its form must be conditioned. Following his logic of *reciprocal causation*, however, this content generates a form that is only *indirectly* conditioned. Due to the self-positing form of its simultaneous and reciprocal emergence, the form of this axiom is directly or "immediately unconditioned" (ibid.). The form of conditionality checks and limits the form of unconditionality of the supreme axiom. Schelling describes this reciprocal causation parallel to the reciprocal production and limiting of Plato's τὸ πέρας and τὸ ἄπειρον: "If the I should posit only itself, then all possible forms would be exhausted by the form of the unconditioned, an unconditionality that would condition nothing" (ibid.). Regarding modality, the form of being conditionally posited falls under the form of actuality (*Wirklichkeit*) (I/1, 108). This form is the basis for the derivation of the axiom of sufficient reason and the form of the synthetic proposition.

Form of Conditionality Determined by Unconditionality = Consciousness

This form is the exemplar for the disjunctive syllogism and betrays a strong family resemblance to Reinhold's conception of consciousness that integrates the heterogeneous forms of the first two perspectives. At this point Schelling runs into the same conceptual difficulty Kant had when attempting to articulate how the third category in each class is *both* product and condition of the first two forms. But unlike Kant and Reinhold, Schelling considers this logical impossibility through the lens of organic form, putting to use Kant's category of *community*, in which the position of the third—*das Dritte* of *das Band*—always comes first in playing the role of a mediating unity.[57]

To posit a mere duality of opposites leads to a negative dialectic in which each term must cancel the other out: in Schelling's *ordo generativus* it is impossible for a duality to generate a genetic dialectic capable of creation, namely, self-organization. Such a dialectic can occur only under the unifying auspices of a coordinating third term, of a binding relation that brings together, but also sustains the interaction of opposing forces. Reciprocity inverted is mutual exclusivity. To the extent that the first two forms are posited, they are mutually exclusive, and thus incapable of sustaining their reciprocal engendering—unless mediated and united in a third common ground. From the standpoint of reflection and the first two forms, the third is posited only because these two forms are mutually exclusive (I/1, 99). From this perspective, the third emerges as nodal point or standing wave rising out of the interference patterns produced by the first two forms. But while this abstract presentation results in a relatively determinate picture, its subordination to the principle of contradiction renders it incapable of acknowledging and explaining the third term of relation. Moreover, this acceptance of a presupposed duality fails to convince when its systematic ramifications are pursued: the *complete* dependence of consciousness on the generative interplay of form and content completely destroys the value of an autonomous moral agent, and therewith, freedom. If the third (empirical consciousness) is simply the result of the interaction of the two engaged in reciprocal generation, and depends on that generative force to endure, then that third is confined to absolute dependence (Spinoza). While this arrangement satisfies our desire for a linear order, it fails to account for the fundamental stochastic dimension of our reality. In a clear reference to the category of *community*, from the perspective of the unifying relation, the *relatum* itself is the condition of the first two forms of productive interaction:

> There is a third element (*ein Drittes*) which, as the condition of the relation between two things that mutually exclude each other, relates to the conditions of this relation as the entirety of conditions [relate] to individual conditions. (I/1, 99)

The three forms relate as parts to whole in an organism: the whole of the third is the condition of the relation of the parts, which in turn are the conditions of one another, and likewise of the whole. There is an asymmetry in the exchange of conditioning exerted in this triad. Conceptualized as an inverted cone, with *das Dritte qua* whole as center point on which it rests, the conditioning exchanged vertically between the whole and the subset of *Ich* and *Nichtich* is qualitatively different from the horizontal conditioning exchanged between the mutually exclusive *Ich* and *Nichtich*. That is, the entire form of consciousness must *simultaneously bind (vertically) and separate* (horizontally) the reciprocal causation of the *Ich* and the *Nichtich*—an inexponible feat Schelling can only account for through the disjunctive logic of organic form.

He captures this two-phased modulation in his definition of the modality of this form of consciousness as "actuality determined by possibility, which is necessity" (I/1, 109).[58] This necessity of consciousness results from the coercion of finite existence; it is the limiting basis of our fundamental convictions of existence (immanent preestablished harmony), and the limiting source of the a priori parameters of reflective thought. These natural limits of our empirical lives provides the necessity Schelling promised at the beginning of the *Form Essay*, in that they provide "a principle (*Princip*) that would not only furnish an *Urform* as the root of all particular forms, but would also give the reason for its *necessary connection* with the particular forms that depended on it" (I/1, 87; emphasis mine). The necessary connection at play here is of course that of living existence itself. Following Plato's anthropology of mind dependent on an ensouled body, since it is an embodied living conscious I, it is *unconditioned in content*, and thus capable of positing itself, thereby completing the entire cycle of the unity Schelling presents in linear fashion. We end where we began in a simultaneous snapshot of the organic form of Schelling's I.

Disjunctive Identity

What is this new composite form of proposition? In this admitted "sketch (*Verzeichnung*)" of a proposed theory, Schelling offers us no clear answer (I/1, 89). Based on his position that this *Urform* arises simultaneously, there is only one form of reasoning we have discussed that could articulate this spontaneous generation: that of disjunctive *community and reciprocal causality*. This, however, requires that we harmonize this organic form with the obvious identity expressed through the form 'I = I'. Schelling attempts to address this problem in his discussion of the modality of the forms. The account we provided earlier is analytic: we took the inexponible whole of the unity of self and consciousness and reduced it to a linear series. What we must now do is attempt to place these components back into their respective "positions" as a processive unity.

As we have just seen, the content of the I of consciousness is unconditioned. This explains how and why Schelling can claim that the axiom 'I = I' is an identity only as regards content, not form (I/1, 106).[59] Because this content is unconditioned, it can only enjoy a modality of possibility. As a possible unconditioned, it can only be expressed through a categorical judgment in which the subject and predicate *are to* (should) constitute their content (*Logik*, §24; Ak IX, 105). What distinguishes this *Urform* 'I = I' from every other proposition is that "it is not conditioned by a superior proposition but rather through itself" (I/1, 109). This is due to its content, not its form. Schelling derives two points from this. Because it conditions itself this proposition also stands under the modality of *actuality*, and because it is not conditioned by a higher proposition it also stands under the modality of *necessity*. Schelling advances this line of reasoning to justify his expansion of Kant's limited definition of analytic propositions as simply identical propositions: "It is therefore clear that identical propositions express merely a particular form that stands under the general form of analytic propositions" (ibid.). From this it follows that although every identical proposition must be categorical, not every categorical proposition must have the form of identity (ibid.).With this, Schelling argues he has created the opening for a new form of proposition that, although its form looks like conventional logic's statement of identity, it is not. It is rather the "exterior form" of being unconditionally self-positing, "which is necessarily induced by its content" of the unconditioned (I/1, 109, n. 2). The emphasis is on the "exterior form" of self-positing, an exterior form that is the disjunction of the *Urform*, and as such is a form external to the apparent form of identity. It is this exterior form that supplies the most general genus of form from which the forms of analytic and synthetic propositions are derived. The form of identity is conditioned by the *Urform*. "One can therefore recognize in the form of identity only that form as the *Urform*, which in the form of identity is no longer conditioned"—that is, the exterior form of disjunction (I/1, 109). This is possible only by recognizing the content of the *Urform* as unconditioned. Once this is recognized, it becomes impossible for the form of identity to be the *Urform*, if it is a *conditioned* identity, since the *Urform* must instead be the form of the unconditioned self-positing of the I itself. This, according to Schelling, explains the "paradox" that only as a categorical proposition—a characteristic derived from the unconditioned content, and thus standing under the modality of possibility—can this proposition be flexible enough to be "the principle of all content and of all form of a science" (ibid.). The *principle* of all content and all forms of knowledge is thus the categorical proposition of freedom expressed in the unconditioned content of 'I = I'. The *content* of this categorical proposition supplies the *Urform* with its unconditioned *content* that induces the form of the *Urform*, that is, unconditioned self-positing. This unconditioned form, however, can only be expressed through the composite form of proposition that combines both the analytic and synthetic forms of proposition. By all indications the form of this proposition is that of a disjunctive form of judgment. Since this logical form is consistently associated with the *Urform*, and since only this form can integrate and coordinate an opposition of forms, the form of the *Urform* must be that of a disjunctive unity.[60] Seen through the genetic lens of his analysis of organism, the proposition 'I = I' is the formulaic expression of how *one unity can simultaneously be both cause and effect of itself*. Repulsed by Kant's disembodied idea of the human self, Schelling posits an identity whose content is unconditioned, but whose form is fluid enough to account for the fact of our conditioned and thus alienated consciousness. On the other hand, however, it is also powerful enough to articulate the absolute causality of freedom that offers the ideal of completeness, namely, of a generative unity. Its content is unconditioned identity, but its form is that of estranged (living) disjunction. This formal characteristic of the *Urform* demands that Schelling employ the progressive method of the dynamic categories and begin his system of philosophy with *das Ganze* of an unconditioned first magnitude. But this first magnitude is not the whole of the cosmos. It is instead the unmediated fact of living "empirical existence" whose absolute necessity *coerces* us to acknowledge it. Recall his analysis of Plato's understanding of soul and mind: they can only exist together in a three-way relationship of reciprocal grounding, which we can understand only if we *first* posit the idea of the whole *qua* life. Mind is dependent on the whole, that is, life. Hence, at this unconscious, limbic level, that which is beyond the mind coerces us to acknowledge it. The first magnitude in this series is not the mind, but the *entirety* that is the living organism. It is the entirety that forces us (*es wird uns dazu gezwungen*) to acknowledge it as the condition for our ability to even begin our discursive activities. It is the immanent transcendental condition of all thought. As Schelling describes this *absolute causality of Freedom* in 1796:

§8
If I should master the world of phenomena and legislate nature according to moral laws, then the causality of freedom must *reveal*[*61] itself through physical causality. Now *freedom* as such can only announce itself through original autonomy. Thus this physical causality must—even if it is heteronomous according to the object, i.e., is only determinable through laws of nature, it must nonetheless according to its principle, i.e., be attainable through no law of nature. This freedom must unite autonomy and heteronomy.

§9
This causality is *life*. Life is autonomy in phenomena; it is the schema of freedom, insofar as it reveals itself in nature. I become therefore necessarily a *living* being (*Ich* werde daher notwendig *lebendiges* Wesen). (I/1, 248)[62]

The use of the passive voice here is precisely the point. The "absolute natural necessity" Schelling begins with is not the *Tatsache* of freedom, but the fact of his "existence" as a living natural *being*, which is therefore the schema of freedom (A 418/B 446). 'I = I' stands under the modality of an iteration of the necessity of living consciousness. It is only because of the necessity of the unity imposed on our consciousness that Schelling's *Urform* demonstrates the necessary connection between its unity and every other form of individual knowing: beginning with the first magnitude of the idea of the whole is equivalent to beginning with the ἕν of Plato's unity *qua Einheit*. Its living necessity binds us to a self-organizing and self-regulating order (cosmos of the ζῷα νοητά) that imposes the idea of unity. The condition for our being compelled to think this idea of unity is not the *result* of thinking, but rather the cause of this thought is transcendent to the circle of reflection.[63] He makes this decisive point succinctly in 1797 through a reference to Aristotle: "λόγου ἀρχὴ οὐ λόγος, ἀλλά τι κρεῖττον (The starting point of reason is not reason, but something stronger than reason)."[64] Thinking is not the cause of thinking, rather the cause of thinking is something much stronger than mere thought, that is, the intentionality of a living, conscious being. Following Plato, the first idea that imposes itself is that of unity, the idea of the ἕν, that is the condition *qua* first magnitude for reflective thought. It is the unity within which reflection occurs and the common ground presupposed by this modality of thinking. Finally, it is this necessary imposition of the idea of unity that determines Schelling's understanding of what he will later call an immanent, preestablished harmony. Just as Plato argued before him, if we are not the source of the life that imposes its unifying force of self-organization, then the fact that we are a living unity is dependent on the totality of conditions that sustain us, a totality that we are compelled to consider as a whole.[65]

This necessary dependence of the living self on nature is, however, only one leg of the triad that is Schelling's generative *Urform*. To remain in this modality of necessity is to ignore his explication of this constraint as the result of the interaction of possibility and actuality. As he will ask in his next essay, *On the I*, do we consider ourselves free in this living consciousness? Since this modality of necessity is the result of the interaction of possibility and actuality, Schelling can provide the honest but frustrating answer: yes and no. While the actuality of the external world is captured through the hypothetical propositions employed by the natural sciences, the possibility of the unconditioned, the possibility of freedom and autonomy realized is, as we have seen, captured by the categorical proposition employed in the historical world of humanity. All three of these modalities of Schelling's *Urform* constitute a generative nexus of ideas that he will use throughout the course of his career to develop his system. Emerging from this *ordo generativus* his system betrays the elements of both systematic unity and organic development. Contrary to a static aggregate of principles and signs, Schelling's system evolves as it develops. The changes are sometimes seemingly abrupt, but only if we ignore the immanent perspective we have been exploring. The proposition 'I = I' is a disjunctive identity in which the copula becomes transitive and binding, as it mediates the *reciprocal* modulation of subject and predicate. Echoing Oetinger's description of the absolute before creation as "indifferent,"[66] Schelling cryptically alludes to his *Urform* as expressing "absolute reason" in the first pages of his *Presentation of My System of Philosophy*: "One attains to it through the reflection on that which is posited in philosophy between subject and object, and which clearly must be something that relates indifferently to both" (I/4, 114). Attempting to articulate the moment before creation, Schelling makes use of the triadic form of immanent generation. As the organic form—the DNA of his system—this eternal relational *Urform* is its "center point of gravity" around which all irregular orbits and physiognomic transformations occur. It is the focal form that guides every iteration of Schelling's philo-sophical evolution. As perhaps his most astute reader, Charles Sanders Peirce, realized, if philosophy is to be truly organic, it can do its work not by dichotomy, but by trichotomy:

> Among the many principles of Logic that find their application in Philosophy, I can here only mention one. Three conceptions are perpetually turning up at every point in every theory of logic, and in the most rounded systems they occur in connection with one another. They are conceptions so very broad and consequently indefinite that they are hard to seize and may be easily overlooked. I call them the conceptions of First, Second, Third. First is the conception of being or existing independently of anything else. Second is the conception of being relative to, the conception of reaction with, something else. Third is the conception of mediation, whereby a first and second are brought into relation.[67]

Following the genetic logic Schelling extracts from Plato, this third would correspond to the τò κοινòν which alone deals with 'empirical existence.' The first and the second, like the τò πέρας and τò ἄπειρον, are separate "only in the *Vorstellungsvermögen*" (*TK*, 70). But "if the talk is about *empirical* existence, then" firstness and secondness "are present only in connection with each other," mediated through the category of *community and reciprocal causation* (ibid.). By integrating all three of these ideas Schelling's organic form of philosophy both reveals its historical lineage and indicates its generative power to unify the oppositional dualities of our thinking. In the concluding chapter, we will see how this organic form actually *is* the DNA of Schelling's philosophical world, as it informs and guides the first iteration of his philosophy.

6

Freedom and the Construction of Philosophy

With this acknowledgment of the eternal within all things the philosopher sublates the last estrangement (*Entzweiung*) between the phenomenal world and the things in themselves. He recognizes that there are not two worlds, but rather one true world, which is not beyond or above the phenomenal, but is rather right here in this one. (I/6, 274)

The Dynamic Process: Producing the System of Identity

We have argued that the *Form Essay* presents Schelling's synthesis of Plato's triad of divine causes and Kant's dynamic categories, articulated through Fichte's formula 'I=I', understood as a statement of disjunctive identity. The goal of this strategy is to advance an organic form of unity that will overcome the debilitating dualities established by the regressive methodologies of reflective analysis. Although he too makes use of the regressive method, he does so only after having established the parameters of system via the employment of the progressive method. Schelling achieves this integration of the regressive and progressive methods through his inversion of Kant's categories, so that the relational class precedes the mathematical, and within the relational class, the category of *community* precedes those of causality and substance. Working within Kant's own transformed structures, the world of exponible concepts becomes nature viewed as an inexponible dynamic whole.

This inversion supplies Schelling with the organic form and conceptual tools required to construct a system whose inner dynamic is animated by the very nature he seeks to account for. The challenge is to develop a system that can integrate and harness the positive content of sensuous nature, thereby expanding its explanatory power and scope, while strengthening its capacity to support the moral development of humanity. He claims that the most comprehensive and productive model for philosophy is organic, where this term signifies, in its broadest possible meaning, the positive capacity for self-organization. The framework proposition of his philosophy is synthesized by the category of *community and reciprocal causation*: to generate a comprehensive explanation of natural phenomena we must begin from the necessary idea of the whole, from the comprehension of the absolute magnitude of an unconditional unity, in order to guarantee systematic coherency and development. As he writes in 1799:

> there is no true system that would not at the same time be an organic entirety. For if in every organic entirety everything is reciprocally supported and sustained, then this organization as an entirety must precede its parts; the entirety cannot emerge from its parts, but rather the parts must emerge from the entirety. Thus it is not we who know nature [a priori], but rather nature *is* a priori, i.e., every individual member within it is determined from the beginning through the entirety, or through the idea of nature in general. But [if] nature is a priori, then it must also be possible to know it as something that is a priori, and this really is the meaning of our position. (I/1, 279)

The epistemological possibilities of this inversion are comprehensive. There comes a point at which the mechanistic analysis of a subject no longer promises an expansion of knowledge. In many cases, the exclusive allegiance to one method proves counterproductive. Contrary to his reputation as the German Idealist whose sole service is that of a bridge between Fichte's Subjective and Hegel's Absolute Idealism, Schelling offers an epistemological structure grounded in the facticity of organic life and actual existence that, if fully understood, lends little support to this "textbook" reputation. Parallel to the argument Plato advances in the *Philebus*, Schelling accepts the restrictions of existence as his paradigm of necessity. Following the trajectory of his inversion of the categories, Schelling inverts Kant's understanding of necessity: whereas for Kant rational certainty exerts a stronger necessity over the knowing mind than empirical certainty, for Schelling it is the involuntary dimension of our embodied existence that determines the ideal of certitude. Our consciousness is not an otherworldly Gnostic power momentarily trapped in this alien organic body; rather our consciousness is itself the dependent product of our embodied nature; a dependent and restricted nature that informs our understanding of certitude. A priori and a posteriori are not related to *before* or *after* experience, but rather derive from necessary or not necessary in experience, since "originally we know nothing at all other than through experience and by means of experience, and only to this extent does all our knowledge consist of empirical propositions" (I/1, 278).

This inverted path of modernity's epistemological trajectory has even wider system ramifications. The subsumptive logic of a Cartesian cogito, in which the subject's disembodied reason dictates laws to nature, is replaced by an organic reason through which "nature is her own law giver" (I/1, 96). Calling upon our capacity for *conscientia* and *Mitwissenschaft*, the epistemological shift required to comprehend the whole ruptures the linear and exponible framework of reflective consciousness. In Kant's own words, such a comprehension generates "a retrogression and removes the time-condition" (*KU*, 107), thereby removing the sequential condition of reflection. Schelling exploits Kant's momentary rupture of discursivity to interject a third element (*das Dritte*) into the interplay of reflection, namely, the productive imagination. An unruly and second-class citizen of Kant's analytic and thoroughly linear *Gemüt*, the imagination and its power to build contraries into one (*Einbildung*) becomes not only the binding and generative engine of Schelling's epistemological model, but is more precisely the means whereby the autoepistemic structures of nature manifest themselves in consciousness.

Within such a monistic dualism, there can be no categorical difference between nature and mind. Instead, Schelling constructs a continuum of nature filled out by a plurality of reciprocally interacting forces that stretches from the initial conditions of creation's absolute involution to the ever more complex phenomena of nature, eventually attaining to organic life and its most complex manifestation, human consciousness. The process culminates in the creative activities of "reason," which Schelling construes as "nothing else but imagination in the service of freedom," as it produces the ideas and ideals of the moral law that extend beyond the limits of the present into the domain of the future, namely, the moral law (I/3, 559). Throughout this construction he is guided by the form of identity, but an organic conception of identity, fluid enough to serve as the mediating copula capable of coordinating opposing forces. This is a relational bond that unites, and in uniting is the whole within which difference occurs. As we have seen, Schelling justifies this dynamic account of nature through an appeal to Kant's distinction between *Weltbegriff* and *Naturbegriff*, and the respective methodologies whereby they synthesize the absolute:

Since the ultimate cause of natural phenomena is itself not a phenomenon, one must renounce the ability to realize this, or one must simply
posit it in nature. However, what we put into nature has nothing other
than the value of a presupposition (hypothesis), and the science that is
thereby grounded must also be as hypothetical as the principle itself.
This could be avoided in only one way, namely if that presupposition
itself were as non-arbitrary and necessary as nature itself. Accepting
what must be accepted, for example, that the concept (*Inbegriff*) of
phenomena is not just a world, but is rather nature, i.e., that this
entirety is not simply a product, but is rather simultaneously productive, it then follows that in this entirety it can never come to the
absolute identity, because this would usher in an absolute transformation of nature, in so far as it is productive, into nature as a product, i.e.,
an absolute stillness; that oscillation of nature between productivity
and product must appear therefore as a universal duplicity of principles
through which nature is sustained in incessant activity, and hindered
from ever exhausting itself into its product. The universal duality as
principle of all explanations of nature is therefore just as necessary as
the concept of nature itself. (I/3, 277)

Consistent with the disjunctive logic of community, the necessary concept
of nature as a dynamic whole requires an original duality of forces to
account for both the products and productivity of nature. To negotiate
this triad of forces, Schelling makes use of the strategy employed in the
Form Essay: construe identity as the unconditional unity of the whole,
which can only be a whole if it simultaneously and incessantly engenders
the play of the reciprocal forces of productive nature. The metaphorics
of the sphere are implicit in this account of the initial conditions of the
dynamic process. Identity is thus to be conceived as the absolute unity of
an infinite sphere which, somehow, is capable of satisfying its transitive
function as the common parameter that sustains and coordinates the
polarity of forces that animate that sphere.

Consequently, to pursue and demonstrate conclusively that this
relational unity of forms is the axis around which Schelling's thinking
revolves, we must consider how it manifests itself in the development
of his philosophy. Our first task is to review his account of how such a
"center of gravity" functions in the system of human knowing:

One must have found Leibniz's "perspectival center of gravity" from
which the chaos of the different opinions, which from every other
standpoint appear totally confused, shows consistency and agreement.

In order to find what Leibniz found,—that which even in the most contradictory system is actually philosophical [and] also true,—one must keep in mind the idea (*Idee*) of a universal system that provides context and necessity to all individual systems,—as opposed as they may be,—in the system of human knowing (*Wissens*). Such a comprehensive system can first fulfill the obligation of uniting all the conflicting interests of all other [systems], to prove that as much as they appear to contradict the common understanding, none of them has actually demanded something meaningless, so that for every possible question in philosophy there is a universal answer possible. For it is manifest that reason can propose no question that would not already be answered within it.—So just as in the seed nothing emerges that was not already united within it, likewise in philosophy nothing can come to be (through analysis) that was not already present (in the original synthesis) in the human spirit itself. For this very reason a common (*gemeinschaftlicher*) ruling spirit permeates all individual systems earning this name; every individual system is possible only through deviation from the universal archetype (*Urbild*), to which all taken together more or less approach. This universal system is however not a chain which runs upwards, where it hangs onward into infinity link-by-link, but rather an organization, in which every individual member is in relation to every other [member] reciprocally cause and effect, means and ends. Thus too is all progress in philosophy only progress through development; every individual system which earns this name can be viewed as a seed which slowly and gradually, but inexorably and in every direction advances itself in multifarious development. Who has once found such a center of gravity for the history of philosophy is alone capable to describe it truly and according to the worth of the human spirit. (I/1, 457)

The system of human knowing envisioned by Schelling is an organism of knowledge that, as if through our genes, has revealed its generative power from Plato onwards. The shared (*gemeinschaftlicher*) spirit of this system, its *Urbilder*, are all themes we have seen Schelling use in his attempt to construct an organic form of unity. The contrast between the regressive and progressive methods are even present in his account of the sequential step-by-step approach of inferring one's way to the infinite versus that of the progressive method of dynamic nature, where we must first presuppose the whole or unity of this self-organizing system, in order to even frame our investigation. This is a necessary step if our primary objective is to construct a philosophical system that will lay bare the genetic history of spirit's development. As he phrased the matter in 1797:

> Philosophy, accordingly, is nothing other than a *natural history of our Geist*. From now on all dogmatism is overturned from its foundations. We consider the system of our ideas, not in its *being*, but in its *becoming*. Philosophy becomes *genetic*; that is, it allows the whole necessary series of our ideas to arise and take its course, as it were, before our eyes. From now on there is no longer any separation between experience and speculation. (I/1, 23)[1]

The answer to overcoming the divide between experience and speculation lies in a radically different way of conceiving the logic of causal relation. Against the universal employment of a mechanistic model of external causality, Schelling introduces an alternative, and indeed, more original conception of an organic model of reciprocal causality.

In arguing this we are proposing an interpretation of Schelling's *Urform* of 'I = I' that is counterintuitive, to say the least. To review, the reading I am advancing posits that the content of this original form is expressed through an unconditional categorical proposition of identity, standing under the modality of possibility. Its form, however, we read as *disjunctive*. This reading is the only way to impose some degree of consistency on Schelling's insistence that this original form articulates three forms and axioms simultaneously. In the face of the requirement that this form be capable of articulating the triadic, reciprocal causation of the category of *community*, the logical form of the disjunctive proposition seems to be the only alternative to what would otherwise be the needless addition of other logical forms to an already complex arrangement.

Our first step in confirming this thesis is to examine his use of the disjunctive syllogism, which, as we have seen, was the form of judgment Kant fully introduced only in the B version of his first *Critique*, and in which Schelling saw the logical structure of an organic form of unity. This form of judgment supplies the oppositional dynamic that animates his entire system of thinking on nature, freedom, and art. What he must account for in all three of these realms is a differentiating unity, based not on subordination but on coordination, not on subsumption but on disjunction. The only pattern of thought that presents itself as a candidate to account for such a unity is found in the third *Table of Judgments*, in the relation of disjunctive judgment.

To confirm our reading we turn now to the only remaining text that provides an account of Schelling's transcendental logic, his posthumously published *System of All Philosophy and of the Philosophy of Nature in Particular* (1804), commonly referred to as his *Würzburger Lectures*. Pursuing our subsidiary thesis that Schelling's methodology is more organic and complex than the standard narrative appreciates, we are looking for evidence that will confirm that his so-called Identity System should be read as a transcendental schematic of what is actually his system of freedom.[2]

We begin by noting that Schelling clearly states what his transcendental logic *is*. It is the *construction* of "the entire system of universal knowledge" from the "system of necessity determined by possibility and actuality (*Wirklichkeit*)" (I/6, 514). Using the same three categories of modality employed in the *Form Essay* a decade earlier, Schelling here designates a transcendental logic which, through its very construction, shows how the ideal system of knowing (possibility) arises *simultaneously* through and with the real system of being (necessity). By means of this construction, this logic provides not only an account of the identity of thinking and being, but also provides an account of *why* our forms of thinking and knowing are the way they are. Because it does not merely state *what* logic is, but attempts to integrate and reunite logical structure and being, Schelling maintains that his transcendental logic is a science of reason (*Vernunftswissenschaft*) in the same sense that the "Greeks before Aristotle" understood their science of logic to be (I/6, 529). That is, logic is not a man-made construction whose isomorphic relation to nature is mere coincidence, but rather our way of thinking does, in this regard, actually manifest the structure of nature.

He makes equally clear what this logic is *not*. It is not the system of universal knowledge as it is usually derived by means of sheer abstraction. For what is so derived can only be "a mere reflexive totality (*eine bloße Reflexions = Totalität*)" that is "merely a philosophy of common knowledge" and "common understanding (*gemeine Verstand*),"—a mechanical form of thought he sees at work in Kant's system (I/6, 515). Characteristic of modernity's division and separation of form from experience, a logic such as Kant's can aspire to be nothing more than a *reflective* totality, since it is purely conceptual, that is, purely formal and ideal, devoid of any positive content. Because it abstracts from experience it excludes the material and intuitive immediacy of life. This type of system can only be a "sheer abstraction of the habitual use of reason," a logic that merely formalizes the rules of the common understanding, and thereby fails to provide an account for *why* these rules are formalized in this way (I/6, 525).

To provide what Kant failed to, Schelling posits the disjunctive form of logical relation as the highest principle of his logic: "The disjunctive syllogism presents the highest totality so to speak, divided, in that it contains all the conditions required to determine its object" (I/6, 526). He also designates the disjunctive as the logical form of the "intuition of the imagination (*Einbildungskraft*)," which he sets as equivalent to Kant's aesthetic judgment (I/6, 500). The determinative role disjunctive judgment plays in Schelling's logic is demonstrated in his construction of the syllogism. Following the same order of the *Form Essay*, the syllogism incorporates the three concepts of possibility, reality, and necessity, and is the "highest totality" through which *reflective knowing* expresses the necessity determined by possibility and reality (the necessity of consciousness). The major premise is the articulation of reflection and it expresses a mere possibility in the form of a categorical judgment; for example: "everything physical is susceptible to decomposition." The minor premise is one of subsumption and it posits a reality in the form of a hypothetical judgment: "the atom is something physical." The conclusion is the reflection determined by the subsumption—a possibility determined by a reality—and must therefore be a necessity that can only be expressed through a disjunctive judgment that establishes the identity of difference in the first two premises: "the atom is therefore susceptible to decomposition" (I/6, 525).

Through the use of the disjunctive judgment as its conclusion, Schelling claims that this construction of the syllogism can articulate the absolute identity of the difference of its constituent terms. Consequently, this "syllogism is for the *potenz* of reflection the highest expression of the form of the Absolute" (I/6, 526). The absolute identity of the two different terms is expressed through the "*Terminus medius, major* and *minor*." In the following syllogism, Schelling finds that "B is the absolute identity of A and C," whereas A and C are yet both different from B:

A = B	(Reflexion)	[categorical]	[possibility]
B = C	(Subsumption)	[hypothetical]	[reality]
A = C	(*Vernunft*)	[disjunctive]	[necessity]

The mediating flexibility of the disjunctive relation enables Schelling to conceive of how two different terms can be judged as being identical to a third, and conversely, how that third can be judged to be identical to two terms which, when considered among themselves, are different.

Consequently, in the concluding proposition of this syllogism, the terms A and C, which in relation to B are one (*Eines*), are nonetheless "*disjungirt*," and only through the disjunctive relation are they posited as equal. This example illustrates two complementary points central to our reading of Schelling's idea of identity. The first is his use of the term *Eines* to describe a relationship of identity, thereby suggesting that in form, the relationship of identity can be read as articulating a unity. But more importantly, this example clearly shows that Schelling understands the relationship of identity as a disjunctive relation, which, as we have seen, is precisely the logical form Kant uses to parse the dynamic of organic life. Only the relational category of *community and reciprocal causation* can articulate the generative opposition of the disjunctive unity Schelling sees in the relationship of identity. Only organic form can parse the unity of difference that animates the relationship of identity.

In these lectures we also come across a brief analysis of the *Urform* we have been pursuing, in which Schelling makes use of Plato's terms, and comments on the order in which they are perceived relative to one's standpoint. In his derivation of the concepts of necessity, he claims that

> In this class there fall the concepts of the unlimited (ἄπειρον), the limit (πέρας) and *das Dritten* (which, however, considered *absolutely*, is the first). (I/6, 521)

He adds that this inversion of the order of perception is such that what is perceived from the standpoint of reflection in the previous scenario is actually the end result, namely, the synthesis of the unlimited and the limited. From the standpoint of the absolute (of the unconditioned whole, of production), the third, however, appears first in the unmediated experience of what always goes before thinking, the absolute magnitude of unity, wherein the opposition between the possible and actual is seen as a necessary identity. Kant could not account for this, since he never raised himself above the standpoint of the reflexive consciousness (I/6, 523). Schelling, on the other hand, if our grasp of his reading of Kant is correct, finds the conceptual tools to delineate the standpoint of the absolute in the intuitive comprehending of the sublime that Kant himself claims leads to the removal of the time series.[3]

The removal of the time series is a simultaneity the experience of which touches on the eternal—a point of contact Schelling alludes to in his *Bruno Dialogue* of 1802. In this literary presentation of his system, he discusses the informing of eternity into the infinite and the finite. The infinite form of logical judgment is the categorical, whereas the finite form is that of the hypothetical. But due to its integration of difference in a moment outside time, "the form which participates most with the eternal" is that "of the disjunctive" (I/4, 297). Considered again in the form of a syllogism, the major premise stands always in an infinite or categorical relation to the minor premise, thereby limiting the minor premise, with the result that the minor premise must be finite and hypothetical. The conclusion is then of necessity the disjunctive, which "unites within itself the former as well as the latter" as an expression of eternity (I/4, 297).

Of systematic importance is Schelling's conception of how this third form of disjunction and reciprocity always relates to its constitutive forms. Contrary to Kant, Schelling holds that the third member of such a triad does not, outside the inverted world of reflexive consciousness, *emerge* from the synthesis of the preceding members. Rather, just as he wrote in the *Timaeus Commentary*, it is the third member that is always the condition of possibility of the preceding two. This inverted order reflects Schelling's unwillingness to accept Kant's rather dogmatic proclamation that the third member of each class of category magically emerges—"through a special Actus of the understanding"—from the "combination of the second with the first." Perhaps reflecting his "dogmatic use of pure reason," Kant simply makes these declarative summations, while failing to provide reasons for *why* or *how* these operations occur. As Schelling points out:

> Yet we cannot understand what it is that *constrains* the human spirit at all to *construct from opposites* everything whereof it has an intuition and cognition, unless we consider the *primordial dualism* in the human spirit that Kant elaborated in his practical philosophy, but merely *presupposed* everywhere in his theoretical [philosophy]. (I/1, 408)

The *primordial dualism* Schelling refers to is none other than the same dualism we have seen him draw from Plato's cosmogony, a dualism that provides not only for the "possibility of matter and a world construct in general," but also for "the entire mechanism and organism of nature" itself (I/2, 74). However, as organic nature illustrates, the whole must ultimately precede its parts; consequently, only the third category of reciprocity can therefore account for the synthesis of the first two terms, which from the standpoint of reflection should in turn create the third.

Accordingly, Schelling's conception of the nature of logic and reason betrays the same structural imprint of the organic form we are pursuing. In one of the subsidiary triadic cycles of concepts, derived from the initial triad of possibility, reality, and necessity, Schelling posits the concept as "the mere schema of possibility or of reflexion," and characterizes *Reason* as an *"organism"* (I/1, 524). He writes that "[t]he entire sphere of concepts stands under the mere schema of possibility or of reflexion, although within this sphere the entire *organism of reason* again expresses itself as determined through possibility, reality and necessity" (I/1, 524, emphasis mine). Schelling of course correlates this "organic reason" with the disjunctive form of judgment, since it is this logical form that alone proves capable of accounting for the manner in which parts and whole relate both systematically and in organic nature.

The fact of nature's self-organization allows Schelling to apply this logical schema of reciprocity to account for what he considers the symbiotic relation between form and content evident in organic life. The fact that organic life best illustrates the concrete interconnectedness of these abstract categories opens a promising line of attack on Kant's systematic separation of form and content:

> Thus, organization constructs itself only out of organization. In the organic product, for this very reason, form and matter are inseparable; this particular matter could only arise and come to be along with this particular form, and *vice versa*. Every organization is therefore a *whole*; its *unity lies in itself*; it does not depend on our choice if we think of it as one or many. Cause and effect is something evanescent, transitory, mere *appearance* (in the usual sense of the word). The organism, however, is not mere appearance, but is *itself* object, and indeed an object subsisting through itself, in itself whole and indivisible, and because in it the form is inseparable from the matter, the *origin* of an organism, as such, can no more be explained mechanically than the origin of matter itself. (I/3, 24)

The regressive method of analysis that views nature as an aggregate sum total of appearances is incapable of accounting for the immediacy—and simultaneity—of the union of cause and effect in an organism. Schelling sees in this a model for how to articulate a different relationship of the subject to the world of nature.

Beginning from the absolute dynamic whole of nature, the first step he undertakes is to integrate the same and the other of nature and *Geist* by elevating nature to the status of unconscious *Geist*. The second step roots human nature in organic nature: mind is dependent on body for its functioning. If, for the sake of argument, we accept these positions, we easily see an answer to Kant's difficulty of where 'pure reason' gets the idea of nature's purposiveness (*Zweckmäßigkeit*). Clearly, the directional force of purpose does not arise in the reversible time sequence of our human 'pure reason', but is rather a constitutive drive and thus *irreversible* drive of nature itself, as seen in the capacity for self-organization witnessed in the evolutionary process of nature itself. In his treatment of Fichte's *Wissenschaftslehre*, Schelling makes this point when he argues that

> The system of the world is a type of organisation that has formed itself from a common center. Even the powers of chemical matter are beyond the borders of the merely mechanical. . . . the steady and continuous course of nature towards organisation clearly betrays enough of an active drive, which, . . . from moss, in which there is hardly a trace of organisation visible onwards to the most noble form, is controlled by this one and the same drive, which works according to one and the same ideal of purposiveness, . . . to express one and the same archetype (*Urbild*), *the pure form of our Geist*. (I/1, 386)

This is an archetype that is none other than the organic form we have been considering, which in its "most noble form"—the pure form of our spirit—is freedom. The possibility for an organism to be simultaneously its own cause and effect is the schema, the model for spirit's highest act of this form of causation, the free self-determination of self-conscious spirit. This continuity of organic form throughout nature's system of self-organization gives the lie to the inherent purposiveness of this world system. And indeed, this organic form of life and freedom reaches beyond humanity to the absolute itself. From the standpoint of *absolute knowing*, the Absolute as Identity can only be described as an organism:

> §190
> The organism is the immediate image (*Abbild*) of absolute substance, or Nature, considered as such. For both gravity and light are the equally eternal and necessary attributes of the absolute substance. But precisely these two attributes are also in the organism as one and the same, or they are subordinated as attributes to a *common* organism. . . . The organism therefore is in species also the most perfect expression of that universal relation of the world of appearance to the absolute, from whose power this world of appearances is the *contrafigura* (*Gegenbild*)

or organ. The organism *in specie*, because it is in itself a totality, an *Allheit*, is precisely the most immediate *contrafigura* and organ of the absolute Identity. (I/6, 376)

The Self *Versetzt*: Freedom as the Postulate of Philosophy

It "is a fundamental mistake to attempt a theoretical grounding of theoretical philosophy" (I/1, 399). With these words, Schelling accuses Kant of committing a grave error when he attempts to ground his theory of pure reason in pure reason. What one produces through such an attempt can only be circular, since the principles of one's explanation must be of a different nature than what one is attempting to explain.[4] This problem becomes even more acute when one attempts to ground a *system*: "*System* we call only such a whole as *supports itself*, something that is contained within itself and presupposes no external ground for its movements and its coherence" (I/1, 400). Schelling bypasses the entire metaphorics of grounding and foundation, since these foundational terms presuppose a philosophical framework determined by a mechanistic "*ordo mathematicus*" in which our world is ultimately reducible to matter. Schelling rejects this type of philosophical frame for many reasons, chief of which is its inability to explain the self-organizing dynamic of nature's evolution, particularly as this dynamic manifests itself in human freedom. As we have seen, Schelling's understanding of the ultimate reality of our world has more in common with string theory than scientific materialism. If one's "physical" universe is ultimately the manifestation of the interaction of oppositional forces, the metaphorics of grounding will always fall flat. That is, if, like Schelling, one interprets material substance as the emergent "standing waves" of a gravitational field, then the promise of "foundations"—and a correspondence theory of truth—becomes irrelevant.

> Anyone who has followed us attentively thus far will perceive for himself that the beginning and end of this philosophy is *freedom*, the absolute indemonstrable, authenticated only through itself.—That which in all other systems threatens the downfall of freedom is here derived from freedom itself.—In our system being is merely *freedom suspended*. In a system that treats being as primary and supreme, not only must knowledge be reduced to the mere copy of a fundamental being, but all freedom likewise becomes merely a necessary deception, since there is no knowledge of the principle, whose stirrings are apparent manifestations of freedom. (I/3, 376)

To be self-grounding in this sense a system must establish an equilibrium of forces that sustains its position and shape. But as Kant's example illustrates, this equilibrium must be the product of the tensive interplay of *oppositional* forces. That is, *knowledge* cannot be explained by *knowledge*. Just as "the forces that constitute our universe" cannot be reduced to matter, Schelling insists that his system of knowledge cannot be reduced simply to *our* knowledge; rather it must postulate a principle that is categorically different from our knowledge:

> Now that which alone surpasses all our cognition is our faculty of transcendental freedom or the will. For as the limit of all our knowledge and activity, it alone is by necessity incomprehensible, indissoluble—according to its nature it is the most unfounded and the most indemonstrable—[and] precisely because of this, the most immediate and most evident [element] in our knowledge. (I/1, 400)

The nature of our reason and knowing is not atomistic, nor is it hermetic: it cannot be accounted for, in and of itself, on its own terms. To provide an insightful account of our knowing, we must posit a principle *outside* our sphere of knowledge from which to begin. The point of leverage Archimedes envisioned, and even Kant believed to have found, Schelling now claims as his own. To apply the lever from within the sphere of our knowing, and thereby hope to move the entire system, is impossible; at best, such a procedure would allow us to merely rearrange individual components within that system. The lever must instead be placed beyond the theoretical dimension of the system, since to determine this standpoint from within that system in a "theoretical manner" results in a circular and "contradictory" position (I/1, 400).

But as Schelling points out, Kant himself had already claimed to have discovered this point of global leverage, namely, "what Archimedes was in need of yet did not find: a firm standpoint where reason could apply its lever, not to the present or some future world, but strictly to the *inner idea of freedom*" (I/1, 401). What Schelling disputes is Kant's attempt to sequester this idea of freedom within his critical program, and indeed, only within *one branch* of his entire system, that of his practical philosophy. In contrast, within Schelling's system it is the postulate of the absolute Will that provides the categorical variance required by both the theoretical and the practical philosophies. And while the system remains self-contained, since the postulate of the absolute Will serves as the axis around which both philosophies circle, it is centered and focused by an inexplicable and unfounded force that lies beyond the specific orbit and trajectory of theoretical knowing.

The absolute Will is that *pure consciousness* that "exists within us" which, "independent of external things [and] not dominated by any external power, *supports* and *activates* itself." The "Absolute Will" is thus synonymous with "Absolute Freedom," and is therefore the "source of all self-consciousness," of which we can only become conscious through a "free *act (freien Handlung)*" (I/3, 366). Because we know these absolute elements only as a *limit*, that is, because we have no positive theoretical knowledge of them, we are not permitted to call them principles (*Grundsätze*). Because the Absolute Will is the most unfounded element in our knowledge, so too is self-consciousness: as both are the condition of any knowing, from the theoretical standpoint they can only be *postulated*.

Because the first principle of philosophy must serve *both* theoretical and practical philosophy, this postulate must simultaneously unite and express both a theoretical and practical component. Schelling specifies the theoretical aspect as the "demand for an original (transcendental) construction" of the Self (I/1, 451). Following Kant's definition of *construction* in his logic, this genetic creation is a "free" or "voluntary act *(willkürliche Handlung)*"; it is a construction through which we exhibit—in an "intuition *that is not empirical*"—a *schema* that corresponds to the concept we are creating.[5] This construction is brought about through the powers of the inner sense *qua* productive imagination and, accordingly, is infinite in its freedom of expression. To limit and focus this boundlessness of free construction, Schelling introduces the *practical component* of this postulate, namely, the "compulsory force" of the categorical *should (das Sollen)* (I/1, 446, 448): "The postulate from which philosophy proceeds will therefore require something of which everyone at least *ought* to be conscious, even if he *is* not" (I/1, 446). The "object" of this ought is of course "*the most original construction of the inner sense*," namely, the "one by virtue of which the 'I' itself first originates" (I/1, 448).

The Method of Construction: *Einbildung* as the *In-Eins-Bildung* of Duality

In direct violation of Kant's doctrine of method, Schelling adopts the procedure of construction as the methodology for his philosophy. Only this productive method of construction can supply the possibility of envisioning the dynamic dualisms of our estranged existence. His criticisms of Kant's prohibition are illustrative for what they tell us, not only about Kant, but what they disclose about Schelling's methodology. After reprimanding Kant for having presented philosophy as little more than a dogmatism working exclusively with logical analysis, Schelling proceeds to laud him for having been perhaps the first to grasp its potential power:

> He describes construction thoroughly as the equalization of concept and intuition, and demands for this a non-empirical intuition that, on the one hand as intuition, is singular or concrete, while on the other hand, as the construction of a concept, it must articulate universal validity for all possible intuitions that belong under that concept. Whether the object which corresponds to the universal concept triangle is projected in pure or in empirical intuition is entirely indifferent to its capacity to articulate the concept's universality undamaged, for even in the empirical intuition, only the act of constructing the concept in and of itself is considered. (I/5, 128)

The two decisive points made here concern the "equalization of concept and intuition" and consideration of the act (*Handlung*) of construction "in and for itself." The first point provides a way of mediating and unifying the opposing spheres of the intellectual and the sensible, so that these two heterogeneous spheres can be united, while still preserving the integrity of each. The second point provides for the linkage of this methodology with Schelling's conception of freedom, since every act of construction is, by definition, a *free* or voluntary act.

Schelling is highly critical of the argument Kant advances to deny philosophy access to construction. Not only is it inconsistent within the context of Kant's own *Transcendental Doctrine of Method* that ends the first *Critique*, but it is also inconsistent with the central tenets of his *Transcendental Doctrine of Elements* that begins the first *Critique*. Schelling's first objection questions the obvious ambiguity of Kant's unfortunate use of the expression "non-empirical intuition." The apodeictic certainty that construction generates presupposes that the mathematician *must* be capable of apprehending *in concreto*, in his pure non-empirical intuition, the expression of the union of polar opposites. Kant himself says as much in his *Logic*, when he writes that "in mathematics one uses reason *in concreto*, but the intuition is not empirical; rather one here constructs something for himself, *a priori*, as object of intuition" (*Logik*; Ak IX, 27). Moreover, the "apodeictic proof" of construction can only be evidenced in what Kant calls non-empirical "intuitive cognitions" (ibid.). But what is a non-empirical intuitive cognition? It certainly does not conform to the definition of a pure intuition, since the pure, subjective form of sensibility is incapable of providing an "intuitive cognition." It appears that if Kant's account is to remain internally consistent, he must make room for a form of internal intuition that is intellectual, a position of course, that directly contradicts his repeated declarations that such an intuition is impossible. "For we cannot in the least represent to ourselves the possibility of an understanding which should know its object, not discursively through categories, but intuitively in a non-sensible intuition" (A 256/B 311). Yet in the *Doctrine of Method* he makes what seems to be the opposite claim. "For the construction of a concept we therefore need a *non-empirical* intuition" (A 713/B 741). Kant's own presentation of the geometer's method of construction provides the very representation (*Vorstellung*) he elsewhere deems inconceivable.

Moreover, if philosophy is really only limited to concepts devoid of all intuition, then the only task it can fulfill, as Kant himself notes, is the analytic exposition of a priori synthetic propositions; a point to which Schelling poses the rhetorical question: "Is this then Kant's opinion, or has this later section forgotten the earlier sections," in which Kant claims to be doing more than simply engaging in analysis? (I/5, 133). But then Kant does make the qualification that these synthetic a priori propositions are *transcendental propositions*, a special class of principals that contain within them the a priori synthesis of *possible* empirical intuitions. But then how does Kant account for the genesis and construction of *these* synthetic propositions? According to Schelling, he does not have to, since "[i]t is also quite right that he has not constructed them, because more properly speaking he has taken them by analogy from experience," that is, he has employed the regressive method and abstracted them from experience (I/5, 134). Such inconsistencies are ultimately necessitated by, and follow from, Kant's theoretical framework, "according to which, in the human spirit there is nothing but empty concepts and empirical intuitions, and between both an absolute hiatus" (I/5, 134).

That the standpoint of reflexion must involve itself in contradictions is obvious when one examines Kant's own use of "construction and pure intellectual intuition" in the *Transcendental Deduction* (I/5, 129). Schelling argues that if we want to understand the entire mechanism of the schema as employed in this deduction, we should first look to Kant's writings on logic and mathematics. In both we find a doctrine of construction which has as its essential element the production of the infamous third element—*das Drittes*—which in this case is the generation of the *schema*. As Schelling repeatedly demonstrates, the entire *Transcendental Deduction* is an example of synthetic construction, which, of course, is the very method Kant denies philosophy in the *Doctrine of Elements*.

The *Deduction* provides us with virtually every element of construction. There is the universal concept in need of a singular figure to mediate between concept and the images of the manifold, a singular figure that *somehow* provides the possibility for the reproductive imagination to produce the images of sensible objects. Following the model of mathematical construction, "pure a priori imagination" supplies the productive power to create the "monogram of the schema, while the schema itself then expresses the rule whereby sensible images are subsumed under the schema's universal concept (A 142/B 181). It would seem to follow from this that the schema is also constructed *"entirely through imagination* in pure intuition . . . completely a priori, without having borrowed the *Muster* from any experience" (A 713/B 741). For just as the generation of the schema for a triangle must adhere to certain universal determinations in its construction, so too must the production of the schema for a dog adhere to the a priori "formal conditions of sensibility, namely those of inner sense" (A 140/B 179).

But at first glance, it appears that in the *Transcendental Deduction* the generation of the schema for the "pure sensible concepts" involves an *empirical* element, whereas the mathematician's construction requires a "non-empirical intuition." For example, while in the construction of algebraic figures there is no apparent linkage with a priori forms of sensibility, in the *Deduction* Kant explicitly links the generation of the schema for these sensible concepts to the transcendental determination of time. But this is only an apparent difference. Schelling points out that the symbolic constructions of *arithmetic* are only possible within the formal condition of time as it subsists in the reversible time zone of the pure a priori. In the construction of mathematics, the universal formal condition of time determines the shape of the schema produced. Yet the schema so produced is still "something particular (*ein einzelnes*)." And it is precisely in this power of construction to exhibit the universal *in concreto* that Kant locates the productive and truly synthetic nature of this method. Indeed, it is this very act of construction that provides the *apodeictic certainty* characteristic of mathematical knowledge; a certainty generated purely through the compelling evidence of non-empirical intuition, which alone is capable of cognizing the manifest contradiction of a universal *in concreto*. The question Schelling thus poses is this: is a non-empirical intuition also required to construct the schema for a sensible concept?

Schelling argues that it must, if Kant is to remain consistent with his analysis of the method of construction in the *Doctrine of Method*. Indeed, when faced with the task of explaining the process of schematism in the *Deduction*, Kant himself makes unqualified use of examples taken from the construction of mathematical concepts:

> Indeed, it is the schemata, not images of objects, which underlie our pure sensible concepts. No image could ever be adequate to the concept of a triangle in general. It would never attain that universality of the concept, which renders it valid of all triangles; it would always only be limited to a part only of this sphere. The schema of the triangle can exist nowhere but in thought. It is a rule of synthesis of the imagination, in respect to pure figures in space. Still less is an object of experience or its image ever adequate to the empirical concept; for this latter always stands in immediate relation to the schema of imagination, as a rule for the determination of our intuition, in accordance with some specific universal concept. (A 140/B 180)

Again, we encounter the same elements and method of construction.[6] Again, we find the schema, an intellectual element of thought, uniting and mediating the universal concept with a specific intuition. Sensible images are incapable of fulfilling this function, because they are capable of delimiting only a local region of the concept's universal scope. Hence the need for an intellectual schema, a product of pure a priori imagination (*Einbildung*), which exists nowhere but in our minds; a product of pure imagination that mediates universal concept and individual intuition, "hovering" as it were, between determinacy and indeterminacy, quantity and quality.

It is this third power of the imagination that is so decisive for Schelling. His usage of the terms "intellectual intuition" and the "productive imagination" sometimes obscures this point, but these two terms are used by him to describe different aspects of the same productive power. Intellectual intuition is the *window through which we see into* the productive imagination. Conversely, intellectual intuition is the *screen* onto which the productive imagination projects its visions. But it is the power of *Ein-bildung* that allows us to mediate and *make one* the dualities of the universal and particular *in concreto*.

The schema functions as the capstone of Kant's entire transcendental deduction. As the last essential stone inserted into the top of the arch, it is the schema that carries the entire weight of Kant's deduction. Addressed through whichever metaphor we choose, the common ground or the capstone, Kant's use of the schema's figurative power, along with the ambidextrous nature of its generative source, the productive imagination, suggests to Schelling a solution to the problematic question of the common ground that should unify *Sinn* and *Verstand*, intuition and concept. Overlooked by Kant, he sees in this faculty the source of a *productive* model of knowing which will enable him to conceive of how the dualities of *reflection* can be mediated; a model that informs what Schelling calls the "standpoint of Production," in contrast to the Kantian "standpoint of Reflection." Focusing on the essential role played by this figural power in Kant's own construction, Schelling argues that only the productive power of the imagination is capable of setting such a capstone in place, since it alone provides the figurative mortar to keep it there, by integrating difference into one (in the literal sense of *Ein-bildung*). Moreover, Schelling insists that Kant's embrace of "non-empirical intuition" begs the question of the systematic necessity of intellectual intuition. In Schelling's reading, the solidity and *construction* of Kant's entire edifice depends on his sustained, yet tacit, use of intellectual intuition to access the powers of the productive imagination. Indeed, Schelling conceives of the act of construction as being nearly synonymous with the act of intuition.

Problematic: All Philosophy Is Construction

If the alpha and omega of Schelling's philosophy is freedom, and construction is a "voluntary (*willkürlich*)" or "a free act (*eine freie Handlung*)," it follows that the former adopt the latter as its method of choice. That construction is in fact an act of freedom is due to its origin in the power of the productive imagination. For whereas the thought of the common understanding is governed by the laws of formal logic, the very etymology of *Einbildung* provides for the possibility of creative disobedience, of envisioning the infinite *in-form-ing* the finite, of the universal informing the particular, or of the intelligible world informing the sensible. The constructed triangle is but a schema that unites the universal in the particular; it is a figure which is a particular *informed* by a universal. Likewise with the schema of a dog: the schema unites the terms of the universal concept and the particular intuition. The act of construction is thus the productive creation of a unity of differences.[7]

It appears that we have once again encountered in this triadic dynamic of construction the logic of disjunction and its category of *community and reciprocal causation*: out of the reciprocal interaction of two opposing forces, a third emerges that, while informed by the contraries, is not reducible to them. However, this similarity is only partially correct. The preceding account presents this act of informing as a unidirectional informing of the particular by the universal, when in fact what Schelling requires is reciprocal informing, whereby *the particular also informs the universal*. Adhering to the logic of disjunction, the relation between terms cannot be restricted to one of the "subsumption of intuitions under pure concepts" (A 138/B 177). The dynamic at work is not the vertical top-down assimilation of quality to quantity, and neither is it the complete absorption—and thus negation—of the particular qualities into a universal magnitude. Instead, the logic of disjunction posits both a horizontal and vertical coordination of terms.

The process of construction is merely the manifestation of the original productive powers of nature in the sphere of the human imagination; it is the manifestation of nature's productive powers as *Geist*, revealing itself within humanity's imagination. The generative power at work is that of the productive interplay of opposing forces, including those of form and matter. At every level or dimension of reality, this generative power of oppositional forces is operative: "Thus organization constructs itself only out of organization. In the organic product, for this very reason, form and matter are inseparable; this particular matter could only arise and come to be along with this particular form" (I/2, 45). It is only by adopting this spiraling model of reciprocal interaction that Schelling can account for the dynamic whereby Nature—and therefore humanity—incessantly develops in a seemingly never-ending process of self-differentiation.

Accordingly, the theoretical dimension of Schelling's postulate of philosophy demands "an *original* (transcendental) construction" of the Self (I/3, 451). The term *postulate* is taken from mathematics, and employed with the express intent of presenting philosophy as comparable, in this respect, to the science of geometry. Both begin with "*the most original* construction" which, incapable of being demonstrated, can only be postulated (I/1, 444). The primordial construction for the geometrician is the straight line, which, as unlimited, is also the construction of unlimited space. The evidence for this postulate must be produced by the individual geometer himself, through the act of constructing the line either *via* the imagination, or together with the aid of the external senses. There is, however, an essential difference in how the geometer and the philosopher employ construction: whereas the geometer has access to external intuition to support his activities, the philosopher does not.

The "organ" of construction is the indeterminate Kantian "inner sense," which Schelling coordinates with the imagination in intuition.

Thus, whereas the mathematician is never directly concerned with intuition, the philosopher is actively engaged, in the most direct way possible, with the act of construction. Through this activity of construction, philosophy establishes itself as a productive science that depends on the imagination as much as art does (I/3, 351). But whereas art, like geometry, is directed outwards "to reflect the unknown," the production of the philosopher is turned inwards to disclose the unknown in intellectual intuition.

What the philosopher constructs exists nowhere but in the imagination of that thinker. Because the act of construction must be a truly free act, it cannot be about reproducing a given object. If it is, one forsakes autonomy in exchange for a derivative heteronomy. Consequently, since the method of construction is the method of transcendental philosophy, strictly speaking, the system we are considering can only exist for one person—in this case, Schelling. If we cannot be compelled to engage in this "free act" of construction, and what we construct must bear our signature imprint, then it follows that each one of us must create our own system:

> The student must be immersed, so to speak, in the transcendental method. Hence the first principle must already be his own construction, which is required of (and left to) him, so he learns at the outset that whatever originates for him by means of this construction is nothing beyond it, and that it exists only to the extent that he constructs. (I/1, 447)

To a certain extent, Schelling uses the method of construction as a conceptual tool to erect the edifice of his theoretical system. When we are working under the restrictions of reflexion, using both the inner and outer senses, there is a clear distinction between the subject and its object. In this context, to construct is to create a systematic narrative or theoretical framework through which the philosopher can account for unknown phenomena. To this extent, this use of construction parallels its use in any theoretical science that seeks to interpret data that is underdetermined.

Yet there is another, more fundamental employment of this method that occurs when we direct our attention exclusively inward. Like Kant, the sole aim of theoretical philosophy for Schelling is to account for practical philosophy, and the goal of both is not speculation, but *action*. However, when the method Schelling employs is itself an *act* directed inward, the reflective distinction between knower and known is not always possible. The activity of construction at this degree of interiority and intensity is one of a true *creatio ex nihilo*, for there is no "thing," no *Gegenstand* present, until one begins to construct it. The activity of self-construction is thereby itself an essential component of practical philosophy contained within the theoretical.

An Aesthetic Philosophy

Construction in philosophy is neither about discovering the true structures of an external reality nor about claiming to have discovered some type of universal truth. Such attempts can only prove a philosopher's arrogance and simple-mindedness; arrogance because that philosopher then imposes her constructions on others, and simple-mindedness because she assumes truth to be something found and not made. Schelling is not merely making hyperbolic claims when he states that his philosophy is an aesthetic philosophy. There are significant systematic reasons for his belief that of all forms of scientific thinking, "philosophy contains the most freedom, *and is therefore just as much art as science*" (I/5, 141).[8]

If philosophy is not primarily an analytic activity, then there can be no definite concept of what philosophy is. If philosophy is primarily a synthetic enterprise, if it is a matter of creation, then there must be as many philosophies as there are (original) philosophers. Although we are born *to* philosophize, we are not born philosophers; philosophy is not an innate power of the mind, it must instead be developed and cultivated if it is to arise. Schelling makes this point quite clear when he writes:

> It is throughout a work of freedom. It is for each only what he has himself made it; and therefore the idea of philosophy [is] only the result of philosophy, a universally valid philosophy, however, [is] an inglorious chimera (*ruhmloses Hirngespenst*). (I/2, 11)

To claim that there can be no universally valid philosophy is not, however, to maintain that the activity of philosophy is futile. To preclude the possibility of our ever attaining to the absolute truth does not entail that there is no absolute truth. Rather Schelling's position is simply this: that as finite human beings, existing and living in a contingent world such as ours, it can only be counterproductive for a philosopher to make the claim that he is in possession of such an absolute truth. Indeed, Schelling does posit an absolute truth, and in quite a traditional way: it subsists in the divine understanding. However, this is a normative truth, which constitutes the ever-receding horizon of our finite understanding. It is the "riddle" of our Spirit and its existence which, "marvelously deluded, seeks itself, and in seeking flies from itself" (I/3, 628); it is the truth of an "eternal and original unity" which "in nature and history is rent asunder, and in life and action, no less than in thought, must forever fly apart" (I/3, 628). Philosophy is the creation of the individual, in which she attempts to integrate that which has flown asunder, and seeks to dispel the delusions that separate her from herself, others ,and nature. But philosophy and philosophical systems are not written from the perspective of the divine understanding:

> Most philosophical systems are merely the creations of their authors—more or less well thought out—comparable to our historical novels (e.g., Leibnizianism). To proclaim such a system as the only possible system is to be extremely restrictive [and results in] a dogmatic system. I assure you that I do not intend to contribute to such [thinking]. (I/7, 421)

That Schelling believed philosophical systems should be read as historical novels, and thus as literature, should not come as a surprise if we take him seriously when he asserts that philosophy and art are two sides to the same coin. If we take him at his word, and for a moment assume that he considers himself to be engaged in a process of constructing an aesthetic philosophy, his position as it is expressed here follows from, or links directly to, what he writes about the nature of *modern* art.

In contrast to the collective world of antiquity, the modern world is one of individuals. And whereas the ancient world was one of eternal and imperishable order, in the modern world "change and transformation are the reigning law."[9] With no universally valid *mythos*, the modern poet

> is called to structure from this evolving (mythological) world, a world of which his own age can reveal to him only a part. I repeat: from this world he is to structure into a whole that particular part revealed to him, and to create from the content and substance of that world *his* mythology.[10]

The examples Schelling provides are of the great modern poets who have achieved this: Dante, Shakespeare, and of course, Goethe. Their success lies in being able to articulate their own respective "mythological circle." That they were able to do this was a result of their having adhered to "the fundamental law of modern poesy" which is none other than *originality*.[11] This originality emerges from the power to interpret one's own time and place, and then articulate this interpretation as a consistent symbolic universe which—and here it gets problematic—by chance expresses the spirit of that entire age. The individual is thus responsible for creating his own "poetic circle for himself" so that, in accordance with the law of originality, the more original that poetic circle is, the more universal does its meaning have the chance of becoming. In the absence of a universal mythology, the mythological circle produced by the individual thinker or poet provides the vehicle for the intuition of the infinite within the finite.

The Construction of the Self: Theoretical Philosophy and Unconscious Nature

Before the self initiates the act of self-construction, it undergoes an unconscious development driven by the necessity of our organic nature. It is in Schelling's construction of this preconscious epoch that time arises for the self. In contrast to Kant's determination of transcendental time in the realm of the pure a priori, Schelling locates the source of this restricting force in the unknowable sphere of the unconsciousness (*das Unbewußte*). This fact highlights perhaps most clearly the fundamental difference which exists between their respective standpoints of reflexion and production.

Accordingly, in contrast to Kant's stated goal of providing for the possibility of synthetic a priori knowledge, Schelling instead seeks to account for the singular *fact* of our knowledge in general. Purposely avoiding the distinction between a priori and a posteriori, he replaces these traditional divisions with the interplay of conscious and unconscious mind.[12] Simply put, Schelling seeks to account for that "natural and necessary prejudice"—that "compulsion (*Zwang*)"—whereby we are compelled to involuntarily believe that "external objects are real" and that "we exist" (I/3, 344). Questions which, when reformulated into the jargon of philosophy, assume the familiar form of: how can I explain the *identity* of subject and object in my knowing?

The goal of Schelling's system is thus "to explain the indestructible connection of the I with a world which is necessarily thought as external to it, via a preceding transcendental past of a real or empirical consciousness," an explanation which must lead to what Schelling calls a transcendental "history of self-consciousness" (I/3, 399).[13] The conception of philosophy that emerges from this standpoint is fundamentally historical. Grounded in the *postulate* of the autonomy of the will, both theoretical and practical philosophy have the task of presenting a history of the self in its twofold nature. The object of theoretical philosophy is the history of the unconscious self *qua* nature, whereas the object of practical philosophy is history, both at the species level and at the level of the individual person. The former domain of nature is characterized by unconscious, and thus necessary, activity, whereas the latter is characterized by the self-conscious actions of free, moral agents.

The point at which Schelling locates the identity of subject and object is in the self-consciousness of each one of us, for it is only in our self-consciousness that we experience the "feeling of *compulsion*" that accompanies and defines our primordial prejudices about our existence. The unavoidable compulsion of the self to believe that it exists, is both sustained by, and the product of, the reciprocal interaction of the never-ending opposition of nature's productive polarities. In the human self, this primordial dualism manifests itself in the tensive interplay of the infinite *qua* unconscious and the finite *qua* conscious *Geist*.

There is therefore no categorical divide between Nature and Spirit, or the sensible and intelligible worlds. Rather the difference between the two is always only a question of their respective limitations. Sensible nature is but unconscious Spirit, and conscious Spirit is but nature elevated to self-consciousness.[14] Yet it is only through the mutual interaction and restriction of these conflicting directional forces that self-consciousness can emerge. The condition of possibility for self-consciousness is, as for every other element of reality, for it to be simultaneously unlimited expansion and a limiting contraction. For it is only through such tensive conflict that factual limitations (*faktische Beschrankung*) and finitude can emerge:

> An activity, for which there is no longer . . . resistance, never returns back into itself. Only through the return into oneself does consciousness emerge. Moreover, for us, only a restricted *Realität* is *Wirklichkeit*. (I/3, 324)

The only possible locus for the identity of subject and object is in self-consciousness. What is unconsciously primordial in the self "is the conflict of opposing directions in the self" (I/3, 393), out of which the mediating factor of consciousness emerges as *"an activity that wavers between opposing directions"* (I/3, 393). Self-consciousness, as the nodal point of this oscillation, is the dynamic, relational identity generated by this duality.

Before we move to consider the following three epochs of Schelling's transcendental history of the self, it must be noted that what he provides here is his construction of the genesis of self-consciousness. In the same manner as his account of the dynamic emergence of form and content via his *Urform* in the *Formschrift*, here too he offers a linear account of a process that actually occurs in virtual *simultaneity*, as if Piaget's developmental curve were compressed into that moment in which the infant distinguishes its reflection and becomes aware of itself *für sich*. But instead of a mirror providing the foil for this awakening, Schelling uses the three restrictions of time to generate consciousness's three-dimensions of past, present, and future.

First Epoch: Productive Intuition of Sensation through the Restriction of the Past

In this first epoch of the history of the self, Schelling must account for how it comes to intuit itself as limited, which is to say, he must account for the fact of our primordial sensation *qua* productive intuition of an external world of objects. This sensing is by its nature blind and unconscious, and represents but the most dulled and diffuse potentiation of the powers of intuition.[15]

Transcendentally regarded, the sensory object is nothing other than outer intuition itself, cut off from the self. What must be accounted for is the process whereby this outer intuition becomes separated from the unconsciously productive self. To do this, the nature of the boundary that "cuts off" the self from the objective reality of the object must be defined, but in such a way that we can still account for the fact that the self is ultimately responsible for the production of that object. What Schelling seeks is an account of the primordial limitation of the self that will provide for the compulsion that accompanies all true sensation and cognition. In short, he must account for a restrictive limit that can provide for the factual ("*faktische*") secondness of experience that eluded Fichte's Not-I. The reality of this *preconscious* limitation will, he claims, "only demolish an idealism which sought to bring forth the original limitation freely and with consciousness, whereas the transcendental version leaves us as little freedom in that regard as even the realist could desire" (I/3, 408).[16] However, to avoid a rigid Kantian dualism, the sensation of resistance provoked by the 'other' must not be of a wholly different kind than the self:

> the judgment that the impression proceeds from an object presupposes
> an activity that is not limited to the impression, but moves *beyond*

the impression. The I is, therefore, not what feels, unless there is an activity in it that goes beyond the limit. (I/3, 413)

Schelling employs this argument against the Kantian *thing in itself*. The compulsion to move beyond limits reflects the fact that to be aware of a limit presupposes that one has already transcended that limit.

The boundary that limits the activity of the object can only be explained by a ground external to both its nature and the nature of the self; it must lie somewhere "wholly outside consciousness," but yet still be capable of intervening "in the present phase of consciousness" (I/3, 463). In striving to overcome this boundary, the self discovers that the ground of this boundary lies in a state of consciousness beyond the present one. That is, it lies in a moment that is behind the present one, and thus in the *past*:

> The reason why the self finds itself limited in this action cannot lie in the present action, but rather in one that is *past*. So the self in its present action is limited *without* its consent, but that it finds itself so limited is also the whole of what is contained in sensation, and is the condition of all objectivity in knowledge. (I/3, 409)

What allows Schelling to make this distinction of a *qualitative* difference between a past and present state of the self is his use of the unconscious. It is this power of the involuntary, indeed *limbic necessity*, that enables him to account for how the ground of the self's limitation emerges from within that self, and yet only appears to the conscious mind as being external to it. Schelling writes:

> So in order that the limitation shall appear to us as a thing independent of ourselves, provision is made for this purpose, through the mechanism of sensation, that the act whereby all limitation is posited, as the condition of all consciousness, does not itself come to consciousness. (I/3, 409)

The boundary that limits the activity of the object can only be ex-plained by a ground external to both its nature and the nature of the self; this ground must lie somewhere "wholly outside consciousness," but yet still be capable of intervening "in the present phase of consciousness" (I/3, 463). The reality (*Wirklichkeit*) of Schelling's time results from the fact that, seen from the standpoint of production, "time appertains at once both to inner and outer sense" (I/3, 517). This is because, at this strata of the genetic construction of the preconscious self, time itself must be "an object of outer sense" and hence *real* (I/3, 517).

Propelled by the dynamic generated through the interaction of finitude and the infinite, the self cannot remain at rest in this epoch. The moment of the first restriction of a material finitude has occurred, but this moment is counteracted by the force of the unrestricted, leading the self to struggle onward to overcome this boundary.

Second Epoch: Transition from Blind Intuition to Reflection through the Restriction of the Present

In the previous epoch, the self has been completely fettered and bound in its unconscious production of the object world. In the second epoch the self must break out of this blind producing and become aware of itself *für sich*, as having sensations. This will occur through the second restriction of time, which generates the present. What distinguishes this level of restriction from that of the first epoch is that the self now becomes aware of the nature of the "common boundary" that sets the present off from the past. Whereas in the previous epoch the self could merely *feel* the constraint of a restriction, in this phase it becomes capable of self-awareness as a result of the disclosure of the present. Accordingly, as all of these three epochs are but linear constructions of a process that occurs in virtual simultaneity, we resume right where we left off: in the feeling of constraint.

In the incapacity to return to this past state of consciousness, the self *"feels"* itself restrained and experiences "a state of constraint" (I/3, 464). This "feeling of being thus driven back to a stage that it cannot in reality return to" generates "the feeling of the *present*" (I/3, 465). The genesis of self as distinct from object thus springs from the feeling of being "trapped in a present," of being "held fast in a particular moment of the time series" (I/3, 481). An attenuated sense of self-awareness begins with this feeling, and with it, the empirical self first becomes aware of external objects. In this the self "becomes an object to itself *as* pure intensity, as activity that can extend itself only in one dimension, but is at present concentrated at a single point" (I/3, 465). Moreover, it is this constricted activity of the self, of its becoming an object to itself, which brings forth our *awareness* of time as limit. From this it is clear that for Schelling time is no longer merely a formal condition of intuition, but has rather become *constitutive* of the empirical self: "Time is not something that flows independently of the self; the self itself is time conceived of in activity" (I/3, 465).

In an inversion of Kant's determination of a temporality defined by the formal requirements of an analytic unity of consciousness, Schelling here presents a self whose consciousness emerges from the restrictive influence of time, and is thus subordinate to, and limited by, its temporal restraints. This conception of time goes beyond the reversible, quantitative mode of time conceived as parallel to number, and instead advances time as an irreversible restraint and limit to the empirical self, thereby establishing the possibility of a factual and real *historical time*, capable of creating a *qualitative* and material difference between a past and present moment. Schelling incorporates this restrictive time as a limit that defines the qualities of objective objects, and thus of determinateness, when he writes that " . . . a magnitude in time we call *quality*," and "only by virtue of its quality does any given object become something determinate" (I/3, 381). And it is this qualitative determinateness (*Bestimmtheit*) that in turn creates the bond we share with all humans: "The original limitation, which we have in common with all rational beings, consists in the fact of our intrinsic finitude" (I/3, 409).

The object thereby distinguished from the self must appear as the negation of the self's pure intensity, "that is, it will have to appear as *pure extension*" (I/3, 465). Through this second limitation of time, the inner and outer senses divide, and in the instant that the self becomes aware of the present, it finally perceives the *space* inhabited by an external object.

This development requires that Schelling construct the intuitions of the infinite and the finite from the self's new awareness of time and space. Time restricts the self, trapping it within the present moment as a "pure intensity"; conversely, this restriction negates the intensity of the outer sense, thereby producing the pure extension of space. From this it follows that

> Both are opposed to each other, precisely because they mutually restrict each other. Both, for themselves, are equally infinite, though in opposing senses. Time becomes finite only through space, space only through time. That one becomes finite through the other means that one is determined and measured through the other. (I/3, 468)

Inner and outer sense separate at this level of awareness. However, this potency of awareness does not cancel out the sensation produced in the previous epoch. At a blindly unconscious level, the inner and outer senses remained conjoined, thereby producing the *qualitative facticity* of immediate experience.

Following the dynamic of Schelling's construction, the first and second potencies of production now come into opposition with one another in order to propel the self towards the next epoch. In doing this, the first and second potencies of producing are displaced (*versetzt*) by the third potency whose emergence we will presently address (I/3, 481). The dynamic at work however, is not merely one of a restrictive past and present pushing the self forward. Rather the self is *pulled* forward by the pole opposing the restrictedness of finite time; that is, it is pulled forward by the *eternal*, as that expansive force engaged in the reciprocal interaction with the contractive forces of time. For the future will not disclose itself until the self attains to the *absolute act of the will* that marks the transition into full self-consciousness. This transition also marks the end of theoretical philosophy and the beginning of the practical.

Third Epoch: From Reflection to the Absolute Act of the Will

Schelling draws a clear distinction between the concept of time generated from the Kantian "standpoint of reflexion" and the time that emerges from his "standpoint of production." Within the former, "time is merely a form of intuition of inner sense" (I/3, 516). It is generated through the mere observing of the *succession* of presentations that exist *only within us*. Yet the *coexistence* of objects and substances— objects that are the very condition for the possibility of inner and outer sense—can only be intuited outside us. Through abstraction, the standpoint of reflexion "abolishes" the schematism of time. Grounding its reflection in the intuitionless concept of logical form, reflection derives its categories from logic, and therewith derives the unity of its self from a postulate of logical unity. Because of this, time is entirely removed from consideration as a possible constitutive factor in the derivation or construction of either of these essential structures, and is instead merely superimposed onto these structures after their outline has been determined by the dictates of logical form.

Schelling points to the sophism of Zeno's paradox as a simple example of the problems that emerge for the standpoint of reflexion when time is removed through abstraction. Through the introduction of the concepts of mechanics, the attempt is made to mediate the transition from A to -A, from rest to motion, by describing that transition as mediated by an infinity. However, this transition must still occur in a finite period of time. Hence, "from the standpoint of reflexion" the construction of time is "utterly impossible, since between any two points on a line an infinity of others must be supposed" (I/3, 519). This paradox is the result of the removal of "the original schematism of intuition" from the reflective model of the self.

The standpoint of production however, has the conceptual resources required to account for Zeno's paradox. The productive self, which is constantly striving for "identity of consciousness," finds that "this combination of contradictorily opposite states is possible only through the schematism of time. Intuition produces time as constantly in transition from A to -A in order to mediate the contradiction between opposites. By abstraction, the schematism, and with it, time, are abolished" (I/3, 518).

As in the constructions of mathematics, only intuition "can picture an infinite within the finite; that is, a quantity in which, though itself finite, no indefinitely smaller part is possible" (ibid.). This is because from the productive standpoint time is originally already an object of outer intuition, so that there can be "no difference between *presentations* and *objects*" (I/3, 516).[17] Since originally time is the universal link between inner and outer senses, it is also the link between intuition and concept. As we saw in the previous epoch, time is the mechanism that limits and restricts, and thereby generates the individuating force that produces the objects and concepts themselves. From this it follows, that if the categories "are originally types of intuition, and hence not separated from the schematism" of time, then the entire mechanism of the categories will allow itself to be derived from the relation of time to pure concept, on the one hand, and to pure intuition, or space, on the other.

The Derivation of the Categories from Time

Because categories are originally intuitions, they are for Schelling "modes of action, whereby objects themselves first come about for us" (I/3, 472). Consequently, since these objects arise through the restrictive influence of time, the first class of "dynamic categories" must then parallel the mediation of time, and be capable of presenting "inner and outer sense as still united" (I/3, 519). The only class of category capable of achieving this is that of *relation*.

As we have noted, Schelling understands the triadic relation among this class of categories quite differently from the relation advanced by Kant. Whereas Kant held that the third member of each class "always arises from the combination of the second category with the first" (B 110), Schelling maintains that the first two categories "are possible only mutually through one another, that is, they are possible only in a third, which is reciprocity" (I/3, 520). The interrelation among the three is such that only through the addition of the third member are the previous two possible. The triad cannot be reduced to a "dyadic subject-object relation."[18] For the first two alone are purely ideal; only through the third category do they become real, because it is through the third category that the previous two acquire the transcendental schematism of time (I/3, 447). Thus, the condition for the possibility of the first category of the class of relation is the third member of that class, *reciprocity*. The first two members, substance and causality, are only possible in that they "mutually presuppose the other" (I/3, 522), which is to say, that they can exist only in a *reciprocal* relation with each other. The first category of substance and accident is only intuitable through the second category, that is, through the category of causality. But both are possible only in that "we add the transcendental schema of time" (I/3, 520):

> Substance is intuitable as such only by being intuited as persisting in time, but it cannot be intuited as persistent unless time, which has so far designated only the absolute boundary, flows (extends itself in one dimension), which in fact comes about only through the succession of the causal sequence. But conversely, too, that any succession occurs in time is intuitable only in contrast to something that persists therein, or, since time arrested in its flow = space, [time arrested in its flow is then] that [which] persists in space, and this in fact is substance. Hence, these two categories are possible only mutually through one another, that is, they are possible only in a third, which is reciprocity (ibid.).[19]

Consequently, in every class of category, the relation between the first two categories is always similar to that obtaining between space and time, and the second category in every class is necessary to append the transcendental schema of time to the first category of each class. Significant however, is the fact that for Schelling the mathematical categories can only arise from the standpoint of reflection, such that each of these categories, in their exclusive employment of reflection, "abolish . . . the unity of inner and outer sense" (I/3, 520). In doing this they abolish constitutive time, and it is only if time is reintroduced into these categories through the category of reciprocity, that the unity of inner and outer sense can be restored. From the intuition of space and time, Schelling derives the category of substance and accident; from the intuition of time *qua* succession, that of cause and effect; and from the intuition of *organic nature* arises the category of reciprocity.

Transition to Practical Philosophy: The Absolute Act of the Will

The postulate around which Schelling's entire system revolves is that of the absolute autonomy of the will. Schelling determines this act as having both a practical and theoretical aspect. The theoretical aspect of this postulate demands an absolute abstraction that will be "the beginning of consciousness"; but such an act must also be at the same time a practical act, "explicable only through a self-determining" (I/3, 533). This act of self-determining is further defined as a "*willing*," which provides the "complete solution to our problem of how the self recognizes itself as intuiting" (I/3, 534). Yet though this act of the will may provide a "complete solution," the solution provided does not submit to a theoretical analysis, nor does it allow itself to be explicated as a theoretical grounding for Schelling's system. Rather, this absolute act of the will, by definition, refuses to submit to a theoretical justification. Thus, it must posit its validity "by means of categorical demands":

> But now this act is an absolute abstraction and, precisely because it is absolute, can no longer be explained through any other in the intelligence; and hence at this point the chain of theoretical philosophy breaks off, and there remains in regard to it only the absolute demand: there *shall* appear such an act in the intelligence. However, in so saying, theoretical philosophy oversteps its boundary, and crosses into the domain of practical philosophy, which alone posits by means of categorical demands. (I/3, 224)

By situating the absolute act of the will in a categorical demand, Schelling unites both theoretical and practical philosophy. However, as an act that unites these two domains, how can this postulate of autonomy be said to apply to both? Where in the realm of Nature, of the preconscious self, does the principle of autonomy manifest itself?

Schelling conceives of the autonomous self as essentially one that *realizes* the moral law. The primordial autonomy of the self does indeed determine its actions, but it does so without being aware of this self-determination *for itself (für sich)*. The result is that "the self both gives itself the law and realizes it in one and the same act, wherefore it also fails to distinguish itself as legislative, and merely discerns the laws in its products, as if in a mirror" (I/3, 535). This preconscious mode of self-determination finds the subject locked in a synthetic relation with the object; a relation that is simply of a subject to an object, of the ideal to the real. In the conscious mode of reflection, after the act of self-determination, the self assumes an ideal standpoint that allows it to consider the productive activity of the unconscious self in both its ideal and real activities. For this reason, the conscious self "is no

longer ideal, but *idealizing*." Consequently, the producing self "in practical philosophy, is no longer intuitive, that is, *devoid of consciousness*,
but is consciously productive, or *realizing*" (ibid.). The motivating and
driving contradiction, the creative tension that propels the practical self,
is thus the product of "the duality of the self that both idealizes (projects ideals) and realizes" (I/3, 536). The domain of practical philosophy
must therefore be a field in which the self can project the ideals of the
moral law and then realize them.

What must now be addressed is the motivating cause that impels
the self to an absolute act of the will. The construction of this cause,
however, is thwarted by the fact that within the linear evolution of
the self, the point we are now attempting to account for occurs at the
beginning of the self's temporal order, and therefore at the "empirical
starting point of consciousness" (I/3, 538). However, "in consequence
of the original mechanism of thought," to account for a *thing* neces-
sitates imposing the calculus of causality upon the issue at hand, and
causality requires a temporal sequence. Yet what we are attempting to
explain here is the very genesis of that temporal sequence. To continue
with his analysis, Schelling must therefore argue that if this genesis
of time refuses to submit to the sequential logic of causality, its motivating "cause" must be *unconditional*. But to maintain that something
is unconditional is to suggest that it is inexplicable, and this is a
suggestion that Schelling cannot allow to stand without qualification.
Consequently, he must posit yet another contradiction to be resolved,
namely, that this act, the genesis of time and self, "has to be at once
both explicable and inexplicable" (ibid.). The task thus becomes to again
find "a mediating concept" to resolve this contradiction and provide
some way of explaining an action that must simultaneously remain
inexplicable.

For an act of the self to be inexplicable implies that this act is not
the result of an anterior activity of the self. However, since the self *is*
precisely *its activity* of constant producing, the cause of this act must
lie outside the self. This act of self-determination must still somehow
arise within the self, for it is ultimately a productive and free act of
the self that must be explained. There must be a mediating concept,
a "something which contains the ground of free self-determination,"
which in turn must be "a producing on the part of the intelligence,
although the negative condition of this producing must lie *outside* it"
(I/3, 538). The self must therefore provide the "negative condition" for
this act through a type of "nonaction." The external act will in fact
be only an "indirect ground" of the act in the self; an indirect ground

which, as such, must "coexist" with the self in a relation of "indirect reciprocity" (I/3, 539). Therefore, "by the contradiction noted above" Schelling is "led on to a new principle," namely, that *The act of self-determination, or the free action of the intelligence upon itself, can be explained only by the determinate action of an intelligence external to it"* (I/3, 540). A "necessary condition" of the act of self-determination is the determinate action of another individual upon the self. To mediate the contradiction of causality and the genesis of time—two phenomena which occur on the vertical axis of the evolution of the self—a lateral force is required; a force which, while perpendicular to the trajectory of the self's development, is yet structurally parallel to the form of the self.[20] This force can only be provided by another self who shares our nature, and who thus "coexists" with the self in a relation of indirect reciprocity. With this, Schelling successfully incorporates the dimension of intersubjectivity as a necessary condition of self-consciousness. Even so, Schelling has still not yet attained to the "mediating concept" required to explain the inexplicable ground of the act of self-determination. For what must be explained is the mechanism whereby an external agent can be an indirect cause of a "free" action of the will, without corrupting the integrity of the autonomy of that act.

The free act of self-determination presupposes that I have willed this act, and that this act has occurred only because I have willed it to occur. Thus to act freely, I must have already "willed the willing." However, the concept of willing only comes to be through this act. "This manifest circle," Schelling notes, "is eliminable only if willing can become an object for me prior to willing. This is impossible through my own agency, so it will have to be simply that concept of willing which would arise for me through the act of an intelligence" (I/1, 542). To escape this circularity, Schelling must propose that the condition for the possibility of willing is generated in the self—without its consent—through the encounter with another intelligence, and that this condition assumes the explicit form of an unconditional "demand." It is the concept of the unconditional demand that mediates the contradiction whereby the act of the self must at once be both explicable and inexplicable. For that another intelligence places a demand on the self does not necessitate that the self conform to that request. But "by means of the demand the action is *explained, if it takes place,* without it *having* to take place on that account" (I/1, 543). The self's act of determination maintains its autonomy, for the self is by no means constrained to respond to this demand. The space within which the self chooses to respond—its autonomy—is, by definition, that which cannot be explained or accounted for a priori, since if this were possible the unpredictable nature of freedom would be destroyed. Yet if the self yields to the demand of the other, its actions are explicable, "It may ensue, as soon as the concept of willing arises for the self, or as soon as it sees itself reflected, catching sight of itself in the mirror of another intelligence; but it does not have to ensue" (ibid.).

A condition of my self-consciousness is then not only that I intuit other intelligences outside me, but that they make a moral demand of me, for within this framework, how else could I realize myself *qua* individual, that is, as not being like the other? This limiting fact is the *restriction* that posits in the individual self something that is *negated* by its interaction with other intelligences; a negation that in turn allows the intuition of the actions of other intelligences as being other than my own. Hence, before the self is conscious of its freedom, *its freedom must have been already restricted.* And with this, Schelling introduces the dialectic of freedom and necessity to parallel that of the finite and infinite. The absolute form of either equals the other, whereas empirical freedom exists for the self only within the limiting parameters of temporal finitude and the restrictions imposed upon us by other intelligences. With the "restrictedness . . . of individuality" Schelling has arrived at the "synthetic point or pivot of theoretical and practical philosophy" and has with this "really arrived in the territory of the latter" (I/3, 552).

Time and Historicity

Time and individuality arise for the self in its act of free self-determination. With the autonomous act of the self, Schelling leaves the domain of theoretical philosophy and enters the realm of the practical, that is, of the experience of self-consciousness *für sich.* Thus, whereas the object of theoretical philosophy is the activity of the self prior to consciousness, that is, nature, the object of practical philosophy is the autonomous activity of the *will*, whose field of performance is none other than that of experience *qua* history.[21]

The problematic of freedom and necessity—following the formal dynamics of infinitude and finitude, unlimited and limited—appears in Schelling's discussion of time and its determinative role in our lives. For example, the particular succession of time into which one is "thrown and posited" (*hingeworfen und gesetzt*; I/3, 485) is not something that one's will has any control over; it is rather something that happens to you. As a condition of restrictedness, the time which one becomes aware of in the act of self-knowledge "is not determined by you, insofar as you are this individual, for to that extent you are not the producer, but yourself belong to the product" (I/3, 484).[22] It is this constitutive time, as that force which provides for the possibility of a past, which determines your individuality.

For if we were to take away this original restrictedness, time and all individuality would dissolve into an absolute intelligence that would remain "unaware of itself as such" (ibid.). The boundary that separates absolute intelligence and conscious intelligence is therefore restrictedness, finitude, and time: "For pure reason there is no time, for it *is* everything, and everything at once; for reason, insofar as it is empirical, everything comes into being, and what arises for it, is all merely successive" (I/3, 485).[23] Considered from the standpoint of temporality, the absolute intelligence encompasses everything that was, is, and will be. For this absolute intelligence to "become a determinate" and individual intelligence it must submit to the restriction of time, which will produce "an empirical infinitude engendered through succession of presentations" (I/3, 487). The empirical self has the continuous "feeling" of being restricted, a feeling that is *provoked* by time, yet simultaneously *sustained* by the self's awareness of the infinite. As our entire existence depends on activity, our existence must find its expression in continuous productivity. As Schelling makes clear, there is a "*necessary* striving to sustain the continuity of the representations, that is, an *eternal producing*," in which the self moves from a past and "inevitably aims at something in the future" (I/3, 384). But at what does the self aim at in the future?

The answer of course lies in the imagination. Echoing previous accounts of this faculty advanced by Kant and Fichte,[24] Schelling provides an account of how, as a result of the opposition generated by the infinity of freedom and the "finitude" of our temporal existence, "an activity must arise which wavers in the middle between finitude and infinity"; an activity which mediates "between the theoretical and the practical" projects of reason that he terms "imagination" (I/3, 558). The power generated by such a polarity must of necessity produce something, "which itself oscillates between infinity and finitude" (ibid.). The products of such an oscillation he terms "Ideas" and opposes them to "concepts," and this state of productive imagining he terms "reason" as opposed to "understanding." Conversely, what is commonly called reason is within Schelling's *System* "nothing else but imagination in the service of freedom" (I/3, 559). Thus, when the reflexive activities of the understanding fail to provide a mechanism whereby the self can visualize how the moral law should be realized in the future, the self must rely on the productive powers of the imagination to create and *bring forth* possibilities of how the future should be. The self is led by this process into "a new realm, into the realm of the creative and realizing activity of reason" which Schelling earlier described as follows:

> What lies beyond the real world are the *Ideas*, i.e., not as objects of speculation but of action, to that extent therefore of a *future* experience (but nonetheless still of experience), something that should be realized in reality. (I/3, 465)

The Tense of the Absolute: Futurity

Just as the third member of every triadic class of categories is the condition of possibility for the other two members, the future is the condition of the possibility of the past and present. The construction of substance occurs under the category of the past, whereas the awareness of causality arises in the present. However, both are made possible only through the reciprocity of the future. The past can be grasped only in concepts, the present through intuition, but the future is accessible and present only through the imagination:

> With the spirit striving to disengage itself from the present, the present becomes, in and through this activity, a *past*. The past meanwhile, attains presence only in the *concept*. Yet the soul, whose productive activity is infinite, ceaselessly strives for *reality*, and thus involves a continuous progression from the *concept* to the *intuition*, from the intuition to the concept, from that past to the present, and from the present to the future. (I/3, 385)

Only the future, in its reciprocal fluidity, can enable us to move between and among the tenses. The unconscious status of theoretical philosophy's domain lies in an irretrievable past; the conscious state of practical philosophy's domain lies in the immediacy of moral decision; but it is the future as the sphere of imagination and hope that provides our power for aesthetic production, informing the past and the present, and thereby making both bearable.

The future tense is ultimately the sphere of the infinite and of unity. In articulating this position, Schelling advances three dimensions of time. The first dimension is that of the future, the second is that of the past, and the third, that of the present. Among these, "the ruling (*herrschende*) dimension" is that of the future, since it is the future dimension that is "properly speaking the time in time." The future is a time within this time because its essence is to mirror eternity within time (I/6, 277). The dimension of futurity reflects the eternal in the present now. It mirrors the totality of time because it is itself the "privation of totality," and "the expression of *Nicht-Totalität*" (I/6, 276). Futurity is thus a force resistant to the closure of an objectified Absolute. Consequently, the denial of the future could only occur through "the completed affirmation, totality (*das vollendete Affirmirtseyn, die Totalität*)," which can only be an infinite intension that "time eternally lacks" (I/6, 275).

It is a principle of Schelling's philosophy that reality equals the rupture of the whole, and that finitude is fundamentally a sphere of contingency. The possibility of both the self, or of the Absolute, ever becoming totally objectified, is categorically ruled out. It is ruled out in the name of the *infinite* freedom that animates both: "if the appearance of freedom is necessarily infinite, the total evolution of the absolute synthesis is also an infinite process, and history itself is a never wholly completed revelation of that absolute" (I/3, 603). A complete revelation of the Absolute would complete history. However, for history to complete itself, the objective world would have to become a "perfect manifestation of God, or what comes to the same thing, of the total congruence of the free with the unconscious" (I/3, 603). But if this were to ever occur, freedom itself, the infinite power that defines our nature, would dissipate. In the dimension of particularity, for the self to completely objectify itself for itself, it would have to wholly overcome the rupture that constitutes our dualistic, alienated (*entzweitetes*) consciousness.

However, to say that such a complete objectification of the absolute could occur, that history could end, or that man could overcome the restrictions of his finitude: all this presupposes a conception of an otherworldly utopia that Schelling simply finds both irrelevant and downright unappealing:

> For if we were ever to fulfill our purpose and realize the absolute, then there would indeed be no other law for every individual, and for the entire species, than the law of their perfected nature, consequently all history would cease; hence the feeling of boredom that attaches itself to every idea of an absolute state of reason (like the idea of a theater piece in which all the major roles are played by perfected beings, or the lecture of a novel . . . where idealized people appear, or a Christian poem

of the heroes in which angels—the most boring beings of all—play all the major roles). (I/1, 473)

The Endless Process

With this, we approach the end of our attempt at understanding Schelling on his own terms. Having focused almost exclusively on a small number of his earliest writings, extending from roughly 1790 to 1804, we have followed his own interpretive strategy and sought out his "fundamental thought" to serve as the pole star of our investigation. To review, I have argued that this fundamental thought is more accurately a *form* which, just as he argued in his *Form Essay*, is shaped by the organic logic of disjunction. Rooted in Kant's understanding of the disjunctive syllogism, this form of inference provides the young Schelling with the desired means not only to unite Plato's eternal form of reasoning with Kant, but also supplies him with the key to presenting an organic form of philosophy which, grounded in the self-organizing dynamic of life, provides him with a natural schema of freedom. What is essential in this organic form is the dynamic of relation (*Verbindung*), not what is related: the relation of unity sustains the field in which oppositional elements emerge. The possibility of Plato's *same* and the *other* is what is common to both, and this is their unity, their identity. And with Kant: the possibility of *Sinn* and *Verstand* is what is common to both, the whole within which these parts emerge. This self-differentiation of the whole occurs according to the organic logic of reciprocal coordination, both horizontally between parts, and vertically between parts and whole, a reciprocal coordination that again follows the organic logic of disjunction as found in Kant's dynamic category of community and reciprocal causality; the same category that accounts for how a living organism can be both cause and effect of itself, and in this sense can be seen as free. Finally, to demonstrate the explanatory power of this interpretive strategy I have presented in this last chapter an account of Schelling's thought over this fourteen-year period as if it were guided by this organic form. Given enough time, I believe we could continue with this strategy throughout Schelling's entire fifty-four-year career, and find that throughout he consistently "oriented" his work by keeping this form "before his eyes." Needless to say, the portrait of Schelling's philosophy that emerges from this departs mightily from the various accounts of his work that have been advanced over the years.

Due to reasons previously noted, Schelling's demand that philosophy be as free as it is creative does not lend itself to the "groupthink" of a school of followers. Consequently, his philosophical profile has been chiefly defined for posterity by that one person in his life who betrayed him the most, namely, his one-time friend and colleague, Hegel. The distorted portrait of Schelling that emerges from Hegel's most notorious accounts of him has proven an irresistible temptation to those more inclined to accept the judgment of others than actually to read Schelling. Hegel's charge that Schelling, having carried out his philosophical education in public, was the Proteus of German Idealism, has provided the template for most subsequent treatments of Schelling. When faced with the sheer number of pages written about such diverse topics as theology, legal theory, transcendental philosophy, as well as *Naturphilosophie*, it is understandable that one might be inclined to focus on that one aspect of Schelling's work that works best with one's field of interest or school of thought. Expanding our focus to include the entirety of Schelling's career only makes the problem more acute, since we then have to wrestle with an even broader array of work generated over five decades of writing: at twenty-five he presents his *System of Transcendental Idealism,* while at sixty-six he announces the "existentialist system" of his Positive Philosophy. Yet whereas most have seen these differences as supporting Hegel's verdict of, at best, philosophical inconsistency, I would like to suggest these "differences" in Schelling's works demonstrate the robust productivity of an organic form of philosophy which, oriented towards an open future, values the risks of discovery more than the certitude of method. Rather than an embarrassing weakness, we should see these differences as C. S. Peirce did, namely, as an indication of a "truly scientific mind" more committed to the pursuit of truth than "the trammels of system." At the very least this approach will allow us to read Schelling as he himself read Kant, by first assuming that Kant's thought can make sense, and then figuring out how he must be read in order to support this hypothesis. Calling on Peirce once again, we could call this an abductive method of interpretation, which leads directly to the type of immanent reconstruction of Schelling's philosophy that that we have carried out.

The challenge of such an immanent reconstruction, of reading Schelling on his own terms, is daunting, since he insists that to do this we must consider all of his work. He makes this point quite clear in his Berlin lectures of 1841:

> I do not at all expect to be judged according to prejudices and provisional remarks alone. Whoever seeks to listen to me, listens to the

end. It could very well be that in this case he would find something completely different from what, commensurate with his existing and somewhat narrow opinions, he expected to find. (II/3, 143)

The need to do this, to evaluate Schelling's work only after one has heard him to the end, is due to the very nature of his way of doing philosophy that we have been considering: what he is presenting "does not consist of a series of finished propositions that can be put forth individually," since "its results are generated in a continuous but thoroughly free and animated progression and movement, whose moments do not allow themselves to be captured in the memory, but rather only in the spirit" (II/3, 21). In terms now familiar, we encounter in this self-description the dynamic of an organic development in which individual moments can only be understood within the full context of his philosophy. Pointing once again to the creative fundament of doing philosophy, Schelling warns his audience that he does not offer "finished propositions" to be memorized, but individual "moments" that can only be captured through one's own active participation. Once again applying Schelling's words to understanding his philosophy, it is clear that if we are to remain true to his own terms we cannot treat each "moment" of his "free and animated progression" as resulting in a "finished proposition" that can be captured in the memory, as one might do with, for example, a logical method that can then be imitated by others. Rather, the Herculean challenge he appears to be throwing down for us is to follow all of his work as it unfolds in a free but continuous progression, trying throughout to construct for ourselves, in our own spirit, the moments which together reveal the meaning of his philosophy. While the limited scope of the current investigation is unable to meet the breadth of this challenge in its full expanse, I have made the case that organic form is the fundamental thought that directs the development of his work.

As we have seen, this development does not follow the Cartesian deductive model, but is rather based on the recursive employment of this Urform, whose dynamic generates the ever-present triadic principles that structure and inform Schelling's work. Regardless of how seemingly confused and contradictory his work may appear at first glance, upon closer examination one begins to see the imprint of this organic form of reasoning. As in his reading of Leibniz, one must find the "'perspectival center of gravity' from which the chaos of the different opinions, which from every other standpoint appear totally confused, exhibits consistency and agreement" (I/4, 457). To do this requires that one "keep in mind the idea of a universal system that provides context and necessity to all individual systems—as opposed as they may be—in the system of human knowing." Implicit in this position is the claim that our reality is simply too multifaceted and dynamic to be captured in just one description, demanding instead an ongoing process of iterative description. Since all knowing is grounded in the experience of our world, and our world (consciousness and nature) is constantly changing, then what we can claim as true will be the result of the recursive application of our patterns of thought to experience. These descriptions in turn reinforce and modify the principles that guide our pattern of thinking, completing the cycle or loop of the dynamic growth of knowledge. This iterative process demands that we consider things repeatedly, sometimes from different perspectives and with different trajectories, acknowledging thereby the fundamentally developmental nature of the "organization" that is "the system of human knowing":

> For this very reason a *common* (*gemeinschaftlicher*) ruling spirit permeates all individual systems earning this name; every individual system is possible only through deviation from the universal archetype (*Urbild*), to which all, taken together, more or less approach. This universal system is, however, not a chain which runs upwards, where it hangs onward into infinity link-by-link, but is rather an *organization,* in which every individual member is in relation to every other [member], reciprocally cause and effect, means and ends. Thus too is all progress in philosophy only progress through *development;* every individual system which earns this name can be viewed as a seed which indeed slowly and gradually, but inexorably and in every direction, advances itself in multifarious development. (I/4, 457)

Seen in this context, this passage has a different meaning from what we encountered in the first paragraph: this iteration draws our focus to Schelling's explicit identification of the organic form of philosophy and its developmental process of self-differentiation, whose telos aims at a future more complex than the past. From this standpoint of unceasing growth, there is no good reason to assume that there is only one unchanging, precise, and exhaustive description of our world in general, and *especially* of what is *most important* to us. Our world has many descriptions—the fiction is to believe that it only has one.[25]

Obviously, to see Schelling as Peirce did challenges us to reframe our expectations of what philosophy does, requiring us to reconfigure our understanding of *system* and how it is ordered. But what are our options if mathematics cannot supply us with the *Urform* of all knowing, and if an axiomatic deductive model no longer offers a way of showing how the many knowledges are one? It's as if we face the problematic dilemma of the oenophile who, after a night of too much Gigondas, drops his keys in the dark on the way home, yet rather than feeling around in the dark, opts to look for them where there is light, under the street light. Used to only the sight of discovery, our oenophile would rather look in vain all night, than use the more immediate sense of touch to search for his keys. While sight generates results more quickly, it only works in a limited sphere of experience. Feeling and touch, on the other hand, while slower in exploring our world, offer a vastly more immediate and yet universal scope of experience. A person blind from birth can thrive, but a person incapable of feeling and touch is forever exiled from experience. A similar point can be made about consciousness and the relation between conceptual and intuitive thought: a person incapable of rational thought still experiences emotion, but a human lacking all self-awareness would not even be able to experience emotion. Yet like our inebriated lover of wine, the seductive promise of conceptual thought's quick precision can lead to dependence on this one way of seeing the world. The resulting exclusion of intuition results in a way of experiencing the world that Schelling likened to an intellectual sickness that "makes permanent the separation between humanity and the world, in that it considers the world as a thing in itself, which neither intuition or imagination, nor understanding or reason, is capable of reaching" (I/2, 14). As we have seen, Schelling's "whole philosophy proceeds from the standpoint of intuition, not that of reflection, occupied, for instance, by Kant and his philosophy" (I/3, 456). It is here, in this immediate act of awareness that humanity finds its unity with nature and the epistemological footing that enables us, as members of the larger organization of nature, to function as the autoepistemic organ of nature, whose apparent knowledge *of* nature is at this most important level a participatory "knowing with (*Mitwissenschaft*)" nature (I/9, 221 [Erlanger Vorträge—1821). The common ground that unifies us with nature, this identity locates the beginning of thinking and deliberation in the *fact* of existence, whose chaotic power is the real ground of the cogito's reflexive determinations. This inversion of Kant's order grounds Schelling's system in the dynamic experience of life, an epistemologically problematic field that he orders through what I have been calling an organic form of thinking.

It is perhaps here that we can see and appreciate the role this organic form plays throughout Schelling's work, connecting as it does the initial and final stages of his philosophical development. In his first book, the *Weltseele* of 1798, he writes that "our philosophy cannot proceed from the mechanistic (what is negative), but rather must start with the organic (what is positive)" (I/2, 349). Pointing towards the very factors that will inform the distinction between Negative and Positive Philosophy in his final system, Schelling presents the organic as what is positive in nature's self-organizing system of creation as opposed to the static and formulaic *results* of this process. Both the *Weltseele* and his Negative and Positive Philosophy reveal the imprint of his *Urform*, providing for us what Schelling claimed to have found for Leibniz, the "'perspectival center of gravity' from which the chaos of the different opinions, which from every other standpoint appear totally confused, exhibits consistency and agreement" (I/4, 457). A "center of gravity" whose form in turn reveals the trace of the "universal archetype (*Urbild*), to which all [systems], taken together, more or less approach." Like the self-similarity found in a fractal, each philosophical system (worthy of this name) presents an iteration of philosophy's *Urbild*. The equation at the root of a mathematical fractal however, differs greatly from Schelling's archetype of philosophy. Other than the specificity of number, it is a form of thinking which, like Kant's schema, straddles the boundary between literal and figurative and is, in this sense, more of a symbol than a formula. Just as Kant presents Plato's idea of the perfect Republic as an "archetype (*Urbild*)" and "maximum" (A 317/B 373), Schelling understands the universal archetype of philosophy as mediating the maximum of the absolute. As such, any description of this form is as problematic as the disjunctive logic that attempts to articulate it. Nonetheless, describe it we must, and so we close this investigation with a brief justification of our attempt to describe this organic form of reasoning. Kant's words about understanding Plato, enthusiastically used by Schelling to understand Kant, we now employ to explain our reading of Schelling:

> it is by no means unusual, upon comparing the thoughts which an author has expressed in regard to his subject, whether in ordinary conversation or in writing, to find that we understand him better than he has understood himself. As he has not sufficiently determined his concept, he has sometimes spoken, or even thought, in opposition to his own intention. (A 314/B 370; cf. I/5, 188)

In contrast to Schelling, who, when necessary was willing to read Kant "against even the original meaning of his words" (I/1, 155), our attempt at articulating Schelling's organic form of philosophy has pursued a more harmonious strategy. Following his claim to "understand Kant better than he understood himself" (I/5, 188), the argument of this work has sought to make explicit Schelling's "fundamental thought" that provides the key to unlocking what, in my view, "he *had* to have intended if his philosophy . . . [is] . . . to prove internally cohesive" (I/1, 375).

Appendix

Eulogy Sung at Hahn's Grave[1]

[1]   Slumber gently your decaying limbs,
       Dust from most eminent man—rest here!
       Nobles of my land! All weep
       A tear for him! Lament with me!

       Here the sheath, but raised up
       Over all spheres is the spirit
       Spirit from God, wrested away from mortality,
       To there where the veil of humanity sunders!

[9]   Ha, in light alters the transfiguration,
       Stands in angel's robe before God's throne
       Gaze now freer through the world—even though
       Allowed him some views of the creator while here!

       Did he not dare to speak, with astute demeanor.
       Still mortal, the forces of nature?
       Did his eyes not plunge through the cosmos and earth's dale
       Searched and found the purest trace of the deity?

[17]   Heard he not the harmony of the soul? Heard
       And understood he not the language of the spirit?

Did you never see the fire, that nourished his eye,
Never see the deep look in his appearance?

Oh he faded, died, in death's slumber
Sunk down lies here the sheath!
Were tears ever just and sorrow
O then weep, you nobles, weep with me!

[25]   Oh he died, of the wise, roll down tears,
For the most eminent man tear-stained!
But . . . weep not, we will see him again,
Where death's slumber unites us!

There, where Hahn, the guide now complete
In the light of immortality
Unclouded views, coarse sheath removed
Joyful now gaze through time and eternity!

[33]   Where he now mixes the jubilant singing in heavenly
Song! Ha there now he praises
Him the all-merciful—sinks back onto the throne
Inspired with thanks!—O brother weep no more!

But his name lives here! Often celebrate
His majestic memory,
So often then to renew the resolve,
To thus dedicate ourselves to wisdom here!

[41]   Friedrich W. J. Sch. In B.

Notes

Preface

1. Manfred Baum for example, has recently called for "the story of his philosophical development [. . . to] be rewritten." Manfred Baum, "The Beginnings of Schelling's Philosophy of Nature," in *The Reception of Kant's Critical Philosophy—Fichte, Schelling, and Hegel,* edited by Sally Sedgwick (Cambridge: Cambridge University Press, 2000), 199.

2. The full passage reads: "You ask whether I know of anybody but Delboeuf and myself who have treated the inorganic as a sort of product of the living? This is good . . . my views were probably influenced by Schelling,—by all stages of Schelling, but especially by the *Philosophie der Natur.* I consider Schelling as enormous; and one thing I admire about him is his freedom from the trammels of system, and his holding himself uncommitted to any previous utterance. In that, he is like a scientific man. If you were to call my philosophy Schellingism transformed in the light of modern physics, I should not take it hard" (January 28, 1895; in R. B. Perry, *The Thought and Character of William James* [Boston, 1935], vol. II, 416f.).

3. G. W. F. Hegel, *Briefe von und an Hegel,* edited by K. Hegel (Leipzig: Dunker & Humboldt, 1887), vol. I, 138.

Chapter 1. Life as the Schema of Freedom: Schelling's Organic Form of Philosophy

1. "[W]e take nothing more from experience than is required to *give* us an object of outer or of inner sense. The object of outer sense we obtain through the mere concept of matter (impenetrable, lifeless extension), the object of inner sense through the concept of a thinking being (in the empirical inner representation, 'I think'). As to the rest, in the whole metaphysical treatment of these objects, we must entirely dispense with

all empirical principles which profess to add to these concepts any other more special experience" (A 848/B 876).

2. *KrV*, B viii.

3. II/5, 109, 108.

4. *KrV*, B vii. Compare B xxxv, where he advances the ultimate goal and method of his critical "purge" of metaphysics as a "dogmatic procedure of reason" whose defining dogma is the denial of "progress in pure knowledge," i.e., the denial of change or evolution in the principles or structures of human reason. See also the *"dogmata"* of his transcendental a priori synthetic propositions (the ideas of reason) at A 736/B 764.

5. I/5, 273.

6. I/5, 110.

7. I/7, 100.

8. *WMV*, 92.

9. Immanuel Kant, *De mundi sensibilis atque intelligibilis forma et principiis*; Ak II, 394.

10. *WMV*, 94.

11. January 28, 1895; in R. B. Perry, *The Thought and Character of William James* (Boston, 1935), vol. II, 416f.

12. I/3, VI. While this myth does serve the purpose of glorifying the alienation of the cogito, like all myths, it limits its believer's freedom, thereby debilitating the individual's capacity for further self-differentiation.

13. To prove his point, Schelling cites Goethe's words from *Faust*:
    Were not the eye filled with sun
    How could we see the light?
    If god's own power did not live in us
    How could the divine entrance us? (I/9, 221)

14. A not too insignificant point about the way in which a theory of truth, in this case the correspondence theory of truth, in establishing the rules of the game, predetermines what will be accepted as true knowledge; a point which becomes painfully if not absurdly clear when considering the nature of the subject and its capacity for self-knowledge.

15. Gustav Leonhard Plitt (Hrsg.), *Aus Schelling's Leben in Briefen*, 2 Bde. (Leipzig: S. Hirzel, 1869–1870), I, 37 (hereafter cited as *Plitt*).

16. Over the past twenty-five years there have only been four significant English treatments of Schelling. All clearly demonstrate a tendency to fragment Schelling's work, while presenting the aspects they do consider on terms that are often inhospitable to the spirit of his thinking. Alan White's *Schelling: An Introduction to the System of Freedom* (1983), offers up a Hegelian reading of one moment in Schelling's philosophical development. Andrew Bowie's provocative *Schelling and Modern European Philosophy* (1993), provides an *apologia* of Schelling as an early Postmodernist, but only by ignoring those essential elements of Schelling's work—most notably the theological—that do not conform to this reading. As his title indicates, Edward Beach's *The Potencies of God(s):*

Schelling's Philosophy of Mythology (1994), confines itself to an analysis of Schelling's later work on mythology, while failing to even mention— much less integrate—Schelling's first published scholarly work on myth, carried out while still a student in Tübingen. Conversely, focussing on the earlier Schelling, Dale Snow's brilliant *Schelling and the End of Idealism* (1996) itself ends less than half way through Schelling's career in 1812, thereby failing to address the final and arguably most important phase of Schelling's career, namely, his existential critique of Hegel's panlogism advanced in his Berlin lectures on *Positive Philosophy*.

17. Paul Ricoeur, *De l'interpretation*; essai sur Freud (Paris: Editions du Seuil, 1965), 35.

18. "I am a schoolmaster who has to teach philosophy—who, possibly for that reason, believes that philosophy like geometry is teachable, and must no less than geometry have a regular structure. But again, a knowledge of the facts in geometry and philosophy is one thing, and the mathematical or philosophical talent which procreates and discovers is another: my province is to discover that scientific form, or to aid in the formation of it" (G. W. F. Hegel, *Briefe von und an Hegel*. Ed. K. Hegel (Leipzig: Dunker & Humboldt, 1887), vol. I, 138.

19. Schelling's final judgment in 1841 reads: "The fundamental thought of Hegel is that reason relates to the in-itself, the essence (*Wesen*) of things, from which it immediately follows that philosophy, to the extent that it is a science of reason, occupies itself only with the whatness (*Was*) or the essence of things" (II/3, 60).

20. Accordingly, the theoretical dimension of Schelling's postulate of philosophy demands "an *ursprüngliche* (transcendental) construction" of the Self (I/1, 451). As we will see later in chapter 6, the freedom of the act of construction demands *autonomy of creation* that rules out as heteronomous the adoption of an external techne or method. In Schelling's transcendental method, "the student must be *immersed*, so to speak, in the transcendental method. Hence the first principle must already be *his own construction*, which is *required* of (and left to) him, for him to learn at the outset that whatever originates for him by means of this construction is *nothing beyond* it, and that it exists only to the extent that he constructs" (I/1, 447). Consequently, since "philosophy contains the most freedom, . . . [it] *is therefore just as much art as science*" (I/5, 141).

21. For example, in the space of twelve years between 1792 and 1804, before the age of thirty, Schelling produced thirty-four essays and books for publication—more than enough material to fill five volumes of his collected works. While the breadth of topics covered in this period is extensive, they might nonetheless be divided into seven areas of focus: 1) myth and biblical criticism; 2) commentary on ancient and Platonic philosophy; 3) the development of his own philosophy articulated through the vocabulary of Fichte's program; 4) the construction of his own philosophy of nature and 5) complementary system of transcendental idealism; 6) the development

of a philosophy of art; and 7) philosophical criticism and commentary. The challenge is to show how these writings cohere in a systematically significant manner. Hartmut Kuhlmann is a lone voice who argues that the diverse work of the young Schelling was in fact united by a vision, in what he calls Schelling's "proto-system." See his *Schellings Früher Idealismus* (Stuttgart-Weimar: Verlag J. B. Metzler, 1993), 11. Strangely however, he also makes the rather dubious claim that aesthetics plays no role in this embryonic system (Kuhlmann, 19).

22. As Schelling often does, he paraphrases here a passage taken from Leibniz, but as provided by Jacobi in the latter's *Ueber die Lehre des Spinoza* (1789) he cites a passage taken from Leibniz's third letter to M. Remond de Montmort, found in his *Recueil de div. Pieces par des Maizeaux* (Tom. II, p. 417, *Op. omnia*, Tom. II, Part I, p. 79). The frequency with which Schelling makes use of ideas found in Jacobi's works has been employed by some as evidence testifying for Schelling's dependence on Jacobi. But as the case here shows, Schelling is using Jacobi to get at Leibniz, whose work in Latin he was more familiar with than his letters in French. Sandkaulen-Bock sticks with the Jacobi factor, and advances Jacobi's *Spinozabriefe* (1785) as the determinative factor in shaping Schelling's first thoughts, setting him on a course that, while close to Fichte's, was destined to become more concerned with correcting the lifeless determinism of Spinoza's *Ethics*. Because an unconditioned principle cannot be a thing (since it is *"unbedingt"*), Spinoza's absolute must be life itself, which, like Jacobi's intuition of a personal God, we grasp through an intellectual intuition that is itself the manifestation of the productive activity of the 'self'. See Sandkaulen-Bock, *Ausgang vom Unbedingten* (Göttingen: Vandenhoeck & Ruprecht, 1990), 39ff. Annemarie Pieper defends a similar position in her "'Ethik à la Spinoza' Historisch-systematische Überlegungen zu einem Vorhaben des jungen Schelling," *Zeitschrift für philosophische Forschung* 31, 1977: 545–564.

23. See, for example, *KrV*, B 112, and *KU*, 407. We will discuss this epistemological point in detail later in chapter 3.

24. Compare *KrV*, A 838/B 866.

25. In his lectures on the philosophy of mythology, given at the Berlin Academy in 1847, Schelling makes the following point about his "genetic connection" with Kant: "But it is the numerous writers of history who have recently discovered contemporary philosophy that are no less clear about the genetic connection mentioned above, and those others who imagine all of the later work as a merely accidental, arbitrary and unfounded extension beyond Kant—these also are less in the position to provide the definitive judgment of that point in the structure of the Kantian Criticism on which the later developments connect as a necessary consequence. This point, in my opinion, lies in Kant's doctrine of the ideal of reason" (II/1, 283, note 1).

26. Hindcasting is a scientific method for testing mathematical models, usually

dealing with chaotic systems of nature such as tsunamis, climate change, earthquakes, and so forth. Models are tested using data of past events to see how accurately they would have predicated these events. An accurate prediction of past events demonstrates the model's success, but only in explaining what has already happened.

27. The italicized passages in full quotation marks occur in *Section I, Book II* of *The Transcendental Dialectic*, in Kant's discussion of the "System of *Weltbegriffe*" that synthesize the unconditioned (*KrV*, A 408/B 435; see in particular *KrV*, A 411/B 438, and A 414/B 441). The seamless blending of Kant's and Schelling's words illustrates the latter's fidelity to the goals of the former.

28. A possibility of a coordinated aggregate in which conditions mutually determine one another is a possibility Kant must deny, since thought for him can only be discursive (sequential): "unconditioned only as it may exist in the series of appearances . . . substances . . . cannot exist in community. They are mere aggregates, and contain nothing on which to base a series" (*KrV*, A 414/B 441). In the regressive mode, reason can only consider that which submits to the form of the time sequence.

29. Kant insists that this progressive approach serves no definite purpose because it cannot determine a conclusion. This is because the series is engaged in the *process of becoming* and therefore opens out towards the possibility of the future; a fact that would require the progressive synthesis "of the whole series of all future alterations" (*KrV*, A 336/B 394). Since the dynamic categories determine the progressive strategy, it does not follow the logic of subsumption, but rather that of a productive coordination (*Wechselwirkung*), thereby precluding the possibility of closure. Precisely because of this, Kant concludes that "reason can be quite indifferent as to how far this advance extends *a parte posteriori*, and whether a totality of the series is possible at all" (*KrV*, A 331/B 388f).

30. For the most thorough treatment in English of the philosophical dilemmas faced by those who immediately followed Kant, see Frederick C. Beiser, *The Fate of Reason: German Philosophy from Kant to Fichte* (Cambridge, MA: Harvard University Press, 1987).

31. Reason's demand for unity is unconditional and is thus never sought as a means to an end, but rather only as an end in itself. The experiential and redemptive ramifications of realizing this imperative will be briefly discussed in what follows.

32. *KrV*, A 665/B 693.

33. *KU*, 117f.

34. Because this relational category of community and reciprocal causality articulates "coordinated aggregates" that "do not constitute a series," Kant denies that they can synthesize the unconditioned, and are thus "not adapted" to synthesizing a transcendental idea (*KrV*, A 414/B 441). He appears to change his mind however, in his discussion of the *sublime* in the third *Critique*, a point we examine in chapter 3 (cf. *KU*, 266).

35. *Phil.*, 29b–30c. It is important to keep in mind that for Plato and the Ancient Greeks, unity, the state of oneness, and the number one, are all expressed through the same word, ἕν. When a Plato or Plotinus speaks of the One, they are in a very important sense also speaking about absolute unity per se (cf. Plato's *Parmenides*, 130b–c). A similar understanding holds true in German, where *Einheit* means both unity and oneness.

36. *On the Possibility of a Form of Philosophy in General* (1794), (I/1, 85f).

37. *TK*, 15. Schelling refers to *Timaeus* 68e5–69a1. It is important to keep in mind that Schelling is freely translating, if not transcribing, Plato's Greek in a "sketchbook of ideas" he most certainly never thought would be published.

38. See the sole source for all of these texts, Michael Franz's excellent commentary and transcription of Schelling's notes "Über Dichter, Propheten, Dichterbegeisterung, Enthusiasmus, Theopneustie, und göttliche Einwirkung auf Menschen überhaupt" and "Über den Geist der Platonischen Philosophie," in his *Schellings Tübinger Platon-Studien* (Göttingen: Vandenhoeck und Ruprecht, 1996). Until the recent publication of Schelling's notebooks from his time as a seminary student in Tübingen, only Werner Beierwaltes had examined how Platonism influenced Schelling's works and German Idealism. See his *Platonismus und Idealismus* (Frankfurt am Main: Suhrkamp Verlag, 1972), as well as his recent article "The Legacy of Neoplatonism in F. W. J. Schelling's Thought," *International Journal of Philosophical Studies* 10:4 (2002): 393–428.

39. *TK*, 35f.

40. In this context he refers to *Philebus* 16b5–c7, and uses it as cross-cultural evidence supporting his account of a *universal human nature* which, grounded in our free use of reason, is delimited by the human experience of alienation:

"... there certainly is no better road (ὁδός), nor can there ever be, than that which I have always loved, though it has often deserted me, leaving me lonely and forlorn.

"What is the road? Only tell us."

One which is easy to point out, but very difficult to follow; for through it all inventions of art have been brought to light. See; this is the road I mean.

"Go on; what is it?"

A gift of the gods to men, as I believe, was tossed down from some divine source through the agency of a Prometheus together with a gleaming fire" (*AA*, I/1,127).

Plato's association of Prometheus and his form of all-knowing justifies the young Schelling's inclusion of this passage in his *Magistardissertation*, as proof of reason's interest in the origin of evil. Both Prometheus and Eve demonstrate freedom in choosing to defy the gods in their desire for knowledge, and both suffer the same pain that comes with attaining their goal, namely, the knowledge of, and desire for, an ideal they can never possess. Plato continues to describe this "road" or form of all-knowing in the following words: "and the ancients, who were better than we and lived nearer the gods, handed down the tradition that all things which are ever said to exist are sprung from one and many and have inherent in them the finite and the infinite. This being the way in which these things are arranged, we must always assume that there is in every case one idea of everything and must look for it—for we shall find that it is there" (*Phil.* 16c8–d1).

41. Following the direction of inquiry specified by the aforementioned dedication, Schelling's "commentary" addresses the ontological question of creation and how the divine interacts with the natural—a theme his other notebooks address from the epistemological standpoint of Plato's accounts of divine manias, enthusiasm, and prophecy. Consequently, the *Philebus* is cited once for every three citations from the *Timaeus*. Substantively, however, the importance of the *Philebus* passages would justify renaming this text to a "Commentary on Plato's *Timaeus* and *Philebus*."

42. I/1, 89.

43. I/1, 227.

44. I/2, 356.

45. I/2, 55.

46. The text cited here is my translation of Schelling's sometimes very loose translation of Plato. He frequently does not clothe the transcribed Greek terms in their appropriate form, and I have decided to reproduce such terms exactly as he rendered them. This gets confusing, so please keep in mind that these notes on the *Timaeus* and *Philebus* are from a student's notebook in which he recorded his thoughts on these texts. He is not concerned with rendering Plato precisely, as much as he is concerned with extracting the spirit of Plato's thoughts. The freedom he takes with his rendering of Plato's words reflects this. And in some ways this is a gift, because his free translations reveal more to us about his own agenda and interests than if he had hewn closer to the letter.

47. *TK*, 31f.

48. *TK*, 70.

49. This description matches almost exactly Kant's characterization of the *Naturbegriffe* of the dynamic categories in the first *Critique* (cf. A 418/B 446).

50. Schelling's formulation echoes the "center point of gravity for interpreting the history of philosophy" cited previously : "Who has once found such a center of gravity for the history of philosophy is alone capable to describe it truly and according to *the worth of the human spirit*" (I/1, 457, my emphasis).

51. As we will later see, Kant opts to articulate the form of systematic unity through a very similar triad of logical principles—unity, plurality, and continuity—that match up well with Plato's limited, unlimited, and the common mean.

52. *Phil.*, 15d7.
53. It is fascinating to consider how Schelling must have read Kant after having learned how to read philosophy through a study of Plato in his original Ancient Greek (at the age of twelve). While Kant does acknowledge that Plato's theory of ideas warrants imitation, Schelling surely saw other aspects of Kant's architectonic that leaned heavily on Plato. This had to have made for a much different reading of Kant than those of his contemporaries, such as his roommates at the *Stift*, Hölderlin and Hegel.
54. I/7, 371.
55. A 407/B 434.
56. *TK*, 33.
57. "The So-Called 'Oldest System Programme of German Idealism' (1796)," translated by Andrew Bowie, in *Aesthetics and Subjectivity* (Manchester: Manchester Press, 1990), Appendix A, 266f. Contrary to Pöggler and others who see in this document both the penmanship and brilliance of Hegel, it is clear to those familiar with Hegel *and* Schelling that only the latter could have developed the ideas expressed in this fragmentary manifesto.
58. In a letter to Hegel (21.7.1795), Schelling confides that he had originally wished to write his dissertation as a satire of the Orthodox's handling of heretics (*"de praecipius orthodoxorum antiquiorum adversus haeriticos armis"*), but was unable to do so in light of the religious authorities. Schelling's second dissertation did, however, deal with the subject of heresy, but in a more "non-heretical" fashion, by showing how the early church had seriously erred in prosecuting Marcion for heresy (*Briefe von und an Hegel*, Bd. I, 27–28).
59. This telos can be thought of as Kant's Transcendental Ideal, as what is sacred and thus divine, as what is not yet, but should be. But we should not understand this telos in the Aristotelian sense of the circular causality of a predetermined teleology. Rather, within Schelling's framework of a divinity that does not yet exist, this telos symbolizes an open future animated by a utopian form of causality. More of this in chapter 6.
60. This is a position consistent with his earliest writings on hermeneutics and myth, found in the essays written before his first *Magistardissertation* of 1792. See *Plitt*, I, 44f.
61. *PO*, 250.
62. For Homer's usage of τὸ αγαθὸνατηος, see Hom. Il. 2.673 and Hom. Od. 17.381, respectively. Plato typically uses this term in this sense as an adverb. See *Theaetatus* 161b, 169e, *Protagoras* 319e, and *Parmenides* 128b.
63. I/1, 472.
64. As we will see in the following pages, the organic ordering of this form, as archetype, informs every iteration of Schelling's philosophy, creating a strikingly consistent pattern of self-similarity.
65. Appendix A, lines 13–16.
66. As Aristotle himself admits, there is, *in a sense*, little difference

between the formal cause that initiates, and the telos that completes. A philosopheme first expressed in the words *ego sum qui sum*.

Chapter 2. Beginnings: Theosophy and Nature Divine

1. Friedrich Wilhelm Joseph Schelling, in *Schellingiana Rariora*, edited by Luigi Pareyson (Torino: Bottega D'rasmo, 1977), 5. The deceased colleague was the Reverend M. Eheman, from the neighboring town of Degerschlacht.
2. Letter to Hegel, 4.2.1795 (*Briefe von und an Hegel*, Bd. I, 21).
3. *Plitt*, I, 2. According to Plitt, Schelling spent the vast majority of his free time in his father's library, taking full advantage of the extensive collection befitting a leading scholar in Oriental languages.
4. Although not enrolled in the same courses, Schelling and Hölderlin shared the same teachers and headmaster, and more importantly, both shared the affection and fatherly tutelage of Schelling's uncle, the deacon Nathanael Köstlin. For Hölderlin, he was private tutor and the "father" he had lost years before; for Schelling he was not only his host—Schelling lived at his house for two years—but as we will see, Köstlin was most likely one of the first who introduced Schelling to the teachings of Württemberg's leading Pietist thinkers, Friedrich Christoph Oetinger and Philipp Matthäus Hahn, who occasionally visited his house. The strength of the tie each enjoyed with Köstlin is testified to by the fact that the first letter in the critical editions of Schelling and Hölderlin's correspondence is addressed to this charismatic teacher and father figure. Volker Schäfer, "Neue Daten zu Schellings Schulzeit in Nürtingen," *Jahrbuch der Deutschen Schillergesellschaft* 33 (1989): 13–17.
5. *Plitt*, I, 20.
6. This compact biography is not meant as a hagiography of the young genius Schelling (although these facts do go a long way in accounting for his later ideas on philosophy). It is rather the first step in an argument whose aim is to present an accurate and convincing portrait of a thinker whose ideas are at once as original as they are traditional.
7. *Plitt*, I, 22.
8. Such talent also signifies a consciousness that must have been sorely out of place in the everyday world of human affairs. Accustomed to an almost unchallenged mastery of the world of knowledge, Schelling proved time and again over the course of his life how poorly he dealt with challenges to that mastery.
9. Perhaps the clearest historical example of this is provided by John Wesley, who while visiting a Pietist community in Herrnhut enjoyed a conversion experience that led him to return to England and found the Methodist movement.
10. This is from Wittgenstein's *Investigations*, where he is attempting to articulate the primitive and thus unspeakable foundation of our language:

"But what is the word 'primitive' meant to say here? Presumably that this sort of behavior is pre-linguistic: that a language-game is based on it, that it is the prototype of a way of thinking and not the result of thought" (Ludwig Wittgenstein, *Philosophical Investigations* [New York: Macmillan Company, 1960], #341).

11. Isaiah Berlin presents the thought of J. G. Hamman as indicative of the Pietist's position regarding the relationship between conceptual analysis and brute experience (Isaiah Berlin, "Hume and German Anti-Rationalism," in *Against the Current* [New York: Penguin Books, 1980], 165). Hamman held that all men had the possibility of enjoying a direct experience of God's presence anywhere and at any time, *if* they allowed themselves to be open to such immanent transcendence. The world of nature itself thus becomes the medium through which the divine presence is mediated; God's presence manifests itself in and speaks through the world of nature, at least "to those who have eyes to see and ears to hear" (ibid., 167). Although a friend of Kant, Hamman repeatedly charged his fellow Pietist with creating a theoretical "castle in the air" that mistakes "words for concepts, and concepts for realities" (Letter to Jacobi, 11.14.1784, cited in ibid., 168). While such conceptual analysis may play an essential role in logical, economic, and technical activities, it not only fails to provide access to the real world, it makes it impossible. Instead of diving into the chthonic sensuousness of life—of Goethe's "stream of the world"—one remains instead trapped in the study, enclosed within a "virtual" world of possible experience.

12. Hamman, letter to Jacobi, 11.14.1784, cited in ibid., 168,

13. Wilhelm August Schulze, "Oetingers Beitrag zur Schellingschen Freiheitslehre," *Zeitschrift für Theologie und Kirchengeschichte* 54:2 (1957): 214. For the only English account of Schelling's formative years, see Fritz Medicus's one-page summary on the first page of "The Work of Schelling," *CLIO* 13:4 (1984): 349–367.

14. He is the father of the future first wife of the young Friedrich Schelling, Caroline.

15. *Plitt*, I, 5.

16. Cited in Gottfried Mälzer, *Johann Albrecht Bengel: Leben und Werk* (Stuttgart: Calwer Verlag, 1974), 343.

17. Ibid., 343.

18. *Plitt*, I, 373. Schelling's request, as expressed in a letter from 7.8.1802, presupposes that his father knows Oetinger well enough to distinguish his exceptional works from the mediocre—a point that would require him to be familiar with a good part of Oetinger's oeuvre. Given a man of such intellectual talent and curiosity, who obviously had a love of collecting books, it is highly improbable that J. F. Schelling himself did not own some of Oetinger's writings. The date of this letter is accepted by most commentators as signifying the beginning of Schelling's manifest interest in Theosophy. This reading, however, does not stand up to very significant

facts we know about Schelling's intellectual life prior to this letter. He was already very familiar with this universe of thought, as we will see in his eulogy to Hahn (1790), and in his request for his father's copy of Souverain's, *Le Platonisme dévoilé* (Loeffler's translation), as well as his correspondence with Oberreit (both in 1796). If he was capable at the age of twelve of reading Plato in Greek and Leibniz in Latin, then he was certainly capable of grasping the ideas we are about to consider.

19. Friedrich Christoph Oetinger, *Sämtliche Schriften*, hg. von Karl Christian Eberhard Ehemann (Metzingen: Franz, 1972), 2: VI, 63 (hereafter cited as *SS*).

20. While Plitt informs us that J. F. Schelling was skeptical of such prophetic speculation, his knowledge of Oetinger's work would have brought him into close contact with the teachings of Böhme. For although Oetinger would routinely criticize the shoemaker for his mystifying use of figurative and vivid expressions, the central core of his own teachings—particularly his earliest work—were directly derived from Böhme's. Heinz summarizes the relation between Böhme and Oetinger as follows: "Böhme became for him the measure for the philosophers known to him. Nonetheless, he saw himself neither in a slavish dependence on him, nor as an imitator; indeed, whereas in his youth enthusiastic agreement predominated, in his later years he saw it necessary to distance himself from different substantive points" (Reiner Heinz, *Bengel und Oetinger als Vorläufer des deutschen Idealismus* [Münster: Westfälischen, 1969], 60).

21. Schulze, "Oetingers Beitrag," 214. It appears that the maternal side of the family tended more towards Theosophical pursuits than did the paternal.

22. This last characterization of Oetinger and Hahn as "leading Pietists of the time" again raises the question of how Pietism and Theosophy relate to each other. Jantzen's characterization of Oetinger and Hahn is indicative of most research into the cultural roots of German Idealism: Both are presented as leading *Pietists*, that is, as official and guiding figures of an established church, and thus thinkers whose ideas would be representative of that church's orthodoxy. However, when we examine the research into Oetinger's influence on Schelling he suddenly emerges as a leading *Theosophist* of his time. From this perspective, Oetinger is presented as the leading figure of a confused heterodoxy that stands in opposition to the official teachings of both Pietism and the Bible. The same is even more true for Philipp Matthäus Hahn (1739–1790) who—Jantzen's characterization of him as a "leading Pietist" notwithstanding—had his writings censored by the *württembergische Konsistorium*. Cf. Walter Stäbler, *Das System Philipp Matthäus Hahns und seine Beanstandung durch das württembergische Konsistorium* (Stuttgart: Calwer, 1992), 23–47; and Jörg Jantzen, "Editorial Report," *AA*, I/1, 36.

23. His teachers at Latin school sent the young man home because they had concluded that there was nothing more for them to teach the prodigy.

What did the bored young mind do up until this dismissal with his spare time? Plunder the books and mind of his uncle.

24. Friedrich Christoph Oetinger, *Biblisches Wörterbuch*, hg. Von Julius Maberger (Stuttgart: Steinkopf, 1849), 164 (hereafter cited as *Wörterbuch*).

25. Ibid., 173.

26. Ibid., 2: 5, 295.; *SS*, 2: 5, 289.

27. Ibid., 2: 5, 92.

28. *Wörterbuch*, 304.

29. Letter from 1748, cited in Großman, *Oetingers Gottesvorstellung*, 103.

30. *Wörterbuch*, 314.

31. Heinz, *Oetinger als Vorläufer*, 85.

32. *SS*, 1: 2, 48. Matter is generated by the interaction of the two fundamental forces of attraction and contraction. The generation of matter begins in darkness (preponderance of contractive force) while the process culminates in light (expansive force).

33. *SS*, 2: 5, 170. Following Holy Scripture, life is the essential predicate of God. Accordingly, Oetinger argued against the rationalists that God "is an inner movement, [a] working, [an] overcoming of forces; otherwise one has no concept of God. If one abstracts everything living from God then God is nothing (*ein Nichts*)" (ibid.). There is also an unmistakable Platonic flavor to Oetinger's correlation of life and self-movement; a taste that increases in strength as our argument progresses.

34. *SS*, 2: 2, 205f.

35. *SS*, 2: 2, 201f. He continues: "God hides his wisdom and reveals his freedom." In the debate between Leibniz and Clark, Oetinger sides with the later: while Leibniz subsumed God's actions under the principle of what is *best*, Clark posits God as absolutely free, standing *above* Leibniz's principle.

36. Heinz, *Oetinger als Vorläufer*, 72.

37. The unifying bond that distinguishes the creator from the created is the integrating force of love. As Pseudo-Dionysius wrote, "What is signified by God's eros is a capacity to effect a unity" (Pseudo-Dionysius, *The Divine Names*, translated by Colim Luibheid [New York: Paulist Press, 1987], 709D). It is this power of *eros*—not of *knowing*—that ultimately provides for the unity within God and the possibility of consummating the desire of the created to become whole with itself, nature, and its creator.

38. C. S. Peirce, "Evolutionary Love," *The Essential Peirce*, edited by N. Houser (Bloomington: Indiana University Press, 1992), 357.

39. *Wörterbuch*, 225, 690; cf. *SS*, 2: 2, 237, 348, 354, 360.

40. *SS*, 2: 5, 167, 178.

41. *Wörterbuch*, 453; cf. 2, 5, 401, 134.

42. *SS*, 2: 5, 167, 178.

43. *SS*, 2: 5, 169.

44. *SS*, 2: 5, 179, 178.

45. *SS*, 2: 1, 211.

46. Oetinger followed Böhme in describing God as "eternal freedom," whose actions are his nature. Consequently, creation cannot be described as a necessary emanation of God's goodness, but must rather be described as a sovereign act.

47. *SS*, 2: 2, 383. Heinz notes that for Oetinger "All of nature is the result of a living battle of forces, a polarity, as occurs between light and darkness, matter and spirit. But it is not sufficient for phenomenon to have two sides and exist [as] dualistic and contradictory,—rather, so that they may originate and grow, a 'Trinity' is required" (Heinz, *Oetinger als Vorläufer*, 72).

48. We will see more of this when we turn to Hahn. For further parallels, see also Plato's *Timaeus*, 31c, 36, and 41b.

49. *On the World Soul* (I/2, 345–584).

50. In 1938 Ernst Müller compared Schelling's reinterpretation of Fichte's intellectual intuition with Oetinger's reinterpretation of Böhme's *Zentralschau* (Henry Fullenwider, *Friedrich Christoph Oetinger: Wirkungen auf Literatur und Philosophie seiner Zeit* [Göppingen: Alfred Kümmerle, 1975], 96.

51. This talent for absorption is exemplified by his future immersion in the philosophy of nature: within a year of study, he is publishing articles in scientific journals that do in fact influence and lead to new scientific methodologies and discoveries. The most notable impact Schelling exerted on the sciences came to fruition in the medical understanding of disease as the result of a pathogen, thereby helping to put an end to "humoral pathology." See Nelly Tsouyopoulos, "Doctors contra Clysters and Feudalism: The Consequences of a Romantic Revolution," in *Romanticism and the Sciences*, edited by A. Cunningham and N. Jardine (Cambridge: Cambridge University Press, 1990), 101–118.

52. Plitt writes that "through these connections the young Schelling may well have become acquainted earlier with Oetinger's views" (*Plitt*, I, 4). Schulze's position is stronger. He cites Plitt's conclusion and states that it is virtually inconceivable that Schelling was not exposed to the basic schematic outlines of this alternative Doctrine of Nature in general, and Oetinger's theories in particular (Schulze, "Oetingers Beitrag," 214). Following both Plitt and Schulze, Heinze also considers it highly likely that Schelling was exposed to the writings of Oetinger when he was "still a *Schüler*" (Heinz, *Oetinger als Vorlaufer*, 107).

53. *Plitt*, I, 3; Heinz, *Oetinger als Vorlaufer*, 107; Jantzen, "Editorial Report," *AA*, I/1, 36. No doubt Schelling's namesake and godfather, himself passionately involved with the leading theologians of his day, would have taken an active role in the spiritual development of his precocious godson. It begs credulity to suggest that this godfather, *who knew Oetinger personally*, would not have taken an active role in helping the young scholar understand the theological debates being batted back and forth

by the adults he spent his time with. And again, we are not suggesting that Schelling studied the writings of Oetinger—although it is very likely that he did—rather we are simply arguing that a precocious child such as young Friedrich would have been all too eager to listen and learn from his elders debating the merits of a Böhme versus Oetinger and Hahn.

54. Schulze, "Oetingers Beitrag," 214. See Hahn's entry of 10.6.1784 in his Tagebücher (Philipp Matthäus Hahn, *Die Echterdinger Tagebücher: 1780–1790*, hsg. Martin Brecht *u.* Rudolf F. Paulus [Berlin: Gruyter, 1983], 132). In the "Editorial Report" introducing the eulogy in the critical edition, Jantzen fails to mention this meeting, writing instead that "To prove an acquaintance of the young Schelling with Hahn was not yet possible" (Jantzen, "Editorial Report," *AA*, I/1, 35).

55. The poem was subsequently published in a local newspaper, *Der Beobachter*, Stuttgart 1790, Bd. 1, No. XXXVIII, 5.11.1790; cited in Jantzen, "Editorial Report," *AA*, I/1, 35.

56. Stäbler, *System Philipp Matthäus Hahns*, 5.

57. In 1781 Hahn's teachings were censured by the *württembergische Konsistorium*. See Stäbler, *System Philipp Matthäus Hahns*, 44f.

58. Ibid., 6, 7.

59. Hahn, *Die Echterdinger Tagebücher*, 221.

60. Philipp Matthäus Hahn, *Erbauungsstunden* (Stuttgart: Winterthur, 1779), 17 (hereafter cited as *VTS*).

61. Böhme transforms Newton's attraction and repulsion into the first and second qualities, or "forms of nature (*Naturgestalt*)."

62. As is often the case, these are Böhme's words which Hahn cites and uses to make his own argument. *VTS*, 14f.

63. Hahn's position shows a more sophisticated understanding of psychology than Plato's Artisan God; a position towards the act of creation that Schelling parallels in his analysis of aesthetic intuition and production in the final pages of his *System of Transcendental Idealism* (I/3, 611f).

64. Philipp Matthäus Hahn, *Theologisches Notizen und Exzerpte der Jahre 1766–76*, hsg. von Albrecht Plag (Stuttgart: Calwer, 1989), 434 (hereafter cited as *TNB*). Consider Schelling's mature words in this context: "We know nothing other than what is in experience, says Kant. Very correct; but what is being in experience is precisely what is alive, eternal or God" (I/7, 245).

65. Cited in Stäbler, *System Philipp Matthäus Hahns*, 59. Oetinger's version of this trinity of *Ichheiten* is illuminating in the way he negotiates the oneness of the three—the central conceptual problem Schelling will address in his organic form of identity. Oetinger writes: "God is a particular *Ichheit*, the word too, the Holy Ghost also, for it is called *ekeinos*, *allos* [in the original Greek]. However, that these three should be one in the mathematical understanding is not so. If in 1 John 5:3 it is stated: three are one, then it is not the mathematical one, but rather the true one [of] John 17, which externally is indeed one, inwardly however is a Myrias, an *Inbegriff* of the

concealed many, that proceed from the one, and subsist in the one. From this comes the confusion of the concept of the Trinity . . . but if one goes into this matter too deeply, and on the other hand not deep enough, then one is blinded by this sun" (Cited in ibid., 63).

66. *TNB*, 388.

67. No doubt Hahn's interpretation is in turn dependent on, and to a large extent derivative of, Böhme and Oetinger's work. My presentation of the doctrine of *Tsimtsum* follows the brilliant analysis found in Gershom Scholem's *Major Trends in Jewish Mysticism* (New York: Schocken Books, 1946), 260f.

68. Hahn is tilling a field first systematically worked by Pseudo-Dionysius and his doctrine of the God beyond the Godhead, who dwells in the cloud of unknowing. Others of course worked the field before Pseudo-Dionysius, but (ignoring Proclus for the moment) they had yet to develop systematically the trinitarian dynamic required by Christianity. Plato first employed tripartite schemas for creation and the being beyond being; Philo of Alexandria would have to be counted as the second significant contributor, when he injects the Judaic vocabulary into the discussion; Plotinus would have to be counted as the third. See Werner Beierwaltes's *Proklus: Grundzüge seiner Metaphysik* (Frankfurt: Vittorio Klostermann, 1965).

69. This passage in Ezekiel is the prelude to the infamous Throne Vision, which throughout history has been the foil for Kabbalistic and mystical writings on the true, hidden nature of the deity. Böhme, Oetinger, Hahn, and even the later Schelling, all use this passage in this sense.

70. *VTS*, 22.

71. *VTS*, 20. Hahn follows Oetinger's "Nature is the third out of the two." One of the more heretical positions of Theosophists throughout history has been their conception of an androgynous God. As we can see from this account of a living, productive God, the organic act of production would make sense only if we posit a female and male principle in God. This is precisely what Hahn did: "[he] is not only the father of creation, but also the mother, who has carried everything within her . . ." (ibid., 17).

72. Cited in Stäbler, *System Philipp Matthäus Hahns*, 199. Stäbler notes that while Hahn conceded that it made sense from a pedagogical standpoint to speak about the soul and the body as if they were two different "things," in reality, however, Hahn argued that soul is not "in" matter as a "dagger in a sheath, . . . but rather it is *woven* into matter" as different colored thread in a tapestry (*VTS*, 126).

73. Ibid., 136.

74. Ibid., 175.

75. *TNB*, 394f.; ibid., 321.

76. The term ὁ δεμός appears twelve times; in nine of these, his usage supports Oetinger's employment of the term *das Band*. See *Tim*. 31c; 36a; 38e; 41b; 43a; 73b; 73d; and 77e.

77. The three elements here of the Same, the Other, and the mean between them are suggestive of Kant's trichotomy of logical principles—unity, plurality, and continuity—he uses in the first *Critique* to explicate the systematic unity of unconditional (A 658/B 686ff.).

78. The parallels continue when we consider again Oetinger's account of creation as the dissolution of the "bond of the forces" (*Wörterbuch*, 167, 178), which, originally united by the bond in a state of "indifference" (ibid., 2, 5, 453; cf. 2, 5, 401), spill forth and separate into the productive forces of nature. In the figurative language of myth, Plato provides a similar account in which the three forms of Being, Place, and Becoming move from a state of existing "three in three ways" (τρία τριχῆ) into an imbalanced process of creation: "but owing to being filled with potencies (δυνάμεων) that are neither similar nor balanced, in no part of herself is she equally balanced, but sways unevenly in every part, and is herself shaken by these forms and shakes them in turn as she is moved (*Tim.* 52df.).

79. *TNB*, 267, 359.

80. "Every created spirit, as an *Ebenbild* of the father and of the son, has of course a free will" (ibid., 86).

81. Hahn, *Die Echterdinger Tagebücher*, 102.

82. Ibid., 159.

83. Ibid., 156.

84. *TNB*, 201.

85. Cf. Romans 8:18.

86. *VTS*, 105.

87. Hahn, *Die Echterdinger Tagebücher*, 380.

88. ETB, 266. Stäbler notes that during the 1780s Hahn wrote enthusiastically about Spinoza's doctrine of God, as communicated by Herder's essay "God: A Few Conversations" (Stäbler, *System Philipp Matthäus Hahns*, 296).

89. Hahn confides such thoughts to his *Tagebücher* on 9.8.1788: "Presently one does indeed have the Christian religion in its doctrine, science, words and rituals. But the heart is not inflamed. The spirit of religion is missing. Herder's pamphlet on God shows how so internally near he is to nature, and if one believes, that there is a God, and that he is as connected with the world as gravity is with the body, then one can believe that the spirit of religion is not empty speculation and imagination, but rather a truly divine force that becomes more our own . . . and refines our human nature" (Hahn, *Die Echterdinger Tagebücher*, 352).

90. Hahn, *Die Echterdinger Tagebücher*, 358; 8.22.1788. Hahn continues this passage writing "Our present external religion, as it is practiced by the spiritless Christians, is still very similar to the Masses of former times."

91. Heinze, *Oetinger als Vorläufer*, 67.

92. Ibid., 72.

93. Ibid., 74.

94. Letter dated 4.4.1811, cited in *Plitt*, II, 251.

95. For all we know Schelling could have been alluding to that first time he

met the man at the age of nine; a possibility that does not rule out his later exposure to the teachings of Hahn and Oetinger.

96. The entire poem appears in an English translation (mine) in appendix A.

97. This stanza in particular brings to mind Plato's words used to frame his own inquiry into the divine causes of nature: "Wherefore one ought to distinguish two different kinds of causes, the necessary and the divine, and in all things seek after the divine for the sake of gaining a life of blessedness, so far as our nature admits thereof. . . . " (*Tim.* 68e5–69a1).

98. This reference to Hahn's having heard the "harmony of the soul" constellates Hahn's analysis of the soul as "a *medium conjungendi* for 2 *Extrema*"; a construction that parallels Plato's specific account of how soul unites mind (the Same) and body (the Other) through the continuity of a mean between extremes; the "harmonic mean" of nature, and here at least, in Plato, of the soul as well (*Tim.* 36f). Perhaps a coincidence, perhaps a typical turn of speech.

99. Adolf Beck "Aus Schelling's Jugend: Ein Unbekanntes Gedicht." In "Festgruß für Hans Pritz zum 9.15.1955. Sonderheft des Euphorion" (Heidelberg: 1955), 42–47. Cited in Heinze, *Oetinger als Vorläufer*, 97.

100. Jantzen, "Editorial Report," *AA*, I/1, 33, n. 1. Jantzen cites Guido Schneeberger, *Friedrich Willhelm Joseph von Schelling: Eine Bibliographie* (Bern: 1954), and Hans Jörg Sandkühler, *Friedrich Willhelm Joseph Schelling* (Stuttgart: 1970), 1–8; 24–41.

101. *AA*, I/1, 39.

102. *AA*, I/1, 249.

103. Bowie (1990), appendix A, 266f.

Chapter 3. The Question of Systematic Unity

1. *KU*, 184. Kant continues: "Now this transcendental concept of a finality of nature is neither a concept of nature nor of freedom, since it attributes nothing at all to the object, i.e., to nature, but only represents the unique mode in which we must proceed in our reflection upon the objects of nature with a view to getting a thoroughly interconnected whole of experience, and so is a subjective principle, i.e., maxim, of judgment. For this reason, too, just as if it were a lucky chance that favored us, we are rejoiced (properly speaking, relieved of a want) where we meet with such systematic unity under merely empirical laws: although we must necessarily assume the presence of such a unity, apart from any ability on our part apprehend or prove its existence" (ibid.).We will soon return to the question of this maxim, namely, the idea of the 'maximum.'

2. *KU*, 231.

3. *KU*, 195.

4. As we will see, Schelling will build a parallel between Kant's formulation here and Plato's account of the distinction between the functionality of divine causation and the secondary causes of necessity.

5. *KU*, 94. As Beck points out Kant claims that this definition is given only "in terms belonging to the pure understanding, i.e., categories, which contain nothing empirical" (Lewis White Beck, *A Commentary on Kant's Critique of Practical Reason* [Chicago: University of Chicago Press, 1960], 218). The dynamic of desire and its relation to life and pleasure is the sensuous paradigm for the dynamic of freedom: the capacity to be by means of one's own representations the cause of the objects of those representations. In other words, the capacity of a being to act in accordance with its representations is called life (1797, *MdS, 211*). This is a position remarkably similar to Schelling's programmatic assertion: "Life . . . is the schema of freedom" (1796, I/1, 246). A strikingly similar formulation of the causality of freedom as stated in the *Critique of Practical Reason*: "the practical a priori principles in relation to the supreme principle of freedom are at once cognitions, and have not to wait for intuitions in order to acquire significance, and that for this remarkable reason, because they [the practical a priori principles of reason] themselves produce the reality of that to which they refer (the intention of the will), which is not the case with theoretical concepts" (69). All of which leads Schelling to draw the connection between this process of creating objects of intuition and construction, as well as providing the grounds for claiming that "metaphysics" actually begins in the world of life: "In respect of their object, philosophy and experience have been opposed to each other (as even the name metaphysics indicates). This opposition disappears. The object of philosophy is the real world (*wirkliche Welt*)" (I/1, 464).

6. *MdS*, 356. Anticipations of Fichte: the striving to be the cause of one's own representations, which, as we will see, are the result of an internal, cognitive intuition. One's internal intuition is the cause of the representations whereby the subject becomes its *causa sui*; or, intellectual intuition as construction.

7. It is a "need of understanding" to assume "a finality of objects (here of nature)" to serve as a subjective maxim of judgment; an assumption for which "we are rejoiced (properly speaking relieved of a want)" (*KU*, 184).

8. *MdS*, 41. The practical desire caused by objects of sense is of course the enslaved inclination of "habitual desire" (ibid.).

9. "The specific quality of pleasure on the contrary is perfect at any moment. It is clear therefore that pleasure is not the same as motion, and that it is a whole and something perfect (τῶν ὅλων τὶ καὶ τελείων)" (Aristotle, *Nicomachean Ethics*, Loeb Classical Library [Cambridge: Harvard University Press, 1934], 1174b10). The finality or perfection of the whole is what produces pleasure. That which produces the greatest pleasure because it is pure form (pure actuality inactive to the extent that it is not moving) is contemplation (θεωπητική) (ibid., 1177a18). It is hard to overlook the deeply Aristotelian presentation of finality that Kant here presents, with its emphasis on the relieving of a want through the pleasure of ascertaining a complete whole. A want Kant no doubt sought to relieve in his quest for systematic unity.

10. How Kant mediates sensibility's feeling and intellectual pleasure is hard to grasp given his mechanism of the subject in which the "susceptibility to the representation is called feeling, which is the effect of a representation (that may be either sensible or intellectual) upon a subject and belongs to sensibility, even though the representation itself may belong to the understanding or to reason" (*MdS*, 212, fn.). Feeling as the effect of a *Vorstellung* seems rather ill-equipped to account for the intensity of feelings that enslave our inclinations of "habitual desire."

11. Ibid. This "object," which Kant removes from the representation in this quote, is 1) the aesthetic idea, which is a symbol for the good, that is, freedom, which is the only thought that can be "produced" by the intellect without intuition. This follows from the aforementioned dynamic of desire: the ability to be the cause of one's own representations provides liberation from having one's desire determined by sensible objects (the desire of reason as a form of sublimation).

12. "We call the feeling of this latter kind of pleasure taste" (*KU*, 212).

13. The appeal to a common ground of pure reason leads to the question of how this form of judgment, with its intimate linkage to the individual feeling of pleasure, could possibly display the trait of universal a priori validity enjoyed by principles of pure reason: "The attainment of every aim is coupled with a feeling of pleasure. Now where such attainment has for its condition a representation a priori—as here a principle for the reflective judgment in general—the feeling of pleasure also is determined by a ground which is a priori and valid for all men" (*KU*, 187). Where is the individual feeling of pleasure in this scheme? Like his reduction of evil, pleasure is ultimately a form to be inverted and thus converted to a privation. Like evil, there is no sensual positive power to pleasure.

14. Universal validity for this reflective activity is guaranteed by its "conformity to law in the empirical employment of judgment generally" insofar as this reflective activity conforms to the a priori transcendental rules that govern the "representation of the object in reflection" (*KU*, 190). The feeling of intellectual pleasure enjoyed in a beautiful object generated by an intuition of the cognitive faculty—a pleasure resulting from understanding's want of finality finding satisfaction in the integrated yet free harmony of its concepts with the intuitions of imagination— "occasions" the "concept of a finality" of both beauty and nature (*KU*, 197).

15. *KU*, 338.

16. *KU*, 339.

17. "[I]t is evident that these logical criteria of the possibility of knowledge in general are the three categories of quantity, in which the unity in the production of the quantum has to be taken as homogeneous throughout; and that these categories are here being transformed so as also to yield connection of heterogeneous knowledge in one consciousness, by means of the quality of the knowledge as the principle of the connection" (B 115). These words appear in section §11 of the first *Critique*, added after

Kant composed his *Metaphysical Foundations of the Natural Sciences* and began to realize the difficulties of making a transition from his realm of a "logically possible experience" to that of real, individual, historical experience.

18. *KU*, 351. This *Aufhebung* of the sensible into the intelligible will contrasts sharply with Schelling's reading of Plato's oppositional integration of the sensible and the intelligible as *equal partners* in the generation of their product, *das Dritte*, the common mean of the τὸ κοινόν.

19. *KU*, 339.

20. Cf. Aristotle's *Posterior Analytics*, Loeb Classical Library (Cambridge: Harvard University Press, 1960), 72a7f. The use of the term "ἄμεσος" denotes the lack of a middle term in this unmediated form of knowing the truth of first principles; a modality of knowing that is consequently nondiscursive, since to be discursive this principle would need a "μεσός" or middle term; the most certain modality of knowing which, according to Aristotle, is not an episteme or *dianoia*, but rather a νοῦς, understood as the direct apprehension of the indemonstrable (ibid., 89b1of; 100b5. See also Aristotle's *De Anima*, Loeb Classical Library [Cambridge: Harvard University Press, 1936], Book III, chaps. iv–vii, and compare with Kant's *KU*, 339).

21. Kant writes in the third *Critique*: "The judgment of taste must have reference to some concept or other, as otherwise it would be absolutely impossible for it to lay claim to necessary validity for everyone. Yet it need not, on that account, be provable from a concept. For a concept may be determinable, or else at once intrinsically undetermined and indeterminable. A concept of the understanding, which is determinable by means of predicates borrowed from sensible intuition and capable of corresponding to it, is of the first kind. But of the second kind is the transcendental rational concept of the supersensible, which lies at the basis of all that sensible intuition and is, therefore, incapable of being further determined theoretically" (*KU*, 206). Is this criterion of indeterminability symmetrical with that of the Transcendental Ideal? In the first *Critique* we find: "But the concept of what thus possesses all reality is just the concept of a *Ding-an-sich* as completely determined; and since in all possible [pairs of] contradictory predicates one predicate, namely, that which belongs to being absolutely, is to be found in its determination, the concept of an *ens realissimum* is the concept of an individual being" (A 576 /B 604). Ignoring the dualistic implications of his logically pure God of one-sided predicates: Is the *Ding-an-sich* the inverse of the Transcendental Ideal in the same way as traditionally the simple (τό ἁπλῶς) is the inverse of the whole (τό ὅλον)? See Aristotle's *Nic. Eth.*, Bk. X, iv, 1174a15f.

22. *KU*, 206.

23. *KU*, 340f. Kant tells us in §17 that taste ultimately rests on reason's "indeterminate idea" of a maximum: "Properly speaking, an idea signifies a concept of reason, and an ideal the representation of an individual

existence as adequate to an idea. Hence this archetype of taste—which rests, indeed, upon reason's indeterminate idea of a maximum, but is not, however, capable of being represented by means of concepts, but only in an individual presentation—may more appropriately be called the ideal of the beautiful" (*KU*, 232).

24. *KU*, 340. This supersensible substratum lies at "the basis of the object (and of the judging subject for that matter" (ibid.).

25. Ibid., 314.

26. Ibid.

27. Ibid. Where has he ever provided an example of reason attaining its maximum? In addition, how would this be possible if it is by definition an indeterminate idea? The instance he cites here is that of an artist "emulating" reason's attainment of a maximum. The only instance he provides, as we will see later, occurs through the encounter with the sublime.

28. See his statement: "The ideal is, therefore, the archetype (*prototypon*) of all things, which one and all, as imperfect copies (*ectypa*), derive from it the material of their possibility, and while approximating it in varying degrees, yet always fall very short of actually attaining it" (A 578/B 606). Such imitation is called to mind in the crowning section of the first *Critique*, "The Architectonic of Pure Reason," when Kant writes: "Now that which we call science, the schema of which must contain the outline (*monogramma*) and the division of the whole into parts, in conformity with the idea, that is, a priori, and in so doing must distinguish it with certainty and according to principles from all other wholes, is not formed in technical fashion, in view of the similarity of its manifold constituents or of the contingent use of our knowledge *in concreto* for all sorts of optional external ends, but in architectonic fashion, in view of the affinity of its parts and of their derivation from a single supreme and inner end, through which the whole is first made possible" (A 833 /B 861f). The telos is the condition of possibility of the whole, which is the condition of possibility of the parts (i.e., the logic of community and reciprocal causation).

29. Compare the respective triadic constructions of Plato, Philo of Alexandria, Pseudo-Dionysius, and Kant:

Plato	Philo of Alexandria	Pseudo-Dionysius	Kant
The Good beyond Being (*Rep.* 509 b8)	The Existent of Ex. 3:14	The Supreme Godhead of *The Divine Names* (649b4)	Transcendental Ideal
τὸ πέρας	Lord (Yahweh)	Nous	Unity
τὸ ἄπειρον	God (Elohim)	Ousia	Plurality
τὸ κοινὸν	Lord-God	Zoa	Continuity

30. "The transcendental concept of reason is, therefore, none other than the concept of the totality of the conditions for any given conditioned. Now since it is the unconditioned alone which makes possible the totality of conditions, and, conversely, the totality of conditions is always itself unconditioned, a pure concept of reason can in general be explained by the concept of the unconditioned, conceived as containing a ground of the synthesis of the conditioned" (A 322 /B 379).

31. Kant provides an account of the "genesis" of these ideas in the all-important first section of the Antinomy of Pure Reason: The System of Weltbegriffe: "In the first place we must recognize that pure and transcendental concepts can issue only from the understanding. Reason does not really generate any concept. The most it can do is to free a concept of the understanding from the unavoidable limitations of possible experience, and so to endeavor to extend it beyond the limits of the empirical, though, still indeed, in terms of its relation to the empirical" (A 408 /B 435f). Put simply, transcendental ideas are like the theoretical constructs of contemporary science that proved the undoing of Logical Positivism: every theory includes "pattern statements" that can never be tested directly against reality. However, these very pattern statements provide the context—the whole—within which the "detail statements" of a theory can be tested against reality.

32. "Further—what we need here no more than mention—concepts of reason may perhaps make possible a transition from the concepts of nature to the practical concepts, and in that way may give support to the moral ideas themselves, bringing them into connection with the speculative knowledge of reason" (A 329 /B 386). Freedom is the only transcendental idea of which we have a priori knowledge as the condition of the possibility of the moral law. The ideas of immortality and God are only conditions of the necessary object of a will that has been determined by the moral law, that is, through the practical use of pure reason. How this position harmonizes with the role of beauty as the symbol of the Good in the third Critique is an issue we will turn to later.

33. I am calling this last maxim the "moral visage" in a very loose sense.

34. In the third Critique, he presents this set as the determinative and reflective forms of judgment.

35. Cf. A 411 /B 438.

36. B xxiii, n.a.

37. "If, however, the universal is admitted as problematic only, and is a mere idea, the particular is certain, but the universality of the rule of which it is a consequence is still a problem. Several particular instances, which are all certain, are scrutinized in view of the rule, to see whether they follow from it. If it then appears that all particular instances that can be cited follow from the rule, we argue to its universality, and from this again to all particular instances, even to those which are not themselves given. This I shall entitle the hypothetical employment of reason" (A 646 /B 674f).

We will see that the only maximal schema Kant can provide to guarantee the systematic unity of his program is the deistic idea of God.

38. A system or series of homogeneous members can never be self-grounding according to Kant's own logic. As he points out, an actual totality requires "a first member of the series" that is qualitatively different from the members that constitute it (A 418 /B 446). Ultimately, Kant must ground the series of appearances in the totality of the noumenal. To do this, he must employ a synthesis other than the regressive, and he needs a quantum other than all other quanta, that is, a sublime *absolute Maß*.

39. "Pure reason is in fact occupied with nothing but itself" (A 680 /B 708). The problem with intellectual onanism is that it fails to produce new life, and thus develop and grow. But then Kant's goal is to establish principles of a reason, eternally frozen (frigid?), which, in emulating logic, never change and develop (B viii).

40. "Reason makes this demand in accordance with the principle that if the conditioned is given, the entire sum of conditions, and consequently the absolutely unconditioned (through which alone the conditioned has been possible) is also given" (A 409 /B 436). This only applies of course to the possibly unconditioned synthesized by the mathematical categories, not the actually unconditioned of the dynamic.

41. The progressive synthesis of the *Naturbegriffe* does not appear at all in the first *Critique*. It only resurfaces in the third *Critique* when Kant introduces the aesthetic idea of the sublime.

42. The precise meaning of the adjective "objective" is to be understood in reference to the term "postulate" mentioned in the same passage: as we will see, Kant equivocates regarding the systematic connection of objectivity and postulates. At times, he very clearly denies that a postulate can be said to have objective validity, whereas when rebutting the "problematic" Cartesian idealism, he appears to argue that the postulates of experience and the law of causality are not circular, and therefore have objective force. More of this in the sequel.

43. This seems to be an inconsistency in Kant's method. Compare his account of why apagogic proofs are not acceptable in transcendental philosophy, where the only form of proof he claims to accept is the "direct or ostensive proof" (A 789/B 817).

44. Remove this principle and, as Plato writes in the *Parmenides*, one opens up the possibility of "tumbling into a bottomless pit of nonsense" (*Parmen.* 130d8). Both Plato and Aristotle recognize the need for some ultimate point of definition and solidity that will serve as the positive condition of significant speech *qua* episteme. Both phrase their respective positions in terms of essence and accident, and argue there must be a first essence in order for scientific discourse to occur. Kant's transcendental principle of reason, understood as the conceptual underpinning of his Transcendental Ideal (the *Inbegriff* of all possible predicates), serves a similar function. Aristotle writes in the *Metaphysics*: "if everything said is accidental, if

some accidental always signifies the predication to the subject, nothing will be first or primary. Then predication must proceed into infinity. However, this is not possible (*Met.* 1007a). Plato expresses a similar intellectual vertigo later in the *Parmenides*: "everything must have a class and absolute essence . . . if there is someone who in turn will not allow that there are forms of things, paying attention to all these objections and problems, not allowing even some idea defining one particular thing, he will then have nothing to turn his thinking to, have nothing on which to fix his thought, and thus not allowing ideas of each of the things to always be the same, he will thoroughly destroy and ruin the capacity for significant discourse" (*Parmen.* 135d). Plato's *genos kai ousia auta kath auta* is ultimately the ἕν *qua Einheit* that supports his system. Kant appears to be making a similar argument for *Einheit* as the condition of possibility of system.

45. In German the last sentence reads: "Diese Verrnunfteinheit seit jederzeit eine Idee voraus, nämlich die von der Form eines Ganzen der Erkenntnis, welches vor der Bestimmten Erkenntnis der Teile vorhergeht und die Bedingungen enthält, jedem Teile seine Stelle und Verhältnis zu den übrigen a priori zu bestimmen" (A 645/B 673).

46. "πολλαίτε αἱ συνάπασαι ἐπιστῆμαι δόξουσιν εἶναι καὶ ἀνόμοιοίτινες αὐτῶν ἀλλήλαις." The phrase αἱ συνάπασαι ἐπιστῆμαι is most likely the source for Schelling's idea of the *Urform*.

47. A 653/B 681f.

48. A 661/B 689.

49. This is the same logical problem first addressed by Plato in the *Timaeus* of mediating unity (same) and diversity (other) through a continuum of means: "But it is not possible that two things alone should be conjoined without a third; for there must needs be some intermediary bond (δεσμῶν) to connect the two. And the fairest of bonds is that which most perfectly unites into one both itself and the things which it binds together; and to effect this in the fairest manner is the natural property of the proportion" (*Tim.* 31b9–c4; cf. 36f).

50. *Phil.* 15c2: "These are the questions . . . about this kind of one and many, . . . which cause the utmost perplexity, if ill solved, and are, if well solved, of the greatest assistance." And further at 15d5: "We say that one and many are identified by reason, and always, both now and in the past, circulate everywhere in every thought that is uttered. This is no new thing and will never cease; it is, in my opinion, a quality within us which will never die or grow old, and which belongs to reason itself as such."

51. As shown in his use of the disjunctive form of syllogism to resolve the antinomies of reason, Kant also adopts it to mediate the principle of continuity of forms, since this form alone is capable of mediating the twofold aspect of reason alluded to in the second introduction to the first *Critique*, when he makes the following methodological remark regarding his teaching that the object is to be taken in the twofold sense of appearance *and* as a thing in itself: "In dealing with those concepts and

principles which we adopt a priori, all that we can do is to contrive that they be used for viewing objects from two different points of view—on the one hand, in connection with experience, as objects of the senses and of the understanding, and on the other hand, for the isolated reason that strives to transcend all limits of experience, as objects which are thought merely. If, when things are viewed from this twofold standpoint, we find that there is agreement with the principle of pure reason, but that when we regard them only from a single point of view reason is involved in unavoidable self-conflict, the experiment decides in favor of the correctness of this distinction" (B xxvii; cf. B xix).

52. Evidently Kant did not have enough time to fully correct the second edition of the first *Critique*, for in §11 that he added to the *Table of Categories* he raises a methodological point that calls into question the additive form of synthesis he has just performed (B 109f). Schelling makes this point in the *Form Essay*, reiterating Kant's own questions about why all a priori division is by dichotomy, yet each class of category has three members. Although Kant does attempt to address this in a footnote in the third *Critique* (*KU*, 197, n.), the methodological point is deadly: either the third emerges out of the previous two, or an original trichotomy must somehow be supposed. In §11 Kant tries to have it both ways (B 108). Schelling inverts this: the third is the condition of possibility of the second and third. Following Aristotle's distinction between the order of reality and the order of discovery, the third is prior in reality, while in terms of the order of discovery, it is the latter.

53. Kant explains how these three principles relate by an appeal to what I call *epistemic positionality*: "The systematic unity, prescribed by the three logical principles, can be illustrated in the following manner. Every concept may be regarded as a point, which, as the station for an observer, has its own horizon, that is, a variety of things that can be represented, and, as it were, surveyed from that standpoint. This horizon must be capable of containing an infinite number of points, each of which has its own narrower horizon; that is, every species contains subspecies, according to the principle of specification, and the logical horizon consists exclusively of smaller horizons (subspecies), never of points that possess no extent (individuals). But for different horizons, that is, genera, each of which is determined by its own concept, there can be a common horizon, in reference to which, as from a common centre, they can all be surveyed; and from this higher genus we can proceed until we arrive at the highest of all genera, and so at the universal and true horizon, which is determined from the standpoint of the highest concept, and which comprehends under itself all manifoldness—genera, species, and subspecies" (A 658/B 686f). What Kant is describing here is the dynamic of his transcendental deduction and its synthetic unity of apperception: "Synthetic unity of the manifold of intuitions, as generated a priori, is thus the ground of the identity of apperception itself, which precedes a priori all my determinate

thought" (B 135). The ground of the identity of apperception is the a priori synthetic unity of the manifold: the ground of the identity is clearly the *Inbegriff* of all possibilities for determinate thought, which is *the whole that precedes its constituent parts of the manifold and unity*. See also the "Stufenleitern" of the genus of *Vorstellung* at A 320/B 376f: from each rung on the ladder, the horizon looks decidedly different. Schelling adopts this fluidity of position, and attempts to integrate it into his system.

54. Kant holds that these principles of "systematic unity" contain "ideas for the guidance of the empirical employment of reason . . . which reason follows only as it were asymptotically, i.e., ever more closely without ever reaching them" (A 663/B 691).

55. The role the disjunctive syllogism plays in the ensuing chapters justifies this rather extended citation from Kant's discourse on the Transcendental Ideal: "For only in this one case is a concept of a thing—a concept which is in itself universal—completely determined in and through itself, and known as the representation of an individual. The logical determination of a concept by reason is based upon a disjunctive syllogism, in which the major premise contains a logical division (the division of the sphere of a universal concept), the minor premise limiting this sphere to a certain part, and the conclusion determining the concept by means of this part. The universal concept of a reality in general cannot be divided a priori, because without experience we do not know any determinate kinds of reality that would be contained under that genus. The transcendental major premise which is presupposed in the complete determination of all things is therefore no other than the representation of the sum of all reality; it is not merely a concept which, as regards its transcendental content, comprehends all predicates under itself; it also contains them within itself; and the complete determination of any and every thing rests on the limitation of this total reality, inasmuch as part of it is ascribed to the thing, and the rest is excluded—a procedure which is in agreement with the 'either-or' of the disjunctive major premise and with the determination of the object, in the minor premise, through one of the members of the division. Accordingly, reason, in employing the transcendental ideal as that by reference to which it determines all possible things, is proceeding in a manner analogous with its procedure in disjunctive syllogisms—this, indeed, is the principle upon which I have based the systematic division of all transcendental ideas, as parallel with, and corresponding to, the three kinds of syllogism" (A 577/B 605).

56. A 663/B 691.

57. Kant contradicts or qualifies himself seriously when he writes in the same paragraph: "Nonetheless these dynamic laws are constitutive in respect of experience, since they render the concepts, without which there can be no experience, possible a priori" (A 664/B 692).

58. Continuity to mediate the two maxims in antinomic relation: contraries or contradictories? Neither and both: disjunction.

59. Due to his insistence that transcendental philosophy is a science of concepts devoid of intuition, Kant must deny the ideas of reason the possibility of a creative productivity from which such a schema could emerge. In sidestepping the problems of Plato's construal of the ideas as potential causal agents, Kant nonetheless runs into his own mechanical problem when he accepts them as regulative: how to explain the process whereby these ideas provide a rule for their application in both the theoretical and practical employment of reason.

60. In the first *Critique*, he uses this term in only two other passages to describe how reflective judgments of theoretical reason provide "an analogon for practical judgments" of "doctrinal belief" (A 825/B 853). He writes here that "But in many cases, when we are dealing with an object about which nothing can be done by us, and in regard to which our judgment is therefore purely theoretical, we can conceive and picture to ourselves an attitude for which we regard ourselves as having sufficient grounds, while yet there is no existing means of arriving at certainty in the matter. Thus even in purely theoretical judgments there is an analogon of practical judgments, to the mental entertaining of which the term 'belief' is appropriate, and which we may entitle doctrinal belief" (ibid.).

61. Kant uses "analogon" again to express the same process of arriving at a pragmatic belief at A 830/B 858. After only using this term five times here, he ceases to use it at all in the ensuing *Critiques*. In the third *Critique*, however, he does refer to analogy as mediating the concept of a symbol: "All intuitions by which a priori concepts are given a foothold are, therefore, either schemata or symbols. Schemata contain direct, symbols indirect, presentations of the concept. Schemata effect this presentation demonstratively, symbols by the aid of an analogy (for which recourse is had even to empirical intuitions), in which analogy judgment performs a double function: first in applying the concept to the object of a sensible intuition, and then, secondly, in applying the mere rule of its reflection upon that intuition to quite another object, of which the former is but the symbol" (*KU*, 352).

62. These correspond roughly to the three *Weltbegriffe* specified in Kant's table of cosmological concepts (A 415/B 443): unity = quantity, division = quality, and one principle = origination, that is, relation.

63. "Vollständige" is a term we will soon see Schelling apply as his first definition of Plato's principle of systematic unity: τό ὄν.

64. This definition highlights the importance Kant affixes to being able to negotiate the traditional aporia of all scientific knowing, namely, how "the forms of knowledge collectively are many" (*Phil.* 13e8). Regardless of his claim to revolution, there is no escape from the problems of the tradition: he must still address the same perennial aporia that has forever plagued philosophy. Moreover, in making his appeal to an absolute *Einheit* for his system, he is forced to follow Plato's lead and make a similar division

between the unconditioned "archai" of unity and the necessary principles of the conditioned world: whereas the later can be known directly, the former, as the condition of possibility of the latter, cannot.

65. Nicholas of Cusa would be perhaps the most eloquent proponent of the traditional reading: "Thus the Maximum is the Absolute One which is all things. And all things are in the Maximum . . . and since nothing is opposed to it, the Minimum likewise coincides with it, and hence the Maximum is also in all things" (Nicholas of Cusa, *De Docta Ignorantia*, translated by J. Hopkins [Minneapolis: Banning Press, 1985], 51). This coincidence of opposites parallels the dynamic at play with Kant's *Ding-an-Sich* and the Transcendental Ideal, as well as with Aristotle's simple (τό ἁπλῶς) as the inverse of the whole (το ὅλου). See note 192 ???? above[[AU: provide correct note number and chapter here]].

66. A schema of Kant's architectonic may prove helpful at this point:

Syllogistic Form	Transcendental Ideas	Maxims of Reason	Logical Principle
	synthetic a priori propositions with objective but indeterminate validity when employed as rules for possible experience	subjective, heuristic principles of reason when applied to actual experience (A 662/B 690)	for each Maxim; (A 658/B 686)
Continuum of abstraction	Schema given in idea	Analogon of a schema given by idea of a maximum	no schema
Categorical (concepts of the understanding)	Psychology object is soul and immortality	Unity (thinking subject)	Genera, Homogeneity
Hypothetical (sensible intuition)	Cosmology object is the world and freedom	Manifoldness (series of conditions of appearance)	Species, Specification
Disjunctive (productive imagination *qua* schema)	Theology object is God	Continuum (all objects of thought in a system)	Continuum, Continuity of forms

67. Obviously, Kant must improve on this formulation if he is to provide a more binding necessity than programmatic declaration (or is this the dogmatic use of reason?).

68. "There is a great difference between something being given to my reason

as an object absolutely, or merely as an object in the idea. In the former case our concepts are employed to determine the object; in the latter case there is in fact only a schema which no object, not even a hypothetical one, is directly given, and which only enables us to represent to ourselves other objects in an indirect manner, namely in their systematic unity, by means of their relation to this idea" (A 670/B 698).

69. *KU*, 313. The closest Kant comes to an analysis of the "generation" of the ideas of reason is when he provides the definition that they are the categories extended to the unconditioned. He is constrained in providing a more thorough account of this genetic question by his understanding of transcendental philosophy as a science that works exclusively with "dogmata"—concepts taken from tradition—since he denies philosophy the power of constructing its concepts (A 736/B 764).

70. Ibid., 315.

71. Ibid.

72. Ibid. Aesthetic ideas are to beauty what ideas of reason are to systematic unity; but both sets of ideas are ultimately regulated by the idea of the maximum.

73. *Nic. Eth.*, 1174b10.

74. With this definition we can see why the dynamic unconditioned must take this form. Kant continues: "The division in disjunctive judgments thus indicates the coordination not of the parts of the whole concept, but all the parts of its sphere. There I think many things through one concept; here one thing through many concepts, e.g., the definitum through all characteristics of coordination" (*Logik*, §29; Ak IX, 108).

75. What Kant calls for here is a power of intuition that that seems remarkably close to the type of intuitive understanding Kant forcefully rejects in the first *Critique*. For an insightful and thorough analysis of the intuitive understanding and intellectual intuition in Kant's third *Critique*, see Eckart Förster's "Die Bedeutung von §§76, 77 der Kritik der Urteilskraft für die Entwicklung der nachkantischen Philosophie [Teil I]," *Zeitschrift für philosophische Forschung* 56:2 (2002): 169–180.

76. Or then, perhaps his elliptical comment in the first *Critique* of how the "significance" of the *Naturbegriffe* "will appear later" points ahead to this last critique (A 420/B 448).

77. It is the necessity of violence, or the violence of necessity, that transforms the sensuous into the acceptable attire required to gain entry into Kant's Kingdom of pure Reason: "In this modality of aesthetic judgments, namely, their assumed necessity, lies what is for the critique of judgment a moment of capital importance. For this is exactly what makes an a priori principle apparent in their case, and lifts them out of the sphere of empirical psychology, in which otherwise they would remain buried amid the feelings of gratification and pain (only with the senseless epithet of finer feeling), so as to place them, and, thanks to them, to place the faculty of judgment itself, in the class of judgments of which the basis of an a

priori principle is the distinguishing feature, and, thus distinguished, to introduce them into transcendental philosophy" (*KU*, 266).

78. *Logik*, §29; Ak IX, 108.

79. The arc of this presentation has forced me to leave out material on Schelling's analysis of enthusiasm (*Begeisterung*) in Plato's philosophy. Throughout his career, Schelling referred to this phenomenon in tones of fascination and desire. Whether it be the influence of the true mystic and prophet Hahn (his eulogy was in 1790, the Platonic notebooks date from 1792), or the theoretical connections of Kant's system as accessible through enthusiasm—or both factors together—Schelling appears extremely interested with the topic. One need but read the headings in his notebooks. Such an interest coupled with his intellectual vigor would never miss the anomalous systematic nexus surrounding the sublime and *Begeisterung*. As we will see in the next chapter, he attributes Plato's insights into the "sublime supersensible substrate" of harmony of form between humanity and the world as having inspired his *begeisterte* language. For transcribed excerpts from these notebooks as well as penetrating analysis, see the excellent work of Michael Franz, *Schellings Tübinger Platon-Studien* (Göttingen: Vandenhoeck & Ruprecht, 1996).

80. *KU*, 251.

81. Immanuel Kant, *Religion within the Limits of Reason Alone*, translated by T. Greene and H. Hudson (New York: Harper & Row, 1960), 38f.

82. The non-inspired audience of art would also be open to the harmonious play of faculties set off by the genius' work of art, and thus to that extent be capable of access to the aesthetic ideas. Only the genius is capable of realizing these ideas in a material medium.

83. *KU*, 344. The entire passage reads: "Consonantly with this, GENIUS may also be defined as the faculty of aesthetic ideas. This serves at the same time to point out the reason why it is nature (the nature of the individual) and not a set purpose, that in products of genius gives the rule to art (as the production of the beautiful). For the beautiful must not be estimated according to concepts, but by the final mode in which the imagination is attuned so as to accord with the faculty of concepts generally; and so rule and precept are incapable of serving as the requisite subjective standard for that aesthetic and unconditioned finality in fine art which has to make a warranted claim to being bound to please every one. Rather must such a standard be sought in the element of sheer nature in the subject, which cannot be comprehended under rules or concepts, that is to say, the supersensible substrate of all the subject's faculties (unattainable by any concept of understanding), and consequently in that which forms the point of reference for the harmonious accord of all our faculties of cognition—the production of which accord is the ultimate end set by the intelligible basis of our nature. Thus alone is it possible for a subjective and yet universally valid principle a priori to lie at the basis of that finality for which no objective principle can be prescribed."

84. B 114, §12.

85. *KU*, 347.
86. *KU*, 351.
87. Ibid.
88. Significant is Kant's insistence that nature be denuded of "an objective finality" and the accompanying ability to "fashion its forms for our delight," since such an objective check and limit of our imagination would in Kant's mind denigrate the freedom of human reason. Examining the choice between a judgment of taste forced by nature and the freedom of subjective imagination, Kant clearly prefers the autonomy of the latter over the heteronomy of the former. However, would he not have to concede that there are some forms of nature that possess an objective finality insofar as it is incapable for us to find them pleasing? If the beautiful is the symbol of the good, then what is the symbol of the repulsive that provokes physiological disgust and even involuntary reactions of discomfort? He grants the possibility of disgust provoking displeasure (*KU*, 312). However, just as Kant is forced by his theology of reason to denigrate evil as a privation of the good, so too is he forced to denigrate this disgust to a "strange sensation, which depends purely on the imagination" (ibid.). In denying the possibility of nature to determine real, "objective finality" in the experience of disgust, Kant remains consistent with his systematic subsumption of nature to the reason of man.
89. *KU*, 352.
90. *KU*, 353.
91. *KU*, 344, 255. Kant provides the following summary of the three different ways in which he uses this predicate "supersensible" at the end of its "deduction" in §57: "Firstly, there is the supersensible in general, without further determination, as substrate of nature; secondly, this same supersensible as principle of the subjective finality of nature for our cognitive faculties; thirdly, the same supersensible again, as principle of the ends of freedom, and principle of the common accord of these ends with freedom in the moral sphere" (346). The first use of supersensible answers the antinomy of reason for the cognitive faculty in its theoretical employment (truth-nature-cosmos); the second sense addresses the antinomy of reason generated by the aesthetic use of judgment and its resulting feeling of pleasure or displeasure (beauty-human-soul); while the third sense resolves the antinomy of reason generated by the faculty of desire in its attempts to wield practical reason to legislate itself (the Good-God).

Chapter 4. The *Timaeus Commentary*

1. The epistemological interest is clear when we remember that Theopneusty is a theory of divine inspiration, whereby the spirit of the deity literally breathes knowledge into men, and then makes them communicate its knowledge as revealed truth.
2. *Tim.* 68e5–69a1.

3. As pointed out earlier, Schelling does not transcribe the Greek accents when making entries in his notebooks. Accordingly, Greek text cited from his notebook appear as they do in his text. Terms I introduce will be fully attired.

4. 46c, 29e, 68e; cf. *Phaedo* 99b, 106d5.

5. He follows a similar strategy in the "second sailing" of the *Phaedo*, when he attributes the many different manifestations of beauty to the one cause of beauty καθ αὐτὸ (100c).

6. This is Kant's definition of freedom as found in his momentary discussion of the dynamic categories applied to the dynamic world of nature in his *The System of Weltbegriffe* in the first *Critique* (A 418/B 446).

7. As Schelling will write regarding Spinoza in his treatise *On the World Soul*: "Spinoza said the more we know individual things, the more we know God, and with steadily increasing conviction we must now call out to those who seek the science of the eternal: come here to physics and know the eternal!" (I/2, 378).

8. For Plato truth is not the normative ideal it is for the modern. What drives Plato instead is the ideal of ethics, which is simultaneously that of beauty: truth enters on a subsidiary level of importance as a predicate that determines other subjects' relation to this Janus-faced Ideal of τὸ καλόν and τα αγατηον.

9. *Studienheft* §28, cited in Franz, *Platon-Studien*, 291f.

10. Ibid., 290. The etymology and original meaning of enthusiasm in German is quite clear: *Begeisterung* is an infusion of the divine spirit. This would have been an obvious point to Kant and Schelling.

11. For Schelling the creative actions of the poet and genius refuse to be packaged and communicated like a techne. The creative gift is instead something that an individual must develop and acquire on one's own. Schelling reads Socrates' *Daemon* as signifying that essential dimension of *philosophy itself* that is not a method or skill to be learned, but is rather an activity that one can only understand by actually doing it: "One could <u>learn</u> nothing from Socrates.—Whoever could not comprehend his *Geist*, listened to him in vain, whoever wanted to learn something by heart, for him Socrates had nothing. One could not learn philosophy from him, rather only philosophizing. To this belonged, however, more than just listening to him. Many remained on the surface of the Socratic teachings, as long as they were with him, *edoxan einai ti*, because they had become used to his ways. But his *Geist* did not go over into *them*. *C'est tout comme chez nous*" (cited in Franz, *Platon-Studien*, 317). This reading of the irreducible individual dimension of philosophy should come as no surprise in light of Schelling's position towards the Gnostics, and their prioritizing of individual experience and consequent speculation over the secondhand faith mediated by doctrine: the art of philosophizing cannot be "learned by heart" at the feet of a teacher, but must be instead developed within oneself. The figure of the *Daemon* signifies the inability of method

to serve as the sufficient condition for either philosophizing or creating works of art.

12. §15, cited in Franz, *Platon-Studien*, 293. Again, I have reproduced the typography Schelling uses in his notebooks.

13. §16, Franz, *Platon-Studien*, 294.

14. G. E. Lessing, *Die Erziehung des Menschengeschlech* (Leipzig: Deutsches Verlagshaus Bong & Co., 1877), Bd. V, 77.

15. Kant, *Religion*, 143.

16. Renaissance commentators such as Herrera (1580) made the obvious connection between Plato's genius and Aristotle's agent intellect (M. Menendez Pelayo, *Historia de las ideas esteticas in Espana* (Madrid: Santander, 1962), II, 71). Voltaire characterized genius as a form of "active imagination" (ibid., II, 78).

17. Plato, *The Republic*, Loeb Classical Library (Cambridge: Harvard University Press, 1935), 532b.

18. *TK*, 71–72.

19. Consequently, the degree of precision and discipline demonstrated is of a much different quality than we have seen in his speculations regarding divine epistemology. While different in tone and style, the substance of his commentary on the *Timaeus*, however, does not in the least conflict with what I have examined in his other notes.

20. *TK*, 71–72.

21. Kant's elite class of discursive transcendental propositions, which magically contain within themselves the "synthesis of possible intuitions," which, however, are *not* provided a priori, is perhaps the most baffling aspect of his science of cognition: "All our knowledge relates, finally, to possible intuitions, for it is through them alone that an object is given. Now an a priori concept, that is, a concept which is not empirical, either already includes in itself a pure intuition (and if so, it can be constructed), or it includes nothing but the synthesis of possible intuitions which are not given a priori. In this latter case we can indeed make use of it in forming synthetic a priori judgments, but only discursively in accordance with concepts, never intuitively through the construction of the concept" (A 718/B 747). How can discursive principles be the basis of a synthesis?

22. *TK*, 13. This text was begun in sometime in January or February of 1774, and ended a few months later that year, sometime in May or June. The editors point out that besides orthographical analysis, the most significant factor in establishing the date of this text's composition is its total absence of Fichtean terminology. At this time, it appears that Schelling is still working with an exclusively Kantian framework, employing only a limited use of Reinhold's terminology surrounding the *Verstellungsvermögen*.

23. *Phil.*, 15d9. As we saw earlier, Schelling cites this triadic form in his Magistar of 1792 to prove the universal nature of the idea that the origin of reasoning is likewise the origin of freedom. This is the earliest

evidence of his familiarity with Plato's eternal form. The extent however, to which Plato's account of the triune nature of all productive and binding relationships permeated the intellectual environment of Schelling's upbringing—particularly Hahn's analysis of the forces of nature and the relationship of the soul as the third that connects the mind and body—strongly suggests that Schelling was familiar with this form of reasoning since at least the age of fifteen when he composed the eulogy for Hahn. See *AA*, I/1, 127, n. K, where he cites *Phil.*, 16b5–c7.

24. Franz emphasizes the importance of §65 of the *Critique of Teleological Judgment* for Schelling's reading of Plato.

25. "What then is *jenes geheime Band*, which binds our Geist with nature, or that hidden organ through which nature speaks to our mind or our mind to Nature?" (I/2, 55). In the Anglophone world, only Dieter Sturma has addressed, and then only briefly, Schelling's use of the Platonic idea of "das Band." See Dieter Sturma, "The Nature of Subjectivity: The Critical and Systematic Function of Schelling's Philosophy of Nature," in *Critical Philosophy: Fichte, Schelling, and Hegel*, edited by Sally Sedgwick (New York: Cambridge University Press, 2000), 216–231.

26. See §CXVIII: "The completely real i.e. that being in which the entire Idea or *Natura Naturans* presently lives (XXXIII), is therefore necessarily a threefold in unity and in the threefoldness individual and indivisible. For it is the expression of the threefold Band, that as such is nonetheless only One: the expressed fullness of A=A" (I/7, 233).

27. Cf. II/1, 38: "This third is the *alles verknüpfende* Band. . . . "

28. *Phil.*, 18D.

29. *TK*, 23.

30. Translations of Plato's text will be indicated as Loeb's or my own translation of Schelling's German translation of the original text.

31. Again, Schelling does not transcribe the various accents that accompany the Greek vocabulary. When I cite his text, they will remain bare; when I introduce Greek terms they will be fully attired.

32. Schelling writes: "αλητηεια however, is what for example he means by επιστημη in the Meno and the Gorgias. (γενεσισ⁻ουσιαˆδοχα·επιστημη)" (*TK*, 23, n. 1).

33. Except for the χῶρα (the "void"), all of Plato's reality has form. Indeed, it is when Plato describes matter in the *Timaeus* that he references the "theory of ideas" (*Tim.* 51bf).

34. His argument for creation is more declarative than convincing: as a requirement of our cognitive hardware that refuses to process the datum of an uncaused event, we are forced to posit a reason or cause for what occurs in the sensible world. Since everything perceived through experience and the senses is in becoming, it must have had a beginning initiated by a cause that itself was not in the process of becoming, but is instead fully complete. "And that which has come into existence must necessarily, as we say, have come into existence by reason of some cause" (28c5). Schelling

notes: "(One sees from this why Plato explained the original matter as something invisible)" (TK, 24). As something invisible the original matter is posited as coeternal with τὸ ὄν.

35. TK, 23.

36. Ibid., lines 23–24.

37. Further on we will examine his application of Kant's critique of the ontological argument to the τὸ ὄν of the ideas.

38. Possible translations of τὸ παραδειγμα are first *pattern, model, exemplar, precedent, example*; further, *lesson, warning*, or *argument*; finally, in law, *precedent*.

39. In the midst of researching his dissertation on Marcion, Schelling parenthetically comments directly after this passage: "(An idea no Moses and no Jew has come across)" (TK 27). That is, Plato's deity is not a wrathful or jealous deity.

40. *Hom. Od.* 15.324 and 9.27 respectively.

41. For Homer's usage of τὸ αγαθὸνατηος, see *Hom. Il.* 2.673; *Hom. Od.* 17.381, respectively. Plato typically uses this term, in this sense, as an adverb. See *Theaetatus* 161b, 169e; *Protagoras* 319e; and *Parmenides* 128b.

42. Plato's use of τόὄλον lends further support to reading this passage as a testimony to the ideal of the complete *qua* whole.

43. According to Plessing, who at the time was one of the leading historians of philosophy, Plato's ideas are immaterial substances, that must be "seen" in a divine intellectual intuition before coming into existence. Schelling charges that Plessing's interpretation of Plato's Ideas as existing entities presupposes their physical existence, which, he holds, cannot be compatible with their supersensible status. In his *System der Platonischen Philosophie*, Tennemann refers to Plessing's interpretation of Plato's Ideas as being in opposition to his own. See Baum, "The Beginnings of Schelling's Philosophy of Nature," in Sedgwick, 206–208.

44. Schelling does not cite this passage.

45. Schelling refers to the following parallel passage in the *Philebus*: "Surely σοπηια and νουσ could never come into being without soul" (30c8).

46. TK, 28.

47. TK, 29. The problem Schelling is addressing here stems from the question of how to mediate the seemingly formless matter᾿ ἄπειρός with the limiting form of the νοῦς᾿ πέρας᾿. We will discuss this issue in detail in the next section.

48. Schelling argues that this follows from Plato's words "νοῦν δῌ αὖ χωρὶς ψυχῆς ἀδύνατον παραγενέσθαι τω" at 30b2.

49. *Thol. Ar.*, 6.

50. Schelling's words cited from TK, 29.

51. Schelling must have conceived of this low-intensity soul of matter as possessing just enough energy to keep it in a chaotic flux of disordered movement.

52. Like interpreting a face or contemplating the *eidos*. To be consistent, the parts then conversely interact both among themselves laterally, and vertically feedback to affect the nature of the whole.

53. Schelling follows Kant almost word for word here. Compare the third *Critique*: "daß die Theile desselben sich dadurch zur Einheit eines Ganzen verbinden, daß sie von einander wechselseitig Ursache und Wirkung ihrer Form sind. Denn auf solche Weise ist es allein möglich, daß umgekehrt (wechselseitig) die Idee des Ganzen wiederum die Form und Verbindung aller Theile bestimme" (s. 291, 17–21, AA. 33, 13–17). And from Schelling: "Also als ein Wesen, deßen Teile nur durch ihrer Beziehung auf das Ganze möglich sind, deßen Teile wechselseitig sich gegen einander als Mittel u. Zweck verhalten, u. sich also einander ihrer Form sowol als Verbindung nach wechselseitig hervorbringen . . . umgekehrt die Idee des Ganzen wiederum als vorausgehend, u. a priori die Form u. die Teile in ihrer Harmonie bestimmend" (*TK*, 33).

54. The type of causation at work in the category of *community* does not follow the linear model of a series in which the movement of cause to effect flows in one direction. As Kant notes: "This is a quite different kind of connection from that which is found in the mere relation of cause to effect (of ground to consequence), for in the latter relation the consequence does not in its turn reciprocally determine the ground, and therefore does not constitute with it a whole—thus the world, for instance, does not with its Creator serve to constitute a whole" (B 112). We see here clearly how even in a discussion of the dynamic categories, Kant still insists on the supremacy of the mathematical series: if he were to be consistent, and apply the dynamic synthesis he prescribes for this class of categories in the Transcendental Dialectic, he would see that this account of the relationship of creator to world is in error. For in the dynamic synthesis, not only does the linear relation of subsumption give way to the reciprocal causality of *Wechselwirkung*, but the totality of the series is qualitatively different from the members of that series. Thus, the Creator becomes the whole qualitatively different from the members of its "series" qua parts, which *nonetheless forms one unity with those parts*: this is a form of causality that provides the only possible model for conceiving how the parts of an organism relate to each other and to the whole. Accepting this model of the relationship between creator and created however, would entail accepting Hahn's proposition that God needs creation as much as creation needs God. The epistemological ramifications of a thoroughgoing organic causality of reciprocal determination: not only does the whole determine the part, but the part must also determine the whole, thereby requiring an autoepistemic structuring built into Nature. Or as Schelling will later phrase the matter, that man is with god a *Mitdichter* of creation (alternative model of the self vis-à-vis Descartes' cogito).

55. The dynamic of *Wechselwirkung*, however, is inapplicable to Plato's understanding of the relationship between the divine understanding and its members.

56. The close proximity of the term *sublime* and "discovery of a supersensible principle of form and harmony of the world in ourselves" constellates the role of the sublime in Kant's third *Critique* as the only means of delivering to reason the intuition and idea of an absolute magnitude *qua* maximum. As we will see, it is this experience that Kant ultimately devises to supply his system with the "absolute whole" required to ground it, and thereby keep it from infinitely spinning in the ethereal void of possible experience. To make the constellation complete, the surplus of sensual data the sublime delivers can only be assimilated by Kant's architectonic through the dynamic categories: this is the only instance of his application of this category to experience in which it generates the force of necessity required of the unconditional. Whether or not Schelling consciously makes these connections remains to be seen.

57. "πολλαίτε αἱ συνάπασαι ἐπιστῆμαι δόξουσιν εἶναι καὶ ἀνόμοιοίτινες αὐτῶν ἀλλήλαις. The phrase αἱ συνάπασαι ἐπιστῆμαι is the source for Schelling's idea of a "form of philosophy *überhaupt*."

58. Baum and Franz do an excellent job of laying out the basic contours of the debate surrounding the status of Plato's ideas, both from a historical perspective as well as in the specific historical context of Schelling's work. In many ways Schelling sees Plato's Ideas as serving an analogous function to Kant's logical conditions of knowledge, namely, as "subjective forms according to which one represents the world" (*TK*, 69). Consistent with one of the oldest traditional readings dating back to at least Philo of Alexandria, Schelling suggests that the Ideas originate in the divine understanding and then "are made possible in human understanding [*Verstand*] through the intellectual unity [*intellektualle Gemeinschaft*] of men with the origin of all being" (*TK*, n. 37). Given the contours of the nominalist-realist debate of the Middle Ages, there were in Schelling's time two major modern schools of thought on the status of Plato's Ideas. Following the nominalists, the Cambridge Platonist Ralph Cudworth (1617–1688) argued that the Ideas are concepts of God, whereas the German historian of philosophy Johann Jakob Brucker (1696–1770) maintained that they are eternal and self-subsistent, knowable only through pure noesis. In the critique of his contemporary Plessing, Schelling makes it clear that he follows the more Neoplatonic reading of the nominalists. See Baum's discussion of this in his "Beginnings of Schelling's Philosophy of Nature," 206–207. Yet the most important source for Schelling's position here has yet to be explored, namely Loeffler's translation of Matthieu Souverain's *Le Platonisme dévoilé*, a book which, after visiting with Loeffler in Leipzig, he asks his father for in a letter of 29.4.1796. Hans Wagner was the first to have pointed this out in his "Die Idee der Philosophie bei Schelling: Metaphysische Motive in seiner Frühphilosophie," in *Hans Wagner zum 60. Geburtstag*, edited by Harald Holz (Freiburg: Alber Karl, 1977), 31ff.

59. Franz points out that, contrary to most of his contemporaries, Schelling makes a clear distinction between the ontological status of Plato's *archai* and his Ideas, arguing that the former are causes of the empirical, whereas

the latter belong to pure being. See Franz, *Schellings Tübinger Platon-Studien*, 212–215.

60. See *TK*, 39, 5–25.

61. Nor do other translations that I know insert this term in the passages Schelling here translates. It should be pointed out, however, that the translator of the Loeb edition of the *Philebus* chooses to interject *form* into the passage I just cited—and modified by removing his term *form* so the passage would be in literal agreement with the Greek. The Greek reads literally "the knowledges collectively are many," whereas Fowler smoothes the rough edges of an ancient language by writing "the forms of knowledge collectively are many" (*Phil.*, 13e8).

62. "1ne bei Plato durchaus herrschende Idee" (*TK*, 36).

63. Schelling uses this phrase "ursprüngliche Form" throughout the *Form Essay*, written four to six months after this commentary.

64. "ὡς ἐξ μὲν καὶ πολλῶν ὄντων τῶν ἀεὶ λεγομένων εἶναι, πέρας δὲ καὶ ἀπειρίαν ἐν αὐτοῖς ζύμφυτον ἐχόντων"(*Phil.* 16c7).

65. "που τὸ μὲν ἄπειρον δεῖξαι τῶν ὄντων, τὸ δὲ πέρας"(23c8).

66. The order is once again not of the mathematical synthesis, but of nature "viewed as a dynamical whole" (A 417/B 446).

67. He writes: "take hotter and colder and see whether you can conceive of any limit of them, or whether the more or the less which dwell in their very nature do not, so long as they continue to dwell therein, preclude the possibility of any end" (24a8–12).

68. This specific passage parallels Kant's discussion of how only the fact that sensations have degree can be known a priori (A 176/B 218). Schelling reiterates this point, noting how the "continuous increase and decrease in sensation is the necessary form of all sensation" (*TK*, 60).

69. The reading Schelling has just provided correlates almost exactly to Kant's table of ideas at A 415/B 443: "1. Absolute completeness (*Vollständigkeit*) of the Composition; 2. Absolute completeness in the Division; 3. Absolute completeness in the Origination; 4. Absolute completeness as regards the Dependence of Existence."

Chapter 5. On the Possibility of a Form of All Philosophy: The *Form Essay*

1. Kant's last reference is to his *Metaphysical Foundations of Natural Science* (translated by J. Ellington [Indianapolis: Bobbs-Merrill, 1970]).

2. Although he fails to treat Schelling thoroughly in his major studies of this "constellation" of thinkers, Dieter Henrich nonetheless claims that Schelling's early philosophical work is most accurately understood as the methical employment of Fichte's philosophy to address the shortcomings of Reinhold's *Elementarphilsophie*. Once again, Schelling emerges in this narrative as a derivative figure lacking any independent character as a philosopher; a position which says more about the scope and color of Henrich's vision than it does about Schelling's work. For an

example of this, see his *Grundlegung aus dem Ich: Untersuchung zur Vorgeschichte des Idealismus Tübingen—Jena (1790–1794)*, Vol. 1 and Vol. 2 (Frankfurt am Main: Suhrkamp Verlag, 2004), 1551–1699. Henrich's student, Manfred Frank, follows the general contours of this narrative of Schelling's early development, but accounts for Schelling's differences with Fichte by appealing to the influence of Hölderlin, who he claims supplied Schelling with the idea of the 'absolute I' as an ontologically prior identity of self and nature. Frank bases this claim on a brief four-hundred-word piece Hölderlin wrote sometime between the end of 1794 and the beginning of 1795. In *Urtheil und Seyn* Hölderlin presents self-consciousness as an example of judgment (*Ur-theil*) that presupposes an original unity of self and nature. Schelling had himself explored this theme in his first *Magisterarbeit* (1792) on the myth of the Fall (*AA* I/1,127). See Manfred Frank, *Eine Einführung in Schellings Philosophie* (Frankfurt am Main: Suhrkamp Verlag, 1985). Jacobi's *Spinozabriefe* is alleged to be just as much—if not more—of an influence on Schelling's early work. See Sandkaulen-Bock's *Ausgang vom Unbedingten: Über den Anfang in der Philosophie Schellings* (Göttingen: Vandenhoeck u. Ruprecht, 1990), 13–18. For a more extended discussion, see Frank's *Unendliche Annäherung: Die Anfänge der philosophischen Frühromantik* (Frankfurt am Main: Suhrkamp Verlag, 1997), 67–114.

3. May 11, 1794 is the date given in *AA*, I/1, 250.

4. *Recension des Aenesidiemus* appeared on February 11 and 12, 1794, in numbers 47–49 of the *Jenaer Allgemeine Literaturzeitung*. "Ueber den Begrif der Wissenschaftslehre oder der sogenannnten Philosphie, als Einladungsschrift zu seinem Vorlesungen über diese Wissenschaft" appeared in May of 1794.

5. *AA*, I/1, 252. Jacobs points out that Schelling also probably heard Fichte in Tübingen both on May 2 and during his stopover from the 11th through 13th of June (ibid.). Schelling presumably began to study Fichte's *Recension* at this time. Jacobs does not, however, agree with those who suggest that Schelling actually spoke with Fichte (ibid., 251). Jacobs, curiously enough, fails to mention Fichte's *Recension des Aenesidiemus* as a significant influence on Schelling.

6. Hegel, *Briefe von und an Hegel*, hrsg. von V. J. Hoffmeister, 2 Bde. (Hamburg: F. Meiner, 1969–1981), I, 12.

7. *AA*, I/1, 127.

8. *AA*, I/1, 251.

9. *F. W. J. Schelling: Briefe und Dokumente*, hg. von H. Fuhrmans, 3 Bde. (Bonn: H. Bouvier, 1962–1973), I, 41.

10. Even Manfred Frank is forced by his own interpretative *Vorverständnis* to admit *confusion* when faced with the apparent dissonance of Schelling's first works of *Idealism* and *Naturphilosophie*. In what is the finest introduction to Schelling's philosophy available, Frank writes, "Wir konnten beobachten, daß Schellings frühste Schriften, vor allem

diejenige (1795), ... *die Abhandlungen zur Erläuterung des Idealismus der Wissenschaftslehre* (1796/97) und [die] *System des transzendentalen Idealismus* (1800)—sich so weit wie möglich dem idealistischen Ansatz anbequemen. Verwirrenderweise kennt diesselbe Zeit bereits die ersten Ansätze einer Naturphilosphie, in deren Namen Schelling eines Tages die Anmaßung der Wissenschaftslehre zurückweisen wird, die Philosophie überhaupt und im ganzen zu erschöpfen" (Frank, *Eine Einführung in Schellings Philosophie* (Frankfurt am Main: Suhrkamp Verlag, 1985), 72). If our thesis is correct, there is actually an intellectual center of gravity from which we can understand Schelling's dual-pronged strategy as complementary, instead of contradictory.

11. "πολλαίτε αἱ συνάπασαι ἐπιστη'μαι δόξουσιν εἰ'ναι καὶ ἀνόμοιοίτινες αὐτω'ν ἀλλήλαις" (*Phil.* 13e8).

12. Fichte introduces his technical term of *Tathandlung* to describe the *deed* whereby one intellectually discovers the first principle of his *Wissenschaftslehre* in the *Aenesidiemus Recension*: "But such a principle does not have to express a *Tatsache*; it can also express a *Tathandlung*" ("Review of *Aenesidiemus*," in *Fichte: Early Philosophical Writings*, translated and edited by D. Breazeale [Ithaca: Cornell University Press, 1988], 64). Schelling's use of the necessary *fact* (*Tatsache*) of organic self-determination, instead of Fichte's mentalistic *Tathandlung*, designates that point on which these two philosophers will never agree: the role of nature in philosophy. In locating the fact of freedom in all organic life—indeed, the entire cosmos—Schelling shows just how different his approach is from the standpoint of Fichte's more modern standpoint of subjective idealism.

13. These are Schelling's words from his *New Deduction of Natural Rights* (I/1, 249, §9).

14. As we will see, the self-positing of freedom is a mere possibility, not a fact.

15. Schelling uses this formulation in 1797 to describe the nature of organic life in the introduction to the first edition of his *Ideen zu einer Philosophie der Natur*: "Every organic product carries the ground of its being in itself, since it is cause and effect of itself" (I/2, 23). This is the perspective from which we have been exploring his programmatic statement of 1796, "life . . . is the schema of freedom," whose full context concerns the *causality of life*: "Life is autonomy in appearance; it is the schema of freedom, insofar as it reveals itself in nature. I am therefore necessarily a *living* being (*Wesen*)" (I/1, 246, §9). This passive state of the subject in the face of being necessarily a living organism denotes that strata of existence whose modality Schelling will designate as necessary, thereby deriving this modality not from "a priori" certainties, but from a *necessity in experience*: "originally we know nothing at all other than through experience and by means of experience, and only to this extent does all our knowledge consist of empirical propositions" (I/3, 278).

16. The status of this "I"—whether it is the "absolute I" or the "empirical I"—is a question we will address later.

17. He writes in the *Timaeus Commentary* that "In general Plato considers everything in the human soul as divine activity, or rather presents it as such, that emerges in our ideas lacking any empirical cause and empirical development (like virtue), or at least lacking easy to notice empirical causes, and lacking easy to notice empirical development (as for example, enthusiasm)—in short everything in which the empirical data is either completely missing or is difficult to find (cited in Franz, *Platon-Studien*, 290).

18. Sandkaulen-Bock would no doubt read this passage as evidence of Schelling's dependence on Jacobi (cf. Sandkaulen-Bock, *Ausgang*, 15f). We would concur only *if* Schelling 1) adopted other characteristic terms and strategies employed by Jacobi, and 2) he was not, on the contrary, working with a consistent set of Kantian terms and methods.

19. A 418/B 446. Although we will discuss this point later, it is essential to our reading of Schelling's method that we grasp the extent to which he uses and transforms Kant's methods in ways the master suggests, but of course explicitly forbids.

20. As Kant asserts in his *Logic*: "In a science we often *know* only the *cognitions* but not the *thing presented* by them; consequently there can be a science of that whereof our cognition is not knowledge" (*Logik*; Ak IX, 72). In his *Metaphysics of Morals*, Kant elaborates on this and provides a definition of philosophy as metaphysics that links this definition of the science of pure Logic to his theoretical employment of reason: "A *philosophy* of any subject (a system of rational knowledge from concepts) requires a system of *pure rational* concepts independent of any conditions of intuition, that is, a *metaphysics*" (*MdS*, 375). As a science of pure form, Kant's method explicitly denies the very *Inhalt* Schelling demands *his method* incorporate.

21. This is only an apparent contradiction. Kant proceeds to develop a new "third strategy" of a priori synthesis that (providing the model for *Hegel's logic*) somehow "creates" concepts merely through the interaction of concepts. See his account of the "disciplined" and "dogmatic employment" of pure reason that begins at A 713/B 741.

22. Kant continues: "From this it follows: (a) That in philosophy we must not imitate mathematics by beginning with definitions, *unless it be by way simply of experiment* [Kant's thought experiment of "possible experience"]. For since the definitions are analyses of given concepts, they presuppose the prior presence of the concepts [Kant's acknowledgment of the potential circularity of his presentation], although in a confused state; and the incomplete exposition must precede the complete. Consequently, we can infer a good deal from a few characteristics, derived from an incomplete analysis, without having yet reached the complete exposition, that is, the definition. In short, the definition in all its precision and clarity

ought, in philosophy, to come rather at the end than at the beginning of our enquiries. In mathematics, on the other hand, we have no concept whatsoever prior to the definition, through which the concept itself is first given. For this reason mathematical science must always begin, and it can always begin, with the definition" (A 730/B 758), a feat mathematics executes through the construction of its concepts.

23. "Now one concept cannot be combined with another synthetically and also at the same time immediately, since, to be able to pass beyond either concept, a third something is required to mediate our knowledge. Accordingly, since philosophy is simply what reason knows by means of concepts, no principle deserving the name of an axiom is to be found in it. Mathematics, on the other hand, can have axioms, since by means of the construction of concepts in the intuition of the object it can combine the predicates of the object both a priori and immediately, as, for instance, in the proposition that three points always lie in a plane" (A 732/B 760).

24. Kant's use of the organic model of explanation to describe his architectonic was surely one of the many "hints" that Schelling read as indicating Kant's true aspirations, which of course could not be achieved in the mere propaedeutic of Critique: "Systems seem to be formed in the manner of lowly organisms through a *generatio aequivoca* from the mere confluence of assembled concepts, at first imperfect, and only gradually attaining to completeness, although they one and all have had their schema, as the original germ, in the sheer self-development of reason. Hence, not only is each system articulated in accordance with an idea, but they are one and all organically united in a system of human knowledge, as members of one whole, and so as admitting of an architectonic of all human knowledge, which, at the present time, in view of the great amount of material that has been collected, or which can be obtained from the ruins of ancient systems, is not only possible, but would not indeed be difficult. We shall content ourselves here with the completion of our task, namely, merely to outline the architectonic of all knowledge arising from pure reason; and in doing so we shall begin from the point at which the common root of our faculty of knowledge divides and throws out two stems, one of which is reason" (A 836/B 863).

25. "But, as the magnitude of the measure has to be assumed as a known quantity, if, to form an estimate of this, we must again have recourse to numbers involving another standard for their unit, and consequently must again proceed mathematically, we can never arrive at a first or fundamental measure, and so cannot get any definite concept of a given magnitude. The estimation of the magnitude of the fundamental measure must, therefore, consist merely in the immediate grasp which we can get of it in intuition" (KU, 98).

26. Kant changed his mind after attempting to provide a metaphysical foundation for the empirical sciences: he was forced to add §11 to the second edition version of the Table of Categories in order to explain just how such a community and reciprocal causality works (B 109f).

27. "It was a magnificent idea of Plato's, that could easily send him into *Begeisterung*, that he should look for the harmony of the beings of nature (*Naturwesen*), not merely amongst themselves but also of each individual with itself [*Gemeinschaft*], not in with the method of empirical research, but rather in the investigation of the pure forms of the *Vorstellungsvermögen* itself. No wonder that he expressed *this sublime idea* in a language which, uncommon to the usual philosophical language, actually soars,—that his language itself is the work of a philosophical *Begeisterung*,—that *through* such a discovery of *a supersensible principle* of form and harmony of the world in ourselves [such a language] necessarily must have arisen" (*TK*, 34, bolded emphasis mine). Kant writes in the third *Critique*: "Yet, from an aesthetic point of view, enthusiasm is sublime, because it is an effort of one's powers called forth by ideas which give to the mind an impetus of far stronger and more enduring efficacy than the stimulus afforded by sensible representations" (*KU*, 124, emphasis mine). It is clear that Schelling understands Plato's divine inspiration and Kant's *Begeisterung* as forms of revelation, of the genius of man speaking the language of nature. Rüdiger Bubner also makes this connection between Plato's divine inspiration and Kant's theory of genius as the voice of nature. Klaus Düsing advances a similar position, but also fails to offer up any evidence to substantiate his position. Whereas Bubner and Düsing advance Kant as the source of Schelling's interest in these teachings of Plato, I am arguing that this is the result of his early interest in Plato, fostered in large part by the Platonic framework of his Pietist upbringing. See Klaus Düsing, "Schellings Genieästhetik," in *Philosophie und Poesie I: O. Pöggeler zum 60. Geburtstag*, edited by Annemarie Gethmann-Siefert (Stuttgart: Frommann-Holzboog, 1988) and Rüdiger Bubner, *The Innovations of Idealism* (Cambridge: Cambridge University Press, 2003), 14.

28. Kant continues: "Therefore, since the time-series is a condition of the internal sense and of an intuition, it is a subjective movement of the imagination by which it does violence to the internal sense—a violence which must be proportionately more striking the greater the quantum which the imagination comprehends in one intuition. The effort, therefore, to receive in a single intuition a measure for magnitudes that it takes an appreciable time to apprehend, is a mode of representation which, subjectively considered, is contra-final, but objectively, is requisite for the estimation of magnitude, and is consequently final. Here the very same violence that is wrought on the subject through the imagination is estimated as final for the whole province of the mind" (*KU*, 107).

29. Although he never explicitly forbids or denies this modality of comprehension, it follows from his exclusion of substances in *community* that any aggregate must be excluded as an transcendental idea since its *Vorstellung* would be inexponible: "Now in space, taken in and by itself, there is no distinction between progress and regress. For as its parts are coexistent, it is an aggregate, not a series. The present moment can

be regarded only as conditioned by past time, never as conditioning it, because this moment comes into existence only through past time, or rather through the passing of the preceding time. But as the parts of space are coordinated with, not subordinated to, one another, one part is not the condition of the possibility of another; and unlike time, space does not in itself constitute a series. Nevertheless the synthesis of the manifold parts of space, by means of which we apprehend space, is successive, taking place in time and containing a series" (A 412/B 439). The violence of the sublime is also required to supply the reverence and awe we experience in the face of the moral law.

30. Schelling does not just demand a unity of knowledge; the phrase quoted reads in its entirety "the ultimate unity of knowledge, of faith (*Glauben*), and of will" (I/1, 112).

31. Schelling's intent in this particular context differs slightly from the manner in which I have presented it here. He writes in full: "There is no other basis for this agreement of the oldest traditions in the explanation of the origin of human evil, . . . than the consideration of the universal human nature; anyone that only somewhat penetrates this nature, will very quickly catch sight within us of a peculiar conflict, namely [of] an overpowering principle of action in us that drives us over the narrow limits of our senses to higher things; he will conclude that out of this results the limitlessness of all our wishes and thoughts which never allow themselves to be satisfied; he will discover an excessive drive of human nature in the search for happiness and conclude that so far as we follow this drive, a greater decrease in power in us appears, which no happiness can offset: he will hear the domineering voice of reason and a limitless respect of the demands of necessity, but on the other hand the temptations and lure of sensual nature, which domineering reason concedes but an all too small share in our development to completeness; and he will observe—to the extent that this matter allows itself to be captured in words—how the spirit of man, which lies in miserable conflict with itself, oscillates between both sides back and forth" (*AA*, I/1, 127). From the very beginning of his career, writing as a seventeen-year-old, Schelling refuses to simply subsume the sensual under the intelligible, and instead seeks to check reason's domineering voice—an obvious allusion to Kant—and instead coordinate and reconcile the sensual and the intelligible. As we saw in his *Timaeus Commentary*, only this ideal of integration is worthy of τὸ καλόν.

32. Kant described his critical program to Lambert, as a "quite special, though negative science" (Letter of September 2, 1770 [Ak X, 98], cited in the introduction to Kant's *Opus postumm*, translated and edited by E. Förster [Cambridge: Cambridge University Press, 1993], xxix). Unlike the cartographer of old, Kant liberated himself from the use of pictorially based scales as he sought to develop pure ideas of reason that would provide noetic support for Lambert's general graphical grid, which was used to

depict systematic relationships between measured quantities. However, as we have seen with Plato's divine class of cause, the conditions of continuous space and time cannot themselves be elements of space and time. While the use of a static two-dimensional plane provides an elegant stage on which to present a transcendental philosophy of virtual experience, it fails as an explanatory framework for the multitude of dimensions that make up the real world of a nonlinear and dynamic space-time continuum. As the *Opus postumm* demonstrates, the impossibility of making an *Uebergang* from his transcendental world to the phenomenal world was a central occupation of his last writings (see *Opus postumm*, 100–199 [How is physics possible? How is a transition possible?]).

33. Schelling first mentions the phrase "intellectual intuition" in the *Of the I* essay.

34. *Tim.* 51d–52.

35. Reflective consciousness always comes in after the fact. The point is that this magnitude of knowing is inaccessible to discursivity.

36. This is precisely his reading of the relation between eternity and time in the *Timaeus* (*TK*, 62).

37. I/1, 100, n. 1.

38. This is what happens to Kant in the transcendental deduction when he is forced to make the statement that "I know myself, like other phenomena, only as I appear to myself, not as I am to the understanding" (B 155).

39. A method of construction we discuss in the next chapter.

40. Not, strangely enough, *Fichte's* formulation 'I am I'. Schelling is inconsistent in his use of terms to describe this proposition I = I; most often it is an axiom, but occasionally it appears as a theorem.

41. It can only be made progressively more real through the "*realizierende Vernunft*" of practical philosophy. A proof, which, as Schelling will continuously point out, is as never ending as the ongoing development of creation itself.

42. A series of infinite regress common to Kant's regressive method and Derrida's infinite deferral of meaning: both occur in a differential structure of a series of conditioned conditions that lacks an unconditioned first member to provide the positive meaning characteristically generated by living humans (*intentional subjects*).

43. A strategy, however, that does not seek to deny the efficacy or necessity of our use of the regressive method of analysis, but rather aims only at qualifying it. Though similar, Schelling's is not the same as Jacobi's critique of rationality's limits and dangers. It is instead a critique of a dogmatic adherence to established critical doctrine, a Kantian Scholasticism, as it were.

44. *Logik*, §37; Ak IX, 111.

45. The premise of his argument is the continuity of elements that constitute nature and man (P1): as living beings we are of the same substance and nature as the elements of the rest of creation (*Tim.*, 29b). Concede this

premise, and Plato's second proposition (P2) follows: that we are not the source of these elements and living nature, but rather the world beyond us is the source of ours and all other creatures' being (ibid., 29c8). Having established these two points Plato specifically addresses the question of the unity of creation, using the organic unity of the living body as the paradigm of this ἕν. "When we see all the aforementioned elements gathered into a unity, do we not call them a body (σῶμα)?" (ibid., 29d8). If yes, then we should apply the same reasoning to the universe considered as a whole, that "would likewise be a body, being composed of the same elements" as ourselves (ibid., 29e). Based on P2, Plato asks whether our body derives nourishment from the larger body of nature or vice versa. He concludes that since we derive life, and therewith unity, from the larger organism of nature, the same relationship of dependence must exist regarding soul and mind: humanity is not the source of ensouled mind, rather the larger organism of nature is the source of this ordering power within us (ibid., 30d3f). Consequently, the form of this ordering ensouled mind derives from the objective order of living nature.

46. Once again, a reminder that Schelling inconsistently uses the terms *Prinzip* and *Grundsatz* to name this ultimate axiom 'I = I'.

47. Immanuel Kant, *Metaphysical Foundations of Natural Science*, translated by J. Ellington (Indianapolis: Bobbs-Merrill, 1970), 11, n. 8; emphasis mine.

48. As a further clue to Kant's efforts to address the anomaly in his paradigm, in this discussion he glosses the obvious differences between his logical definition of disjunction and his definition of *community*: contrary to his presentation, the characteristics of the former do not flow seamlessly into the characteristics of the later. The most glaring difference is the character of the relation among the members and parts coordinated by the whole: in a disjunctive proposition "if one member of the division is posited, all the rest are excluded and conversely," whereas the category of *community* specifies that the members of division "simultaneously and reciprocally" condition one another (B 112). The former is a negative act of exclusion, whereas the later is a positive act of mutual engendering that also (somehow) includes separation.

49. See his dismissive analysis of *"Kraft"* in the Regulative Employment of the Ideas (A 648/B 676f).

50. This approach also explains how Kant can assert that the third member of each class of category is simultaneously a *Stammbegriff* and the result that "arises from the combination of the second category with the first" (B 110). For remember, "[i]t must not be supposed, however, that the third category is therefore merely a derivative, and not a primary, concept of the pure understanding. For the combination of the first and the second concepts, in order that the third may be produced, require a special act of the understanding, which is not identical with that which is exercised in the case of the first and the second" (B 111).

51. This passage is preceded by an explanation of these two shifts in perspective that we have already seen in his analysis of Plato's three forms in the *Timaeus Commentary*: "The *Ich, Nichtich,* and the *Vorstellung* are *given* (subjectively) only through the *Vorstellung* and the latter is given in consciousness. But what has been said thus far shows that they can be given through the *Vorstellung* and thus through consciousness only insofar as they themselves are antecedently posited (objectively, i.e., as *independent* from consciousness), either unconditionally (like the *Ich*) or conditionally (but conditioned by the unconditioned, not by consciousness)" (I/1, 100, n. 1).

52. An unfortunate habit of reflective analysis that leads to an inverted understanding of the cause of this duality, whereby the result of a duality reflected in thinking is accepted as an originary divide rooted in ontology. Thus, by reflection, does the effect of thinking itself become its own cause.

53. In the fourth stanza of his eulogy for Hahn, Schelling writes of the divine forces of nature. As Hahn interpreted the interaction of these expansive and contractive forces through the use of trichotomy, it is reasonably safe to infer that Schelling was well acquainted with this modality of synthesis. In addition, lodged in the middle of the *Timaeus* passage Schelling analyzed, is Plato's account of the need for three in synthesis: "But it is not possible that two things alone should be conjoined without a third; for there must needs be some intermediary bond (δεσμὸν) to connect the two. And the fairest of bonds (δεσμῶν) is that which most perfectly unites into one both itself and the things which it binds together; and to effect this in the fairest way" (*Tim.* 31c).

54. We once again encounter the problematic circle of the unconditioned. This is not a problem for Schelling however, since the circular character of his argument is in this context a necessary proof that he has successfully reached the limit of the absolute: "Of necessity, either there can be no ultimate axiom, or it can exist only by reciprocal determination of content by form and form by content" (I/1, 97).

55. *TNB*, 394f.

56. This composite form of expression is most likely the (one) root of his idea that only symbolic or artistic forms of expression are capable of articulating the *relatum* that unites his theoretical philosophy of nature and his practical philosophy of consciousness and history.

57. Oetinger's compact *"Sprichwort"* that "Nature is a third out of two" would be easily assimilated by a boy of Schelling's genius (cited in Heinz, *Oetinger als Vorläufer,* 89).

58. Continuing our parallel reading of Kant and Schelling, note how for Kant it is the character of the "assumed necessity" in the idea of the sublime which allows it to be accepted as an a priori principle. In other words, the necessity of the sublime is what feeds and supplies the idea of reason, the idea of a necessary absolute whole that should unify reason. Consequently,

it is the sensible that must provide pure reason with its necessary unity. "In this modality of aesthetic judgments, namely, their assumed necessity, lies what is for the *Critique* of judgment a moment of capital importance. For this is exactly what makes an a priori principle apparent in their case, and lifts them out of the sphere of empirical psychology, in which otherwise they would remain buried amid the feelings of gratification and pain (only with the senseless epithet of finer feeling), so as to place them, and, thanks to them, to place the faculty of judgment itself, in the class of judgments of which the basis of an a priori principle is the distinguishing feature, and, thus distinguished, to introduce them into transcendental philosophy" (*KU*, 117).

59. An identity of content is precisely what Kant denied his form of unity, expressed in his formulation of the cogito, the "*Ich denke.*" Since for Kant all thinking is judging, his "*Ich denke*" is a semantic placeholder for the purely formal and ultimately analytic *unitas* (*simplicitas*) of a logician's judging. Kant links thinking and judging with uncharacteristic directness in the following summation of his critical strategy: "I looked about for an act (*Handlung*) of the understanding which comprises all the rest, and is distinguished only by the various modifications or *momenta*, in reducing the multiplicity of representation to the unity of thinking in general: I found this act of the understanding to consist in judging" (Immanuel Kant, *Prolegomena*, translated by P. Carus [La Salle, IL: Open Court, 1994], 86).

60. Following the inner dynamic of his explication of this trichotomy, it would appear to follow that this new form of proposition would be *symbolic*, in the sense of a form of expression that articulates the form of consciousness of empirical existence, that is, that articulates the infinite in the finite. This would then position this new form of proposition in the aesthetic domain of the imagination (*Einbildung*). In his *Würzburger Lectures* of 1804, this is precisely what he does, designating the disjunctive as the logical form of the "*Anschauung der Einbildungskraft,*" which he sets as equivalent to Kant's aesthetic judgment (I/5, 500). The disjunctive is the form of the sublime, which Schelling equates with the beautiful, since they both mediate the infinite in the finite.

61. Schelling writes in a footnote to this, "The proper expression that belongs here!" (ibid.).

62. The living elements of organic nature both exist separately *für sich*, and yet simultaneously exist within the wider entirety of an ecosystem. The nature of such organisms is one of unceasing qualitative development and self-differentiation. Considered from the logical level, the linear model of a subordinating logic is not capable of accounting for the reciprocal interaction of living organisms: "Every organic product carries the reason of its *Dasein* in itself, for it is cause and effect of itself. No single part could arise except in this whole, and this whole itself consists only in the reciprocal causation of the parts" (I/2, 23).

63. A Schellingian point: if the universe betrays self-organizing "habits" or forces, and we are part of this universe, our minds are merely a more complex 'system' of that same self-organization, whose higher level of complexity and thus intensity enables us to turn back on nature and cultivate or destroy her. Knowing the divine essence thus becomes a knowing of the whole self-organization in the vein of a Hahn—that is, as mystic—but also as "scientist": "all knowing is a striving for communion with the divine essence, a participation in that original knowledge" that is the "organism of the whole" (I/7, 218).

64. "And the starting-point of reason is not reason but something stronger than reason." Aristotle, *Eudamian Ethics*, Loeb Classical Library (Cambridge: Harvard University Press, 1934), 1248a28; cited at I/2, 217.

65. A dynamic whole, which, if we as a species wish to continue, must be recognized as an organic unity and not a mechanical aggregate, elements of which we can destroy at will, not expecting this to impact the health of the entire organic world system.

66. Oetinger, *Wörterbuch*, 453.

67. For Peirce's most succinct statement of his use of trichotomy, see the essay I just cited from, "Trichotomic," (p. 296), but also in the same volume his "One, Two, Three: Kantian Categories," and "A Guess at the Riddle," all three in *The Essential Peirce* (Bloomington: Indiana University Press, 1992), 242–297. The influence Schelling had on Peirce was "enormous," or so he says in a letter he writes to William James on January 28, 1894: "Dear William,— . . . You ask whether I know of anybody but Delboeuf and myself 'who has treated the inorganic as a sort of product of the living'? This is good. An instance, no doubt, of that wonderful originality for which I am so justly admired. Your papa, for one, believed in creation, and so did the authors of all the religions. But my views were probably influenced by Schelling,—by all stages of Schelling, but especially by the Philosophy of Nature. I consider Schelling as enormous; and one thing I admire about him is his freedom from the trammels of system, and his holding himself uncommitted to any previous utterance. In that, he is like a scientific man. If you were to call my philosophy Schellingism transformed in the light of modern physics, I should not take it hard . . . . " (R. B. Berry, *Thought and Character of William James* (Boston: Little, Brown & Co., 1935), Vol. II, 416).

Chapter 6. Freedom and the Construction of Philosophy

1. Decisive is the insistence that there is no categorical difference between nature and man; they do not stand in opposition as *Subjekt* and *Gegenstand*, since "The system of Nature is at the same time the system of our mind." Because subject and object reflect two different epochs of the same historical process, the realm of spirit *qua* speculation is no longer

separated from the realm of nature *qua* experience, thereby removing the dualism between metaphysics and physics.

2. Schelling only described his system *once* as his *"Identitätsystem"*—a move he made under considerable pressure and which he came to regret.

3. He also criticizes Kant for believing that he could approach the absolute through the regressive method of a *zurückschließen* (I/6, 524). "This philosophy dealt completely with the concepts of finitude, and sought to climb up to the absolute by means of a regress through intermediate terms, through the concepts, which are sheer negations of the absolute itself, to determine the absolute" (I/6, 524).

4. Cf. I/4, 529.

5. *Logik*, §94; Ak IX, 139; §102; Ak IX, 141; Ak IX, 23. Kant makes a provocative comment about the definition of philosophy in §103, when he notes that "arbitrarily made concepts" are "synthetically defined" not through construction, but through *"declarations*, since in them one declares one's thoughts or renders account of what one understands by a word" (Ak IX, 142). At the very least, this brief remark sheds light on what Kant means by the *dogmatic use of reason* and the acceptance of concepts from tradition.

6. The only element missing is Kant's use of the term *construction* to describe the methodology he employs. But as we have seen, if Kant's intent is to deny philosophy the use of this methodology, while nonetheless employing it himself, he is certainly not going to explicitly mention that fact.

7. For as construction is an act of freedom, this third thing, this constructed figure of unity, must be something *new* and unique, an emergent entity, that is thus as incapable of being reduced to its producing terms as it is possible to reduce life to the sciences of chemistry and physics.

8. The most insightful and thorough treatment of Schelling's aesthetics is to be found in Dieter Jähnig's monumental work, *Schelling: Die Kunst in der Philosophie* (Pfullingen: Neske, 1969).

9. I/5, 444.

10. I/5, 445.

11. Ibid.

12. Schelling provides the following account of how he outflanks the a priori—a posteriori: "In that we displace (*versetzen*) the origin of the so-called a priori concepts beyond consciousness, where we also locate the origin of the objective world, we maintain upon the same evidence, and with equal right, that our knowledge is originally empirical through and through, and also through and through a priori" (I/3, 527). Kant, because he starts with the *gemeine Bewußtsein*, simply finds the a priori "so to speak, lying there, and thereby involves" himself "in the insoluble difficulties" which any defender of the a priori must wrestle. Schelling continues: "To become aware of our knowledge as a priori in character, we have to become aware of the act of producing as such, in abstraction from the product. But in

the course of this very operation, we lose from the concept, in the manner deduced above, everything material (all intuition), and nothing save the purely formal can remain" (ibid.). We do have formal concepts, which we can, if we want to confuse ourselves, call a priori concepts; but these concepts do not exist *prior* to experience: they are instead the *product* of "a special exercise of freedom," that is, of abstraction.

13. Years later he refers to the system of 1800s history of self-consciousness as "a transcendental history of the I" (I/10, 93).

14. "[T]he sensible cannot differ from the supersensible in *kind* but only in respect to its *limitations*" (I/1, 398).

15. It is a common misunderstanding of Schelling's philosophy to construe his concept of "intellectual intuition" as somehow being a form of knowing that lays claim to *"Erkenntnis"* proper. This is not the case. The intuition of which he presently speaks is a *productive intuition*, which is but the preconscious condition for conscious knowing: "Intuition does not yet involve any consciousness, though without it, consciousness is not even possible" (I/1, 368).

16. Schelling's most succinct criticism of Fichte's subjective Idealism appears in his work of 1806, *Exhibition of the True Relation of the Philosophy of Nature to the Improved Fichtean Doctrine*: "In the last analysis what is the essence of his [Fichte's] whole opinion of nature? It is this: that nature should be used . . . and that it is there for nothing more than to be used, his principal, according to which he looks at nature, is the economic-teleological principle" (I/7, 37).

17. Systematically, this formulation anticipates Schelling's definition of the beautiful as the infinite finitely displayed.

18. Carl Apel on Peirce, *From Pragmatism to Pragmaticism*, translated by J. M. Krois (Atlantic Heights, NJ: Humanities Press, 1970), 122.

19. "Being in our system is freedom suspended" (I/3, 376).

20. To account for the similarity in life form, Schelling infers from the postulated existence of "a common world" that "that which remains when I remove the determinacy of this individuality must be common to us both, that is, we must be alike in regard to the first, the second, and even the third kind of restrictedness" (I/3, 543).

21. To return again to the programmatic mantra of the young Schelling: "In respect of their *object*, philosophy and experience have been opposed to each other (as even the name metaphysics indicates). *This* opposition disappears. The object of philosophy is the *wirkliche Welt*" (I/1, 464).

22. As a particular intelligence, it is necessary that you perceive this succession into which you have been "pitched and posited" as itself necessary (I/3, 485). It must appear as a "predetermined series independent of yourself," which you lack the power to create in any other way than the one in which you experience it. For your entire awareness of yourself as an individual depends on this. "For what lies beyond your consciousness should appear to you as independent of yourself, is precisely what constitutes

your particular limitation. Take this way, and there is no past; posit the latter, and it is just as necessary and just as real—no more, that is, and no less—as the limitation" (I/3, 484).

23. But only in reciprocal action with the absolute self—if the absolute self were cut away from the finite self, the restrictedness would cease, the restrictive intensity of time would cease, and the finite self would dissipate into an unrestricted and infinite extension of space.

24. Kant, third *Critique*, §49; Fichte, *Wissenschaftslehre* I, 217f. Schelling himself writes in the *Abhandlung*, "from the reciprocal interplay of the opposing activities of space and time, there emerges a third, communal one . . . this spontaneous activity of the spirit that is operative in intuition, Kant justly ascribes to the *imagination* because this faculty . . . is the only one capable of exhibiting in one communal product the negative and positive activities" (I/1, 357).

25. Granted, theoretical constructs and literary constructions by definition can be determined by, and are thus susceptible to, one true description.

Appendix: "Eulogy Sung at Hahn's Grave"

1. Originally published in *Der Beobachter*. Hrsg. Von Theophil Friedrich Ehrmann. 3. Jg. Stuttgart 1790. Bd. 1. No. XXXVIII vom 11.5.1790.

Index

$4 22.^{00}$ ✓